The Family Romance of the Impostor-Poet
Thomas Chatterton

BOOKS BY LOUISE J. KAPLAN

*The Family Romance of the Impostor-Poet
Thomas Chatterton (1988)*

*Adolescence: The Farewell
to Childhood (1984)*

*Oneness and Separateness:
From Infant to Individual (1977)*

The Domesday Dictionary
(with Donald M. Kaplan and Armand Schwerner) *(1963)*

THE FAMILY ROMANCE OF *the Impostor-Poet* Thomas Chatterton

Louise J. Kaplan

University of California Press
Berkeley   Los Angeles

Selections from *The Complete Works of Thomas Chatterton* edited by D. S. Taylor and B. B. Hoover, reprinted by permission of Oxford University Press.

Quotations from Judith Rossner's discussion at the Council for Psychoanalytic Psychotherapists printed by permission of Judith Rossner.

Selections from *Adolescence: The Farewell to Childhood* by Louise J. Kaplan, copyright © 1984 by Louise J. Kaplan. Reprinted by permission of Simon & Schuster, Inc.

Selection from "The Poet's Quest for the Father," by Stanley Kunitz. *The New York Times*, February 22, 1987. Copyright © 1987 by The New York Times Company. Reprinted by permission.

University of California Press
Berkeley and Los Angeles
First Paperback Printing 1989

Copyright © 1987 by Louise J. Kaplan

All rights reserved. No part of this book may be reproduced or transmitted in any form or by any means, electronic or mechanical, including photocopying, recording or by any information storage and retrieval system, without permission in writing from the Publisher.

This edition is reprinted by arrangement with Atheneum Publishers, an imprint of Macmillan Publishing Company

Library of Congress Cataloging-in-Publication Data
Kaplan, Louise J.
The family romance of the impostor-poet Thomas Chatterton / Louise J. Kaplan.
p.   cm.
Bibliography: p.
Includes index.
ISBN 0-520-06565-4
1. Chatterton, Thomas, 1752–1770.   2. Psychoanalysis and literature.   3. Poets, English—18th century—Biography.
4. Imposters and imposture—Great Britain—Biography.   5. Literary forgeries and mystifications—History—18th century.   I. Title.
II. Title: Thomas Chatterton.
PR3343.K38 1989   821'.6—dc19   [B]
88-27937   CIP

10 9 8 7 6 5 4 3 2 1

Printed in the United States of America

To Donald

Cut is the branch that might have grown full straight
And burnèd is Apollo's laurel bough.

> —CHRISTOPHER MARLOWE
> *Dr. Faustus*
> (Inscribed upon the frame of
> Henry Wallis's painting *The
> Death of Chatterton*)

CONTENTS

INTRODUCTION *1*

PART I
THE WORLD OF SIR WILLIAM CANYNGE:
Chatterton's Fifteenth-Century Father *13*

1 The Death of Chatterton *15*

2 A Fatherless Boy Grows Up in Bristol *33*

3 Scoundrels Galore *55*

4 Fabricating a Father *77*

5 Petty Lies, Practical Jokes, and Historical Hoaxes *105*

PART II
A NOBLE INSANITY OF THE SOUL:
Chatterton's Search for an Eighteenth-Century Father *121*

6 The Rage of Satire *123*

7 Freedom of the Press, Revolution, and Obscenity *143*

8 The Great Impostor Becomes a Garden-Variety Narcissist *163*

9 The Makings of a Romantic Hero *191*

10 Narcissism and Melancholia *213*

11 The Rowley Controversy *237*

NOTES *259*

INDEX *291*

ILLUSTRATIONS

COVER: *The Death of Chatterton* (1856), by Henry Wallis. The model for Chatterton was George Meredith. Reproduced by permission of the Tate Gallery. See first note in Notes: Chapter One, p. 261.

FRONTISPIECE: *Chatterton* (18th century) from the collection of George Weare Brackenbridge, Esq. One of the several spurious portraits of Chatterton. The portrait is said to resemble his sister, Mary. Courtesy of Avon County Reference Library, Bristol, United Kingdom.

CHAPTER ILLUSTRATIONS: By Thomas Chatterton. Reproduced by permission of The British Library (with the exception of the illustration for Chapter Six, see below).

ONE Church with steeple from "The Rolle of Seyncte Bartlemeweis Priorie." Thomas Rowley.

TWO Seal for Deed of Foundation of a Chapel, from the reign of King Richard, purportedly by the fifteenth-century priest Thomas Rowley, as transcribed from the original eleventh-century drawing from "Nine Deeds and Proclamations."

THREE Towre Gate, the "thyrde and laste Ybuilden by Brightricus," as transcribed by Thomas Rowley in "Towre Gate."

FOUR Tomb of Alward Prepositor of Redclift, as transcribed by Thomas Rowley from "Three Tombs."

FIVE A Silver Coin of Brightrick, as transcribed by Thomas Rowley from "Fragmentes of Anticquitie."

SIX "Flattery's a cloak and I will put it on." Illustration by Chatterton from his notebook copy of his acknowledged satirical poem "Intrest thou universal God of Men," October 27, 1769. Reproduced by permission of the Rare Book and Manuscripts Division of Butler Library, Columbia University Library.

SEVEN Jacet Corpus Ceolwardae of Alward Prepositor of Redclift, as transcribed by Thomas Rowley from "Three Tombs."

EIGHT Score from the Chapel from "The Rolle of St. Bartholomeweis Priorie."

NINE Statue of Sir John de Berkeley from "The Rolle of St. Bartholomeweis Priorie."

TEN Tomb of Aelle the Caesar of Bristol, as transcribed by Thomas Rowley from "Fragmentes of Anticquitie."

ELEVEN Window in the Hall wythe peyncted Glass (Rowley has drawn in his usual rough manner and is here copied) from "The Rolle of St. Bartholomeweis Priorie."

xi

TO THE READER

I REGARD the Notes for this book as an essential adjunct to the main narrative and not merely as a bibliography or reference section in the customary scholarly tradition. I strongly recommend them to your attention. In order not to interrupt the flow of the narrative with footnotes and asides, I thought it best to refer the reader to the Notes for these interesting and informative details. There are numerous passages that a reader is likely to question: "How do we know this?" The Notes cite the sources that support these passages, and occasionally fuller amplification, qualifications, and additional facts are also given. Because of the still-disputed and somewhat overlapping chronology of Chatterton's writings, the reader will also want to refer to the Notes for clarification.

ACKNOWLEDGMENTS

I AM immensely grateful to Geoffrey Langley, county reference librarian of the Bristol Central Library and his assistant M. E. Bridge for their generous cooperation and the easygoing, friendly way they made available to me numerous manuscripts relating to the Rowley controversy. I also thank Prof. Margaret Hunt and Susan Grabstein for their research and thoughtful suggestions on various aspects of mid-eighteenth-century English social history.

For their contributions to some special aspects of psychoanalytic theory, I am especially indebted to Phyllis Greenacre and Jacob Arlow. Greenacre's writings on the family romance of the artist and the relationships between creativity and imposture and Arlow's highly original contributions on character perversions are central to my understandings of Thomas Chatterton's character. Arlow also offered some very constructive suggestions.

Helen Foster, a British child analyst, became my most valuable assistant and supporter. With characteristic good nature, wit, and ingenuity she fulfilled every one of my exotic and, I imagine, sometimes very dull research assignments. She interviewed various Bristol citizens familiar with the Chatterton story and uncovered volumes and manuscripts inaccessible to me in the United States. It was Helen who alerted me to the wonderful Bristol librarian, Mr. Langley. Most of all, Helen believed in my project, appreciated the documents we read together, and sustained my spirits when the going was rough.

The Family Romance of the Impostor-Poet
Thomas Chatterton

INTRODUCTION

THOMAS CHATTERTON was in many ways a typical adolescent. During the seventeen years of his life, he was an exuberant player in the artistic, intellectual, religious, political, and sexual adventures we have come to expect of not-quite-adults. Even his suicide marked him as a typical, if extreme, example of the *Sturm und Drang* image of adolescence. But he was not merely an ordinary adolescent. He was an impostor, and indeed he grew up in the precise family environment that is believed to promote imposturousness. He was a fatherless boy raised by an adoring, idealizing mother and sister, both of whom encouraged his tendencies toward grandiosity and exceptionality. Chatterton was an artistically gifted boy whose poetic talents flourished during adolescence.

In fact I came to Chatterton through my work on adolescence. While sorting out my research and notes for the concluding sections of my last book, *Adolescence*, I thought that Thomas Chatterton, the now nearly forgotten eighteenth-century poet who became an emblem for the English romantic movement, would be the ideal figure to represent the prototypically male disorder, the impostor. However, as I looked further into the circumstances of his life history, I found that his imposturous deeds and indeed his character were far more out of the ordinary than I had expected. I had imagined impostor types to be more straightfoward—obvious con men and manipulators. But Chatterton was different. In the first place, he was not even a genuine plagiarizer. A plagiarizer imitates or appropriates the writings of another person and represents them as his own original work. He is a pure and simple faker, whose motives of financial reward and personal aggrandizement are relatively uncomplicated. But Chatterton actually wrote the poems that he pretended were written by a fifteenth-century priest. He never took on the identity of another person the way a true impostor would. Furthermore, it was nearly impossible to discern where his genuine artistic passions left off and his criminal impulses began.

Felix Krull, Thomas Mann's brilliantly realized fictional confidence man, an out-and-out liar, cheat, and plagiarizer, was decidedly better suited to my immediate purposes. Some of the ambiguities in Chatterton's character are also present in Krull. As Mann commented on his novel, "It is in essence the story of an artist; in it the element of the unreal and illusional passes frankly over into the criminal." But despite this general ambiguity, Mann's fictional confidence man exemplifies with greater clarity the language and mentality of the criminal than could Thomas Chatterton, who never quite grasped the criminal nature of his poetic enterprise and who never had a Thomas Mann to give artistic shape to his confused mental life.

Krull was the example I selected to use in *Adolescence*, but I could not abandon Chatterton. I had grown attached to him and wanted to give him a book of his own, a biography that would do justice to the richness and complexity of his life, particularly to the peculiar relationship between artistic creation and falsehood that is expressed in his literary endeavors. I was intrigued by the dilemmas of his moral character, his motives for writing imposturous poetry, and the external circumstances and internal motives surrounding his suicide.

Another facet of Chatterton's imposturousness commanded my attention. Obviously, a man who pretends to be another man has an uncertain sense of personal identity. What is not so obvious is that underlying that manifest uncertainty of selfhood is a fragility of *masculine* gender identity. As psychoanalysts have come to appreciate, an impostor's sexual orientation is as ambiguous as his moral orientation. The sexual dilemmas are not whether the impostor's sexual orientation is homosexual or heterosexual; the dilemmas concern the perverse quality of his relationships with his sexual partners, whether they are male or female. Impostors are predisposed to acquiring sexual perversions such as sadomasochism, transvestism, fetishism, exhibitionism, voyeurism. And when they become involved in less-complicated sexual relations with women they nevertheless are pseudogenital in the psychological sense; that is, while they are able to employ their penises without ritualized or manifestly perverse scenarios, they emphasize scoring, performance, orgasm in the partner not as the giving of pleasure but as vanquishment and defeat. They view erection as risk, enmity, deception, survival.

Unlike Felix Krull, who we are told courts and seduces married and unmarried women, Thomas Chatterton's actual sexual behavior remains a mystery. He was rumored to be a profligate, a libertine, far too enamored of too many of the young ladies in his Bristol neighborhood, far too well acquainted with the mantua-makers and dulcineas of London. One widespread theory had it that he committed suicide because he was afflicted with syphilis or perhaps an untreatable gonorrhea.

INTRODUCTION

What is certain is that under his own identity he wrote a few scandalous works, among them an obscene poem celebrating the size and marvelous abilities of an exhibitionist's penis and a doggerel verse deriding a capacious vagina and that in the last year of his life he wrote as a freethinker on all matters—religious, political, social, and sexual. Though some critics would cite these writings as evidence of Chatterton's sexual perversions, such "wild" hypotheses are unfounded. The significant issues concern the unique and puzzling relationships between Chatterton's acknowledged freethinking writings and the conflicts expressed in his imposturous works, which were noble, pure, and saintly.

My special interest in the relationships among artistic creation, falsehood, and perversion, which Chatterton's life illustrates, began in my clinical work where many years ago I encountered several overtly perverse patients who were simultaneously caught up in various fabrications of reality—pathological lying, hoaxing, plagiarism, swindling. About fifteen years ago, I took into treatment a nine-year-old boy who, quite unknown to anyone in his family, was consumed by a secret voyeuristic involvement with the live-in housekeeper, an attractive forty-year-old woman who was unconsciously seductive toward my patient. It was not until the second year of analysis that my patient alerted me to his voyeurism.

From the beginning I worked with the boy to modulate the severe anxieties that had brought him into treatment. He was terrified that his parents would abandon him. His day-fantasies and dream life were haunted by outer-space creatures that were poised to hack off, burn off, or otherwise mutilate his arms, legs, ears, eyes, and penis. The year after my patient and I began to address the connection between his voyeurism and these terrifying abandonment and mutilation anxieties, puberty arrived, and the surface clinical picture altered. His overt perversion diminished considerably. His anxieties became more manageable. For some time thereafter, however, his considerable intellectual and creative energies were put in the service of convincing me, his teachers, and his family that events that were untrue were true. He had become a pathological liar. At that juncture, I remembered something crucial about the relationship between perversion and pathological lying. Otto Fenichel, a disciple of Freud's, put it: "If it is possible to make someone believe that untrue things are true, then it is also possible for true things, the memory of which threatens me, are untrue."

Sexual perversions in men center on a fear of the female genitals. The true things that are to be falsified are the penisless female genitals—the vagina, the labia, the tiny erect clitoris. Pathological lying and imposturousness can make these undeniably true facts of life at least momentarily deniable. Petty lies, hoaxes, practical jokes, plagiarisms, and imposturous acts—known as character perversions—originate in the same anxieties and serve similar purposes as manifestly sexual perversions such as fetishism, voyeurism, exhibitionism, transvestism. The analyst Jacob Arlow, who first identified the perverse nature of these denials of reality, illustrated the connections between character perversions and sexual perversions:

> The petty lie is the equivalent of the fetish—it is something which is interposed between the individual and reality in order to ward off the perception of true reality and to substitute instead perceptions which facilitate ambiguity and illusion, both of which can temper for the patient the harsh reality of female anatomy.

Coincidentally, during the same period I was engaged in a prolonged diagnostic evaluation of a five-year-old boy who was in analysis with a colleague of mine. The boy demonstrated a conscious wish to be a girl and an impulse to dress up in his mother's clothing—an impulse that he resisted valiantly but his mother subtly encouraged.

I was struck by the similarities in family background and psychological dynamics of these two boys. The prominent features of each developmental history were an absent or absentee father and a mother who had unsettled the child's narcissistic balance by inviting the fantasy that he had the power to gratify her every wish and desire and eventually fulfill her own exalted version of masculinity. When the exalted maternal ideal of masculinity replaces or overshadows the masculine ideal as represented by the father, this produces the emotional hothouse in which manifest perversions and character perversions, including certain failures of identification such as imposturousness, seem to flourish.

Literary imposture occupies its own niche within imposturousness. It flourished in England during the eighteenth century. The century started off with George Psalmanazar, a French impostor who, in his mid-twenties, came to London posing as a native of Formosa and after translating the Anglican catechism into Formosan, a language he invented, produced (in Latin) the totally fictitious *Historical and Geographical Description of Formosa*. At the century's end, William Henry Ireland fabricated two "lost" Shakespearean plays, *Vortigern and Rowena,* and *Henry II.* And in between were literally scores of others.

INTRODUCTION

The masks of the literary impostors of the eighteenth century were diverse; some were manufacturers of fake legal documents, some printers of spurious books, some tellers of false tales, some creators of some form of false literature. But as I have pointed out, the literary impostor is not, strictly speaking, a plagiarizer. He is more complex in that he represents his own hard-won labors as having originated in someone else's mind. He claims to bring lost documents to light, and in so doing dupes the world into believing that something which is not true is true.

Thomas Chatterton, one of the more famous eighteenth-century impostor-poets, can be distinguished from his fellow literary impostors by the poetic verisimilitude he brought to the long-ago past that he invented. An interpretative reading of Psalmanazar's exotic Formosa or James Macpherson's glorified Irish heroes might also reveal a psychological longing for an ideal father figure. But Chatterton's fabrication of the fifteenth-century Sir William Canynge, the noble merchant prince through whom he tried to fill in the gaps in his own identity, represents a longing for a father that is startlingly transparent. As I embark on this full narrative of that young man's literary exploits and brief, tragic life, I hope that my explorations will enrich the psychoanalytic perspective on the dynamic relationships among creativity, falsehood, and perversion. I hope also that I can communicate to readers outside the psychoanalytic profession something of the richness of the psychoanalytic version of the relationship between sexuality and morality.

While I have not yet made explicit the two main themes of this narrative on the life of Thomas Chatterton, it must already be apparent that I am speaking of imposturousness as a male rather than a female disorder. In the course of relating the tale of this young man's life, I shall be exploring the psychological ramifications of the absence (and by extension of the presence) of a father in a boy's life.

One of my motives in writing about a father-son relationship was to redress the balance at a time when at last so many women writers have been appreciating the depth and meaning of the mother-daughter bond. Since female relationships play so large a part in the upbringing of impostors and impostor-poets, I will be inquiring into mother-son, sister-brother bonds and what these might mean in the father's absence. But my major emphasis will be on the longing for a father, a universal human longing that is all the more significant because we have begun to live in a father-absent culture, where large numbers of boys and girls are being raised in households made fatherless by illegitimacy, abandonment, divorce, and most recently the decision of women to bear and bring up children as single parents. Lest I give the impression that this turn of events might hasten us toward a matriarchal paradise, I want to underline that I am exploring not a positive or potentially beneficial phenomenon but the detrimental effects of an absence.

The week I was preparing this introduction, Stanley Kunitz published an article for the *New York Times Book Review* entitled "The Poet's Quest for the Father," in which he concludes:

> Out of 20th century American poetry emerges, as a collective creation, the mythic image of the absent father. His absence explains why he haunts the modern imagination. He has died of natural causes, or by suicide, or in the wars of the century. It is astonishing how many American poets have lost their fathers at an early age. . . . Often the father is more than absent; he is lost, as he has been lost to himself for most of his adult life, crushed by his burdens, rendered impotent by fatigue and anxieties, reduced to a number, a statistical integer, in the army or the factory or the marketplace. The son goes in search of the father, to be reconciled in a healing embrace. In that act of love he restores his father's lost pride and manhood. Perhaps he also finds himself.

I agree with Kunitz that the absent father can serve as an inspiration for poetry and that poetry can act as a healing embrace between father and son. And I appreciate how earlier in the essay he offers an impressive list of women poets who have written about their fathers. Even so, as he points out, "The song of daughters is different from that of sons, and the scope of my essay does not permit me to add to its complications." With this crucial distinction I also concur, because I regard *The Family Romance of the Impostor-Poet Thomas Chatterton* as a biography about masculine psychology as distinct from, though not, as I shall be explaining, dichotomous with, feminine psychology.

A few words concerning the reasoning that led to my original choice of the impostor as a representative of masculine conflicts are in order here. In the concluding section of my book on adolescence I contrast two rare emotional disorders that come to fruition during puberty, one of them prototypically feminine, the other prototypically masculine. The prototype for the feminine disorder, anorexia nervosa, is a typically adolescent, typically feminine solution to the dilemmas of becoming an adult. It entails the pursuit of a caricature of femininity—a pure and saintly attitude toward all forms of desire (not merely the avoidance of food); a nymphlike physical appearance devoid of body fat, hips, breasts, or any other grown-up feminine attribute. The moral and sexual life of the anorectic have been arrested at a childlike ideal of what it means to be female.

When it came to conceptualizing the male counterpart to anorexia, I was confronted with all the paradoxes inherent in contemporary research and thinking on issues of femininity and masculinity. Therefore I adopted a few strategies that I hoped would minimize the ideologies and intellectual shortcomings that usually result from these paradoxes.

The first of these was to avoid the statistical and normative solutions that have been promulgated by quite a number of feminist writers. Phyllis Chesler's influential notion, for example, that women internalize aggressive feelings while men externalize them was derived from a more or less numerical base: men are victimizers—killers, robbers, burglars, muggers—while women are victimized—they destroy themselves, succumbing to depression and hysteria. Women tend to become mental patients rather than criminals. Among psychotics, the men are the violent paranoids, the women the self-mutilating, silly hebephrenics. Men are sadists while women are masochists. This sort of head-counting approach to mental illness is often supplemented by the assumption that masculinity is synonymous with being strong and active while femininity is associated with being weak and passive.

I was wary of such dichotomizing of feminine and masculine traits. Such approaches to the gender dilemma also claim that one set of traits—feminine or masculine—is better than the other. While it is tempting to succumb to the appeal of the superiority of "the feminine approach to science," "the feminine universe," "feminine dialogue," "feminine morality," I am generally suspicious of the motives underlying any "better or worse" interpretation of the differences between the sexes. Often, I believe, when people dichotomize differences they regress to the very stereotypes they are so conscientiously striving to avoid.

I started with some basic numbers. Anorexia, a rare disorder in its full-fledged primary form to begin with, is rare in males, who comprise at most ten percent of all anorectics. The impostor, also a rare disorder in its primary form, is with few exceptions nonexistent among females. When I intentionally selected these apparently dichotomized disorders, I did not intend to demonstrate that females are more likely to solve gender dilemmas by manipulating their bodies while men are more likely to solve these dilemmas by manipulating others. I wanted to demonstrate how a seeming dichotomy, when explored from a psychoanalytic developmental perspective, reveals other more subtle dynamic issues. The anorectic and the impostor are distinctly different disorders but both are aftermaths of a developmental arrest in which an "absence of the father" usually exerts a significant influence.

When no one comes along to intrude on the intimacies of the mother-infant dialogue, the child's moral sense continues to be dominated by the concrete prohibitions and permissions of the nursery. The "voice of the father" (or any powerful third force that makes it clear to the child that his mother is not his possession) awakens the child to the complex moral authority of the larger social order. The father's presence in the mother's life and the mother's presence in the father's convey to the child the painful but necessary knowledge of the differences between the sexes and the generations. This bitter reminder that he is small, vulnerable, deficient in grown-up desires and capacities motivates a young child to become like his powerful parents and acquire some of their moral authority. Thus, in exchange for banishment by his parents, the child is permitted to participate in the principles of law and order that govern the social world in which he will grow up. The primitive nursery morality that gathers its dreadful power from the possibility of abandonment, absence, weaning, mutilation, and defilement is tamed and to a large extent replaced by inner conscience and the less awesome anxieties that arise from guilt. The primitive gender ideals of femininity and masculinity are also modified. As development proceeds, they become less stereotyped and rigid, more humane and rich with complexity.

The anorectic and the impostor represent alternative sex-gender scripts that never evolved beyond the simplified ideals of femininity and masculinity conveyed to a child during infancy. These infantile ideals, if unmodified and enriched by later development, will eventuate in pathological solutions to the dilemmas of arriving at genital maturity during adolescence. Neither the anorectic nor the impostor dares to risk the challenges of adult gender identity offered by the adolescent process. Though these pathological solutions are typically feminine and typically masculine, they cannot be construed as paired opposites with assigned valuations such as weak/strong, clean/dirty, good/bad, subjective/objective, passive/active. They are examples of what happens to a sex-gender script when the infantile gender ideal as conveyed by the mother during the earliest months and years of life does not confront the challenges posed later on by the three-person socialized version in which the father also plays a part. A weak articulation of the oedipal triangle—an "absence of the father"—leaves both boys and girls extremely vulnerable to unfocused, generalized anxieties about abandonment and mutilation. The anorectic and the impostor are prototypes of all who remain in the never-never land of moral and genital ambiguity because they are too frightened

INTRODUCTION

to assume the complex demands of adult moral responsibility and adult gender identity.

Thomas Chatterton, though he did suffer from a character perversion, was *not* a full-fledged impostor. He was a youth who struggled to find a way toward adult moral life and gender identity despite the absence of an actual father in his life. Because he was artistically gifted—a poet who could portray his quest for an adult ideal of manhood—he left a record of these struggles for all of us.

In conclusion I will relate an incident that occurred a few months before I completed this life of Chatterton, during a discussion period after I had presented a paper based on the life of Chatterton at a psychoanalytic conference. Since my paper dealt primarily with the borders between art and crime described earlier in this introduction, I requested that Judith Rossner be the official discussant rather than a psychoanalyst. Rossner recognized immediately that I was writing about the meaning of literary impostures and pathological lying, and in keeping with the spirit of the occasion, she decided to play a literary prank on the audience—the invention of a female literary impostor. Her invention was so convincing that many listeners thought they remembered reading Nell Shapiro's "A Servant's Diary," a "lost" manuscript purportedly written by one Estella Martinez and then "discovered" by Nell.

Judith Rossner told the audience she wanted to stimulate discussion on an issue that concerned her:

> The question that recurred as I read Louise's paper had to do not with its accuracy but with the limitations of her observations on Chatterton and on literary impostors in general. That is to say, all of her references, as well as those of Dr. Chasseguet-Smirgel, were to men, but they set me to thinking about women and imposture.

Rossner went on to point out that after all girls did have a head start on castration anxiety and that in any event

> As a bored world becomes increasingly determined to erase those sexual distinctions that seem to have been crucial in arresting mankind's boredom, we shall doubtless see an increasing number of women supplying their missing pieces by faking advanced degrees ... performing surgery they know almost as well as if they'd really gone to medical school ... selling millions of gallons of corn oil stored in nonexistent storage tanks in New Jersey ... and publishing manuscripts they've found in their grandmother's

attics that are later revealed to have been written and placed there by themselves.

This was in fact the issue that dominated the discussion period, which dealt not only with the general problem of creativity and imposture but more specifically with the premise that women did have and were entitled to have the same perversions and character perversions as men. At first my male colleagues on the panel took a professional view and supported my thesis that the perversions and character perversions I had described were primarily male territories. Before too long, however, a few of them lost their analytic objectivity and began to react like ordinary besieged men. They began to blur the distinctions between technical language and everyday usage. One analyst, for example, found himself defending the commonplace notion that women were just as guilty of exhibitionism as men. Didn't they sit in front of the mirror all day, trying on clothes, putting on makeup, and so on? Strange alliances were made. Some feminist members of the audience supported this male analyst's argument by proposing that prostitutes and specialty call girls were as perverse as their male clients. Quite a few agreed that when it came to petty lies women were more accomplished than men. Equal rights had won the day.

Before presenting my paper I had discussed my premises with a few writers and psychoanalysts. One of them, William Grossman, predicted what might happen: "You'll see. The minute you begin to illustrate a few of the ways in which men and women are different you will get dozens of examples of how they are alike. Just listen. You will gather more fascinating and useful data than if you had set up months of interviews directly addressing the questions, 'Do you know of women who engage in perverse sexual acts like exhibitionism, fetishism, voyeurism?'; 'Do you have female patients who are practical jokers, impostors, or pathological liars?' " He was right.

That afternoon's discussion encouraged me to begin the research for my next book, which will examine female perversions and character perversions and their resemblances to or differences from male perversions and character perversions.

For now, I return to *The Family Romance of the Impostor-Poet Thomas Chatterton,* which is much less a sinister tale of sexual perversion than it is a study of the slender border between art and crime. I expect that some readers may question whether Thomas Chatterton's fate was in fact prototypically masculine. But I imagine even they will consent to my general thesis that, for Chatterton at least, an "absence of the father" stimulated his imposturous acts and also set him on his quest for poetic

INTRODUCTION

nobility. The first part of the *Romance* is about the healing embrace between Thomas Chatterton and Sir William Canynge, the fifteenth-century father through whom Chatterton hoped to find his own manhood. In the second part, we see what happened to Chatterton when he lost that father.

PART I

THE WORLD OF SIR WILLIAM CANYNGE:

CHATTERTON'S

FIFTEENTH-CENTURY

FATHER

ONE

The Death of Chatterton

A young poet commits suicide in his attic room on Brooke Street and becomes an emblem for the English romantic movement. How the romance was created: Jack-and-the-Beanstalk for the impostor; Sir William Canynge for the poet. Myths of burial and reburial, and the endless saga of Chatterton's monument.

ON the evening of August 24, 1770, a 17½-year-old poet by the name of Thomas Chatterton retired to his attic room in Brooke Street, London, mixed some arsenic he had obtained from the neighborhood apothecary with water, drank the potion, and lay down on his bed to await death, which came slowly. Chatterton died in the early hours of the next morning. When his body was discovered that afternoon, the floor surrounding the bed was littered with shreds of paper which were, presumably, the remnants of Chatterton's latest literary efforts. Did these scraps contain lines of the magnificent poetry that would make him the emblem of genius and inspiration for the English romantic poets? Or were they works that Chatterton considered unworthy of his talents? These unanswered questions are among the innumerable small mysteries of the life and death of Thomas Chatterton. Before he was lowered into his grave, his scrupulous landlady, a Mrs. Angel, had the scraps swept away.

Soon to be immortalized in the poetry of his romantic brothers, and later in Wallis's *Death of Chatterton,* which now hangs in the Tate Gallery, Chatterton died penniless, a literary failure, an unsung poet. He was not found stretched out in beatific repose as depicted in the Wallis painting but instead died in convulsive agony from the effects of the arsenic.

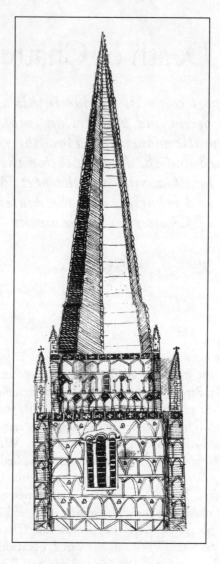

THE IMPOSTOR-POET THOMAS CHATTERTON

Between the time of Chatterton's suicide in 1770 and the beginning of the nineteenth century, the English romantic movement blossomed. A few antiquarians and scholars might wrangle on about whether the magnificent Middle English poetry that came to light after his death was by Chatterton or by a fifteenth-century priest named Thomas Rowley. But, from the romantic period on, Chatterton belonged to the poets.

In 1790, Samuel Taylor Coleridge drafted a version of *Monody on the Death of Chatterton*, "A Monody on Chatterton, who poisoned himself at the age of eighteen—written by the author at the age of sixteen."

> *Now, prompts the Muse poetic lays*
> *And high my bosom beats with love of Praise!*
> *But, Chatterton! methinks I hear thy name,*
> *For cold my Fancy grows, and Dead each Hope of Fame.*

Six years later, when his poetic judgment was more secure, Coleridge began to edit that version and added thirty-six more lines, among which were

> *O Chatterton! that thou wert yet alive!*
> *Sure thou would'st spread the canvas to the gale,*
> *And love with us the tinkling team to drive*
> *O'er peaceful Freedom's undivided dale;*
> *And we, at sober eve, would round thee throng,*
> *Would hang, enraptur'd on thy stately song,*
> *And greet with smiles the young-eyed Poesy*
> *All deftly mask'd as hoar Antiquity,*

For William Wordsworth, born the year of Chatterton's death, Chatterton would be "the marvelous Boy, the Sleepless Soul that perished in his pride." In 1818, when he was twenty-three, John Keats would dedicate his *Endymion*, "Inscribed, with Every Feeling of Pride and Regret and with 'a bowed mind' to the memory of the Most English of Poets except Shakespeare, THOMAS CHATTERTON." Keats thought of Chatterton as the soul of romantic poetry, "Where we may soft humanity put on / And sit, and rhyme, and think on Chatterton." And, shortly before his own death at the age of twenty-six, he lamented the untimely death of Chatterton:

> *O Chatterton! how very sad thy fate!*
> *Dear child of sorrow—son of misery!*

How soon the film of death obscur'd that eye,
Whence Genius mildly flash'd and high debate.

Percy Bysshe Shelley had a mournful phrase for Chatterton: "Chatterton / Rose pale, his solemn agony had not / Yet faded from him . . ." George Gordon Lord Byron, in his flamboyant manner, complained of the vulgar displays of elegance in some of the young poets of his day. He contrasted them with others, including Chatterton, whose purity he admired. "Burns is often coarse but never vulgar, Chatterton is never vulgar, nor Wordsworth."

The week of Thomas Chatterton's death, a butcher boy who was tossed and gored by an overdriven bullock, a paupered widow who stabbed herself to death in Carnaby Market, a salesman who dropped dead while bargaining at the door of the Red Cow all found their way into the London daily papers. But there was no mention of the poet who had committed suicide in a garret on Brooke Street.

Thomas Chatterton was born November 1752, three months after his father's death, in the bustling port city of Bristol, England. Visitors to Bristol in the eighteenth century did not have much that was positive to say about the city, although they did note its predominance in trade. Daniel Defoe, in *A Tour Thro' the Whole Island of Great Britain*, portrayed Bristol in 1720 as "the greatest, the richest, and the best Port of Trade in Great Britain, London only excepted." By Chatterton's day Liverpool had outstripped Bristol as a port of trade, but Bristol, with its close to fifty thousand inhabitants, was nonetheless the second-largest city in England. Accounts of Bristol's commerce often mentioned the thirty or so awesome pyramidal glass houses there and the city's vast variety of crown, flint, and bottle glass. "Ireland and America take off great quantities of these goods, especially bottles, of which nearly half the number are sent out filled with beer, cyder, perry and Bristol water." Another architectural highlight was the enormous sugar refineries. The underpinning of the sugar trade was the slave trade, for which Bristol had been renowned since the fifteenth century. Hard white soap, leather goods, white lead, gunpowder, earthenware, cheese, herrings, salt, woolens, stockings, and hardware were also exported to the rest of England and to all parts of the world from the port of Bristol.

The countryside that eventually became the commercial center of Bristol was destined to become a great port city. Bristol is encircled by riverways: the Avon to the south, and its narrow branch, the Frome, curving across the north of the city. Some five miles westward, the Avon opens to the mouth of the Severn, which itself then turns its waters north to the Irish Sea and south to the English Channel and Atlantic Ocean. Riverways are what made Bristol into a mighty city.

The rivers were also responsible for much of the city's unsavory reputation. Because of the violent tides created by the crossing of the Severn with the Irish Sea, the quays of Bristol had to be built high enough along the shore to accommodate thirty- to forty-foot high tides. The gigantically high quays induced a closed-in, narrow feeling. At ebbtide the river was muddy and filthy, and the sails of the grand ships were barely visible above the quays. Horace Walpole, the first person to detect and condemn Chatterton's forgeries, was, as might be expected, the harshest critic of Bristol. He said bluntly what others would put more diplomatically: "I did go to Bristol, the dirtiest great shop I ever saw, with so foul a river, that had I seen the least appearance of cleanliness, I should have concluded they washed all their linen in it, as they do at Paris."

Bristol also received bad notices on its housing and pavements. "When we consider Bristol as a place of trade and riches we are greatly surprised to find the houses so meanly built, and the streets so narrow, dirty, and ill paved." Or again: "The passerby was not always safe as he walked under these ancient buildings, for their timbers and plaster often fell into the streets." And about the roadways: "They draw all their heavy Goods here on Sleds, or Sledges without Wheels, which Kills a Multitude of Horses: and the Pavement is worn so smooth by them that in Wet-weather tis dangerous walking." After going into the narrowness and sordidness of the Bristol pavements, most writers went on to assault the character of the citizenry:

> We might mention also another Narrow, that is, the Minds of the Generality of its People; for, let me tell you, the Merchants of Bristol, tho' very rich, are not like the Merchants of London; The latter may be said (as of old of the Merchants of Tyre) to vie with the Princes of the Earth; whereas the former, being rais'd by good fortune, and Prizes taken in the Wars, from Masters of Ships, and blunt tars, have inbib'd the Manners of those rough Gentlemen.

Alexander Pope summed it up: "The City of Bristol itself is a very unpleasant place and no civilized company in it."

Whatever else might have been said about the city of Bristol, St. Mary Redcliffe was recognized as one of the most beautiful parish churches in all the world. Thomas Chatterton was raised in the shadow of St. Mary's.

Thirty years before his death, Thomas Chatterton, Sr., a schoolmaster, had taken (some would say stolen) from the Bristol parish church, St. Mary Redcliffe, some ancient parchments which he used to cover the copybooks of his grammar-school students. His wife, Sarah Chatterton, also made sensible use of these parchments by transforming them into embroidery patterns and threading papers for her needlework. The young Thomas Chatterton, upon discovering his father's purloined parchments in various chests and odd corners of his childhood home, became infatuated with their antique beauty and decided that they were far too wondrous to be put to mundane purposes. As he was nearing his sixteenth year, Chatterton, who had up till then seemed a grandiose but otherwise trustworthy boy, put himself foward as the transcriber of the poems and stories that he claimed were written on these parchments. In actuality the parchments contained only some parish accounts and other illegible scribblings. But Chatterton claimed that these markings were medieval English which, when translated, he found to be narratives and poems that had been penned by a monk named Thomas Rowley during the fifteenth century. After a while Chatterton decided that Rowley should be a Bristol parish priest rather than a simple monk. Rowley's exquisite narratives, as Chatterton fabricated them, created a revised history of the old city of Bridge Stowe, place of the Bridge.

For nine months between his sixteenth and seventeenth year, Thomas Chatterton invented a fake Middle English and in the voice of Thomas Rowley composed a body of literature—poetry, poetic drama, historical documents, letters, medical and architectural treatises—that endowed the eighteenth-century mercantile city of Bristol, a city where even priests talked only of money and trade, with a history of artistic sensibility, selfless devotion, virtue, heroism, poetic nobility. Accompanying the fabricated literary documents were designs of heraldic crests, ancient coins, and pedigrees, and drawings of the churches, bridges, gateways, and statuary that were meant to represent the glories of the medieval city of Bristol. All of these the imaginary poet-priest Thomas Rowley had supposedly created for the merchant prince Sir William Canynge, an actual person who had been five times the mayor of fifteenth-century Bristol. According to Rowley's legend, Canynge had donated the money acquired from his slave trade and merchant-ship empire to artistic enterprises of all kinds, but primarily to the rebuilding of St. Mary Redcliffe church, the church where young Chatterton's father had discovered the parchments.

The port of Bristol, Redcliffe parish, and St. Mary Redcliffe church were to play central roles in the romance that Chatterton would create. That he was born after his father's death and raised in a fatherless household by his adoring mother and sister also contributed to Thomas Chatterton's unique fate.

Figuring prominently in any tale of an impostor is an absent or emotionally ineffectual father. In some instances the father dies during the boy's infancy. In others he prefers his older male children, or is denigrated by his wife, or is himself a shabby pretender to social and financial importance. So far as we know, all full-fledged impostors are males, and two sorts of little boys grow up to become impostors: the despised outcasts and the adored ones. Thomas Chatterton belonged to the second category. He was a beautiful and talented boy, a magical son, the focus of his mother's all-loving gaze, a favored child of fortune. Chatterton's central misfortune was to have been born posthumously. That calamity, when combined with the exalted ideals of masculinity that flourished in Chatterton's household, marked him for the role of an impostor. With no fathering presence to represent an alternative and more realistic sense of masculine identity, a little boy is predisposed to becoming a mirroring extension of some exalted feminine ideal of masculinity. And it was Chatterton's fate to have two idealizing women play a prominent role in his upbringing. His mother, Sarah, catered to his eccentricities. His elder sister, Mary, revered her talented little brother. Furthermore, as a likely psychological replacement first for a four-month-old male child who had died two years earlier and then for the father who had died only three months before Chatterton's birth, little Thomas would have been expected to embody whatever fantasies of masculinity that Sarah and Mary might have entertained about those two lost male figures.

To compound these circumstances, something about the little boy himself seemed to promote the idealizations that were already lively in the minds of the Chatterton women. The boy's innate abilities and the fantasies of his loved ones worked hand in hand to produce a remarkable child. Early on in life Thomas Chatterton, like other impostors-to-be, had about him the aura of the exception.

According to his sister's reports, Thomas's "thurst for preheminence" was already apparent when, at the age of four, he began to play with the neighborhood boys. Never did he take the role of follower with his playmates. He was the master. They were his humble servants. He was the commander. They were his obedient foot soldiers. As his ever-loyal boyhood friend Thomas Carey was to recall of those childhood days in his *Elegy to the Memory of Thomas Chatterton: Late of Bristol:*

> *Ere vital utterance could scarce transpire*
> *His infant lips evinc'd a manly soul*

Predicting that heroic mental fire
Which reign'd supreme within the mighty whole.

When Chatterton was five years old and Mary herself around eight or nine, their uncle William Chatterton, a potter, promised to make for the two children some earthenware cups. Originally the potter had thought to have a "lyon rampant" for Thomas's cup. But the little boy asked his uncle for a different design. "Paint me an angel," he requested. "An angel with wings—and a trumpet, to blow my name about."

It was clear from the start that their Tom was an uncommon boy, by and large a loner, always different from the other boys in the Redcliffe neighborhood. Mary took on herself the role of her little brother's calming spirit. She also encouraged his artistic inclinations which, since she herself had a talent for drawing, she could certainly appreciate. For Mary, Tom was a shining star, a hero whose passions for books and writings were his only excesses. And his passion for books is prominent in all accounts of Chatterton's childhood.

The little boy with a thirst for fame did not show promising beginnings. At a young age he was declared an incorrigible illiterate, too much of a dullard to be able to profit from instruction in reading and writing. At the age of five, soon after he acquired his marvelous delft cup with the angel trumpeting his name, he was dismissed from school for learning problems.

Mary was willing to admit that at first her brother had been "dull in learning," and did not know "many letters at 4 years old." But she would highlight the splendid originality of Tom's reading tastes. He "always objected to read in a small book." Mary's account implies that her brother was much too clever to learn to read in the ordinary way. "He learnt the Alphabet from an old Folio musick book of my father's my mother was then tearing up for waste paper, the capitals at the beginning of the verses." Chatterton's mother tells the same story: "He fell in love with the illuminated capitals." Seizing on her son's passion for the antiqued alphabet, Sarah, with the assistance of her learned eight-year-old daughter, proceeded to teach him to read from an antique black letter Testament.

Once he caught on to that glorious alphabet there was no stopping him. He would read ravenously from morning till night. He early on revealed a preference for works of antiquity and historical treatises. At the Colston School, where he was admitted at age eight, he read when he should have been adding columns of numbers. He read when the other boys were at recess. And as a scrivener's apprentice at age sixteen, he pretended to be finishing up his legal copying while actually boning up on the history of Bristol, designing heraldic crests and family pedigrees, and composing poetic dramas.

He was a moody child. Throughout childhood, he was subject to recurrent spells of bleak and incommunicable depression. Even after he had left his imprisoning grammar school and begun to immerse himself in his Rowley saga, "his spirits," reports his sister, "was rather uneven. Some time so gloom'd that for many days together he would say very little and that by constraint." He was often morose. He would sit for long periods of time staring into nothingness. There were storms of passionate weeping. He was absentminded, not hearing what was said to him. On some days he would refuse to come to table altogether. On others, with assumed majesty, he would command his mother to serve him only bread and water as he had more significant feats to perform than eating and drinking. Whenever he heard his mother and sister praising someone or other for a minor accomplishment, he would remind them that "God has sent His creatures into the world with arms long enough to reach anything."

The veneration of his sister and mother was an equivocal piece of luck for Chatterton. The unspoken message that he is expected to fulfill the desires of the grown-up females who worship him is a weighty burden for a little boy. Some little boys are so frightened (and angered) by the idea that they have been invested with such unrealistic power that they manage to fail at everything they set out to do. On the other hand, maternal adoration can be a spur to fame and achievement, an incentive that could as easily press a boy toward imposturous fabrications as toward artistic creations. Young Thomas Chatterton spent a great deal of time imagining ways he might rescue his sister and mother from their dreary Bristol existence. He began to write poetry while in grammar school, and by the time he signed his indenture papers, he had decided to become a famous and wealthy writer. He would buy beautiful gifts for Sarah and Mary. He would deliver them from their life of poverty.

Another of Chatterton's childhood burdens was struggling to patch together a whole impression of the father he never knew. And here too the liability fired his ambitions. What could he make of those scraps of parchment taken from St. Mary Redcliffe Church? Thomas knew that his father had been a schoolmaster assigned to "instructing the boys and finding them pen, ink and paper," and that his father's family had been sextons at St. Mary's for generations. Around the Redcliffe parish, Thomas Chatterton, Sr. was appreciated for his musical tastes and elegant handwriting and for his collection of Roman coins. On the other hand, less salutary views of the senior Chatterton were also common in Bristol. Some neighbors made much of his noisy manners, his fondness for gin and beer, his volatile temper and bullying treatment of his young and less-educated wife. Both images of his father appear as representations of manhood in Chatterton's writing. As young Chatterton approached his own manhood, he created an ideal father who used his fine appreciation of the arts to ennoble the city of Bristol. Sexual vulgarity and overindulgence in food and alcohol, on the other hand, became trademarks of degraded manhood in Chatterton's political and religious satires.

There might have been some relief from young Thomas's anxiety-arousing ambitions, some tempering of his defensive grandiosity, had he gone from the emotional hothouse of his family to an educational environment that provided him with some realistic way to assess his talents. But unfortunately he was sent to Colston's Hospital, a training school designed to crank out obedient apprentices. It was precisely the wrong situation for a talented, imaginative boy who fancied having his name trumpeted over the world.

This contrast between the life of glory and fame that he had freely entertained at home and the paltry circumstances to which he was reduced at Colston's inspired in Chatterton the family romance that would later become the decisive theme of his poetic genius. At the same time, the mortifying discrepancy between his early childhood fantasy of being the rescuer of the women who adored him and his status as a run-of-the-mill grammar-school boy brought out the imposturous tendencies that had been bred in his childhood home.

The family romance is a ubiquitous item of normal childhood. Typically the young child constructs a family romance fantasy to soften the humiliation of being cast out of that sublime Olympus-Heaven-Eden where he was once the adored baby of the Olympian rulers of the Universe. In the typical romance the child imagines that he has been abducted from that magical family and placed temporarily in the home of some ordinary, workaday, not-so-clean, impatient, quarrelsome, but kindly peasants. Superman is a common prototype of a family romance. The child's true mother and father, to whom he will one day return, are noble, grand, strong, magnificent, gratifying, shining with perfection, superior in every way to the humble mother and father with whom he is forced to live. His true family, the one from which he was abducted as an infant, would love only him. His real mother and father would grant his every desire. They would reveal all magical secrets to him. They would reveal magic words. They would be perfect and all-knowing. They would transmit to him the radiance of all their powers. One day he will be restored to the Garden of Eden and to his legitimate rank as the most valued member of the Royal Family.

For a fatherless boy who is worshiped and pampered by the female members of his family, the humiliating discovery that he is a common boy of mortal lineage stimulates more complicated psychological maneuvers than those of the usual child. Chatterton's unconscious strategy was to create two interweaving family romances, each with its own scenario. One scenario would be embodied in the story narrated by the poet-priest Rowley. The other would be acted out in real life through the impostor's relations with those he deceived. Although he did not formulate the literary strategies of his Rowley saga until the second year of his apprenticeship, the shape of that family romance began to form during his years at Colston's.

The life of William Canynge "as wroten by Thomas Rowley" was a straightforward expression of the more or less typical family romance, in which a child is temporarily reduced to a lowly and demeaned status, but because of his patience, honesty, industry, obedience, kindness, innocence, virtue, and underlying if not actual beauty, is at last restored to his legitimate status as a true member of a noble family.

The other scenario of Chatterton's ingenious double-edged solution required an idiosyncratic family romance tailored for an impostor, a person whose anxiety and humiliation can be allayed only by magic and duplicity, a person who feels whole and intact only when he is putting one over. The fairy-tale prototype for an impostor's family romance is the familiar "Jack and the Beanstalk." This seemingly innocent childhood romance captures the essence of the impostor's childhood humiliations and the illusory victory that begins to dominate his existence.

Jack, we recall, lives in a humble cottage with his poor, hardworking mother. His father is dead and thus neatly out of the way as a competitor for Jack's mother's affections. Because Jack is not really as clever as his mother has led him to believe, he is easily duped into trading the cow, Milky White, for a handful of beans, thus failing in the mission on which his mother has sent him. But Jack gets his revenge on the deceiving grown-ups. The beans turn out to be magical after all. Overnight they grow into a beanstalk that reaches beyond the clouds. Jack decides to climb the beanstalk. After climbing and climbing he arrives in the kingdom of the wicked giant. The giant has the reputation of eating up all those who trespass. He especially relishes little boys of Jack's age. But clever Jack hoodwinks the giant, who for all his loud and terrifying mutterings is obviously merely a lazy, foolish, and rather gullible show-off. With the assistance of the giant's wife, who just like his own mother treats the marvelous Jack as an exception, Jack robs the giant of his most precious possessions, not once but three times. First he steals the bag of gold, then the goose that lays the golden eggs, and finally the singing golden harp.

As he abducts the golden harp, it sings out to warn the giant. But it is too late. Jack has already begun to scramble down the beanstalk. The giant follows in hot pursuit. In the nick of time, Jack reaches the safety of home. He grabs his hatchet and chops down the beanstalk. The mighty giant comes crashing to earth. Jack returns triumphantly to his mother and rescues her from her life of poverty.

Every imposture enacts a variation of the redemption aspect of a Jack-and-the-Beanstalk legend. The impostor must constantly reestablish the illusion that he is not small and insignificant, that he is worthy of his mother's ambitions, and moreover that he is entitled to trick the mighty father, overthrow him, and rob him of his powers.

Encouraged as he has been in his role as the divine extension of his mother's exalted ideal of masculinity, the little boy soon catches on that truth and facts, the real appearances of things, can be ignored and supplanted by fantasies and illusions. When one is adored for being the self one is not, the self one is gets lost in the shuffle and never has a chance to grow up. The impostor suffers, therefore, from a profound impairment of his sense of identity. He knows he is not the person he pretends to be. But he feels that he must be greater and more magnificent than the person he really is. The impostor goes through life with two incompatible self-images: the shabby, poorly knit real self and the illusory self that cloaks it. The fundamental ironies of Chatterton's life concern the contradictions between these two self-images. Which is the true Chatterton? Which are his "genuine" literary works—the acknowledged poetry and prose he wrote as a journalist during the last year of his life or the fabricated Rowleys?

After nearly a year of devoted labor in which he managed, during the spare hours of his apprenticeship, to fabricate the world of Sir William Canynge, Chatterton realized that, except for two "respectable" Bristol elders who consciously or unconsciously seemed to have become his collaborators-in-deceit, the world placed little value on Rowley. Publishers either ignored or rejected Rowley's writings. Horace Walpole, the only person of renown to respond positively, grew suspicious, investigated some historical details, and determined that the documents Chatterton had sent him were counterfeit. He advised the young man that he would do more honor to his poor mother to stick to his apprenticeship as a lawyer's scrivener.

Reluctantly and in a fury with Walpole, Chatterton gave up the romance of William Canynge. For a full summer he wrote almost nothing. Finally, in the autumn, the young man revived his literary spirits. He began to emulate the freethinking poets and journalists of his day. While only one Rowley poem was published during Chatterton's lifetime, many of the political and anticlerical poems and political tracts and conventional love poetry he wrote at the beginning of his seventeenth year were published in leading London magazines. Chatterton made up his mind to seek his literary fortunes in London. He had to escape from his mundane apprenticeship and the petty narrows of a Bristol he could no longer camouflage beneath a fabricated aristocratic history.

In April of 1770, Chatterton wrote a "fake" suicide note which he intentionally left open on his desk for his lawyer master to discover. The hoax worked. The alarmed lawyer immediately canceled Chatterton's indentures. Within the week Chatterton had packed his clothing, books, and papers and made his farewells to friends and family. A number of his acquaintances demonstrated their faith by contributing money for his trip to London. Emboldened and cheered by the prospects of his new life as a bona fide writer, Chatterton boarded the One-Day Express for London. "Here I am safe, and in high spirits" begins his letter to his mother dated April 26, 1770.

Just as the romantic movement was fading, the poet-painter Dante Gabriel Rossetti, one of Chatterton's staunchest champions, would revive for a moment the name of Chatterton. "Not to know Chatterton is to be ignorant of the *true* day-spring of modern romantic poetry." In a sonnet written for Blake, he immortalizes Chatterton's association with Bristol:

> *Thy nested home-loves, noble Chatterton;*
>   *The angel-trodden stair thy soul could trace*
>   *Up Redcliffe's spire; and in the world's awed space*
> *Thy gallant sword-play:—these to many an one*
> *Are sweet for ever; as thy grave unknown*
>   *And love-dream of thine unrecorded face.*

The unknown grave that Rossetti alludes to is another of the mysteries of Chatterton's life and death. Chatterton's peculiar destiny followed him to the grave. Just as hardly anyone nowadays remembers the name of Thomas Chatterton or recalls one word of the poetry he wrote, no one knows where his bones finally ended up.

The saga of Chatterton's unknown grave began three days after his suicide and continued for decades. When no family member appeared to identify his body, it was taken to the Shoe Lane Workhouse and placed in a pauper's grave. His death in the Register of Burials was entered as William Chatterton.

A few days later, his family and friends finally received notice of the burial and the details of his suicide quickly became known in Bristol. Even then, before the world at large became alerted to the name "Chatterton," rumors of counterfeiting, plagiarism, forgery, insanity, profligacy, physical disease began to attach themselves to the memory of the dead poet. Debates over whether Rowley or Chatterton had written the ancient poems continued long after most antiquarians were satisfied that Thomas Rowley, parish priest, biographer of the fifteenth-century merchant prince William Canynge, historian of ancient Bristol, poet, dramatist, collector of rare paintings and old coins, was a pure invention of Thomas Chatterton, and that Chatterton was the true and only author of the poetry and everything else purportedly penned by Rowley. All manner of shadowy characters rushed in to claim a piece of the Chatterton action. A few were driven primarily by scholarly ambition. But, for most, the motives were not exactly lofty.

Editors corrupted Chatterton's writings to suit their fancy, while writings not penned by Chatterton were attributed to him. Biographers falsified their data, often so arbitrarily mingling fact and fiction that many of the details of Chatterton's life will never be verified. Of the numerous alleged "life" portraits, among them a Hogarth and a Gainsborough, all are certified counterfeits. The authenticity of his last verses and the location of his final burial ground will remain forever doubtful. The heavens themselves were falsified to fit the hindsight prophecies of an ingenious astrologer, who portrayed the stars at the hour of Chatterton's birth, 6 PM, November 20, 1752, as an "accumulated malevolence" of "malefic rays."

In the 1830s, just as the dust had settled around the Rowley-Chatterton debates, a new Chatterton rumor caught the attention of the public. The rumor was that shortly after his burial, Chatterton's bones had been removed from the pauper's grave in London to be reinterred in the St. Mary Redcliffe graveyard. This sentimental story, a probable fabrication, allegedly originated with Mrs. Edkins, a friend of Chatterton's mother who claimed to have seen the body of the poor dead boy a week or so after his suicide. It was lying in a box in an upstairs room of his childhood home. In 1810 Mrs. Edkins, who for forty years had strictly obeyed the vow of silence she claimed had been imposed on her by Sarah Chatterton, revealed this weighty secret to the Chatterton scholar George Cumberland. To the Edkins fabrication Cumberland appended a few of his own imaginary details.

Cumberland, who over the years had compiled considerable data on the life of the poet, related conflicting accounts of this alleged revelation and supposed event to various other writers interested in the life of Chatterton.

Did Mrs. Edkins lie to Cumberland? Or did Cumberland fabricate her story? Or did subsequent writers on the subject misrepresent them both?

Joseph Cottle, the young and enterprising bookseller who produced with Robert Southey the definitive collection of Chatterton's *Works* (1803), was the first to bring Cumberland's report of Mrs. Edkins's tale to the public. In a note to the 1829 volume of his own *Poems and Essays,* Cottle asserts that Chatterton's remains were removed from the Shoe Lane Workhouse grounds and sent to Bristol in a box constructed by the poet's uncle, a carpenter who resided in London. The coffin arrived at Mrs. Chatterton's house. Then, in great secrecy, in the dead of night, it was brought to the St. Mary Redcliffe Churchyard. A suicide's body was not allowed to lie in consecrated grounds, so the reinterment was attended only by Sarah Chatterton, a sympathetic sexton, and his assistant. By the time Mrs. Edkins supposedly told this tale to Cumberland, all these participants were dead.

A variation of the reinterment scenario appears next in George Cumberland's appendix to John Dix's *The Life of Chatterton.* Here Cumberland reports that his informant was a Mrs. Stockwell. According to Stockwell, Sarah Chatterton, in a burst of generosity which she subsequently regretted, had granted permission to a poor neighbor to bury his dead child over her son Tom's grave in the Bristol churchyard. Mrs. Stockwell, while she had not seen Chatterton's coffin, knew the very spot of the double grave. It was, she said, "on the right hand side of the lime tree, middle paved walk, in Redcliff Churchyard, about twenty feet from the father's grave, which is . . . in the paved walk, and where now Mrs. Chatterton and Mrs. Newton, her daughter, also lie." Cumberland's appendix to the most notorious of Chatterton's discredited biographies has received special citations for unbelievable circumstantial detail.

Any hopes that Chatterton might be buried in Bristol were nearly forgotten when, in 1855, George Pryce, an architectural writer, printed the following statement about Chatterton in his *Memorials of the Canynges Family:* "The bones of the poor lad have rested undisturbed from the period of his death in his father's grave in the churchyard of St. Mary Redcliffe—there to mingle in consecrated ground with those he loved in life." As his authorities the writer cites Dix's appendix by Cumberland and some pages from an 1853 letter written by Joseph Cottle to a friend. The Cottle letter is quoted:

> About forty years ago, Mr. Geo. Cumberland (a descendant of Bishop Cumberland, a literary and highly respectable man whom I well knew) called on me and said, "I have ascertained one important fact respecting Chatterton." "What is it?" I replied. "It is," said he, "that the marvelous

boy was buried in Redcliffe Churchyard." He continued, "I am just come from conversing with old Mrs. Edkins, a friend of Chatterton's mother: she affirmed to me this fact."

Cottle's letter then goes on to deliver a verbatim rendition of Mrs. Edkins's account, though it had allegedly been relayed to him forty-three years earlier.

Three years after he had published the Cottle tale, Pryce recognized that the entire story had been "without the slightest foundation in truth." As for Cumberland's data, that scholar "was not sufficiently careful in examining the veracity of the evidence which he had procured."

Occasionally the various burial fables would be revived among the citizens of Bristol. But, by the end of the nineteenth century, there were only a few die-hard adherents to the reinterment theory. Still, the question of Chatterton's final resting-place has remained a subject of conjecture well into the present century. Fifty years after the poet's suicide, when the Shoe Lane Workhouse was torn down, it is likely that the bodies in the pauper's graveyard were dug up and carted away—where to nobody is sure. One twentieth-century Chatterton scholar suggests: If the bodies were removed in 1828, his may be among those in the additional burial ground for St. Andrew's opened in 1754, and closed a hundred years later, in Gray's Inn Road. If they remained until the market site was sold in 1892—it is now crossed by Farringdon Avenue—they should be in the City of London Cemetery at Little Ilford, consecrated Nov. 16, 1857. To the scholar's comparatively wholesome possibility for poor Chatterton's bones, a scrupulous biographer appends his own sinister commentary: "This does not exhaust all the possibilities." He then quotes from a 1764 text called *Low Life,* "Sextons of parish churches, privately digging up, and sending to the houses of surgeons, the bodies of such people who were buried the preceding night, that died young, and after a short illness, to be anatomized."

Though the city of Bristol could not claim to hold the final remains of Thomas Chatterton, over the years there were commemorative ceremonies to "proclaim our darling Son, / Our pride, our Glory—Chatterton." In 1838 a group of prominent Bristoleans proposed a monument in the poet's honor to stand in the churchyard of St. Mary Redcliffe. Even at that late date, objections were raised on the grounds that Thomas Rowley was the real poet and therefore to honor Thomas Chatterton would be to honor a mere transcriber. Other objections came from those who believed Chatterton to be the true poet. These citizens did not wish to honor the memory of a forger and a suicide.

The money for the monument was nevertheless secured, but then the project ran up against the vehement opposition of the vicar of St. Mary's, who could not tolerate the idea of a monument to an unbeliever, a liar, a forger, a depraved person who had taken his own life in defiance of church law. Surely, the vicar reasoned, to immortalize the memory of such a boy would forever impair the morals of the youth of Bristol. Finally the vicar agreed to the monument but insisted on certain conditions. The monument could be erected on the north side of the church but only on unconsecrated grounds. The vicar also insisted that the monument be inscribed with some lines from his favorite volume of verse, *Night Thoughts*. The rage of Europe, that Ossian-like volume belonged to the literature of melancholy and sentimentality that inspired Goethe's *Sorrows of Young Werther*. The vicar selected some lines that condemned but granted some faint hope of immunity to infidels:

> *Know all, know infidels, unapt to know,*
> *Tis immortality your nature solves,*
> *Tis immortality deciphers man,*
> *And opens all the mysteries of his make.*
> *Without it half his instincts are riddles*
> *Without it all his virtues are a dream:*
> *His very crimes attest his dignity;*
> *His sateless appetite of gold and fame*
> *Declares him born for blessings infinite.*

Chatterton's admirers had no choice but to agree to the vicar's conditions. But on the side of the monument facing the porch steps of St. Mary's they put their own words:

> *A poor and friendless boy was he, to whom*
> *Is raised this monument without a tomb.*
> *There seek his dust, there O'er his genius sigh,*
> *Where famished outcasts unrecorded lie:*
> *Here let his name, for here his genius rose*
> *To might of ancient days, in peace repose!*
> *Here, wonderous boy! tis more than want consign'd,*
> *To cold neglect, worse famine of the mind:*
> *All uncongenial the bright world within*
> *To that without of darkness and of sin,*
> *He lived a mystery—died. Here, reader, pause:*
> *Let God be judge, and mercy plead the cause.*

Soon after the monument was installed, the vestry of St. Mary's decided to restore the North Porch of the church, and the vicar seized the occasion to rescind his reluctant promises. He had the monument taken down so that it would not interfere with the restoration.

In 1857 the obstinate vicar was replaced by one more genial, who permitted the monument to be reinstated near the North Porch, insisting like his predecessor that it stand outside consecrated ground. There the pentagonal monument remained for 110 years: thirty-one feet high, constructed in three stages; a pedestal, a gray limestone shaft, and a statue of a boy in the Colston's School uniform, holding in his left hand a scroll inscribed, "Aella, a tragedie." The offensive lines from *Night Thoughts* were replaced at this time by lines from Coleridge's 1794 *Monody on the Death of Chatterton:*

> *Sweet Flower of Hope! free Nature's genial child!*
> *That didst so fair disclose thy early bloom,*
> *Filling the wide air with a rich perfume!*
> *For thee in vain all heavenly aspects smil'd;*
> *From the hard world brief respite could they win.*

Below, on a simple rectangular tablet, appeared the epitaph that Thomas Chatterton, in one of his bittersweet, half-serious, half-hoaxing moods, had designed as part of the fake suicide note that would enable him to escape from his indentures.

> To the Memory of Thomas Chatterton. Reader, Judge not: if thou art a Christian, believe that he shall be Judged by a Superior Power; to that Power only is he now answerable

In 1967 the monument was taken down once more. The pedestal with its inscriptions and the limestone shaft were demolished. The statue of the Blue Coat boy was placed in a shed, a sort of outhouse adjoining the Thomas Chatterton House.

TWO

A Fatherless Boy Grows Up in Bristol

The narrows of Bristol and lofty spires of St. Mary Redcliffe Church. Family life: The father Thomas and the mother Sarah. The altruistic surrender of Chatterton's sister Mary. A Colston's School inmate: Early religious poems and social satires. The conflict between belief and cynicism. Apprentice to Mr. Lambert: Chained to his ignominious labors, Chatterton tries valiantly to remain true to his beliefs—romantic longings for Miss Polly Rumsey. The ideal of manhood of Sir William Canynge.

ACCORDING to the astrologer Ebenezer Sibley, the causes of Chatterton's suicide lay in the conjunction of the stars. The fate of the poet was already sealed at his birth. Writes Sibley in his *New and Complete Illustration of Occult Sciences* (1797), Chatterton's unfortunate life and dreadful end were presaged by the coalition of the Sun, Saturn, Venus, Mercury and the Part of Fortune, in the sixth house, which presages every species of misfortune that can arise from poverty, and from the chicanery of prostituted women; the immediate effect of the baleful rays of Saturn and Venus. To this fatal conjunction, the approach of Mars potentiated the accumulating malevolence. Save for Mercury who stamped "upon the native so early and so extraordinary a turn for literary pursuits," all other stars were positioned to write the wretched life and fatal end. "This gentleman," said Ebenezer Sibley, "was a native of Bristol, much cele-

brated for his literary productions, and for the originality of his ideas, which rose early in the horizon of his life, and set as prematurely upon its hemisphere, without even allowing him to attain its meridian altitude. In short, this is a very remarkable, at the same time that it is a most unfortunate geniture."

By Sibley's time astrology no longer enjoyed the reputation that it had a little more than a century earlier, when some of the most powerful figures in the land were known to consult the stars in making state decisions. But even in the late eighteenth century, when reason, intellect, and philosophical inquiry had been given more importance, a larger proportion of people than is the case today probably placed some credence in astrology. Others participated enthusiastically in the vogue for books of esoteric and occult knowledge which was a pronounced feature of the so-called Age of Reason. Thomas Chatterton's father reflected both these tendencies. He was "deeply read in Cornelius Agrippa," and like most eighteenth-century editions of Agrippa, his contained the spurious fourth book of *De Occulta Philosophia*. Into his copy of *History of the Holy Bible*, the elder Chatterton entered the age of the moon next to the births of Mary and his son Giles Malpas.

This first Chatterton son, who came into the world December 12, 1750 and died four months later, was named for the wealthy pinmaker who had donated the Pile Street schoolmaster's house in which the three Chatterton children were born. When Thomas Chatterton was an infant the rhythms and sounds of his mother's voice and the bells of the nearby St. Mary Redcliffe Church would have sometimes mingled, sometimes competed for his attention. When he first looked outside the house, he would have seen the lofty spires and archways of St. Mary's. He played commander to his underling playmates in the shadow of her engraved Gothic towers. Even as he wrote home from London to his childhood friend Thomas Carey, bragging of his successes as a freethinking journalist and adventures as a rake who could "make love to all but love none," he confessed his enduring affection for St. Mary's: "Step into Radclift Church, look at the Noble Arches, observe the Symetry the Regularity of the whole. How amazing must that Idea be which Can Comprehend at once all that Magnificence of Architecture, do not examine one particular beauty, or dwell upon it Minutely, take the Astonishing whole into your *Empty Pericranium*."

It is the entire encompassing glory of St. Mary's that Chatterton recommends to his friend. But simpleminded adoration would not do for a sophisticated London journalist. So Thomas recalls some other details from his beloved St. Mary's that serve as analogies to the narrow visions of some of his contemporaries. "Step Aside A Little and turn Your Attention to the Ornaments of a Pillar of the Chapel, you see minute Carvings of Minute Designs, whose Chief Beauties are deformity and Intricacy.... Examine all the Laborious Sculpture, is there any Part of it worth the Trouble it must have Cost the Artist. Yet how Eagerly do Children and Fools gaze upon these littlenesses."

The *Holy Bible*, a few other books, some antique Roman coins, and the scraps of ancient parchment that had come from a coffer in the Muniment Room of St. Mary's were young Chatterton's sole tangible inheritances from his father. But through the family history and legend, his father's family's intimate association with St. Mary's was transmitted to the son he would never know.

On October 17, 1802, Mary wrote to Cottle and Southey, who were about to publish her brother's collected works: "It is unnecessary to inform you by what means the parchments were in our possession. My father received them in the year 1750. He discovered by some writings he found among them that persons of the name Chadderton were sextons of St.

Mary Redclift parish 120 years before. His father had affirmed the family had held that office, to use his own phrase, 'Time out of mind.'" Mary was proclaiming the family lore. Once the Rowley controversy caught fire, she and her mother told the sexton legend to all the scholars and journalists who came to interview them, most of whom received it as gospel. But one eighteenth-century scholar, Michael Lort, never took any testimony about Thomas Chatterton simply for granted, and he did not let the "time out of mind" legend pass his scrutiny either. He inquired of the vicar of Redcliffe, "How many of and for how long have any of the family of the Chattertons been sextons of Ratcliffe Church?" and got the reply, "One only, who died ab't 30 years ago." That sexton was Chatterton's father's uncle, John.

Whether or not the Chattertons had been sextons, we can be certain that the Chatterton family was caught up in the daily life of St. Mary Redcliffe Church, *longe pulcherina omnium ecclesia* ("by far the fairest of all churches"), and resided in the Redcliffe parish or nearby, if not since "time out of mind" at least for a century.

The Redcliffe Parish Accounts list the Chattertons as masons who from 1661 onwards performed odd jobs in the service of St. Mary's. In 1662 a Chatterton "pulled the weedes out of the leads and tower," for which he was paid 00/00/05. Two years later Chaterton (sic) the mason, for work "on the church for stone," received the then munificent sum of 4/18/9. From the 1660s and through the early eighteenth century, Chattertons were paid for work on the tower steps, removing dirt under the churchyard wall, lighting the lamps, and repairing the cross.

Long before Chatterton invented Rowley, even before he learned to read, he could stare at the marble figure of Canynge, whose magnificent tomb lay within the South Transept of St. Mary's. By the time he was seven, Chatterton would have become sufficiently literate to decipher the words inscribed beneath the tomb.

Mr. William Caning, ye Richest marchant of ye towne of Bristow afterwards chosen 5 time mayor of said towne for ye good of ye comon wealth of ye fame. Hee was in order of Priesthood 7 years & afterwards.
Dean of Westbury and died ye 7th of Novem 1474 which said William did build with ye said towne of Westbury a Colledge (which his canons) and ye said William did maintaine by space of 8 years 800 handy crafts men, besides carpenters & masons, every day 100 men. Besides King Edward ye 4th had of ye said William 3000 marks for his peace to be had in 2470 tonnes of shiping.
These are ye names of his shipping with his burthen:

TONNES	TONNES
ye Mary Canings 400	ye Mary Batt 220
ye Mary Redcliffe 500	ye Little Nicholas 140
ye Mary & John 900	ye Margarett 200
ye Galliott 50	ye Katherine of Boston 22
ye Katherine 140	A ship in Ireland 100

If Chatterton's geniture—his stars, his birthplace, his family's association with St. Mary's, his social class, and all other manifest circumstances attending his birth—was one strand of Fortune's work, another was his family genealogy.

Thomas Chatterton, the poet's father, was born August 8, 1713. After attending school at Colston's, serving as apprentice to the freeholder Captain Saunders and for seven years more as an assistant teacher, he became the schoolmaster of The Redcliffe and St. Thomas Charity School on Pile street, "instructing the boys and finding them pen, ink and paper." Around Redcliffe, Thomas Chatterton, Sr. was esteemed for his elegant handwriting and musical tastes. He was said to be "a complete master of the theory and practice of music." When he was thirty-three years old he was appointed a "singing man" of the Bristol Cathedral, a lay clerkship that drew on both these special abilities, as his duties involved the copying of music into books belonging to the cathedral. He was also employed part-time by a London attorney for whom he worked copying deeds. Chatterton's collection of Roman coins was admired by his friends and neighbors. At the time of his death he owned about 150 books and had borrowed many more from his friend Mr. Broughton, the vicar of Redcliffe.

On Monday, April 15, 1748 the 35-year-old schoolmaster married 16½-year-old Sarah Young. Sarah was a barely literate seamstress, sewing teacher, and designer of needlework patterns, but nothing is known about her before her marriage, "and little enough afterwards." She has been depicted as a "decent, plain" woman, without any extraordinary qualities, "a colourless personality," a woman of "no shining abilities." She is routinely dismissed as having had no real effect on her son: "She cannot, anyhow, be classed among the remarkable mothers of remarkable men."

In contrast, young Thomas's father's influences have been highly valued. By some crafty reasoning, even the unpropitious circumstance of the father having died before his son's birth has been promoted as a positive contribution to the boy's eventual fame. "His opportunities considered, Thomas Chatterton, senior, appears a person remarkable enough, and his early death the first of those misfortunes which have rendered his second son at least as notable as have that son's native powers." From that quaint system of reckoning we are led to assume that the son's native powers can be attributed directly to inheritances from his father: the beautiful and precise handwriting that enabled the boy to fabricate the parchments, the love of antiquities and ancient literature that inspired the creation of the ancient history of Bristol. Perhaps even the poetical and musical gifts latent in *A Catch for Three Voices,* which Chatterton's father composed for a festivity held at his favorite Bristol tavern, the Pineapple, provided the source for the boy's sensitivity to nuances of speech and rhythms of language.

A CATCH FOR THREE VOICES

The words and music by MR. CHATTERTON (Father to Thomas Chatterton, the Poet) one of the Choristers of Bristol Cathedral

Other biographers, particularly those inspired by Wordsworth's "marvelous boy" who "perished in his pride," take a dimmer view of the poet's father. They have little sympathy for the schoolmaster's association with the Pineapple, "a club the main object of which seems to have been to promote among its members a habit of excessive drinking." In the more generous interpretations of Thomas Chatterton, Sr.'s love of jolly times, meat, drink, and clothes, he is characterized as "an exuberant" man with "gregarious habits" and a "rough and boisterous conviviality." Less sympathetic accounts describe him as "an ordinary man of ordinary stock" with "no scholarly habit; his mind was not thoughtful," and his musical gifts are categorized according to the circumstances that inspired them. "He knew something about music and even composed a catch for three voices, a kind of drinking song, said to be an extremely dull performance. He sang well, he loved good roaring company at the ale house, he was careless, plodding, unaspiring, and without a trait to distinguish him from his roistering kind. In fact, a colorless person, even in his bibulous way of life not beyond the general custom of his age; for he was not quite a sot."

Those scholars who did not cherish the father will grudgingly concede the worthiness of Sarah's modest character, "a large, motherly soul, simple, unimaginative and affectionate." They contrast her conscientious attitudes with those of her husband, seen as "shiftless and improvident," leaving the poor woman "nothing but a handful of books and a memory none too fragrant." While the sentimental idealizers of Chatterton are willing to grant that his father might have been a man of "more than ordinary ability for his social position and the times he lived in," generally they stress the unwholesome qualities of the heritage that he left to his son.

> He possessed eccentricities which, though harmless in themselves, divided him off from his neighbors, and made him a mark for their observation. He talked little, was absent-minded in company, and was given to walking alone by the riverside, muttering to himself and gesticulating with his arms and, "like all his family was so proud." With such peculiarities and accomplishments in the father it is not very difficult to divine whence the son, the boy-poet, derived his more marked idiosyncrasies, however abnormal they may appear.

Sarah is credited in this account with the more benign influences on her son's character

> She had a fair share of educational qualifications for the times she lived in—times when duchesses wrote and talked ungrammatically, and when

even professors of learned societies did not understand their own language. She was not only a good-hearted woman, with domestic qualities of a high order, but had a strong love for her kindred and worked nobly for their welfare.

Moreover, "from what is known of his mother's disposition, he must have been better cared for than were many children of the poor in those times." A niece thought she had been "one of the best of women." It is generally agreed that whatever her intellectual limitations, Sarah "devoted more care and intelligence to the upbringing of her family than was customary in those days."

Less ominously fatalistic than Ebenezer Sibley's heavenly accumulation of malevolence, but hardly more optimistic, is one biographer's hindsight prediction that the fatherless boy, son of a poverty-bound widow, had entered the world at 6 PM on November 20, 1752, "heavily handicapped for life's race." To succeed at all, such a boy would have had to possess exceptional qualities of mind and temperament or else have been the recipient of exceptional good fortune.

There was much that was exceptional about Thomas's upbringing. Whether or not he actually inherited his mental abilities and temperamental characteristics from his father, he was born into a household that, whatever else its limitations, prided itself on its association with St. Mary's and placed a high value on artistic accomplishment and learning.

It was more in their general attitude toward learning and artistic enterprise than in any absolute belief in Tom's literary antics that Sarah and Mary expressed their faith and support. In fact, they found most of what he wrote incomprehensible and at times even alarming. As Mary would confess, "The language was so old, that I could not understand." The Rowley antiques were to her "all a mere blank, I had no relish for them. This my brother used sometimes to perceive, would grow angry, and scold me for my lack of taste." As for his satirical poetry and political tracts, those freethinking pieces were banned from the household. Thomas's father's mother, a pipe-smoking lady who seems to have had little or no influence on her grandson, regarded Tom as a dear but incorrigibly mad child. She agreed with her daughter-in-law that freethinking would sooner or later involve their Thomas in some terrible scrape. For Chatterton's pre-Rowleyan heroic poetry, particularly the boyish and bloodthirsty *Battle of Hastings,* Mary had not a shred of fondness: "What I sickened my poor brother with, I remember very well, was my inattention to the *Battle of Hastings* which before he used to be perpetually repeating." After a while, sensing his family's incomprehension, Chatterton decided to keep his poetry to himself. However, when he needed an audience he would usually turn to his patient and trusted Mary, and occasionally to his mother. Often before showing his writings to a would-be sponsor, Chatterton would try them out on his sister. All the while he would pretend to be reading aloud from Rowley. Mary's tastes in literature were not entirely arbitrary. The one Rowley that Mary liked immensely was the tragedy *Aella,* a poetic drama recognized as Chatterton's most exquisite creation. As for her judgment on the bloody Hastings poem, no less a mind than George Gregory, the learned antiquarian who was Thomas's first official biographer, expressed an even greater revulsion toward that work. "The mere detail of violence and carnage, with nothing to interest curiosity, or engage the more tender passions, can be pleasing to few readers. There is not a single episode to enliven the tedious narrative, and but a few of the beauties of poetry to relieve the mind from the disgusting subject."

Despite her difficulty in grasping the full extent of her brother's prodigious intellectual and artistic gifts, Mary's sisterly veneration and artistic sensibilities prompted her to do everything within her power to encourage her brother's literary abilities. From the way she presents the story of her brother's life, it is evident that Mary vicariously gratified her own artistic ambitions by fostering those of her younger brother.

The altruistic surrender of her own ambitions in favor of her brother's served as a convenient mask for any rivalrous feelings she might have had. In the eighteenth century only an exceptional woman would have been admitted to artistic, intellectual, or professional circles. It was nearly unthinkable for a woman of Mary's station and social class to nourish hopes of becoming more than a housewife or shopkeeper. The role of governess, which Mary eventually did achieve, was aspiration enough for a poor and slightly educated young lady. Women and younger male siblings, even those from the middle and upper classes, were always expected to defer to the eldest (or only) brother. Most accepted their assigned lot with silent ambivalence. Some, like Mary, were inclined to adopt an altruistic attitude toward their more fortunate brothers. Throughout her brother's lifetime, Mary was Tom's protector, adviser, teacher, and loyal champion. After his death she became a credible and clever informant on the circumstances of his infancy, boyhood, and young manhood, shrewdly rearranging the facts according to the shifting sands of the Rowley controversy.

At the age of eight, Tom left home for the Colston School, and it was there that the family romance of Thomas Rowley and Sir William Canynge began to stir in his mind.

To bear the ignominy of his life at Colston's, Chatterton gradually invented the interweaving fantasies of Thomas Rowley and Jack-and-the-Beanstalk. In the one fantasy he became the virtuous son of the benevolent William Canynge. Rowley's fictional relationship with Canynge clearly represents the wish of a poor but gifted boy to be restored to the position of the artistic son of a wealthy merchant prince. As his own father had rescued the parchments from St. Mary's, so Canynge had been the benefactor and restorer of that very church. And Rowley would bring to Canynge the poems, gold coins, paintings, and statuary that would transform the already powerful man of wealth into a patron of the arts, a noble spirit who could rise above the narrow mentality of the city of Bristol, "where illiteracy joined hands with display."

With the second scenario Chatterton acted out the role of the imposturous Jack who believed he was entitled to put one over on the crude, bumbling giants of Bristol who cared for nothing more in the way of entertainment than to eat, drink, and have a jolly good time at the neighborhood tavern.

Our common sense allows us to appreciate how a boy might seek restitution through rising above his ignominious beginnings by acquiring a status or identity other than the miserable one that had been dealt to him by chance. Even his penchant for revenge might strike a compassionate chord. Do we not sympathize with Jack as he steals from the giant? For who among us has not at some moment or other reproached Nature or Destiny for not having conferred on us greater advantages? We feel entitled to right the wrongs that have been done to us.

Was Chatterton really so different from most boys his age? It is not at all unusual for a boy on the verge of manhood to try to prove himself by assuming grandiose postures and roles. Every adolescent, male or female, will occasionally manipulate others to advance his or her psychological cause. But the difference is that for the potential impostor, lying, cheating, and manipulating become a way of life. His shaky masculine identity is held together by the false images he imposes on others.

Certainly not every fatherless boy surrounded by adoring females is destined to grow up with a defective sense of his own masculinity. What is crucial is the mother's ideal of masculinity and how she conveys that ideal to her son. Not enough is known about the fantasies and attitudes of Sarah and Mary to draw specific connections between their inner lives and the behavior of young Thomas. We can, however, infer from their reminiscences and Chatterton's letters and literary productions that in a general way they unconsciously fostered and encouraged the little boy's sense of grandiosity and entitlement. Chatterton did grow up with the burden of having to be the man of the house. He did construe himself as the rescuer of and provider for his household of women. Even so, many of the anxiety-arousing ambitions engendered by Sarah's and Mary's adoration could have been mitigated by later circumstances. Along the way to adulthood, life provides opportunities for modifying infantile scenarios. Crucial among such favorable circumstances is the chance to identify with an adult man whom the boy can respect and admire. Others are respect and admiration for the talents and abilities one actually possesses and exposure to an educational environment that will enhance such assets.

On August 3, 1760, Chatterton donned the uniform of Colston's Hospital School: a blue robe with orange lining, orange stockings, and a blue bonnet to cover his head, which had been shaved in the rounded form of a tonsure as though he were about to enter the priesthood. Even in that dismal environment in which poetry could not easily blossom and flourish there were some redeeming touches of medievalism. Colston's was founded on the site of a Carmelite priory that had been known as White Friars, and several ancient arches were still standing in Chatterton's day.

Colston's Hospital School was like a benevolent reformatory. The Blue-Coat boys were referred to as inmates. Each had his number. Each wore a brass badge bearing a dolphin, the founder's crest. The boys rose before six, read the scriptures or sang psalms, had their breakfast of beer and bread or water gruel, and by seven o'clock were seated at classes, where they remained until eleven. After a noontime dinner of beer, meat or vegetable, and bread, the inmates returned to their classrooms for four more hours of education, ending at five. Then, following a supper of beer and cheese, the boys were expected to be in bed by eight. The younger boys slept three in a bed; the older ones were promoted to the luxury of only two in a bed.

Except for Thursdays, when he might study "but til three," Saturdays and saint's days when he was permitted to visit his family from one until seven, and Sundays, which were devoted entirely to catechisms and other religious exercises, the six in the morning to eight at night schedule was Thomas Chatterton's daily routine.

For nearly seven years, this contemplative, imaginative boy was consigned to the dullest sort of learning. Had his mother applied for a scholarship to St. John's College at Oxford or even to the nearby free grammar school, perhaps Chatterton would have been exposed to an educational environment more compatible to his temperament and intellectual gifts. He would have read the classics. He would have learned Latin. In the months before he left for London, Chatterton would occasionally admit his worries to his sister: "I wish I knew the classicals, I then could do anything." Mary, in her typical sisterly way, would bolster her brother's spirits by telling him that he knew quite a lot already. And Tom would reply with his characteristic manly bravado, "As it is, my name will live three hundred years."

As it was, Sarah probably had chosen the least damaging school environment then available to a child of Thomas's social class. Oxford was in a perilous state, with low enrollments, little or no commitment to teaching, and an incredibly dissipated student body. Moreover, commoners did not fare well there. Many parents preferred to send their children anywhere but to the universities because of the dissolute habits students picked up there. Some of the grammar schools were as bad. A place like Colston's would have seemed to be the safest option in terms of insuring vocational opportunities.

The poverty-bound Mrs. Chatterton counted herself fortunate that her son had been nominated and accepted at Colston's, where, thirty-seven years before, her husband had enrolled. Sarah was immensely grateful that Thomas would be housed and boarded, and Colston's had the special advantage of being within walking distance. Sarah could have her Tom beneath her roof for at least one day each week. Best of all, becoming a Colston inmate meant that a boy's future employment was practically guaranteed. In its day, Colston's was well-known as a training school whose educational fare of Church of England catechism, reading, handwriting, and accounting arithmetic produced obedient apprentices to drapers, mariners, potters, ropemakers, tobacconists, grocers, and smiths—although only once or twice in a decade would a Colston boy be bound to an apprenticeship as schoolteacher or as attorney's scrivener. Still, it was central to the Colston tradition that each boy at age fourteen or fifteen would be bound for seven years to an apprenticeship suitable to his talents. Colston's itself paid the indenture fee of ten pounds. There were a few strict stipulations. The boys were to be Anglicans only. They could not be apprenticed to Dissenters.

Edward Colston, a native Bristolean born into extreme poverty, had gone on to make considerable money from the slave trade and a variety of other commercial enterprises. In 1710 he founded the school that he named after himself so that future generations of poor boys could have the chance to achieve financial success comparable to his own. Colston, who died a bachelor in 1721, proudly responded to those who would urge marriage, "Every helpless widow is my wife and distressed orphans my children." However, Colston was not the stepfather Chatterton had in mind.

On Colston's Day of 1839 the foundation stone of Chatterton's beleaguered monument was laid in Redcliffe Churchyard. Present-day visitors to Bristol cannot escape the name Colston. Still standing are his two schools and his two almshouses on St. Michael's Hill and in King Street. There is Colston Hall and Colston Parade. On Colston Avenue sits the bronzed Colston himself, propped up on one elbow, leaning on a bronze cane.

Because Colston's ambitions for his little orphans went no higher than providing them with a down-to-earth, practical education to be followed by a commercial apprenticeship, the qualifications he set forth for headmaster were simple and to the point. He "must be a member of the Church of England, of a sober life and conversation, not under five and twenty years, one that can write a good hand and understands the grounds of arithmetic." He was to receive an annual salary of one hundred pounds. Either he or one of his assistants must "attend at their Meals or Times of Devotion to prevent Disorder."

Chatterton did not exhibit the typical signs of potential impostureship while at Colston's. On the contrary, the schoolboy Chatterton was obedient and possibly more trustworthy than most boys his age. As Mary reported it, "He was a lover of truth from the earlyest dawn of reason, and nothing would move him so much as being bely'd. When in the school we were informed by the usher, his master depended on his verasity on all occasions." Chatterton always completed his dreary assignments, if not as brilliantly as he no doubt could have, at least in line with the Colston standards of what was acceptable. He was not even to be counted among the few oddball poetical boys who were permitted to form a group. The headmaster, Mr. Haynes, known to be fond of Chatterton, would later testify that the lad, though quite bright and capable, had never distinguished himself in the poetical realm. A few of the other boys might have written the magnificent Rowley poems, but certainly not Thomas Chatterton. Even Chatterton's school chum, Thomas Carey, who after Chatterton's death composed the elegy celebrating his friend's precocious intellectual and spiritual powers, was convinced that Chatterton was incapable of the Rowleys. "His abilities for his age, were beyond conception great, but not equal to the works of Rowley, particularly at the age he produced them to light." Aside from his general aloofness and his belief that he was made of finer clay than the other Blue-Coat boys, about the only thing that would have designated Chatterton as a potential impostor or possible great poet was his nimble fantasy life. And that he kept discreetly hidden.

When Chatterton was at Colston's, the Blue-Coat boys were, by and large, an orderly bunch. Only two had to be expelled, one for elopement and misdemeanor, the other for theft and misdemeanor. Two generations later, in the mid 1780s, the demeanor of the boys, no doubt infected by the romantic rebellion and political dissension in the air of most of Europe, underwent a change. One boy was expelled "for running away, throwing his school clothes over the wall, and for theft." Five boys had conspired to cut off the usher's hair and had cut up their own coats and made them into trousers. Eight boys were expelled. Six boys had to be flogged. A new boy who had stolen a penknife and run off wearing the coat of the master was sent to Bridewell prison and to further insure his eventual reformation, threatened with a sending to sea. That horrific threat could keep even the most unruly boy in line. As James Boswell commented, "No man will be a sailor, who has contrivance enough to get himself into a jail; for, being in a ship is being in a jail, with the chance of being drowned. The man in jail has more room, better food, and commonly better company."

With the exception of some scurrilous verse written about the mean-spirited headmaster who reigned during Chatterton's first two years at Colston's, the boy whose poetic daring and rebellious, freethinking attitudes made him a symbol of the romantic movement may have been one of the more docile of a generally conformist group of Blue-Coat inmates. While most inmates let off steam and played boisterous games in their free time, Chatterton would sit quietly reading a book or thinking. As it turned out, he was writing poetry and satirical pieces, but he chose to preserve them in his private notebooks or to submit them to the local newspaper rather than to the conventional poetry group at Colston's. We learn about these private writing escapades from Mary as she sums up her brother's stay at Colston's:

> About his 10th year he began (with the trifle my mother allowed him for pocket money) to hire books from the circulating library and we were informed by the usher made rapid progress in arithmetick. Between his 11th and 12th year he wrote a caterlogue of books he had read to the number of 70. History and divinity were the chief subjects, his school mates informed us he retired to read at the hours allotted for play. At 12 years old he was confirmed by the bishop, he made very sencible serious remarks on the awfullness of the ceremony and his own feelings and convictions during it. Soon after this in the week he was door-keeper he made some verses on the last day, I think about 18 lines, paraphrased the 9 chapter of Job and not long after some chapters in Isaiah.

On New Year's Day of 1764 Mary presented him with a pocket notebook into which he might copy his poetry. When he returned the pocketbook to her at the end of the year it was filled with writing, most of which was poetry. Mary was impressed with the beneficial effects of poetic enterprise: "He had been gloomy from the time he began to learn, but we remark'd he was more cheerfull after he began to write poetry. Some saterical peicis we saw soon after."

Of Chatterton's Colston-day writings, which are said to have included numerous satirical, religious, and love poems, only seven have survived. Of these, only the three transcribed from originals in one of Chatterton's Colston notebooks are of certain authenticity. The other four likely Chattertons were anonymously published in *Felix Farley's Bristol Journal.* They had been sent directly to the editor by the Blue-Coat boy.

One of the poems written in Chatterton's notebook was entitled *Apostate Will* and dated April 14, 1764. This fifty-four-line poem, a satirical fable about a Methodist convert whose religious fervor is inspired by avarice, presaged the satirical style and attitudes Chatterton would adopt after he gave up his Rowley romance:

> *But, be his outward what it will,*
> *His heart was an Apostate's still;*
> *He'd oft profess an hallow'd flame,*
> *And every where preach'd Wesley's name;*
> *He was a preacher and what not,*
> *As long as money could be got;*

Another satirical fable composed later that same year, *Sly Dick,* had as its subject a schoolboy inspired to theft by a spritely dream apparition: "A noble Purse rewards thy pains,/A Purse to hold thy filching Gains." However, the same world-weary eleven-year-old had also begun to sing in a Rowleyan voice. The last of the pocket-notebook poems was a straightforward religious devotion inspired by the birth of Christ, the lovely lyric *A Hymn for a Christmas Day.* Traces of cynicism were already marked on Chatterton's character, but the Blue-Coat boy with the tonsured hair had not betrayed the illuminated folio letters and the antique Bible of his childhood. Like the spiraling Gothic towers that rose above the Pile Street cottage, the son of the composer of "A Catch for Three Voices" would rise above his ignominious beginnings and learn to sing from God himself:

> *My Soul exert thy Powers, adore,*
> *Upon Devotion's plumage soar*
>   *To celebrate the Day:*
> *The God from whom Creation sprung*
> *Shall animate my grateful Tongue;*
> *From him I'll catch the Lay!*

In the mid-nineteenth century, after the Rowley controversy simmered down and Chatterton began to be respected as a genuine poet in his own right, scholars searched the 1763 through 1765 issues of Bristol's *Felix Farley* daily newspaper for possible early writings by Chatterton. There they discovered three anonymous poems and a letter which, because their content, form, and style so closely resembled the contents of Chatterton's Colston notebook, have generally been accepted as among the first published works of Thomas Chatterton, written between his tenth and twelfth years.

In the January 8, 1763 issue is a religious poem, *On the Last Epiphany, or Christ Coming to Judgment*, a lyrical narrative of deep religious sentiment. It seems very likely that these sixteen lines are the ones that Mary referred to as "some verses on the last day, I think about 18 lines."

> *Behold! just coming from above,*
> *The Judge, with Majesty and Love!*
> *The Sky divides, and rolls away,*
> *T'admit him thro' the Realms of Day!*
> *The Sun astonish'd, hides its Face,*
> *The Moon and Stars, with Wonder gaze,*
> *At Jesu's bright superior Rays!*
> *Dread Light'nings flash, and Thunders roar,*
> *And shake the Earth, and briny Shore;*
> *The Trumpet sounds at Heaven's Command,*
> *And pierceth thro' the Sea and Land;*
> *The Dead in each now hear the Voice,*
> *The Sinners fear and Saints rejoice:*
> *For now the aweful Hour is come,*
> *When ev'ry Tenant of the Tomb,*
> *Must rise, and take his everlasting Doom.*

Then, appearing one year later, in the January 7, 1764 issue of *Felix Farley* are the three pieces that scholars presume to be the original literary matrix for Chatterton's satirical writings. The central themes of these narratives concern the corruption of religious devotion by commercial greed. They are literary responses to the true story of an actual churchwarden of St. Mary Redcliffe who had recently come under public attack for removing the gold cross from the graveyard and carting away clay from around the graves to use in his brickmaking yard. The first of the narratives seems to be quintessential Chatterton. It displays strong anticlerical sentiments which point in the direction of Chatterton's later freethinking works. *The Churchwarden and the Apparition, A Fable* depicts the greed of the churchwarden, who even in sleep cannot escape his mercenary desires, "But still the pleasing Hope of Gain/That never left his active Brain."

The next of these pieces published in January 1764 was a short poem, *I've let my Yard, and sold my Clay,* a straightforward first-person admission from the churchwarden on his own mercenary act. *Letter from Fullford, the Gravedigger,* the last in the series, is an ironically reasoned satire in which a gravedigger reports on the vandalisms of his headmaster, who "has taken it into his Head to level the Church-yard; and by digging and throwing about his *Clay* there, and defacing the Stones, makes such Confusion among the *Dead.*" The psychological sophistication and literary wit of this satire would certainly exceed the grasp of most eleven-year-olds. The gravedigger uses the churchwarden's venality to justify his own imminent corruption: "And I see no Reason why I may not get a *profitable Job* out of the Church, as well as my GREAT MASTER,—as I find that's the Game nowadays,—tho' Decency, Convenience, or the like, be the Pretence."

These works do appear to be genuine Chatterton. Certainly the letter's theme—the infiltration of Bristol trade mentality into holy works and religious deeds—was to become the creative principle for the two literary voices of Thomas Chatterton. He could speak with sincerity and poetic eloquence for Canynge's benevolence but then a year later turn to the satirical journalism that denigrated every sacred institution of eighteenth-century England: religion, marriage, nobility.

In that Bristol where people gave themselves up to trade entirely, where "the very parsons of Bristol talk of nothing but trade and how to turn the penny," where "all are in a hurry, running up and down with cloudy looks, and busy faces, loading, carrying and unloading goods and merchandises of all sorts, from place to place," the Colston schoolboy was trying desperately to hold on to the uplifting visions and inspirations of St. Mary Redcliffe and Sir William Canynge's marble effigy.

On July 1, 1767, the very day that Chatterton graduated from Colston's, he signed his indenture papers, committing himself to another seven-year term, this time as apprentice "to be educated as a Scrivener," to Mr. John Lambert, a twenty-eight-year-old gentleman, attorney, and member of the Church of England. And as his indentures commanded, during that time "Taverns he shall not frequent, at Dice he shall not play. Fornication he shall not commit. Matrimony he shall not contract, or damage to his said Master within the said Term he shall not do; but well and faithfully shall behave himself in all things, as well in Words as deeds, as a good and faithful Apprentice, according to the Use and Custom of Bristol." When the apprenticeship was over, Mr. Lambert would pay Chatterton four shillings and sixpence and give him two suits of clothing, "one for Holydays and the other in lieu of his salary." Despite his elegant handwriting and his relatively dignified apprenticeship, Chatterton's prospects for the next seven years of his life were dim.

In large urban centers like Bristol and London many apprentices found ways to provide themselves with some of the pleasures forbidden by their indenture papers. Although by the middle of the eighteenth century apprentices were afforded some legal protection, some continued to be "exposed to almost limitless sadism from their masters, mitigated only by the fact that the bolder spirits among them could, and sometimes did sue their torturers for assault." Thus, apprentices might be treated as virtual slaves or they might instead enjoy a life of relative freedom, depending on their own courage, the amount of work required of them, and the whimsy and temperament of their masters.

John Lambert, though he would acquire from some of Chatterton's biographers a rather nasty reputation as a tyrannical and meanspirited man, was actually not a bad sort. After Chatterton's suicide, he was fair-minded in his appraisal of his apprentice's character, praising the regularity of his habits and declaring that he had never had any occasion to charge him with ill behavior or neglecting his work. Lambert's sole complaint about his apprentice was of "a sullen, gloomy temper which showed itself in the family and among the servants by his therewith declaring his intentions to do away with himself."

The office hours at Lambert's were from 8:00 AM to 8:00 PM with one hour off for midday dinner, two hours off each evening, and Sundays free. Chatterton was not overworked by his master. As his sister reported, "He had little of his masters business to do. Sometimes not 2 hours in the day, which gave him an opportunity to pursue his genius." All in all, probably because of his own talents and his father's reputation as a copier of legal documents, Chatterton had been assigned to what most boys would have considered a choice apprenticeship. But to a youth like Chatterton for whom pride was "19th/20th" of his soul, the conditions of servitude, no matter how benevolent, were intolerable.

Rather than pleasing him, the lack of significant or meaningful work at Lambert's was for Chatterton a mortification. The fact that he was assigned to copying precedents and given no important legal copying or other legal work to do signified that Lambert regarded him as the office drudge, a creature only one rung above the house staff. He ate his meals with the servants and shared his bed with the footboy. Chatterton's capacity to retain a sense of inner dignity and hopefulness was sorely tested in those months. He did find a way to remain true to his ideals. The irony was that he could preserve his uplifting visions only through fraudulence and pretense.

After one year at Lambert's, Chatterton began to elaborate the literary devices that would articulate the family romance of Sir William Canynge. By assuming the voice and character of the imaginary poet-priest Thomas Rowley, Chatterton related the history of Bristol as he wished it to be. By becoming Rowley he became the poet-biographer-romancer he wished to be. For the emotional centerpiece of this glorified history of Bristol he invoked the spirit of William Canynge, the rebuilder and benefactor of Chatterton's own beloved St. Mary's Church.

Why did this youth find the answers to his dilemmas and conflicts by calling up the spirit of the past? Early in the twentieth century, the annual Warton Lecture on English Poetry given at the British Academy was entitled "Chatterton." The author of that lecture described the young poet's birth into the famous age of prose and reason, the "understanding age" newly conscious of its good sense and the inestimable blessings thereof. "The new Golden Age, the age of the calm, clear, invincible intelligence seemed at hand.... The future held all the promises. Chatterton arrests attention in that, as a child, instinctively and without instruction, guided by some inward prompting, he turns away from this promising future to the past, the repudiated past." Why, the lecturer wondered, do poets have such a passion for the past? "One might well suppose that if not the eternally disappointing present, the open future would afford a more alluring field for poetic minds. Upon its virgin soil they might to their heart's content, with imagination's aid, erect their airy palaces, or build unhindered the Utopias of their fancies."

But no. Poets, like all the rest of us, look to the past to rectify the humiliations and disappointments of the present. Utopias, even when they are set in some far distant future, are based on a dream of glory, a heavenly perfection we once knew. Hence the word *Utopia,* which means nowhere.

Why then would a young boy with a poetic gift *not* turn to some heavenly past for deliverance from his mean and petty existence? Chatterton's solution to the commonplace dilemmas of a youth on the brink of manhood was unique, but its outlines, his looking backward to an ideal past, are familiar. The heartbreak, disappointment, and grief of the adolescent years, particularly the inescapable knowledge that our parents are not the ideal figures we once imagined them to be, are difficult to bear. By arousing memories of a pure, innocent, and joyous infancy, one can make the disappointing present more endurable.

When an ideal past is evoked, it is always the romance that is revived, never the frustrations and defeats. The romancers would have it that "heaven lies about us in our infancy," or that infancy was "the happy highways where I went / and cannot come again." The goodness that once was is something to which they aspire. Longings for a lost state of perfection can heighten a young man's social awareness as his nostalgia inspires him to consider ways he can improve humanity. Nor is it unusual for an adolescent's social ideals to be mingled with erotic and romantic fantasies which then stimulate him to convert his nostalgia into a yearning for the future perfectibility of humankind. He enters into mystical union with God, Nature, Music, Poetry, Politics, Painting, Dance, Theories of Evolution. In his love affairs with social, political, artistic, religious, and intellectual ideals, even the loneliest of adolescents can expand himself lovingly into the world of others.

The beginnings of Chatterton's love affair with the ancient parchments from St. Mary Redcliffe paralleled the beginning of his interest in the opposite sex. Interweaving with the tale of his heroic creation and tragic loss of Canynge is the story of Chatterton's frustrated love for Miss Polly Rumsey, a lively, vivacious girl whose physical allure was equaled only by her unusual sensitivity to literary matters. Exactly who Polly was remains obscure, but her presence haunts the pages of Chatterton's poetry and prose. Once she had taken hold of his imagination, he was never able to forget her.

One day, toward the end of his fifteenth year, Chatterton confessed his thoughts of love to his sister, indicating that he needed romance to sweeten the bitterness of his temperament:

> Till this time he was remarkably indifferent to females, one day he was remarking to me the tendency sever study had to sour the temper and declared he had always seen all the sex with equal indifference but those that nature made dear, he thought of makeing an acquaintance with a girl in the neighbourhood, supposeing it might soften the austerity of temper study had ocationed, he wrote a poem to her and they commenced corrisponding acquaintance.

Chatterton was altogether correct in his assumptions that love, affection, and erotic longings can sweeten a sour temperament and that ideals can enhance the pride of a lonely and oppressed soul.

As he admitted to his changing attitudes toward the fair sex, Chatterton was expressing an emotional dilemma common to most adolescent boys. While it is not possible to draw correspondences among all adolescents of all times and all places, there are certain stable issues of human development that do prevail. Distancing from matters feminine during early puberty is one such stable issue. The initial signs of approaching puberty awaken in a boy anxieties about his own (usually unconscious) feminine strivings which he senses can only impede his attainment of masculine identity. To a twelve- or thirteen-year-old boy being masculine requires the exclusion of girls and women, whose very existence is a threat. For a fatherless boy like Chatterton, who was keenly aware of his profound and unshakable attachment to "those whom nature made dear," the initial masculine protest might even have been more pronounced. But, as most boys do when they begin to feel a bit more secure about their masculinity, Chatterton at fifteen was able to concede that the characteristics of the opposite sex might have some allure. In these first tremblings of romantic love, affection and eroticism intermingled. Slowly and surely Eros was triumphing over another willing victim.

What was peculiar about Thomas Chatterton was not that he had to look backward to an ideal past before he could confront the realities of the social world in which he actually lived, nor that for him eroticized physical love intermingled with artistic and religious idealism. What did distinguish him was that at the noblest moment of his brief artistic life he was an impostor.

A month or so before his sixteenth birthday, Thomas Chatterton would be transformed from an average apprentice youth struggling with the dilemmas of manhood into a most unusual young man. Mary relates these events:

> About this time the parchments belonging to my father that was left of covering his boys books, my brother carried to the office. He would often speak in great raptures of the undoubted success of his plan for future life. He was introduced to Mr. Barret, Mr. Catcot, his ambition increas'd daily.

THREE

Scoundrels Galore

The celebration of the new Bristol bridge brings Chatterton face-to-face with his two abettors, George Catcott and William Barrett. Fabricating the parchments and inventing a fifteenth-century language. Thomas Rowley, the monk, becomes a parish priest, poet, biographer, historian, and architect. The collaboration between the author of History of Bristol *and the creator of the* Worlde of William Canynge. *The eighteenth-century impostor-poet James Macpherson and his fabricated world of Ossian.*

IT was the creation of one of Chatterton's earliest imposturous narratives that brought him face-to-face with George Catcott and William Barrett, his future patrons. On the occasion of the opening of the new Bristol bridge in October of 1768, the local Bristol daily, *Felix Farley,* published Chatterton's fictitious historical account of the opening of the first stone bridge in 1247. Though the *Bridge Narrative* allegedly was composed two centuries before the days of Rowley, it was written in the fake Middle English that Rowley was about to speak.[1] When the Rowley narratives and Thomas Rowley materialized a week or so later, the minds of Catcott and Barrett had been prepared to welcome him, his fabricated language, and especially his celebrations of Bristol, which would enhance their own reputations and bring esteem to all Bristoleans.

---

[1] At this juncture, because of the complicated chronology of the Chatterton pre– and post–*Bridge Narrative* writings, and the dating of the Rowley-Canynge relationship, the reader is reminded to check the Notes.

Let outsiders say what they would, Bristoleans were proud to be so named. They were particularly proud of their bridge. The earliest chronicles of AD 1051 listed the place as "Brycgstow, place of the bridge," and the city had grown up around this crossing of the Avon between Redcliffe and the commercial center. The opening of the new bridge was a prestigious moment in the history of Bristol. "I believe there has been more noise made about building this single bridge at

Bristol than there has been about erecting both in London." As the city prepared for the opening festivities, Chatterton had the inspiration to link this breathlessly anticipated event with the ceremonies attending the opening of the first stone bridge to replace the wooden ones that had previously spanned the Avon.

By the time the eighteenth-century bridge was completed there had been a decided movement among Bristoleans toward self-improvement in manners and art appreciation. Bristol consisted essentially of a middle class and a lower class. Since there was no aristocracy, the merchants aspired to become royalty themselves, and art and antiquity became the routes to merchant aristocracy.

Did the sixteen-year-old Chatterton, bound to nearly six more years of his ignominious apprenticeship, calculate that his own route to personal aristocracy and preeminence would be through catering to the cultural aspirations of his fellow citizens? It is very likely that this was one of Chatterton's original motives for fabricating the *Bridge Narrative*. But there is no evidence that Chatterton was consciously planning some extended fraud. The opening of the new bridge simply gave the young apprentice an opportunity to express his pride in the history of Bristol, albeit a history colored by his imagination and family romance. He did not plan his prankish bit of history making to be the opening act of his role as an impostor-poet.

Though the *Bridge Narrative* was not a consciously intended, full-fledged imposture, it nevertheless exhibited a facet of Chatterton's character that is very closely allied with imposturousness. Chatterton was beginning to be extremely fond of hoaxing and practical jokes. No doubt he relished the idea of fooling his fellow Bristoleans. The loner schoolboy who had set himself apart from his peers was becoming a more gregarious chap. Mary notes this change in his temperament: "He began to be universally known among the young men. He had many cap acquaintances but I am confident but few intimates." Among his apprentice acquaintances, he was known as the neighborhood ghost writer, who could at a moment's notice whip up just the right kind of love poetry for them to present to their lady friends. Many of Chatterton's future literary productions, including his last will and testament, would have the same uneasy combination of genuine feeling and hoaxing that was expressed in his first imposturous artistic production.

On October 1, 1768, a month or so before the official opening of the bridge to the general public, Chatterton's tribute to it appeared in *Felix Farley's Bristol Journal*.

Mr. Printer

The following Description of the Mayors first passing over the Old Bridge taken from an old Manuscript may not be unacceptable to the Generality of your Readers

The piece was signed *Dunhelmus Bristoliensis*. It began:

> On Fridaie was the time fixed for passing the newe Brydge: aboute the time of the tollynge the tenth Clock, Master Greggorie Dalbenye, mounted on a Fergreyne Horse enformed Master Mayor all thynges were prepared; whan two Beadils want fyrst streyng fresh Stre, next came a Manne dressed up as follows—Hose of Goatskyn, Crinepart outwards, Doublet and Waystcoat also; over which a white Robe without Sleeves, much like an Albe but not so longe, reeching but to his Lends; a Girdle of Azure over his left Shoulder, rechde also to his Lends on the ryght, and doubled back to his Left, bucklyng with a Gouldin Buckel, dangled to his Knee: thereby representing a Saxon Elderman.

Dunhelmus Bristoliensis (Durham man of Bristol) described in comparable lush detail the other major participants in the glorious pageant: a Manne in Armour, six Claryons and six Minstrels, Master Maior, the Eldermen and Cittie Broders, Preestes and Freeres, Parysh, Mendicaunt and Secular. Some of the priests and friars were singing *Saincte Warburghs Song*. With the sound of clarions, the mayor and the eldermen gathered round to sing the *Song of Saincte Baldwyn*. The parade concluded with a Latin sermon preached by Ralph de Blundeville. And then:

> with sound of Clarion theie agayne went to the Brydge, and there dined, spendying the rest of the daie, in Sportes and Plaies, the Freers of Saincte Augustine doeying the Plaie of the Knyghtes of Bristowe, makynge a greete Fire at night on Kynwulph Hyll—

Chatterton even tried to insert a little poetry into the telling of his historical fiction. Appended to the narrative were the songs of Saint Werburg and Saint Baldwyn, with a note to the printer: "If you think the before mentioned and underwritten Songs worth inserting they are at your Disposal—" In the tenth, eleventh, and twelfth centuries, various wooden bridges had crossed the Avon. The songs that Chatterton composed made explicit the connection between the opening of the new stone bridge and the first stone bridge of 1247:

> *Now agayne with bremie Force,*
> *Severn in his auntient Course,*

THE IMPOSTOR-POET THOMAS CHATTERTON

> *Rolls his rappyd Streeme alonge,*
> *With a Sable, Swift and stronge—*
> *Movynge manie a okie Wode—*
> *We, the Menne of Brystowe towne,*
> *Have yreed this Brydge of Stone;*
> *Wyshyng echone it maie last,*
> *Till the date of daies be past—*
> *Standyng where the other stode—*

Guided by an instinctive appreciation of the no-nonsense literary tastes of his readership, the editor of *Felix Farley* chose not to print the songs.

Imagine the stir that was created by the *Bridge Narrative*! Immediately inquiries were made as to the identity of Dunhelmus. All the printer could answer was that the boy who brought him the ancient report was named Thomas Chatterton, a Redcliffe youth descended from the sextons of St. Mary's.

Chatterton was summoned by some city elders. He refused to disclose his sources. He was summoned again and this time coaxed more gently. Whereupon Chatterton claimed that a gentleman who had been employing him to write love verses had recently asked him to transcribe a few ancient documents in his possession. Among them Chatterton had discovered the *Bridge Narrative.* His questioners were unconvinced by such an obvious lie, and finally Chatterton confessed the *real* truth: that the original of the bridge story was written on a parchment found by his father in a large coffer in the Muniment Room of Redcliffe church. The Bristol elders were immensely pleased with this rendition, which added credence to the elegant cultural heritage of Bristol. So satisfied were the wise men of Bristol that not one of them asked the boy to produce the originals. That moment of curious "oversight" on the part of his elders may well have given Chatterton his first inkling of the easy susceptibility of those who unconsciously abet fakery and imposture.

Long after the young poet's death, George Catcott, a tradesman engaged in the manufacture of pewter pots and pans, and William Barrett, a surgeon immersed in the writing of a history of Bristol, sometimes disputed which of them should be remembered as the first to befriend the transcriber of the Rowley narratives. The pewterer's story, which became the accepted version, claimed that a few days after the *Bridge Narrative* appeared, Catcott heard from a friend of Chatterton's about the old writings found in the Redcliffe Church and about the boy who had some of these. Catcott requested an introduction.

During their first meeting, Chatterton had a few Rowleys ready and produced them for Catcott's examination. He used the occasion to retry the first version of the story of their origin: that he had been hired to transcribe them. When Catcott put it to him firmly that he had heard the manuscripts came from St. Mary's, Chatterton once again readily confessed that, indeed, his father had found them there. This encounter proved to Chatterton that the story of the parchments found in St. Mary's had the most appeal, and from that point on he stuck faithfully to that version, which Bristoleans seemed to want so much to believe.

A native Bristolean, born in 1729, Catcott had been renowned since early manhood for his eccentricities and foolish escapades. For most of his adult life, he lived with his brother, Alexander Catcott, the vicar of Temple Church. On his brother's death, he moved in with his unmarried sister Martha, who was delighted to serve as his housekeeper. He never married. Among Catcott's peculiarities were his temperamental outbursts, which he referred to as his "propensities." Chatterton's fakery would have had an irresistible unconscious appeal to a man like Catcott. While not quite a hoaxer, George Catcott certainly had a flair for performing outlandish and pretentious feats and was known as a man who would do almost anything to acquire a name for himself.

On June 25, 1767, Catcott acquired for himself the distinction of paying the first toll on the new Georgian-style Bristol Bridge. Catcott reasoned that, as the first crosser, his name would be linked to the past of his beloved city and then be remembered ever afterwards. For five guineas, he got some workmen to lay down the temporary wooden planks that would enable him to accomplish this first crossing more than a year before anyone else crossed the bridge. The day after the last stone was set in the center arch, he borrowed a horse from his partner, Henry Burgum. Seated on the nag, Catcott rode over the few loose planks laid there for him. As he stood nearby, watching his partner's heroic feat, Burgum was heard to declare, "There go my horse and my ass."

Catcott's feat of being the first Bristolean to cross the new bridge was followed the next year by his climbing 205 feet to the top of the newly built steeple of St. Nicholas Church to deposit two five-inch-square pewter pieces inscribed with his own and his brother Alexander's names.

Chatterton readily discerned Catcott's foolish vanity and propensity for prankish acts as well as his inability to perceive how ridiculous he was. About a year after he met Catcott, the young poet had the fun of describing his patron's escapades in a mocking panegyric, *Happiness:*

> Incomparable Catcott still pursue
> The seeming Happiness thou hast in view
> Unfinish'd Chimneys Gaping Spires compleat
> Eternal Fame on Oval Dishes beat

THE IMPOSTOR-POET THOMAS CHATTERTON

Ride four-inched Bridges clouded Turrets climb
And bravely die to live in after-time.

Much to Chatterton's private amusement, Catcott was thrilled to have his name celebrated in poetry and even more excited when *Happiness* was printed in *Felix Farley*. But at heart Catcott was not a lover of poetry. His favorite author was Charles I. He collected all the monarch's writings as well as many books and prints related to him. On special occasions he put on a ring engraved with a likeness of Charles.

William Barrett, the second of Chatterton's collaborators, was an adopted son of Bristol, but he was nevertheless intensely devoted to the city. He had come to Bristol in 1745, at the age of fourteen or fifteen, to learn the trade of apothecary. After his apprenticeship to a barber-surgeon, where he learned to bleed, shave, and draw teeth, he practiced as apothecary for several years before beginning a steady climb that culminated in 1760 when he was named full surgeon at St Peter's Hospital. When he was thirty-one, after attempting unsuccessfully to move to the more prestigious Bristol Infirmary, Barrett began to invest his personal ambitions in another enterprise.

In 1760, he applied to the mayor of Bristol for access to the town records and decided to become the official documenter of the history of Bristol. He intended his historical treatise to be the consolation of his middle years and old age. Whereas his everyday life as a surgeon was taken up almost entirely by the practice of midwifery, Barrett could aspire to scholarly aristocracy through his investigations into the history of his adopted city. He claimed not to write for profit or fame but wholly for the honor of Bristol. When he met Chatterton, Barrett was a widower with four daughters and a rector son of whom he was very proud. Apparently Barrett also had some special affection for his youngest daughter Sophia, a popular name for girl babies destined to be wise women. He taught her Latin and Greek.

For eight years, Barrett had been plodding through one Bristol document after another. The documents had run out and he had not yet made much headway toward the writing of his projected history. At the time Catcott arranged the meeting between Barrett and Chatterton, all progress on the *History of Bristol* had come to a halt. To Barrett, the boy Chatterton with his ancient parchments from St. Mary's was like a gift from the gods.

A week before the Barrett-Chatterton meeting, Catcott had eagerly taken possession of the young poet's notebook, which contained some stanzas from *Bristowe Tragedy*, about thirty lines from the first version of *Battle of Hastings*, and two short poems on our Ladies Chyrche. This first batch of Rowleys was from the apprentice's pre-Bridge writings and was composed of transcription copies in his own hand. Chatterton presented them to Catcott as samples of what the fifteenth-century monk had written, implying that the ancient parchments contained a great deal more. Catcott did not ask to see the parchment originals.

A week or so after he became acquainted with the surgeon-historian Barrett, Chatterton did produce some "original" Rowley documents written on "original" parchments. Either shortly before he brought his bridge story to the printer or a day or so after the cross-examinations began, the ingenious Chatterton had found some interesting ways to manufacture antique parchments. He was hardly, however, what could be considered an accomplished counterfeiter. His methods were skillful, but of the common, schoolboy variety. The details of one of his techniques was revealed after Chatterton's death by a friend, John Rudhall, who was apprenticed to an apothecary at the time Chatterton was with Lambert. Rudhall saw his friend write on a sheet of foolscap several words in a style of lettering he had never before seen, in a language most strange, "very unlike English." After Chatterton had written these exotic words, he held the foolscap over a candle. The heat changed the color of the ink, blackened the parchment at the edges, and made the whole thing somewhat contracted.

Edward Gardner, a son of one of the senior Thomas's cronies, told of an even more primitive method. According to him, Chatterton would buff a parchment in several places with streaks of yellow ochre. He would rub the ochred parchment into the dirty ground and then crumple it in his hand.

Chatterton's parchment originals were attempts to pass off something new as something old. But unlike a practiced counterfeiter, he did not imitate old documents either in appearance or in the hand in which they were written. The parchment originals were simply a schoolboy's impressionistic version of the olden days. After Chatterton's death, one antiquarian commented on the clumsiness of the boy's methods of manufacturing parchments:

> We remarked some of the Letters to have been written in 4 or 5 different manners; so that the Writer evidently went upon no principles, had previously formed to himself no Alphabet; had a very imperfect random guess at the old Alphabets, & was incapable of imitating any of them truly.

As for the parchments themselves, they were

> . . . evidently stained yellow on the back with oker, to look like old parchment. But the fraud is so unskilfully performed that you may see stains and besmearings on the other side, and if you rub the back with a wet

white handkerchief, it will be stained with oker. He hath also contrived an Ink (than which nothing is more easy) that be very faint and yellow, which being washed with an infusion of galls, would naturally become blacker.

This was hardly the kind of handiwork that should have fooled William Barrett, the possessor of hundreds of genuine fifteenth-century documents. But even years after Chatterton's death, Barrett asserted his innocence. He, like everyone else who had something to gain from believing in Rowley, would also be easily taken in by Chatterton's fabrications.

During the early years of the Rowley controversy, pro-Rowleyan scholars claimed they could prove the authenticity of Rowley's language. The Rowleyans had no difficulty in bringing to light all the evidence they required. The resemblance, they showed, between Rowley's words, syntax, and poetic structure and those of fifteenth-century English was indisputable.

But in 1871 the scholar Walter Skeat demonstrated conclusively how Chatterton had actually fabricated this fake language. What he pieced together was, for nearly a century afterward, the authoritative rendition of Chatterton's sources and methods of language construction.

From Skeat's commentaries we can surmise that, with the exception of the parchments themselves, which were "antiqued" in ordinary schoolboy fashion, everything else Chatterton fabricated proclaimed his magical signature of historical accuracy and pure imagination. Rowley's language was not the helter-skelter fancy some of Chatterton's critics liked to believe. Apparently, when it came to language, the boy had worked like a true scholar and historian. So seriously did he take his language researches that Chatterton himself must have been fairly convinced that Rowley's Middle English was pretty much the genuine article.

For his basic glossary of Rowley's language, Chatterton turned to the then-popular Thomas Percy's *Reliques of Ancient English Poetry* and to Speght's edition of Chaucer. To Chatterton's intuitive but untutored mind Chaucer's poetry had just the right feel for his Rowleys. The next step was to look up some actual Middle English nouns, verb forms, word endings, adjectives, and syntax. For these elements, Chatterton turned to the standard Middle English dictionaries of his day, *Bailey's* and *Kersey*. From this point on, Chatterton did not try for realism. He used his dictionaries, his Chaucer, his history and poetry books as an impressionistic painter would use his palette, mixing the actual phonemic tones and hues with others that were more expressive. Like a true impressionist, Chatterton did not self-indulgently dismiss the real world. Instead his writings were based entirely on his conception of real life in the fifteenth century and his conviction that those olden days had been freer, less formal, more imaginative and creative than the present was. Thus, fifteenth-century language would have its own innate majestic lawlessness. In the world of William Canynge as portrayed by Thomas Rowley, language was not capricious or arbitrary. However, it was fitting that words should be spelled and articulated in harmony with the poetic tone and rhythm that brought out the nuances of that unfettered existence.

Recent scholars claim to have discovered an underlying order and coherence to Chatterton's invented language. They say that Rowley's works are governed by forty-four distinct rules of language development. Spelling is not uniform. Words are frequently omitted if understood. Syntactical inversions are permitted. Verb forms are interchangeable, as are verb endings. Final syllables may be changed for rhyming purposes. The final accent in a line is movable. Double consonants may substitute for single consonants, and single consonants may stand in for double ones. Other precepts are slightly more regular: *it* stands for *ed;* initial *i*'s and *y*'s may be freely added; *t*'s are dropped before *ch; k* substitutes for *tch* or *ch; f* and *v* are interchangeable.

Finally, even with all its underlying rules, Rowley's 1,800-word Middle English comes off as a colorful mixture of standard eighteenth-century words, with Chaucer, *Bailey, Kersey,* and *Percy,* expressing precisely the unlawful-lawfulness that Chatterton wished to achieve. In essence Chatterton had set the English language free to live a life of its own. There is the core Rowleyan vocabulary: *allein*—alone; *lovred*—lord; *mickle, myckelle, myckle*—much; *peynote*—paint; *swote, swotelie, swottellye*—sweet, sweetly. There are the more or less easily recognizable early words: *adente*—fastened or annexed; *affere*—frightened; *alse*—else; *alswai*—also; *amenge*—among. And then, as the Rowley year came to an end, Chatterton created the most liberated Rowleyese: *ammeelde*—ornamented; *asenglave*—part of a lance; *atrametous*—inky; *awhape*—astonished. The easy Middle English of the *Bridge Narrative* which Chatterton had produced for the readers of *Felix Farley* was replaced by a gradually thickening Rowleyese. In March of 1769, when Chatterton sent some of his work to Horace Walpole, that learned man (before he discovered the fraud) was forced to admit that he did not have the language skills needed to decipher some of the words in this fascinating ancient language.

On the first two original parchments that Chatterton fabricated for Barrett were a short Rowley poem, *Song to Aella,* and the *Yellowe Rolle,* an impressive historical document designed specifically to satisfy the historical longings and scholarly lusts of his new friend. These narratives were written quickly, perhaps overnight, and penned in easy-to-read early

Rowleyese. Chatterton recognized immediately that Barrett was cut from more elegant cloth than the foolish Catcott. In Barrett, at least, he had found a kindred spirit who wanted to prove that Bristol had been highly regarded as far back in history as Roman and Saxon times.

The earliest Rowleys make it clear that the family romance fantasy of the Colston years, though not yet put to paper, had been given its literary and narrative structure before the *Bridge Narrative* was written and perhaps as much as three months before Chatterton ever met Catcott or Barrett. The *Yellowe Rolle* parchment, which Chatterton produced so soon after meeting the surgeon, contains a nearly complete conception of what would be invented in the months to come, including the intimate relationship between a merchant prince and an artist who would celebrate his wisdom and benevolence, as well as numerous references to as yet untranscribed pieces that Rowley had composed.

The *Yellowe Rolle* is subtitled, "Of the Auntiaunt Forme of Monies carefullie gotten for Maystre Wm. Canynge by mee Thos: Rowleie." The account begins with what will become Canynge's central ethical principle—the benevolent use of riches:

> Greete was the Wysdom of him who sayde 'The whole Worlde is to no one Creature whereof every Manne ande Beiste is a Member ne Mane lyveth therefore for hymself but for his Fellowe Creeture' Excellent ande pythey was the saying of Mr. Cannges 'Trade is the Soule of the Worlde but Moneie the Soule of Trade' Ande alas Moneie is nowe the Soule of manie—

The title of the second part of the *Yellow Rolle* is a bold proclamation of Chatterton's intentions: *Englandes Glorye revyved in Maystre Canynge.* Here, Rowley praises Canynge's cabinet of ancient "Coynes," "Monyments," and "Instruements of Warre," including "Saxonne Swordes" and "Sheeldes blazonde wyth a Crossee Patee." Before commencing the cataloguing, Thomas Rowley apologizes for his immodesty, "To prayse thys auntyant Repositorye maie not be befyttynge in mee Seeynge I gotten it moste."

Most significantly, *Englandes Glorye* introduces Barrett to a fictitious eleventh-century monk, Turgot, whose poems and historical writings Rowley would discover, translate into more "playne" fifteenth-century language, and donate to the collection of his patron, Sir William Canynge. "The Greete Ledger is a Gemme wordye the Crowne of a Kynge. It contayneth the Workes of Turgotte a Saxonne Monke as followes Battle of Hastynge ynne Anglo Sexonne donne moe playne bie mee for Maystre

Canynge. Hystorie of Bryghtstowe inne Saxonnes Latynne translated for Mr. C. bie Mee." There Chatterton has Rowley doing for Canynge what he himself was doing for Barrett. In this way Chatterton was hinting to Barrett that the Turgot documents that Rowley discovered and translated would certify Bristol as the earliest cultural center and source of English history.

At this point Chatterton was having a love affair with the Bristol of his imagination. The Rowleys represented Chatterton's wish to bridge the past and the present and thus to create a new and better Bristol for the future. Through Rowley's vision of past glories, the merchants and citizens of Bristol in Chatterton's day could aspire to art appreciation, elegant manners, and nobility of character. William Canynge, merchant prince and patron of the arts, would be their inspiration.

On another original parchment "annexed" to the *Yellowe Rolle* and *Englandes Glorye,* Chatterton then wrote out the *Purple Rolle* or *Explayneals of the Yellowe Rolle. Explayneals,* in essence a form of footnote documentation that Chatterton imitated from other historical treatises, was the display case for Rowley's gifts as a scholar. Moreover, nearly every other line in this parchment contains a reference to some aspect of the Redcliffe parish. St. Mary's and Redcliffe emerge as the hub of Bristol history and cultural life.

Shortly thereafter, Chatterton concocted three more original parchments for Barrett. These were meant to exhibit yet another of the marvelous skills of the infinitely talented Thomas Rowley. These suitably antiqued parchments contained Rowley's drawings of the sixty-one ancient coins that he had collected for Canynge's cabinet. Rowley, the artifact collector and translator of "Saxonnes Latynne," was also a drawing master and painter.

Chatterton continued to furnish Catcott with translations. But his heart was with the scholarly Barrett, whose life was devoted to raising up the majestic past of Bristol. The monk Rowley had always been more than merely a poet, but within a few weeks after Chatterton met Barrett, Rowley became a priest whose historical and scholarly interests from then on would continually acquire momentum and variety. Within the month Chatterton manufactured several more parchment originals containing Rowley's drawings of the ancient buildings, monuments, and walls of Bristol, among them Redcliff Wall, Brightric's Church, Eslewin's Tower, Brightric's Palace, and the crowning feat of Chatterton's architectural fantasies, the mighty Bristol Castle with its towers, walls, foundations, fortress. William Barrett gobbled up all these parchments with his characteristic scholarly greed, without hesitation, with no questions asked.

In *The Rolle of Seyncte Bartlemeweis Priorie,* Chatterton's most ambitious historical fabrication, Rowley became an authority on the popular and ecclesiastical architecture of his day and also an expert on literature, drama, and medicine past and present. However, the extensive notes to this document are from the transcriber and editor of Rowley, Thomas Chatterton. The impostor-poet chose this moment in his creation of Rowley (probably in late November 1768) to exhibit his own talents as a contemporary authority on the antiquity of literature, drama, and medicine. For example, for one line of Rowley's on the so-called leprosy of the fifteenth century, Chatterton writes several lines of interpretation, acknowledging himself as an eighteenth-century expert on the symptoms of venereal disease, specifically the secondary and tertiary symptoms of syphilis. Chatterton concludes his commentary on Rowley's brief medical treatise with his interpretation, "All these Circumstances and Descriptions candidly considered I shall not scruple to allow the Venereal Disease to have been known in England long before the time of Columbus, tho not by the same name."

In the months between October 1768 and February 1769 Chatterton was caught up in trying to impress Barrett with his scholarly and worldly knowledge, no doubt hoping that one day Barrett would be as generous with him as Canynge had been with Rowley. Chatterton's desire to please Barrett and Barrett's need for documentation from the fifteenth century made for a mutually exploitative partnership. The surgeon's aspirations for his *History of Bristol* would exert a considerable influence on the growth of the Rowley fantasy and the directions that it would take.

When the Rowleys first came to his attention, Barrett went with Catcott to visit Sarah Chatterton, who gave them her version, which would soon become her litany of the history of the poetry. Her husband had found the parchments in the Muniment Room. He had discovered written on some of them proof that the "Chadderton" name had been since "time out of mind" associated with St. Mary's. After using what he needed for covering his students' books, the senior Chatterton had destroyed most of the old parchments, leaving her a small trunkful for domestic needs.

If Sarah or Mary had their doubts about the authenticity of the Rowleys, they did not at that time mention them to Barrett or Catcott. But when Mary wrote in 1802 to Cottle and Southey, she recorded at least two occasions when she or her mother had suspected that her brother was the true author of some of the poetry. "My brother read to me the Poem on our Ladies Church. After he had read it several times, I insisted he had made it. He begged to know what reason I had to think so; I added, his stile was easily discovered in that poem. He replied, I confess I made this but don't you say anything about it." Sarah Chatterton, Mary reports, had admired the piece on the death of Sir Charles Bawdin *(Bristowe Tragedy),* and asked her son if he had made it. "He reply'd, I found the argument and versified it."

There were similar incidents with Barrett. The highly educated surgeon-antiquarian should have been at least as clever as Mary and Sarah in detecting the modern style beneath the Rowleyan surface, especially in the early days before the Rowleyese had gotten more elaborate. Initially, he did have a few doubts about the Rowleys' authenticity, which is why he had insisted on visiting Sarah Chatterton. He was particularly suspicious of Rowley's account of receiving two hundred pounds, an extravagant sum in the fifteenth century, as payment for collecting a set of drawings for Redcliffe Church. But Barrett began to adapt himself to the inconsistencies and anachronisms in Rowley's accounts. He instead collaborated by alerting Chatterton to Rowley's errors, and educating the boy to more convincing deceptions.

For example, Barrett reasoned to Chatterton that since Rowley's poems were "better than Chaucer" they could not be as old as fifteenth-century work. Chatterton replied that "Chaucer was a fool to Roulie [sic]," then quickly added a few words to Rowley's memoirs, "for I can saie in Troth I was never proud of my Virses sithince I dyd reade Master Chaucer."

On another occasion Catcott and Barrett, whose poetic tastes were not as delicate as those of Mary Chatterton, commented on the beautiful similes and smoothness of the verse in *Battle of Hastings.* Chatterton, flattered by this praise, confessed that the poem was really his own and not Ronley's (sic). Barrett, however, could not tolerate that this incredible historical document, "An Ancient poem called the Battle of Hastynges written by Turgot a Saxon Monk in the Tenth Century and translated by Thomas Ronlie Parish Preeste St. Johns in the City of Bristol in the year of our Lord 1465," was composed by a mere lawyer's scrivener. The surgeon insisted that Chatterton bring forth the poem in its original and thereby prove that it was indeed from the fifteenth century. But Chatterton was too proud and clever to retract his claim to having written beautiful poetry. He did, however, want to remain in Barrett's good graces. As usual, Chatterton negotiated the dilemma brilliantly. He said that he had written the poem Barrett liked so much for a friend, but that he had another much better one on the same subject, a copy of an original by "Ronlie" (sic). Barrett pressed Chatterton to produce the original of this second version. After a week or more had elapsed, Chatterton finally brought in 520 lines of *Battle of Hastyngs by Turgotus translated by Roulie for W. Canynge, Esq.,* written in his own handwriting on plain copybook paper. Barrett was pleased to have been vindicated in his judgment, and promptly forgot all about his wish to see the original. He was impatient for the conclusion and requested that Chatterton find it and transcribe it forthwith. After several more days Chatterton came up with the concluding two hundred lines for his demanding patron. Barrett, though he commented on the ease of versification, actually cared very little for the poetry. But as an historical account linking Hastings with two ancient Bristol authors, Turgot from the Roman days and his translator Rowley from the Saxon days, it was just what Barrett needed for his *History.*

In the interests of consistent scholarship, Barrett then set about to correct and standardize Chatterton's erratic spellings of the fifteenth-century priest's name. In Gothic script it is difficult to distinguish *u*'s and *n*'s, so at first Chatterton was inconsistent in the spelling of Rowley's name. It looked like either "Roulie" or "Ronlie" on the tablet near William Canynge's tomb from which Chatterton had probably taken it. Roulie or Ronlie had been a local sheriff. Finally Barrett set him straight by pointing out to him a 1467 entry of Ricart's *Kalender* where, on the same line, Willelmus Canynges is written down as Maiores and Thomas Rowley as Ballivi. From then on Ronlie was Rowley. And neither Barrett nor Chatterton let the fact that this Rowley was a sheriff disturb them.

Barrett also tried to correct Chatterton's spelling of the hero of the *Bristowe Tragedie.* On hearing the name of the hero as Sir Charles Brandon, Barrett recognized that this gentleman had lived long after Rowley's time. He pointed out the anachronism to Chatterton, who soon returned with the new name of Sir Charles Bawdin. The surgeon then determined that Rowley must have meant Sir Baldwin Fulford. But Chatterton insisted that Bawdin was the way it should be, and so it remained. The surgeon could easily rationalize such errors as the result of the boy's carelessness in transcribing the original poems from parchment to copybook paper.

Chatterton quickly became attuned to Barrett's actual needs, realizing he was not interested in useless copybook pages filled with trivial poetry. Whenever he sensed that Barrett would settle for nothing less than an original parchment he fabricated one, filling it with intricate drawings of the requisite antique statuary, maps, coins, monuments, gates, churches, castles, and heraldic devices. As their collaboration deepened, Barrett and Chatterton would put their heads together to decipher Rowley's parchments, "one assisting the other when at a loss." The jottings and notes that were attached to these parchments are in the alternating scripts of the young poet and the middle-aged surgeon-antiquarian.

Once Barrett went so far in his less-than-conscious collaboration as to submit some pages from his own historical treatise for Chatterton's special Rowley enhancements. The young man supplemented the historian's slumbering prose with several lively drawings of a high cross and some churches, among which was St. Andrews, a pure Chatterton invention. For this church, Chatterton first drew a tall spire, then, supposing that a wall from St. Nicholas Gate would have more authentic charm, he crossed out the spire and surrounded the mythical church with the gate. This drawing was eventually printed in Barrett's *History,* and for nearly a century after that, Bristol antiquarians searched in vain for the ruins of St. Andrews Church.

If Chatterton was conscious that he had duped his collaborator, or that Barrett had taken advantage of his unformed character and youthful aspirations, he never revealed it. Barrett taught him a great deal, including the basics of surgery, and he allowed Chatterton to borrow freely from his extensive library. Chatterton seems to have trusted Barrett's mentorship. He was proud to be associated with a genuine scholar, a man held in high esteem by the citizens of Bristol.

In trying to puzzle through Barrett's side of the collaboration, the way he turned a blind eye to the inconsistencies and corrected blatant mistakes, scholars have sought a rationale for this respectable citizen's manipulations of young Chatterton. Some obscure Barrett's exploitative role by portraying him as a poor duped scholar, a victim of the scheming con artist Chatterton. As Cottle, the bookseller, would put it, Chatterton "approaches every man on his blind side." Other more subtle methods of letting Barrett off the hook are nicely represented by the following scholarly insight: "It is easy, I know, to strain the evidence against Barrett, and one has constantly to bear in mind that absolute honesty was, at that time, scarcely *demanded* of an antiquary."

In that exquisite rationalization there is a substantial truth. Barrett's exploitation of Chatterton's talent for history making was to a great extent a reflection of the emotional and intellectual atmosphere in mid-eighteenth century western European societies. Every age has its impostors. But the phenomenon flourishes in a special climate of belief.

As the Age of Enlightenment, with its professed standards of reason and intellect, advanced, ostensibly leaving behind the superstition and irrationality of the previous era, there grew in people a great hunger for magic, passion, participation, mysteries, dreams. In contrast, those who were the official representatives of "enlightenment," like Voltaire, had contempt for the visions of the recent historical past. According to Voltaire, after the brief glow of illumination from the Greeks and Romans, the human spirit had been lost in the long, dark Gothic night. "Men who think and what is more, men who have taste count but four centuries in the history of the world." Others who shared his narrow view of enlightenment were convinced that only law, philosophy, letters, manners could protect humanity from the jungle of irrationality that might creep up from the Gothic and barbaric past.

The early to mid-eighteenth century, though it saw great advances in the novel and the essay, with the exception of the witty, classical work of poets like Alexander Pope and John Dryden, witnessed something of a decline in poetic sensibility. Even Walpole, whose cool reason and satiric wit placed him at the apex of the literary elite, lamented the absence of poetry: "D'ye see, 'tis an age most unpoetical! Tis even a test of wit to despise poetry."

The eighteenth century brought enormous strides in trade, commerce and industry. But after a few decades it began to be felt that these advances came only at the cost of spirit and imagination. "Bring back the good old days," was the cry. Even as they tried to emulate the elitist literati, up-and-coming middle-class tradesmen yearned for relics from the past. Of the merchants who cared at all about art, a great many resisted satire and classicism, longing instead for less studied, more spontaneous literary expressions.

In England, Shakespeare and Chaucer were especially revered. The desire for antique literary treasures rose to a fever pitch. It became a crusade. And since there were not enough genuine antiques to satisfy the craving, a number of enterprising men began to manufacture "ancient" writings. Some of them got caught, hundreds escaped detection. The fact was that antiquarians themselves were a new breed of literary specialist. Some of them knew very little about their own literary heritage. To distinguish the genuine from the false, the average self-styled antiquarian relied on his intuition, which was generally informed by an enthusiastic wish to believe in the validity of anything supposedly from the past. Impostors and other masters of sleight of hand, like faith healers, gurus, and magicians, flourish in ages where the relentless pursuit of civilization leaves little space for mystery, poetry, imagination.

In 1758 a twenty-three-year-old Scotsman, James Macpherson, a poor farmer's boy, appeared on the literary scene. He had invented a noble past for his fellow Scottish Highlanders, who were considered at that time to be among the lowest of the British, "even lower than the Irish."

He began his fabrication the same year that Chatterton entered Colston's. And only five years later, while Chatterton was composing his satirical fable *Apostle Will,* Macpherson was already rich and famous. Rumors of Macpherson's "discovery," of his fame and popularity among the literati, and of his handsome financial rewards were in the air when Chatterton began to write as Rowley.

Macpherson began much as Chatterton would a few years later—but Macpherson's intent to deceive was *completely* conscious. He showed a recognized Scottish scholar and poet some poems of the North he had translated. Macpherson had figured out that if he could convince the scholar of this literary find, the scholar would not be able to resist spreading the word to his colleagues. His calculations proved correct. In a few months a ripple of excitement spread among the learned men of Scotland. They wanted to see more of these miraculous translations and Macpherson was quick to oblige. Not one of these men ever asked to see the Gaelic originals.

By 1760 Macpherson's *Fragments of Poetry translated from the Gaelic and Erse Languages* had aroused the dormant pride of every important Scottish scholar. The first few fragments Macpherson translated contained clever hints of some larger project. Chatterton would adopt a similar device when he planted the central elements of the Rowley saga in the earliest pieces he showed to Barrett and Catcott. The preface to Macpherson's *Fragments* mentioned an epic poem about the warrior hero, Fingal. It gave an outline of the plot, of Swaran, the king of Sweden, whose brutal invasion of Ireland in the third century was stopped by Fingal, the Scottish king who helped the Irish expel the invaders and then returned home to the Highlands victorious. Macpherson created this thumbnail sketch and then simply sat back and waited for the scholars to take the bait.

Word of Macpherson's extraordinary discovery reached Cambridge, where the lyrical simplicity of *Fragments* captivated Thomas Gray, whose *Elegy Written in a Country Churchyard* would eventually become the most-quoted poem in the English language. By the time he read the *Fragments,* Gray's personal literary sympathies had moved from strict classicism to a romantic adoration of the past—a personal metamorphosis that paralleled the history of poetry in eighteenth-century England. Gray's involvement in ancient poetry transformed him into one of the several truly competent antiquarians of the age.

Here was a man well equipped to distinguish genuine from false antique poetry. But, as he was himself deeply immersed in composing the melancholic *Edda, The Descent of Odin,* Gray wanted very much to believe in Macpherson's discovery:

> I was so struck, so *extasie* with their infinite beauty, that I writ into Scotland to make a thousand enquiries. The letters I have in return are ill wrote, ill reasoned, unsatisfactory, calculated (one would imagine) to deceive one, and yet not cunning enough to do it cleverly. In short, the whole external evidence would make one believe these fragments (for so he calls them, though nothing can be more entire) counterfeit: but the internal is so strong on the other side, that I am resolved to believe them genuine, spite of the Devil and the Kirk. It is impossible to convince me that they were invented by the same man who writes me these letters. On the other hand, it is almost as hard to suppose, if they are original that he should be able to translate them so admirably. . . . In short this man is the very Daemon of poetry, or he has lighted on a treasure hid for ages.

The general consensus was that there probably was a national epic poem hidden in the Highlands that needed to be saved before it perished along with the Gaelic language. A subscription was raised to sponsor Macpherson's expedition into the deeper Scottish Highlands to continue his quest for the epic past. Within six months of wandering about the Highlands, supposedly communing with the primitive natives in Gaelic, Macpherson wrote back to his sponsors that he had been "lucky enough to lay hands on a pretty complete poem, truly epic, concerning Fingal."

By then Macpherson had found an impressive way around the question of original documentation, much more efficient than Chatterton's clumsy method of rubbing parchments in the dust. He told his admirers that Ossian, son of Fingal, who then became the ancient bard of Scotland, transmitted the tales of his father's heroism by way of an oral tradition. Needing no further documentation than the words he had heard from his fellow Highlanders, Macpherson could complete his task of translation with dispatch. The year after Macpherson put Ossian's six-part epic, *Fingal,* to paper, Ossian was declared "the sublimest and simplest bard of all." The year 1763 saw the translation of Ossian's *Temora* in eight books.

The next year the celebrated Macpherson was living in high style as secretary to the governor of Pensacola, Florida.

At first the rest of the English literati were as taken in as the Scottish antiquarians. Walpole was an early sponsor of Macpherson and was much embarrassed when it came out that he had been fooled, one reason why, five years later, he was so edgy about Chatterton. Samuel Johnson was among the first to blow the whistle on Macpherson. Not only had he none of the passionate nostalgia that kept Gray from recognizing the Macpherson forgery as such, but his sharp rational eyes easily pierced through the shallowness of the poetry that everyone else was raving about. "In vain shall we look for the *lucidus ordo* where there is neither end nor object, design nor moral." When asked whether modern man could have written such magnificent poetry, Johnson replied, "Yes, sir, many men, many women and many children."

Johnson's judgment notwithstanding, England continued to have its die-hard Ossian adherents long into the nineteenth century. William Hazlitt, for example, listed four of the principal works of poetry in the world at different periods of history as "Homer, The Bible, Dante and let me add Ossian." There was some debate among the romantic poets. Wordsworth denounced the impudent Highlander for his audacious act of forgery, the worthless poetry, and the false descriptions of the Scottish countryside. On the other side, Burns was an ardent devotee. And the same Byron who could not tolerate the vulgarity of some of his fellow poets imitated the Ossian mode in some of his poems. Even after the romantic period, the levelheaded Matthew Arnold started a temporary revival of Ossian. Essentially, however, even before the eighteenth century was out, the sensible, rational British had more or less come to terms with the idea that whatever their literary merit, the Ossian poems were not authentic.

Not so on the Continent. There Ossianics became the rage. Ossian's works were translated into German, Italian, Spanish, French, Dutch, Danish, Polish, Russian, and modern Greek. No other English author, not even Shakespeare, had such a crowd of foreign admirers. None, except perhaps Byron, was to achieve such fame. Continental opinion held that this was one of the splendors of English literature. The prose poems revealed a glorious English past, where savage warriors like Fingal, Oscar, and Morveen embodied all that was virtuous in the human soul. These Highland warriors were clement to the vanquished and chivalrous to the weak. Their personal morals were pure, their sentiments toward nature generous and open. They treated women with respect. The barbaric Highlanders were as close to nature as man could be. Thus Nature, as she was mirrored in their eyes, was revealed in her true colors, gray and brown, with touches of drab green. It was proclaimed that Ossian was more inspired, more simple, more naive, more barbaric, and closer to nature than Homer. The German poet Voss stated the matter plainly: "What is the use of beauty in nature? The Scotsman Ossian is a greater poet than the Ionian Homer."

Everywhere sensitive Europeans were experiencing what they imagined to be the Anglo-Saxon ecstasy of melancholy, tenderness, openness to feeling. Tears were shed on every page. Macpherson had once said of his discovery that it was "calculated to please persons of exquisite feeling of heart." At the beginning of the nineteenth century, when most Englishmen had lost interest, the Ossian vogue was at its height on the Continent. In Germany especially, where the search for a *Volkpoesie* had caught the nation's imagination, Ossian fit right in. For a time Goethe compared Ossian to Shakespeare and translated selections to recite to his friends. His young Werther speaks of Ossian with a passion equal to his love for Charlotte. On their last evening together he reads Ossian to her. His eyes fill with tears as he speaks, "Star of descending night, fair is the light in the West!" He continues with another set of lines, "The time of my fading is near, the blast that shall scatter my leaves. Tomorrow shall the traveller come; he that saw me in my beauty shall come; his eyes will search the field, but they will not find me." The next day, filled with the soulful melancholy of Ossian, Werther commits suicide. In later years, after Goethe was forced to recognize that Ossian was counterfeit, he expressed contempt for the poetry. He explained away the embarrassment of Werther's poetic lapse by claiming that the inclusion of Ossian at the end of the novel was intended as a sign of the young man's morbidity. While he was sane Werther had praised Homer. Only when he lost his senses did he get so wound up about Ossian.

Lessing, Schiller, and Novalis were also enthusiastic Ossianists. The *Fragments* were set to music by Schubert and Brahms. In France, Lamartine said, "The harp of Morveen is the emblem of my soul." Mme. de Staël and George Sand adored the Ossianic heroes. Napoleon, who had read *Werther* seven times, read Ossian nearly as many. The margins of his copy of *Fingal*, which he read on the way to St. Helena, are covered with exclamations of ecstasy. And a century later, across the ocean in the New World, Walt Whitman sat alone on the shore of Manhattan Island poring over his copy of Ossian.

The impostor-poets of eighteenth-century England, even the most famous—Psalmanazar, Macpherson, Ireland, Chatterton—have been consigned to oblivion along with many of their legitimate counterparts—including Gray and Thomas Warton—who survive only in the classroom and lecture hall. However, Chatterton suffered a fate very different from the other poets of his day and from that of his fellow literary impostors. Though hardly anyone reads his poetry any more, the question of Chatterton's peculiar infamy is still lively. Why was the youth Chatterton treated with such scorn, scholars still wonder, while the more consciously devious

Macpherson, his model and immediate predecessor, became the rage of Europe and was allowed to lead a comfortable and respectable life?

Chatterton had many marks against him. Youth was one. His freethinking mind was another. Macpherson, Ireland, Psalmanazar, devious as they had been, did not have the audacity to write first as a virtuous priest and then presume to write freethinking religious and political tracts or obscene poetry. Nor did they commit suicide. They all lived long enough to settle down and become worthy citizens of the republic. Thirty-five years before his death, Psalmanazar embarked on a written confession of guilt, lamenting his days as a "shameless impostor." Johnson, not a man to be taken in by impostors, developed a profound admiration for the Psalmanazar of the confessional. He reported to Boswell that "he had never seen the close of the life of anyone that he wished so much his own to resemble as that of him for its purity and devotion." Psalmanazar became a highly respected English scholar. Macpherson became a proministerial member of Parliament. And Ireland, the well-known Shakespeare forger, was brought in as a literary consultant on the Chatterton-Rowley case a few years after Chatterton's death.

FOUR

Fabricating a Father

*The Family Romance
of Sir William Canynge
as wroten by Thomas Rowley,
parish priest.*

LIKE Macpherson's Ossian, Chatterton's Rowley was a spokesman for the good old days. Though he was not sufficiently wise to anticipate the discontents that were about to become the plague of modern civilization, Chatterton was certain that the bright glare of reason was no candle to the magical illuminations of the ancient days. However, the young eighteenth-century poet who invented the fifteenth-century world of Sir William Canynge was also devoted to reason. The most honorable men of Chatterton's ancient times embodied his special vision of an eighteenth-century ideal of masculine virtue—a godlike spirtuality humanized and tamed by natural reason.

Chatterton would expend considerable time and energy providing documentation for Barrett's *History*. Although the historical treatises and architectural renderings he produced in Rowley's name were fake, they rang of truth because the boy who fabricated them remained faithful to those innermost purposes which he had stated so boldly in his earliest outpourings of poetry: "The God from whom Creation sprung shall animate my grateful Tongue." Rowley condescended to serve for a time as historian and architect. At heart though, Rowley was a poet searching for an artistic medium that could accommodate the contradictions in his creator's character.

The priest Thomas Rowley, like his creator Thomas Chatterton, had secret longings to become an actor, a theater manager, a playwright. In a footnote to *The Rolle of Seyncte Bartlemeweis*, Chatterton elaborates on Rowley's "great difference between Plays of Mirracle and Maumerys

and the more noble Representations of Fame," distinctions that raised the priest above the "usual Entertainments of the Vulgar" and identified him with the staged plays of the more modern Elizabethan theater. Had it been within the realm of historical possibility, Rowley would have wanted nothing more than to be a second Shakespeare. But Chatterton, who had great admiration for Chaucer, did not always agree with some of Rowley's modern leanings. In his own voice, which sings out in the copious footnotes to the Bartlemeweis *Rolle,* he proclaims, "Our Amusement are the gaudy Children of Fancy, we may paint clearer to the eye but they spoke to the heart." Even after he had given up the fifteenth century and its spectacles and amusements: "I have seen several of these pieces, mostly Latin, and cannot think our ancestors so ignorant of dramatic excellence as the generality of modern writers would represent: they had a good moral in view, and some of the maumeries abound with wit, which though low now was not so then." But there was no essential disagreement between the priest and the scrivener's apprentice on the superiority of poetry and theater over historic reality. The imagined world was more moral and true than the actual one. Throughout his deceitful collaboration with Barrett, Chatterton sought for an image of manhood he could admire and emulate. All along, during the same months that he sat at his desk versifying historical events and fabricating architectural descriptions and drawings, Chatterton was begetting a virtuous father—Sir William Canynge.

Toward the end of the summer of 1768, a few months before the publication of the *Bridge Narrative,* Sir William Canynge first made his appearance. In the context of that first glimpse of his noble merchant hero, Chatterton sketched out the essentials of the romance that would soon follow: the main characters, the setting, the time of the action. Before we hear mention of Canynge, however, we encounter the author of the poem in which he will make his debut. Chatterton introduces the fifteenth-century poet Thomas Rowlie [sic]:

> As the following Transaction happen'd in Bristol the 2nd year of King Edward 4th it deserves to be commemorated as one Instance of the severe Treatmnt. that Prince showed those who oppos'd his coming to the Crown; and as the Story is told in a very affecting mannr. in the following little Poem wrote by Thomas Rowlie Priest, I shall insert the whole as a Specimen of the Poetry of those Days, being greatly superior to what we have been taught to believe. He calls it *Bristowe Tragedy* or the Dethe of Syr Charles Bawdin.

In this tragedy Canynge is cast as a supporting actor. The protagonist, Bawdin, is about to be beheaded and quartered for refusing to declare his allegiance to King Edward, and Canynge intercedes on his behalf. But the king demands absolute loyalty. His justice knows no mercy. And Bawdin, who has been raised according to an analogous set of moral precepts, will not reconsider his act of defiance. When Canynge asks him to think of the feelings of the wife and sons he will leave behind, his friend Bawdin sharply recalls him to the essence of honor. Bawdin, who had been instructed by his father on the code of warriors, never defiled his marriage bed, never ate meat on Lent, and never turned the hungry poor from his door. He had once sworn his allegiance and therefore always would be loyal to *his* king, Henry, and to no other.

Canynge's eloquence and humane courage stand in sharp contrast to the obdurate moral rectitude of the king and of Bawdin, neither of whom will yield from the lofty moral principles which to them are far more important than any human life.

There is no doubt about Chatterton's admiration for Canynge's brand of moral heroism. For the benefit of Rowley's readers the transcriber appends a footnote: "The following Lines, where Canynge intercedes with Edward for the Life of Sir Chas. Brandon [sic] the Hero of the Tragedy, and is answered by Edward are in my Opinion truly elegant and pathetick."

> *My nobile leige! alle my request*
>   *Ys for a nobile knyghte,*
> *Who, tho' may hap hee has donne wronge;*
>   *Hee thoghte ytte stylle was ryghte*
>   . . . .
>
> *Lett mercie rule thyne infante reigne,*
>   *Twill faste thye crowne fulle sure;*
> *From race to race thy familie*
>   *Alle Sov'reigns shalle endure:*
>
> *But yff wythe bloode and slaughter thou*
>   *Beginne thy infante reigne,*
> *Thy crowne uponne thy childrennes brows*
>   *Wylle never long remayne.*
>   . . . .
>
> *My nobile leige the trulie brave*
>   *Wylle val'rous actions prize*
> *Respect a brave and nobile mynde*
>   *Altho' ynne enemies.*

But the rigidity of the king's standards cannot encompass Canynge's tender morality, in which absolute justice is tempered by mercy. As Edward angrily waves away these softheaded notions, the compassionate Canynge "and satt hymm down upponne a stoole, / and teares began to flowe." He is not ashamed to show his pity for the wife and sons of the obdurate Bawdin. Bawdin does not heed his friend's tears nor those of his wife who, "rav'd as anie madde, / and dydd her tresses tere."

The processional to Bawdin's beheading is described with a lush detail and color comparable to the pageantry that will characterize the parade of celebrants in the *Bridge Narrative*. Bawdin's bloody death sets the general tone of the *Tragedie*. But in the midst of the gore and the untamable moral passions of the king and Bawdin, Canynge's temperate, compassionate character has been planted like a small jewel. The fabric of the daily life of Bristowe will be as brilliant and varied as the character of Canynge.

> *Before hym went the council-menne,*
> *Ynne scarlett robes and golde,*
> *And tassils spanglynge ynne the sunne,*
> *Muche glorious to beholde:*
>
> *The Freers of Seincte Augustyne next*
> *Appeared to the syghte,*
> *Alle cladd ynne homelie russett weedes,*
> *Of godlie monkysh plyghte:*

In his final footnote to *Bristowe Tragedie,* Chatterton lets us in on the hidden agenda of Rowlie's poetic mission, the first item of which will be to establish the cabinet of Sir William Canynge as a treasure-house of artifacts and documents hitherto unrecorded in English history. The other major item, a corollary of the first, is to refute *Camden's Britannia,* the then-acknowledged history of England which had allowed to the city of Bristol but a scant page. "I shall conclude this," writes Chatterton, "with remarking, that if Gentlemen of Fortune wou'd take the Trouble of looking over the Manuscripts in their Possession, which are only valued for their Antiquity, it might possibly throw light upon many obscure Passages in and help to establish a more Concise History of our Native Country, than even Cambden's Britannia."

The stage for the opening act of the romance is by now almost in place. Thomas Rowlie's elegant verse has introduced Canynge's compassionate nature and mature eloquence. We have been given an eyewitness account of the natural beauties and cultural pageantry of one day in the life of a medieval city. We have been alerted to the theme of the "Curiosities preserv'd in the Cabinet of Mr. Canynge." Camden's history of England is about to be revised. And, through the partnership of Rowley and Canynge, the mercantile city of Bristol will become the source of the cultural life of England.

Chatterton then extended Bristol's glorious history as far back as possible. His next poem, the *Battle of Hastings,* was the one he claimed to be his own when Barrett and Catcott praised it. In the face of their disbelief, he concocted a second version, by the eleventh-century poet-historian Turgot, which linked Bristol definitely with the glorious battle in 1066. The second *"Battle of Hastings* by Turgotus and translated by Roulie [sic] for W. Canynge Esq." was less gratuitously gory, the poetry more contained and mature.

Chatterton's next bit of history making was entirely personal. He designed an heraldic fantasy, *Craishes Herauldry,* purportedly written by the "Author of the Famous Legend of Beevis of Southampton." With the exception of heraldic entries for the name Rumsey, which he manufactured to honor the family of his Polly Rumsey, the delightful young lady who was sweetening his scholarly temperament, Chatterton got only as far as the letter *C*—just far enough to link his own family name with the family name of Canynge.

The name Canynge has but one entry, for the grandfather of Rowley's patron who, like his grandson (born in 1402) had been destined to be five times mayor of Bristol. In this entry, Chatterton highlights his role as founder of St. Mary's Church.

> 1369 Guillielmus Canynge Founder of the Chirch of oure Ladye of the Redde Clefte in Bristowe, he was Sonne of Robertus Canyng Merchaunt in Bristowe, his Brother Johannes was Lorde Maior of London and himself 5 times Maior of Bristowe.

Directly following the entry for Sir William Canynge's grandfather are ten entries for early variants on the name Chatterton beginning with the eleventh century:

> 1034 Johannes Sieur de Chateau tonne—John Lord of the Castle of Tonne in Normandie wedded Matilda Dawter of Robertus d'etris or Dittris of Normandie who bare three redde Lyonnes on a Bend passaunt regardaunt in a Feelde Or and had issue

This issue runs through entries for three more Chateautonnes, several Chateaton's, culminating at last in the fourteenth-century contemporary of Canynge's grandfather, Bourchier Hungerford Chateaton, who had one issue, a daughter.

As Chatterton reported it, the family name was lost until 1481 when a female descendant of Bourchier Chateaton married Randolphus Chaderton, descended from Randolphus de Chateautonne, born in 1067.

Chatterton's fantasy pedigrees were designed to demonstrate that his family and those of his friends from Bristol were significant personages. The Chatterton name itself he linked to the conquering Normans and the Battle of Hastings. To further embellish his own family's illustrious history, Chatterton borrowed the names of some actual noble families described in *Britannia*—Bourchier, Hungerford, Mandeville. Thomas Chatterton, through his imaginary line of descent, is no longer a fatherless boy raised in poverty by an ignorant mother. He has become the direct descendant of conquering noblemen. And at the same time, William Canynge's grandfather is established as the founder of "the Chirch of oure Ladye of the Redde Clefte in Bristowe." The rebuilding of that most beautiful church by a merchant would count for more than any actual noble lineage. A good merchant who spent his money wisely—as a patron of the arts—could be as famous and renowned in history as any king.

Chatterton then writes *A short Account of Mr William Canynge, an Opulent Merchnt. Native of the City of Bristol, and sole Founder of Saint Mary Redcliff Church in the same City, extracted from the Life of Thomas Rowlie Priest, and principle Author of the Eclogues, Poems &c, contain'd in this Book*. In the first words of that account, William's character is contrasted with that of his common merchant brother Robert, a "Manne after his Fadre's owne Harte, greedie of Gayne, and sparynge of Almes Deedes." William is a different sort of merchant. He is "mickle Courteous." He donates to Rowley "manie Markes." When Rowley presents himself before Canynge to thank him for his generosity, the artist and his patron have their first recorded conversation:

Canynge: Fadre . . . I have a Crotchet in my Brayne, that will neede your aid.
Rowley: Master William . . . if you commaund mee, I will goe to Roome for you.
Canynge: Not so farre distaunt: . . . I ken you for a mickle larned Preeste, if you will leave the Paryshe of our Ladye and travelle for mee, it shall be mickle to your profitte.

And so Rowley accepts his first assignment from Canynge. He will travel to all the neighboring abbeys and priories and gather ancient drawings at a good price. The drawings will be used to enhance the beauties of St. Mary's.

When Rowley returns with the treasures he has purchased, his patron is greatly impressed with the sensitivity of his selections and his excellent bargaining ability: "Fadre you have done mickle well, all the Chattils are more worth than you gave, take this for your paines"—a purse of two hundred pounds. With such a "mickle of Ryches" Rowley was never again to be in need. He settles in a house on the hill nearby his Master William, who was now lord of the house. Rowley caters to Canynge's sentiments for St. Mary's Church by composing a poem in her honor, *Onn our Ladies Chirch*. "Some counyunge Fairie hand / Yreer'd this Chapele in this Lande." For the lines on St. Mary's, Canynge again sent Rowley "mickle good Thynges."

Rowley continues his brief account of this ennobling friendship with a digression on men's relationships with women. Rowley has escaped such relationships altogether by becoming a priest early in life. Rowley's fictional Canynge follows the path of his real counterpart. When the beloved wife of the real Canynge died, he refused the king's order to remarry and, "In all haste toke ordirs upon hum of the gode Bisshope of Worcestre callid Carpynter, and was made preeste and sange his furst masse at Our Lady of Redclif the yere folouyng." This inscription Chatterton would have read on Canynge's tomb in St. Mary's Church. In Rowley's version he, the poet-priest, personally designs Canynge's escape from the unwanted marriage and the wrath of King Edward.

> The Dangers were nighe, unless avoided by one Remmedie, an holie one; which was to bee ordaynd a Sonne of Holie Chirch beynge franke fromme the powre of Kynge, in that Cause and canne be wedded. Master Canynges instauntlie send mee to Carpintar, his good Freende, Bishoppe of Worcester and the Fridaye follouynge was prepear'd and ordayned the next daie; the Daie of Saincte Matthewe; and on Sandy sang his first Masse in the Chirch of our Ladie, to the astonieyng of echone.

From then on, unencumbered by women or family duties, the two men are free to pursue their friendship and devote themselves to good works. The account goes on to the next year when Rowley gives Canynge a present of his poem *Bristowe Tragedie,* for which he was paid "in Hande Twentie Pounds" and "praise it more than I dyd thynk Myself did deserve; for I can saie in Troth I was never proud of my Virses, sithince I dyd reade Master Chaucer." Soon afterwards Rowley becomes the translator of a Saxon manuscript on the "Bloudie Battle of Hastynges" for which he was given "20 Markes." When Rowley goes off to claim the other, more complete, version of this poem, the owner says that he has "brent" it and will have Rowlie "brent" too if he continues to pursue his quest. Apparently this gentleman's wife's family came off badly at Hastings. Says Rowley, "I was faygne content to get awaie in a safe Skynne." This little story represents Chatterton's not-too-elegant ploy to get by without completing the second *Battle of Hastings*.

The rest of the account, which breaks off abruptly after a few more paragraphs, tells of the old age of Rowley. "Nowe growynge Auntiante, I was seized wyth grete Peines, whych dyd cost mickle of Markes to be cured of." Thanks again to the generosity of Canynge, who gives him some more money to fix up his old house, Rowley is able to spend his last days in relative comfort.

It is clear throughout the brief account that the lifelong friendship of Rowley and Canynge was founded on the absence of meddling women-folk, Canynge's "Markes," Canynge's artistic sensibilities, and the versatile artistry of Rowley.

The general outline of the romance of Sir William Canynge arose as a solution to Chatterton's mortification as a Colston inmate. But its details grew organically from Chatterton's adolescent emotional situation. Every adolescent boy requires a society of men to help him escape the lures of femininity. He must ward off not merely the powerful erotic allure of women themselves, but his own feminine inclinations, which he considers to be far more dangerous.

Pubescent boys violently turn away from women. The incessant drawing of military objects and scenes, restlessness, foul language, vandalism, theft, gang conflicts, assaults on "gays" and other sexually threatening feminine types are part of the typical masculine assertion, no doubt captured precisely in Chatterton's earliest version of the bloody battle of Hastings. The scenario underlying these reactions is the boy's desperate flight from the care-giving mother of infancy, the adored and powerful one who first caressed his body, nursed him, rocked him, told him what, how, and when to eat, and seemed to own his body, mind, and soul. In early adolescence, any surrender at all to femininity is tantamount to becoming the passive, receptive infant he sometimes secretly wishes to be. The clamoring insistence on being a man's man is a massive mobilization, an all-out, no-holds-barred, preemptive first-strike defense of the boy's still-fragile, merely incipient masculinity. Mischief at best, violence at worst, is the boy's proclamation of masculinity. Often much of his aggression is directed toward representations of femininity—toward the care-giving environment in general, toward buildings, public monuments, parks. The exhibitionistic, risk-taking acts—brazen, out in the open, catch-me-if-you-can, defiant—are a declaration of masculinity: "I can do anything. Nothing can happen to me. My body cannot be hurt."

Early in adolescence the father is the boy's ally. The boy's idealization of his father is at its height and so he denies everything that might contradict the image of a strong and powerful man. It is understandable that Chatterton, a fatherless boy who had grown up in a household of adoring women, would long even more than the average adolescent boy for a powerful father figure to protect him from women and from his own feminine inclinations. What is striking about Chatterton's romance is that, though it commences with the more-violent masculine virtues of the warring Saxons, it so soon afterwards turns toward the celebration of the rebuilding of a public monument—the marvelous Bristol bridge. Chatterton's bridge hoax was mischief dishonorable in itself, but it was produced in the spirit of honoring his birthplace. During the Rowley year, when he acted as an impostor, Chatterton was a mischievous deceiver, but as Rowley he never attacks or demeans his native city or the citizens in it. Moreover, he selects as a masculine hero one who exemplifies the gentler virtues of compassion and mercy. Sir William Canynge is mayor of Bristol and a mason—a builder of cities. He does not destroy or loot or violate in the name of masculine honor; when his first and only true love dies, he devotes the remainder of his adult life to the priesthood and to his brotherhood of Freemasons. With the help of Rowley he rebuilds and illuminates the marvelous glories of St. Mary's.

The friendship between Rowley and Canynge was strong enough to withstand the disastrous morality of the actual masculine alliances that Chatterton was forced to make. As we have already seen, Chatterton's real-life obligations to his actual patron required that the next act in the romance of Rowley and Canynge be the fabrication of the documents that Barrett demanded for his *History of Bristol*. Though he was forced to invent these documents, Chatterton managed to bring them forth in a spirit of genuine artistry. And, though for the most part entirely false, their historical and architectural details actually extended and deepened the verisimilitude of the Rowley-Canynge romance. Chatterton did not desecrate the architecture of his native city. Instead he designed for its crumbling walls and gates wonders and beauties it never possessed.

To satisfy Barrett's next demands, Chatterton produced transcriptions of Rowley's correspondence with Canynge, as well as fabricating parchment originals of a map of the fifteenth-century Redcliffe neighborhood, deeds, chronicles, and a series of architectural fantasies on the origins of various decaying Bristol buildings, walls, gates, and statuary. The intricate verbal descriptions are accompanied by drawings of comparable intricacy and detail. Before the year 1768 was out, Chatterton had mastered the art of creating history. He returned as quickly as possible to the main narrative line of his family romance.

Chatterton now took hold of the historical impulse and made it his own. Like a novelist, he composed an imaginary history extending his family romance into a further past, *A Discorse on Brystowe by Thos. Rowleie wrotten and gotten at the Desire of W. Canynge Esqur.*

Turgot, the eleventh-century monk-historian, the narrator of the naive epic poem *Battle of Hastings* (versions I and II), tells the ancient history of Bristol. Rowley translates it in somewhat thick Rowleyese and adds his own commentary. Turgot speaks:

> The fyrst noticynge of this my native Cittye yclepen Brightstowe is in Algaruses Dome of Somertowne where it is saide 'Ande the Eldermanne of Kyneriktown or Kynetown-Brigtstowe claymen to paie twayne of Saixes as al Homage' That is, the famous Towne of Kenricus, who on the Banks of Sabrine defeeted the Inhabitens of Caier Bathen Ein Oduna which sayde City of Bathen stooden furtherwards to the City of Welles. In A.D. 638 Sayncte Warreburgus came to Bryghtstowe and preechen to the Folkes of the Cittie. . . .
> then the Menne of Brightstowe repayren from the Hills and received the Faith pytchyng the Cittie over anent Rudcleve and ybuilden a fayre Brydge of Woode over the Tyde, hence was the Cittie called by bad and unskylful Pennesmen Brugstowe Thus muche for the Scite and Name of this auntiaunt Cittie now to saie of the manie Goodlie buyldyngs their forme and buylders in dayse of Yore

Thus, after pitching the city of Bristol across the river into Redcliffe and building the first wooden bridge to connect that ancient city with the rest of England, the men of Bristol could go about constructing their homes, monuments, and churches.

Turgot, Rowley's primary source for eleventh-century history, has his own seventh-century sources. Any errors about history from any of those ancient days could be attributed to Turgot and his sources. There *was* an actual monk named Turgot, who lived around the end of the eleventh century. He may have been a manuscript historian and perhaps also a poet. However, most of the information about Turgot was in Latin and none of his manuscripts were extant. He was just the sort of elusive and unknowable historian-poet Chatterton needed for his documentation of the history of Bristol. The Dunhelmus Bristoliensis signature of the *Bridge Narrative* and the D.B. signature of many of Chatterton's modern writings were derived from Turgot, man of Durham, man of Bristol.

Turgot's bloodthirsty epic poetry and innocent approach to historical documentation were a foil for Rowley, who was in such accounts the comparatively enlightened amender of the textual naivetés and blunt emotionality of the eleventh-century monk. The sly impostor-poet planted a few errors in Turgot for the wise and scrupulous Rowley to discover. Rowley says in a letter to William Canynge: "Turgotte soe putteth Seyntes and Kynges ynne his stories, I wote notte of yette." It also gave Chatterton a convenient scapegoat: all errors concerning pre-Norman history that Barrett might detect could now be attributed to Turgot or the understandable oversights of Rowley. Barrett, who was wearing blinders over his scholarly spectacles, actually detected many fewer errors than the bright-eyed Rowley. Barrett scarcely noticed the Chaucerian allusions in Turgot or the Shakespearean ones in Rowley.

Turgot's discourse establishes St. Mary Redcliffe as the origin of Bristol and suggests that English history began in the countryside that would become Bristol. A wooden church by the name of St. Mary's in the Redcliff section of Brystowe becomes the first Bristol church. "The inhabiters of Rudcleve ybuilden a Churche of Woden Warke casen with a sable Stone and A.D. 644 did the same dedycate to Oure Ladie. . . . It stooden by the Waterre Syde." In the next century, AD 789, "the Woden Chyrche being fallen," King Brightrikus built another one of stone. But, comments the eleventh-century Turgot, "nowadaies it is fallen down." There Rowley puts one of his lengthy footnotes, bringing to the attention of Turgot's readers the two other churches by the name of St. Mary's that preceded the one founded by Canynge's grandfather and repaired to its final glorious state in 1443 by his own friend and patron William Canynge: "This worke now fynished is a true Pycture of the Buylder Greete and Noble, the Glorie and delyght of Bristowe and wonder of Sumerset. of which take yee my Lynes for lack of better." There follows a twenty-four-line poem by Rowley, *Stay curyous Traveller and pass not bye:*

> *Thou seest this Maystrie of a human hand*
> *The Pride of Brystowe and the Westerne Lande*
> *Yet is the Buylders Vertues much moe greete*
> *Greeter than can bie Rowlie's Pen be scande—*

By filling the streets and walls of Redcliffe with more ancient history, monuments, and antiquities than any other section of Bristol, Chatterton establishes his birthplace as the first and culturally most superior neighborhood of the most important city in England. And as supplemented by Rowley's footnotes, St. Mary's Church and her latest builder, Sir William Canynge, become the emotional and spiritual centers of that history. The Turgot history of Bristol ends in 1049. That date is just a few years before Camden's rather unflattering and cursory one-page official history of Bristol begins.

What could Chatterton do next? For a brief moment he must have experienced dejection. He must have felt that Rowley had said all there was to say about St. Mary's, Sir William Canynge, and the ancient history of the Redcliffe neighborhood of Bristol.

But then the next stages of the romance came to Chatterton, and Rowley, the poet-biographer-historian-antiquarian-translator-priest was on his way to becoming an accomplished playwright. "Mr. Catcott left [Chatterton] one evening totally depressed; but he returned the next morning with unusual spirits. He said, 'he had sprung a mine' and produced a parchment containing the *Sprytes.*"

The Parlyamente of Sprytes: On the Dedication of St. Mary's Church was a dramatic interlude. It was commissioned by Sir William Canynge on the occasion of the completion of the rebuilding of St. Mary's and was to be "Plaied bie the Carmelyte Freeres at Mastre Canynges hys greete Howse, before Master Canynges and Byshoppe Carpenterre, on dedicatynge the Chyrche of Oure Ladie of Redclefte." For this event, Rowley-Chatterton simply picks a Turgot-Rowley list of ancient builders and transforms them into characters for the 1443 dedication of St. Mary's.

Sprytes is a parade of the spirits of builders who have been assembled from the past by Queen Mab, the fairy in charge of sprites. The parade begins with Nimrod, the builder of the Tower of Babel, who laments the confusion his pathetically grandiose tower managed to beget. He wishes he could trade places with the constructor of St. Mary's, who will be remembered as a bountiful builder. The two leading roles Rowley assigns to Bythrycke, an eleventh-century contemporary of Turgot, and to Elle, whom Chatterton's footnote lists as "Keeper of Bristol Castle in the time of the Saxons." Elle had appeared in *Discorse* as "a Mercyan Sone hee routted the Danes at Watchette wythe his Brystowians ... but Englande payde dearlie for the Battle he dyed in Brystowe Castle of his Woundes." Elle reappears early the next year as the hero of Rowley's only full-length drama, *Aella.*

The sprites compare their own comparatively poor works to the grandeur of St. Mary's and the noble vision of Canynge:

> *But thou the Buylder of this swotie[1] Place*
> *Where alle the Saynctes in sweete ajunctyon stande,*
> *A verie Heaven for yttes fetyve Grace;*
> *The Glorie and the Wonder of the Lande,*
> *That shewes the Buylders Mynde and Fourmers hande,*
> *To bee the beste thatte on Erthe remaynes;*
> *At once for Wonder and delyghte commaunde,*

---

[1] Chatterton footnoted much of his fifteenth- and eleventh-century narratives and poetry with their eighteenth-century translations. I will hereafter footnote words with a too-impressionistic or thickened Rowleyese: swotie—sweet.

> *Shewynge howe muche hee of the Godde reteynes—*
> *Canynge the Great, the Charytable, and Good,*
> *Noble as Kynges if not of Kyngelie Bloude—*

The tenth-century lord of Bristol Castle, Elle, ends the interlude in celebration of Canynge's noble use of wealth. "Then Canynge ryses to eternal Reste / And fyndes hee choose on Erthe a Lyfe the beste."

Aella: A Tragycal Enterlude, or Discoorseynge Tragedie represents both the culmination of the Rowley saga and the pinnacle of Thomas Chatterton's literary achievements. The works Chatterton produced in the months between the appearances of *Sprytes* in November and *Aella* in February primarily elaborate on already-known events in the lives of Canynge and Rowley, authenticate documents to satisfy Barrett, enhance the verisimilitude of the Canynge romance, and display the versatility and range of Rowley's abilities.

Aella announces Chatterton's as yet tentative decision to seek patronage for Rowley's works outside Bristol. He will remain true to Canynge. But he is disappointed in his Bristol patrons, who pay him nothing for his efforts and care not at all for Rowley's poetic efforts or the marvels of St. Mary Redcliffe. Chatterton is jaded with fabricating history and is eager now to devote himself to the poetic arts. Apparently Rowley has a similar complaint about the fifteenth century. But in contrast to poor Chatterton, whose only patrons are an ardent collector of the writings of Charles I and a plodding historian of Bristol, the fortunate Rowley has the sympathetic ear of Canynge, a poet in his own right who can appreciate the sentiments of a fellow artist. "Canynge and I from common course dyssente . . . Wee wylle ne cheynedd to one pasture bee. / Botte sometimes soare 'bove the trouthe of hystorie."

Aella begins with a letter to Canynge, honoring him for the artistic sensibility that commissioned a poetic drama to celebrate the laying of the first stone of the Redcliffe church. Once again Canynge is shown to be above the mentality of the usual merchant. Moreover, his tastes in literature are much finer than those of the usual patrons of the time, who value only bare historical facts.

> *Straunge dome ytte ys, that, yn these daies of oures*
> *Nete butte a bare recytalle can hav place;*
> *Nowe shapelie poesie hast loste yttes powers,*
> *And pynant hystorie ys onlie grace;*
> *Heie pycke up wolsome weedes, ynstedde of flowers,*
> *And famylies, ynstedde of wytte, theie trace;*

> *Nowe poesie canne meete wythe ne regrate,[2]*
> *Whylste prose, and herehaughtrie,[3] ryse yn estate.*

Barrett was too submerged in his bottomless history to take the hint. Nevertheless, with the tragic interlude *Aella* Chatterton gave himself permission to rise above Barrett's demands for the "trouthe of hystorie." At last he could return to his first love, poetry.

In Rowley's earlier historical accounts Aella was a lord of Bristol Castle who had fought many victorious battles against the Danes. In *Aella*, the battles between the Saxons and the invading Danes are background for the tale of the love and unconsummated marriage of Aella and Birtha. The characters come straight out of *Othello,* with Aella as an Othello consumed by love and jealousy, Birtha as the virtuous Desdemona, and Celmonde as an Iago-Roderigo whose treachery is motivated by his love for Desdemona. Birtha even has a loyal and devoted maid named Egwina.

Act I opens with Celmonde's lament and the prophecy of his treachery:

> *Before yonne roddie sonne has droove hys wayne*
> *Throwe halfe hys joornie, dyghte yn gites[4] of goulde,*
> *Mee, happeless mee, hee wylle a wretche behoulde,*
> *Mieselfe, and al that's myne, bounde ynne myschaunces*
>   *chayne.*
>
> . . . .
>
> *Assyst mee, Helle! lett Devylles rounde mee tende,*
> *To slea mieselfe, mie love, and eke mie doughtie[5] friend.*

Aella and Birtha have just been married and Celmonde cannot honorably possess his adored Birtha. So, with considered malice and calculation, he decides to violate his loyalty to his mighty friend Aella by raping Birtha. The deed will be accomplished while Aella is off at war. Aella returns victorious to celebrate and consummate his marriage with Birtha. But she is gone. He assumes she has been false to him. With scarcely a hesitation the powerful Aella plunges his sword into his chest and breathes his last breaths just as Birtha is brought home to him by the Danish

---

[2] regrate—esteem
[3] herehaughtrie—heraldry
[4] gites—robes
[5] doughtie—mighty

general who has rescued her (in the nick of time before the rape can be accomplished) from the clutches of Celmonde. Birtha dies, apparently of shock, a few moments after discovering the body of Aella.

In its surface narrative, *Aella* is less a dramatic interlude composed by a fifteenth-century monk than a naively conceived eighteenth-century operatic reduction of Shakespeare. Yet some of the finest poetry that Chatterton ever wrote is in *Aella*, even if very few of these remarkable lines concern the interactions, emotions, or personal thoughts of the three main characters. Chatterton often proved himself an insightful observer of human nature: in his conceptualization of Canynge's character, for instance, he grasped more of the subtleties of masculine virtue than could most young men his age. But when it came to the intricacies of devotion, loss, and jealousy, Chatterton was a naif. At the age of sixteen, his poetic strengths were found in his descriptions of battles, nature, lyrical sentiments, and the bolder vices and virtues. Indeed, it is in the battle scenes, which were intended as background for the love story, that some of Chatterton's finest poetry can be found. The glory of battle inspires Aella to think and speak like Henry V:

> *Ye Chrystyans, doe as wordhie of the name;*
> *These roynerres[6] of oure hallie houses slea;*
> *Braste, lyke a cloude, from whence doth come the flame,*
> *Lyche torrentes, gushynge downe the mountaines, bee.*
> *And whanne alonge the grene yer champyons flee,*
> *Swefte as the rodde for-weltrynge[7] levyn-bronde,[8]*
> *Yatte hauntes the flyinge mortherer oere the lea,*
> *Soe flie oponne these royners[9] of the londe.*
> *Lette those yatte are unto yer battayles fledde,*
> *Take slepe eterne uponne a feerie lowynge bedde.*
> . . . .
> *Lyche a rodde gronfer,[10] shalle mie anlace[11] sheene,*
> *Lyche a strynge lyoncelle[12] I'lle bee ynne fyghte,*

---

[6] roynerres—ravishers
[7] for-weltrynge—blasting
[8] lyvyn-bronde—living sword (rage)
[9] royners—ravishers
[10] gronfer—a meteor, a fire exhaled from a fen
[11] anlace—armour
[12] lyoncelle—lion cub

Lyche fallynge leaves the Dacyannes shalle bee sleene,
Lyche a loud dynnynge streeme scalle[13] be mie myghte.
Ye menne, who woulde deserve the name of knyghte,
Lette bloddie teares bie all your paves be wepte;
To commynge tymes no poyntelle[14] shalle ywrite,
Whanne Englonde han her foemenn, Brystow slepte.
Yourselfes, youre chyldren, and youre fellowes crie,
Go, fyghte ynne rennomes gare,[15] be brave, and wynne or die.

And when anyone today recalls lines from Chatterton they are likely to be from the Songes of the Mynstrelles from *Aella:*

O! synge untoe mie roundelaie,
O! droppe the brynie teare wythe mee,
Daunce ne moe atte hallie daie,
Lycke a reynynge ryver bee;
  Mie love ys dedde,
  Gon to hys death-bedde,
  Al under the wyllowe tree.

Whanne Autumpne blake[16] and sonne-brente doe appere,
With hys goulde honde guylteynge the falleyenge lefe,
Bryngeynge oppe Wynterr to folfylle[17] the yere,
Beerynge uponne hys backe the riped shefe;
Whan al the hyls wythe woddie sede ys whyte;
Whanne levynne-fyres and lemes[18] do mete from far the
  syghte; ...

By the time Canynge commissions this poetic drama, his own character has been given color, dimension, and soul. This portrait of Canynge has come to life piece by piece, much as it took shape in Chatterton's mind, much as a fatherless boy would piece together an image of a father he never knew, much even as all of us must eventually reconstruct the images of the parents we once knew.

---

[13] scalle—shall
[14] poyntelle—pen
[15] gare—cause
[16] blake—naked
[17] folfylle—fulfill
[18] lemes—flames

We never see Canynge all at once. We always come across him at a moment in time as he is reflected in one of Rowley's creations. His portrait is built up gradually by way of documents discovered, translated, composed, or preserved by the poet-priest: epic poems in which he appears as a character, letters from him to his family or to Rowley, deeds, views of him from the eyes of others, facets of his own character as they contrast with other, less-noble Bristol citizens, and samplings of his own poetic efforts.

Some of the minor documents were fabricated solely to elaborate a single aspect of Canynge's being—to embellish the details of his physical image, to correct an inconsistency in his family history, to explain away a flaw in his character. A fragment from a letter preserved by Rowley describes Canynge as "talle and stately His Eyes and Haire are jeat blacke hys Aspecte sweete and Skynne blanche han he not soe moche noblinesse yn hys Fygure he woulde bee Wommanysh."

History had recorded that Canynge was a follower of King Edward. Inscribed on his tomb is the notice that he has given three thousand marks to the monarch, who beheaded the warrior hero Bawdin. Yet Rowley as a priest must be loyal to Henry. This difference in political opinion between priest and merchant had to be accounted for. Canynge's loyalty to King Edward had to be justified. So Chatterton arranged for an exchange of letters that would explain Canynge's embarrassingly pro-Yorkist political position.

Canynge begins his explanation to Rowley,

Ye would have me declare for Kynge Henrie— I woulde remayne neutre. Botte I muste perforce be for one of the twayne: successyon ys ne the quere, botte who wylle rule beste: when ones Countrie is abentynge to rewyn Itte ys a fowle thynge even to be neutre— A Kynge shulde bee one who ruleth hys People hymselfe and ne trousteth to untroustie Servantes. Mie Actions shewe me no Ennemie to Goode, but methynketh a holie Seyncte maketh notte a goode Kynge. From the daies of Saxon Governmente to thys presente Englande havethe been undone by Priest-Kynges.

The letter concludes: "Under Henrie we mote have peace but never renome—But doe not thynke I am a Yorkeyst."

Whatever its occasional minor inconsistencies and however often the portrait of Canynge becomes obfuscated by historical shenanigans, certain of his features remain constant. The "time out of mind" legend of the Chatterton family's association with St. Mary's is an unchanging structure around which Canynge's character rises. Canynge's absolute commitment and unstinting devotion to the rebuilding of St. Mary's defines the man that he is. The theme of Canynge's use of riches to enhance the beauties of the world is stitched into nearly every Rowley narrative. On every occasion that Rowley represents Canynge's poetic voice, the merchant prince is speaking out on the benevolent uses of personal wealth.

Late in February 1769, shortly after the composition of *Aella*, Chatterton produced another review of his merchant hero's life. *Lyfe of W. Canynge* documents, in the form of thirteen letters from Canynge to Rowley, all the poetic events that have transpired around the rebuilding of St. Mary's. The letters begin in 1430 with the death of Canynge's father and his inheritance of the money which will make possible his pursuit of art. The two brief letters of 1431 retell the story of his wedding and the death of his wife. More than half of the ensuing letters document the tale of the rebuilding of St. Mary's. In addition to once more underlining the noble character of Canynge, these letters explain the events leading up to his commissioning of *Sprytes* and *Aella*.

In 1432 the letters describe how Canynge opens his Masons Lodge. He makes a speech enlisting the aid of those men who might "beeynge of cleere Wytte counynge and knowlachynge havethe theyre Vapoures subtille and fyne as the dewe whyche ascende the Sonne beames." "I shall therefore streve to drawe togyderre menne of counynge Wytte to advaunce the Glorie of thys oure Towne." Later that year he writes to Rowley telling him of the success of his plan. He has gathered together "Twoe hundreth and thyrtie Freeres, beesydes odhers, Gentylmenn, Maconnes, Carpenters and deelers." Rowley's drawings are shown to the assembly. Iscam, the minor poet who will soon be playing the part of Clemonde in the performance of *Aella*, speaks up in praise of Rowley and his gifts as architect. That very day the rebuilding of St. Mary's gets underway. "all thynges ynne readyness. nowe for a wondrous Pyle to astounde the Eyne." At the conclusion of this letter, Canynge commissions Rowley to "Penne anne Entyrlude to bee plaied uponne laieynge the fyrste Stone of the buyldeynge ande wricte a greete Parte for Iscamme."

There is one other letter from 1432. Chatterton has Canynge write to Iscam rather than to Rowley, thus giving Canynge the opportunity to sing the glories of the ever-modest Rowley. For the first time we hear of Rowley's remarkable acting abilities and thereby of Chatterton's gifts as a theater critic:

Rowleie alleyne culde have plaied Ælle soe fyne. all enseemed properre. no strained Voice ne wrythinge of boddie ne dystortynge of Face, whan Ælle saieth

> *O! speack ne moe: mie hearte flames yn its keste*
> *I once was Ælle nowe bee notte hys Shade*
> *Han all the Fhuyri of Mysfortunes wylle*
> *Felle onne mie benned Head I han beene Ælle stylle*
> *Thys alleyn was unburld of all mie Spryghte*
> *Mie Hounoure frownd at the dulce Wynd*
> *That stealed onne yttte.*

Thenne was the Actyone unyted wythe the Wordes. I saie ne moe. botte next to Rowleies Ælle was Iscammes Celmonde.

The series of letters go quickly on to 1443 and the completion of St. Mary's, when once again Canynge commissions a play from Rowley: "Inne all haste ymake a smalle Entyrlude [*Sprytes*] to bee plaied atte the tyme."

The last letter, dated 1467, has Canynge at the end of his life requesting that he and Rowley "dyspende owre remeyneynge years togyder." Rowley brings the letters to a close with a revelation of the merchant's artistic gifts: not only has that great man employed the townsfolk of Bristol in his ennobling enterprises, he is himself a painter and a poet.

> Heere doethe ende the Letters of Mastre Wm. Canynge who as a Merchante did emploie alle the Radcleve Syde of Brystowe ynne Tradeas a Manne theie wylle dysplaie hymme. As a Leorned Wyseager[19] he excelled ynne alle thynges. as a Poette and Peyncter he was greete ...

There follows one of Canynge's own poems, *The Worlde,* an "Entyrlude" with a father, his son, and six minstrels as characters. The interlude is on Canynge's favorite subject—the proper use of wealth. It begins with the father instructing the minstrels to instruct his son, "To gettynge Wealthe I woulde he shoulde be bredde / And Couronnes of rudde Goulde ne Glorie, round hys Head." The little play concludes with the father furiously dismissing the minstrels, who have taken the embarrassing tack of cautioning his son on the disastrous fates that await those men who devote their lives entirely to financial gain.

Canynge's humorous attitude toward those men who cannot behave according to the ethical principles that guide his life and Chatterton's own satirical wit are simultaneously displayed in the father's dismayed response to the minstrels he has assembled:

---

[19] Wyseager—philosopher (Rowley variant—wiseegger)

> *Howe villeyn Mynstrelles, and is this your rede,*
> *Awaie: Awaie: I wyll ne geve a curse,*
> *Mie sonne, mie sonne, of this mie speeche take hede,*
> *Nothynge ys good thatte bryngeth not to purse.*

Chatterton had begun writing the Rowley-Canynge family romance in October of 1768. It was now late February 1769. At this point Chatterton was struggling to maintain his artistic integrity: he wanted to write poetry but his apprenticeship was strangling him. His escape through Rowley did not seem to be working. He was forced to spend the precious hours of his youth copying legal precedents for Lambert and grinding out history for Barrett.

Poor Chatterton, in spirit so much finer than the father who advises that, "Nothynge ys goode thatte bryngeth not to purse," and yet the issue of money is always with him. How can a poet earn a living writing poetry? It is not enough now for Canynge merely to donate his money to the arts, he must demonstrate the value of artistic enterprise by becoming an artist himself. Chatterton's message in the letters seems to be that a man who patronizes the arts can indeed become an artist himself. Was this designed to capture the fancy of Catcott, who wished so much to acquire a name for himself? Or was Chatterton trying to embarrass both Catcott and Barrett for their mercenary attitudes? Whatever ulterior motive these last Rowleys may have served, they succeeded in still further enhancing the character of Sir William Canynge and deepening Chatterton's romance with the father he wished to have.

And so the next Rowley is *Rowley's Heraldic Account of Bristol Artists and Writers*. He compiles an impressive list of the artists of Bristol, including a John Seconde Abbot of Sayncte Augustyns, "a Manne well learned yn the Languages of yore, he wrote ynn the Greke Tonge a Poeme on Roberte Fitz Hardynge, whyche as nie as Englyshe wyll serve I have thus transplanted." In March, Abbot John will emerge as an important character in the Rowley saga, with knowledge of ancient history, poetry, and painting. Though he will soon be involved in a grander project, for the time being he is merely one of several artists brought up for praise in Rowley's *Heraldic Account*. Canynge still plays the major part. Now the benevolent merchant Canynge is both a poet and a painter.

> And Mastre Canynge hymselfe is ne foule Payncter, or bad Verser.
> Mastre Canynge dyd payncte the depycture of the Kynges, the Vyrgyn, and other matters yn the Wyndowes of the Ysle of the Lord's Table, of hys Poesie see as followeth

Rowley follows up this announcement with a poem of Canynge's *On Happienesse,* and another of his own, *The Storie of Wyllyam Canynge,* which is the only life of Canynge entirely in verse. From his birth he has been "eager gaspeynge after Lyghte." As a child, "He eate downe Learneynge wyth the Wastle Cake." Even "as the dulce downie Barbe beganne to gre" he had men "Wondryng at one soe wyse and yet soe yinge." And when it came time to choose a wife, he had no money to give to his beloved—but he had something much better:

> But Landes and Castled Tenures Goulde and Bighes
> And hoardes of Sylver rousted yn the ent
> Canynge and hys fayre Sweete dyd that despyse
> To change of troulie Love was theyr Content
> Theie lyv'd togeder yn a House adygne
> Of good Sendaument commilie and fine.

And for the culmination of that noble life:

> Next Radclefte Chyrche! Oh Worke of hande of Heav'n
> Whare Canynge sheweth as an Instrumente
> Was to my bismarde Eynesyghte newlie giv'n
> 'Tis past to blazonne ytt to goode Contente.

With the completion of *Heraldic Account* and its embedded life history of Sir William Canynge, the poet and painter, Chatterton readies himself for what will turn out to be his last creation as an impostor-poet. In mid-March Chatterton begins to compose *The Ryse of Peyncteynge, yn Englande, wroten bie T. Rowleie. 1469 for Mastre Canynge.*, but before he is finished he sends this work to Sir Horace Walpole, who soon afterwards declares it counterfeit, thus bringing to an end the glorious family romance of Sir William Canynge. As Rowley and Canynge fade away, Chatterton begins writing in his own name or under one or another of his several pseudonyms, among them his favorite—D.B., or Dunhelmus Bristoliensis.

The most remarkable feature in Chatterton's romance of Sir William Canynge is the uncertainty throughout of the borders between creation and fabrication. From the moment Chatterton met those two Bristolean giants, Catcott and Barrett, he was busily at work concocting his Jack-and-the-Beanstalk duplicities. With only a modicum of coaxing from Catcott and some instructive collaboration from Barrett he became, at least in his relations with these two gentlemen, a clever schemer and a pathological liar.

Each time he perfected a falsehood, Chatterton enhanced his artistic achievement. His creative vision was heightened by having to fabricate the data his patrons desired. If it had not been for Barrett's insistence on historical documentation, the world of Sir William Canynge might have been woven together in sparkling threads of pomp and pageantry. As it turned out, though, Canynge's world, with its fabricated coins, maps, monuments, churches, walls and gates, achieved an impression of artistic truth.

Not all acts of falsification are as ambiguous as the narratives of a literary impostor. Plagiarists, for example, simply appropriate or imitate the work of another and claim it as their own. The motives, on the surface at least, are readily understandable. On the other hand, every creative act is a plagiarism of a sort; every poem, every painting borrows to some degree from the past. Modern poets especially have found their own voices by impersonating sounds, rhythms, and phrases from the past. Life is rendered more bearable when the sounds and rhythms of a past poetic glory are substituted for the rattling emptiness of an actual world.

Every time we try to sort out the issues of authenticity in Chatterton's works, we come to the same ironic point. Those writings for which Chatterton earned the labels "counterfeiter" and "forger" were in fact masterpieces of invention and imagination, while the journal articles he later wrote under his own name or acknowledged pseudonyms were borrowings, sometimes outright plagiarisms from the literary figures of his day. In the Rowleys, when Chatterton borrowed from the past, he did so to make his imagined world more real. His words, phrases, and rhythms are never mere impersonations. With Rowley, Chatterton has not reproduced a literary voice from the past. He has invented a new and completely original language.

It is easy to hold the sexual, religious, and political infidelities of Chatterton's last year of life accountable for the moral outrage that followed his death. But what was more provocative than his later freethinking creed was the cleverness and captivating beauty of the Rowleys. Beneath the calculatedly dispassionate critiques that emanated from the staid eighteenth-century scholarly community participating in the Rowley controversy we detect disgruntled mutterings: "How dare that vulgar stripling outwit us?" "How dare an unschooled boy raised by an indigent woman write such convincing poetry?" "How dare he be so good at it?"

Chatterton was so good at it, both the poetry and the outwitting, not only because he had an extraordinary gift for making imaginary worlds palpable, but because he needed to experience his own self as real and whole. He desperately needed his invented fifteenth-century Bristol and particularly his fabricated benevolent and nourishing father, Sir William Canynge.

Modern-day commentaries on the effects of "father absence" on a boy's life allow us to grasp the complexities and depth of Chatterton's relationship to Canynge. Fortunate is the boy who has an actual father as his ally and sponsor, although without one, a boy may fabricate one and in the process create beautiful poetry or music or painting. Speaking of some of the more fortunate boys—Mozart, Bach, Mendelssohn, Picasso, Bernini—Aaron Esman, a specialist in the psychoanalysis of adolescence, has described the critical role of a father or father surrogate who recognizes and fosters the innate talents of a gifted boy. Esman stresses that "the *early* flowering of creative genius in adolescence is favored by an intense supporting relationship and identification with the father figure." Wisely, Esman qualifies his general thesis. "It is true, of course, that one can find if one looks into the histories of creative persons, data to support virtually any thesis one sets up to account for their creativity." He also points out that "there must be . . . coincidence among innate gift, opportunity and sociocultural support."

There is general agreement that the absence of a father produces an impoverishment of masculine identification, which may serve as a motive for perversion and falsehood but also for certain unique expressions of creativity. The work of art then serves to reconstitute the lost father in fantasy. The death of Freud's father and Freud's mourning for him inspired the creation of *The Interpretation of Dreams*. Freud recognized the connection with his father's death only after the book was completed. Freud writes, "It was, I found, a portion of my own self-analysis, my reaction to my father's death—that is to say, to the most important event, the most poignant loss, of a man's life." George Pollock, a psychoanalyst who has investigated the relationship between mourning and creativity, believes that creation may be an attempt to carry out a mourning process. Furthermore, even though the person might not be successful in completing his mourning, "the intrinsic aesthetic or scientific merit of the work still may be great." In fact, says Pollock, "the creative product may reflect the mourning process in theme, style, form, content and it may itself stand as a memorial." Taking Pollock's general thesis to its extreme, the author of *The Orphans Lead the World* claims his research demonstrates that "all the great leaders in history have been orphans, abandoned children, illegitimate children, or children who have rejected their father."

In one of the definitive summations of the psychological meaning of father absence, the eminent French psychoanalyst Janine Chasseguet-Smirgel states, "Those who have not been able to project their Ego Ideal onto their father and his penis and who subsequently have gaps in their identifications, will feel the necessity, for obvious narcissistic motives, to grant themselves their missing identity by different means, creation being one among others. The work thus created will symbolize the phallus, the gap in the identity being likened to castration ... the subject will be led to create, yet, instead of begetting his work he will fabricate it."

With Chatterton the line between begetting and fabricating is nearly invisible. Chatterton invented more than some history and poems written by Thomas Rowley. He begat his own father, an idealized but believable and complete human being, a man of intelligence, wit, compassion, good judgment, honesty; a man with an extensive personal history, including genealogy, birthplace, and burial ground. With Canynge, Chatterton could fill in the gaps in his own identity. He was fortified and strengthened in the adequacy of his masculinity. Yet central to Chatterton's portrayals of Canynge is an image of masculine virtue that goes against the grain of stereotypical masculinity. Canynge is not a man of warlike temperament or one of those citizens devoted to ale and gluttony and wenching. In some marvelous meeting of poetic craft and psychological necessity, the youth Chatterton took the one tangible inheritance left to him by his father, the decaying parchments from St. Mary's, and composed on them and for them the very father he would have wanted.

The gradual development of Sir William Canynge from his minor role as a nobleman of humane ethical principles to the painter and poet of Rowley's fantasy on Bristol artists is a narrative of a fatherless boy's quest for a satisfactory image of manhood. As the representations of Canynge shift and rearrange, with certain features muting and others becoming more prominent, the relationship between Rowley and Canynge also undergoes its own subtle transmutations.

At first the reader is constantly reminded that Canynge is a benefactor, more than willing to pay Rowley handsomely for his historical researches and poetic dramas. Chatterton's craving for a patron who would support his artistic enterprises is bluntly manifest in these early imaginings on the character of Canynge. Nearly as transparent is Chatterton's wish for a father to take care of him and guide him through the perils of manhood. But by the end of the romance, Rowley has grown up from a mere servant and idealizer of his wealthy patron to the rank of beloved friend and lifelong companion. Thenceforth, the two men will participate in life on an equal footing. Canynge will also learn from Rowley. Both men are artists. Chatterton is no longer satisfied with a father who merely sponsors artistic enterprises and donates his money to the rebuilding of churches. For a while Rowley had been content simply to witness Canynge's glories. Now, as Chatterton begins to long for a father who will admit him to the magic circle of manhood, Rowley begins to create a Canynge who is an artist in his own right. In May, as the Rowley year draws to a close, Canynge writes several short poems and collaborates with Rowley on the tragic dramatic interlude, *Goddwyn,* by writing the prologue and appearing along with Rowley in one of the leading roles. It is uncertain whether this drama was ever completed. Only a fragment has survived. But the working out of an intimate literary collaboration between father and son may be all that Chatterton had intended. In effect, Chatterton was saying that he was becoming a man equal to his father; he was no longer willing to be a subservient child; he wished to be accepted as a real man.

There is another subtext, though, in these last Rowleys, one that reveals the internal conflicts that attended Chatterton's construction of his own manhood. Perhaps, if Rowley's Canynge had been accepted by the world, Chatterton might have retained his belief in the ideal of manhood that the benevolent fifteenth-century merchant prince had come to represent. Canynge was, above all, a man of peace devoted to building and preserving cities, and with Canynge inside him, Chatterton's own soul could be peaceful. But by May of 1769 not only was Walpole's rejection evident, it was becoming clear that no generous patron at all was going to come forth as a sponsor for Rowley's poetry and dramas. In his writings of late April and May Chatterton is already searching for an alternative to Canynge. He writes two Macpherson imitations, Ossian-like sagas in which the heroes are bloody warriors. He also composes a tragic interlude in which Goddwyn and Harold (the good sons) lose out to the bad sons, who convince King Edward to go to war. Among the last of the post-Canynge works of May 1769 is a dramatic eclogue in which the two characters are a father who has seen his son slain in the war and a son who has witnessed the slaying of his father. Says the son, "Sleene in the Warre mie boolie[20] Fadre lies ... Calked[21] from everich joie; here wylle I blede." The father replies, "Our Woes alyche, alyche our Dome[22] shal bee, / Mie Sonne mie Sonne alleyn ystorven[23] ys; / Here wylee I staie ande end

---

[20] boolie—beloved

[21] calked—cast out

[22] Dome—Fate

[23] ystorven—dead (Sonne alleyn ystorven—my only son dead)

mie Lyff with thee." As the father has died, so will the son; as the son has died, so will the father.

Everywhere Chatterton is reveling in warlike and bloody sentiments while simultaneously expressing the sorrow and pain that war inflicts on the poor, the women and children left behind, the fathers, and the sons. With the passing of Canynge, something begins to die in Chatterton.

FIVE

Petty Lies, Practical Jokes, and Historical Hoaxes

Chatterton plays a Cyrano for his Charleston friend, John Baker. Rowley becomes an art historian and composes a history of English painting for Horace Walpole. Walpole discovers the deception and brings the world of Rowley and Canynge to an end. A summer of mourning: The playful romantic becomes an advocate of sexual rakedom.

BUT even before April of 1769, and Walpole's *coup de grace*, Chatterton's correspondence with John Baker, a Bristol friend who was serving out his apprenticeship in Charleston, South Carolina, revealed a sixteen-year-old already becoming disillusioned with romantic love. We see him absorbed by an assortment of literary enterprises but equally concerned with demonstrating a devil-may-care sexual fluency.

Baker was among the favored friends Chatterton celebrated in *Craishes Herauldry*. In September of 1768, Chatterton had designed for the Baker family a brief pedigree going back to 1417 and a heraldic sign and crest. "Name—Baker—Gules a Goat passant Argent by the name Baker Guillams Heraldrye. Crest to Baker. a Goats head Couped holding in his Mouth a Rose barbd proper—."

On January 5, 1769, exactly a week after his arrival in Charleston, Baker wrote a letter to Chatterton in the effusive eighteenth-century manner. He begins with an affirmation of the bonds of "Love, Friendship and evry tender Passion I possess." He alludes to the qualities that make his Bristol friend so dear to him and expresses the hope that he might have

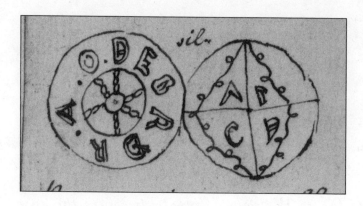

some small share in Chatterton's esteem. After these professions of love, Baker, who had left for South Carolina almost two months before, recounts the full details of his ocean crossing. He then thanks Chatterton for his past poetic favors and asks for yet another. One of Chatterton's beguiling attributes was the easygoing willingness with which, the year previous, he had put his poetic gifts at the service of Baker's courtship of a Bristol lady named Eleanor Hoyland. On the surface the poems he wrote for Baker are pure innocence, completely pedestrian, unremarkable. Yet they exhibit, just as convincingly as the counterfeit Rowleys, all the traits of an imposturous character. Like outright imposturousness, hoaxing and practical joking have the goal of putting one over on an unsuspecting audience.

Chatterton's bent for fooling his audience was given free rein in his Eleanor Hoyland productions. He happily played the ghost writer for his untalented comrade. But Chatterton did not care at all for the very proper Miss Hoyland. He easily expressed for Baker the sentimental sort of love his own proud soul could no longer abide. To Hoyland's name he lavishly invented and not infrequently plagiarized from the lyrical poets of the day some very ordinary lines of love poetry, couched in the formal style he had already learned to mock. Nearly a dozen Hoylands have survived. One, a thirteen-line acrostic, begins:

> *Enchanting is the mighty power of Love;*
> *Life stript of am'rous joys would irksom prove*

THE IMPOSTOR-POET THOMAS CHATTERTON

> *E'en Heavn's great Thundrer wore the easy chain*
> *And over all the World, Love keeps his Reign*
> *No human Heart can bear the piercing Blade*
> *Or I than others, am more tender made*
> *Right thro' my Heart a burning Arrow drove*

John Baker may have pledged his heart to Eleanor, but perhaps to show off to his sophisticated Bristol friend or perhaps because he knew just how to appeal to Chatterton's fondness for amorous banter, after his request for more Hoyland poems, he continues:

> pray my kind love to Miss Rumsey, and remember me to all the Dear pretty Ladies in Redclift Hill, but now I write to you of Ladies perhaps you would be glad to have a Discription of the Girls in this Part of the World I wish it were in my Power to paint their merits in their proper light or to give them the Praise due to their Merit, already I am in Love with twenty, consumedly in Love, so free, so good natured, so affable, so, so so evry thing, so beautiful are the Ladies in this Town that sometimes I fancy myself among the Houri of Paridise. . . .

When after six weeks had passed and he had not yet heard from his enchanting friend, Baker writes again wondering if he has been forgotten. For all the "so, so so evry thing" delights of Charleston, the youth is plainly and painfully homesick.

Later, in the summer of 1770, after Chatterton escapes from his apprenticeship and tries to make a go of it in the vast, impersonal city of London, his letters home to Bristol, though outwardly much braver than those of his Charleston correspondent, reverberate with similar homesick yearnings. But unless one of his correspondents had been emotionally attuned to the desperate sadness beneath his manic braggadocio, no one from Bristol would have guessed how lonely Chatterton was, including Chatterton himself.

Disappointed as Baker must have been when Chatterton did not reply to his first letter, in his second letter he only gives a hint of how much he misses his friend and everything else from Bristol:

> While you are employed in examining and admiring the Charms of your divine Polly (behind the Church Door) I am thinking of you both; no doubt you will soon be tired of such a Correspondent who is always pestering you with his Nonsense, but I cannot let slip any Opportunity of assuring my Chatterton that I am still the same; never a Day passes over my head but I think of you; and heartily wish to be again with so dear a Friend but I

almost begin to think you have forgot me by your not writing me before this Time; and yet I cannot be so unjust as to think you would forfeit your words, so many Times you promised to write by every vessel, I rather think that you did not know of any Opportunity of sending me a Letter.

The letter closes with remembrances to "Jack Fowler, Miss Rumsey, Miss Thatcher, your Sister & Miss Wilkins, and now I have mentioned the young let me like wise mention the old; so remember me to your mother, Mrs. Ewer and Mr. & Jemmy & all our Acquaintance." In addition to appointing him general messenger to his friends in Bristol, Baker commissions Chatterton to fill up a pocket notebook with poetry and to send whatever new books come out "if they are clever" and also "News Papers."

Chatterton was not a reliable correspondent. But his lapse could not be attributed to writer's block or laziness. He had spent the three months before receiving Baker's second letter composing his poetic tragedy, *Aella*, along with the *Lyfe of William Canynge*, and *Rowley's Heraldic Account of Bristol Artists and Writers*. Only two days earlier he had submitted, under the initials D.B., an Ossian-type manuscript, *Ethelgar. A Saxon Poem*, to *Town and Country Magazine*.

On the face of it, Chatterton's reply to Baker on March 6 would indicate that he had no empathy at all for the loneliness and longing of his friend. However, although Chatterton had yet to experience what it meant to be in a strange city, separated from all the familiar faces of childhood, he did have some inkling of his friend's inner state. It simply would have been out of character for Chatterton to expose clear signs of compassion. He seeks instead to cheer Baker with brave news and soaring sentiments: "I have received both your favors, the muse alone must tell my joy." And the muse obeys and inspires in Chatterton some mock lyrical poetry:

> *Oerwhelmd with pleasure at the joyful news*
> *I strung the chorded Shell and 'woke the Muse:*
> *Begin o Servant! of the sacred nine:*
> *And echo joy thro' ev'ry nervous Line:*
> *Bring down th'etherial Choir to aid the Song*
> *Let boundless raptures smoothly glide along.*
> *My Baker's well! oh words of sweet delight!*
> *Now! Now! my Muse, soar up th'Olimpic height.*

The next section of his tardy letter opens with an allusion to the difficulties of being both poet and lawyer's apprentice: "I must now close my poetical Labors, my master being return'd from London." But Chatterton does not let on how oppressive and humiliating is his work as a mere copier of legal documents. Instead, he buoyantly launches into a narrative of Polly Rumsey's betrayal:

> Your celebrated Miss Rumsey is going to be married to Mr. Fowler, as he himself informs me . . . For a Lover Heavens mend him; but for a Husband! O excellent; . . . to find a Spirit so well adapted to the humor of an English Wife, that is, one who takes off his Hat, to evry Person he chances to meet, to shew his staring Horns; and very politely stands at the Door of his Wive's chamber, whilst her Gallant is entertaining her within. O mirabile! what will human nature degenerate into. Fowler aforesaid, declares he makes a scruple of Conscience of being too free with Miss Rumsey before marriage. There's a Gallant for you! Why a Girl with any thing of Woman, would despise him for it.

So went the sixteen-year-old Thomas Chatterton's sentiments on pre- and postmarital fidelity. It was this sort of chin-up cynicism that would become his standard way of reconciling himself to disillusionment. The Miss Rumsey who had softened his studious temper, the sweet lady for whom he had invented a genealogy, was favoring another Bristol youth. But Chatterton certainly was not going to let Baker know how much he had been affected by this rejection. The devil-may-care Chatterton was relieved to be rid of the "Female Machiavel," Miss Rumsey.

The treacherous Fowler disposed of, the unfaithful Rumsey dismissed, Chatterton advances full sail with some rollicking Ossian proclaiming his everlasting loyalty to Baker: "my friendship is as firm as the white Rocks when the black Waves roar around it, and the waters burst on its hoary top, when the driving wind ploughs the sable Sea, and the rising waves aspire to the clouds teeming with the rattling Hail; so much for Heroics." The poetic romp accomplished, next comes some sexual heroics. Not to be crushed by Polly's rejection, not to be outdone by Baker's twenty times in love and his assertion that "one must have a heart of steell covered over with brass and a third Case of Iron to guard against the conquering Eyes of the beauties of Charles Town," Chatterton claims a more extensive triumph for himself: "I have been violently in Love three and twenty times, since your departure and not a few times, came off victorious." He encloses some poems he had written on Miss Hoyland, wryly commenting, "I wish better for her sake and yours."

A week or so after this literary frolic with Baker, Chatterton focused his inventive mind on the pressing matter of how to earn a living as a poet.

He had finally come to terms with the undeniable fact that Catcott and Barrett had no intention of paying him for his Rowleys. Nor were these two self-involved gentlemen, so incapable of rising above the facts of trade or history, going to trumpet Rowley's name to the world at large. Chatterton would have to find a new patron, preferably a very rich man willing to invest his money in artistic enterprises from the fifteenth century. Chatterton hatched a new vocation for the remarkable poet-priest who had already learned to be an art collector and accomplished historian. With his next patron in mind, Chatterton turned Rowley into an art historian.

In 1762 Horace Walpole's *Anecdotes of Painting in England: with some Account of the principal Artists and incidental Notes on the other Arts; collected by the late Mr. George Vertue* had been published to wide acclaim. Vertue had spent a lifetime visiting and cataloguing English art collections. After Vertue's death, Walpole devoted several years to putting his catalogue in order, verifying the references and supplementing the work when he thought it necessary. Walpole, who resided at Strawberry Hill, his pseudo-Gothic estate in Twickenham, was sympathetic to the aristocracy, wealthy landowners, antique collectors, and a few well-known writers of his day. He sent King George III a set of the edited Vertue catalogues and offered his services to the court as a "virtuoso and antiquarian." Around the same time, the virtuoso Walpole had a fling with literary imposture. In 1765, the year that the second edition of *Anecdotes* appeared, the first edition of *The Castle of Otranto,* translated by William Marshall, Gent. from the Italian of Onuphrio Muralto, canon of the church of St. Nicholas at Otranto, was published. At first Walpole palmed off *Otranto* as a translation, but then admitted authorship when the novel became a huge best-seller.

Horace Walpole was the ideal gentleman to trumpet the name of Thomas Rowley to the world. On March 25, 1769, Chatterton sent the following letter in care of Walpole's bookseller.

Sir:

Being versed a little in antiquitys, I have met with several Curious Manuscripts among which the following may be of Service to you, in any future Edition of your truly entertaining Anecdotes of Paintings—In correcting the Mistakes (if any) in the Notes you will greatly oblige

Your most humble Servant
THOMAS CHATTERTON

Appended to the letter is *The Ryse of Peyncteynge, yn Englande, wroten bie T. Rowleie. 1469 for Mastre Canynge.* This prose piece traces English paintings from the early Britons up to those who "payncted the Walles of Master Canynge hys Howse, where bee the Councelmenne atte Dynnere; a moste daintie ande feetyve pereformaunce nowe ycrasede beeynge done ynne M.CC.I." In the middle of that ancient document is a short essay on a Danish glass painter named Afflem, written in the flamboyant style of Ossian but in the language of Rowley. "Forfraughte wythe embolleynge Waves, he sawe his Broder Wyfe and Chyldrenne synke to Deathe: himselfe was throwen, onne a Banke ynne the Isle of Wyghte, to lyve hys Lyfe forgard to all Emmoise. thus moche for Afflem." Then followed some lines of poetry by "Johne Seconde Abbate of Seyncte Austyns Mynsterre was the fyrste Englyshe Paynctere yn Oyles." Thomas Rowley was presented here in a footnote as the transcriber of John's poem. "T. Rowleie was a Secular Priest of St. John's, in this City. his Merit as a Biographer, Historiographer is great, as a Poet still greater: some of his Pieces would do honor to Pope; and the Person under whose Patronage they may appear to the World, will lay the Englishman, the Antiquary, and the Poet, under an eternal Obligation."

Walpole also received an introduction to Canynge. "The Founder of that noble Gothic Pile, Saint Mary Redclift Church in this City: the Mecenas of his time: one who could happily blend The Poet, the Painter, the Priest, and the Christian—perfect in each: a Friend to all in distress, an honor to Bristol, and a Glory to the Church." Was Canynge virtuous enough to inspire the generosity of the great Horace Walpole, who, as it happened, already owned a printing press?

Walpole took the bait. On March 28 he acknowledged Chatterton's discovery. After some polite thank-you's and some hasty commonplaces on the artistic value of the documents Walpole continues:

> Give me leave to ask you where Rowley's poems are to be found. I shoud not be sorry to print them, or at least a specimen of them, if they have never been printed.
> The Abbot John's verses, that you have given me, are wonderfull for their harmony and spirit, tho'there are some words I do not understand.

Chatterton could hardly believe his good luck. He lost no time in replying. On March 30, he dashed off a letter offering some further "Anecdotes and Specimens of Poetry," among them a larger poem of Abbot John and *Historie of Peyncters yn Englande bie T. Rowley*. In commenting on Abbot John's poem, which had been translated by Rowley into his characteristic ten-line stanza with alexandrines, Chatterton makes certain that Walpole knows it to be "inferior to Rowley whose Works when I have Leisure I will fairly Copy and send you." However, not quite halfway through his *Historie,* the impatient Thomas Rowley cannot resist one of his "translations" from the poetry of the ancient days:

> Botte nowe wee bee upon Peyncteynge sommewhatte maie be saide of the Poemes of those daies whyche bee toe the Mynde, what Peyncteynge bee toe the Eyne:
>
> *Whan azure Skie ys veylde yn Robes of Nyghte;*
> *Whanne glemmrynge dewedrops stounde the Faytours[1] Eyne;*
> *Whanne flying Cloudes betinged with roddie Lyghte*
> *Doth on the Brindlynge[2] Wolfe and Wood bore shine*
> *Whanne Even Star fayre Herehaughte of nyght*
> *Spreds the dercke[3] douskie[4] Sheeene alonge the Mees*
> *The wreethynge Neders[5] sens a glumie Lyghte*
> *And houlets[6] wynge from Levyn[7] blasted Trees*
> *Arise mie Spryghte and seke the distant dele*
> *And there to ecchoing Tonges thie raptured Joies ytele.*

Alas, Walpole probably never got to read this charming Rowley. By the time he received this second packet, he had already referred the first samples to his close friend Thomas Gray, the poet, and to Reverend William Mason, the antiquarian. Both these men, former devotees of Macpherson, were quick to certify that the Rowleys were modern forgeries.

Although there is no record of his next letter to Chatterton, Walpole later claimed that he wrote instantly upon hearing that the Rowleys were counterfeit.

> I undeceived him about my being a person of any interest and urged; that in duty and gratitude to his mother, who had straitened herself to breed him up to a profession, he ought to labor in it, that in her old age he might absolve his filial debt; and I told him, that when he sould have made a fortune he might unbend himself with the studies consonant to his inclinations. I told him also, that I had communicated his transcripts to better judges, and that they were by no means satisfied with the authenticity of his supposed MSS.

---

[1] Faytours—travelers

[2] Brindlynge—brindled, having dark streaks on a tawny background

[3] dercke—dark

[4] douskie—dusky

[5] Neders—a serpent or adder, used here perhaps as a glowworm

[6] houlets—owlets

[7] Levyn—lightning

On April 8, Chatterton wrote to Walpole demanding the return of his transcripts of *The Ryse of Peyncteynge, yn Englande* and *Historie of Peyncters yn Englande*. He was exasperated and his smoldering fury came through all too clearly in the first draft of that letter. Barrett, who feared revenge from the vitriolic Walpole, smoothed out the text, toned down the anger, and added an advertisement for himself. "Mr. Barrett who is now writing the History & Antiquities of the City of Bristol, has desir'd it of me, & I should be sorry to deprive him or the World indeed of a Valuable Curiosity." After Barrett's name in the final much abbreviated draft is Chatterton's own additional phrase, "a very able antiquarian."

Walpole's rejection caused Chatterton to vacillate in his allegiance to Thomas Rowley. He received no reply to the considerably toned-down letter he sent on April 8 in which he promised to heed Walpole's advice "by destroying all my useless lumber of literature and never using my pen again but in the law," nor to the letter of April 14, in which he rescinded his vow of reformation, "Being fully convinced of the papers of Rowley being genuine, I should be obliged to you to return the copy I sent you, having no other." Three months later the young poet wrote another letter, this one a lucid testimony that his pride had been sorely wounded by Walpole's snub.

> Sir, I cannot reconcile your behaviour to me, with the notions I once entertained of you. I think myself injured, sir; and, did you not know my circumstances, you would not dare to treat me thus. I have sent twice for a copy of the MS.:—no answer from you. An explanation or excuse for your silence would oblige

But even as Chatterton demanded the return of his manuscript, he was writing the bloody Ossians and eclogues that signaled the end of Canynge's protective presence. By then Chatterton probably had realized that Walpole would never publish him, and so he began to concoct another scheme for making money. In its bare outlines this invention resembled the *Craishes Herauldry* in which Chatterton had linked his family name with that of Sir William Canynge. The *Herauldry* had concluded with a playful entry mocking all those who cared more about family pedigrees than benevolent good works. However, Chatterton's new post-Rowley family pedigree was not just a private hoax to be shared among close friends. It was designed specifically to fool one of the more gullible citizens of Bristol. As much as Walpole may have been tempted by Chatterton's Rowleys, he had not been seduced into believing that something that was not true was true. But Henry Burgum, Catcott's partner in the pewtering trade, was an easy mark.

Though not quite so eager for a reputation as Catcott, Burgum was more than willing to pay a small sum for a noble family pedigree. Early in May of 1769, shortly after the fiasco with Walpole, Chatterton quite miraculously discovered Burgum's lineage among the ancient Rowley parchments. Burgum, a self-educated, newly wealthy man, had become an ostentatious lover of the arts and well-known social climber. *The Account of the family of De Berghams from the Norman Conquest to this Time Collected From Original Records, Tournament Rolls, and the Herald's of March and Garter's Records* by T. Chatterton., a vellum document printed in red and black ink and accompanied by heraldic devices, arms, and authenticating marginal notes, was just what Henry Burgum needed to enhance his prestige in Bristol.

Barrett's writing on Chatterton's documents is nowhere as evident as in his translations of the French and Latin sequences of the de Bergham pedigree. By May, Chatterton had become exceedingly dextrous in wielding the weapons of the learned. He plumped up the pedigree with all kinds of erudition he did not possess, using words and languages he did not really understand simply for their general appearance and impact. Nearly half of this elaborate genealogy and heraldic fantasy, the sections describing the lineages of the so-called Simon I and Simon II, Chatterton had copied, summarized, or paraphrased from the well-known but little-read *Baronettage of England,* by Arthur Collins. The only sections of this fanciful document that Chatterton himself wrote are the prose and poetry dealing with a fictitious de Bergham family, supposedly descended from Alan de Bergham, the third son of Simon III. When composing the pedigree, Chatterton left spaces in the manuscript for Barrett's translations. If there were any doubts about Barrett's collaboration in the Walpole scheme, in the case of the de Bergham pedigree it must be presumed that Barrett knowingly went along with what was an obvious historical hoax.

The discovery of the parchment was an unlikely one, and if nothing else the eighteenth-century puns and double entendres of the heraldic devices and marginal notes should have set a man wise. Yet Burgum was determined to have his glorious pedigree and he willingly paid Chatterton five shillings for it.

For a time, the success of the Burgum hoax took Chatterton's mind off the failure of his Walpole scheme. But by July, still having received no reply from Walpole and still smarting from his rebuff, the sixteen-year-old Chatterton wrote the following lines of verse which he had "intended to have sent . . . to Mr. Walpole, but my sister perswaded me out of it."

Walpole! I thought not I should ever see
So mean a Heart as thine has proved to be;
Thou, who in Luxury nurs'd behold'st with Scorn
The Boy, who Friendless, Penniless, Forlorn,
Asks thy high Favour,—thou mayst call me Cheat—
Say, didst thou ne'er indulge in such Deceit?
Who wrote Otranto? But I will not chide,
Scorn I will repay with Scorn, and Pride with Pride.
Still, Walpole, still, thy Prosy Chapters write,
And twaddling Letters to some Fair indite,
Laud all above thee,—Fawn and Cringe to those
Who, for thy Fame, were better Friends than Foes
Still spurn the incautious Fool who dares—

Had I the Gifts of Wealth and Lux'ry shar'd
Not poor and Mean—Walpole! thou hadst not dared
Thus to insult, But I shall live and Stand
By Rowley's side—when Thou art dead and damned.

This poem, written sometime in late July or early August of 1769, marks a transition in the sentiments and writing style of Thomas Chatterton. Though the poem concludes with Chatterton swearing his everlasting loyalty to Rowley, in essence *Walpole! I thought not I should ever see* is one of the first clear literary statements of the end of the magnificent world of Sir William Canynge, "the Poet, the Painter, the Priest and the Christian perfect in each; a Friend to all in distress, an honor to Bristol, and a Glory to the Church."

The Walpole incident had by this time brought home to Chatterton the futility of hiding behind Rowley. The boy who had sustained his spirits by dreaming of a Bristol more noble than the narrow, mercantile wasteland in which he grew up was no longer able to disguise his disillusionment with the world as it actually existed. With his description of the meanspirited Walpole, whose petty character his poem has so well delineated, Chatterton's pen becomes a weapon. His marvelous, lyrical Rowleys have been rejected. Chatterton will repay scorn with scorn.

Chatterton's statement that he will live and stand forever by Rowley's side is often interpreted as an open admission that he is Rowley. Was Chatterton's sister Mary aware of the implicit confession? Or was her restraining gesture a simple matter of protecting her younger brother from his impetuosity? Mary would reveal a great deal about her brother to the inquirers who visited her after his death, but on the lines to Walpole she was silent. They remained in her possession until 1783, when she gave the manuscript to the family who had employed her as a governess.

The encounter with Walpole, Chatterton's relinquishment of Rowley, and his recognition that Polly Rumsey was lost to him all occurred within the same time frame. For a few months, from June to September of 1769, as he was turning his passions away from the fifteenth-century world of the virtuous William Canynge, Chatterton wrote very little. It was as though his disillusionment with that ideal of manhood had emptied him of inspiration. He seemed to have lost all sense of direction or purpose. Very likely Chatterton's relative artistic silence was the outward manifestation of one of those periods of silent mourning so typical of the adolescent years.

One of the legacies that the adult inherits from the adolescent is the capacity to mourn. This mourning also characterizes mature artists as they negotiate the borders between one phase of artistic development and the next. A child may grieve and protest the loss of someone or something he loves, but he does not recognize the irreversibility of that loss, nor does he accept that the past is gone and will never return. But adolescence itself involves a prolonged mourning for the lost past of infancy and childhood. What is mourned particularly are the childhood idealizations of the parents—their presences, their authority and attitudes. The recognition that childhood is over does not come all at once. The past does not willingly or easily allow itself to be given up. On the way from childhood to adulthood there are numerous excursions back into the past. The past is revisited, remembered in a new way, and then relinquished again. These repeated attacks of loss and disappointment constitute much of the adolescent experience. What the adolescent goes through with such intensity and passion, the adult will later experience in a less chaotic, more even-keeled fashion each time he gives up something or someone he has been attached to.

The adolescent is caught in a dilemma. He wants never to relinquish the idealizations of the past and he also needs equally desperately to move on to the future. At the same time that this conflict claims his energies, the adolescent is also possessed by newly aroused, temporarily unruly genital desires that he must learn to transfer away from the forbidden realm of his family and into the larger social order. Thus, an adolescent feels driven to attach family idealizations and passions to persons, places, and values outside the family.

The adolescent propensity for idealizing the thoughts, values, physical appearance, and philosophies of specially selected members of the adult world is well-known. While he questions the authority and values of his parents, the adolescent seeks in the external world models of perfection with whom he can identify. For a boy like Thomas Chatterton, who had only a shadowy, patchy image of a father on which to base his own masculine identity and self-esteem, the normal tendency to seek ideal father figures outside the family was heightened. Sometimes adolescents select pure and saintly types who represent their own longing to be virtuous and self-sacrificing. Although these new idols are held up as models of the superior beliefs and advanced moral qualities the adolescent is striving for, they are all too often revivals or repersonifications of the sexual, worldly, and moral powers that were once attributed to the parents. The new idols are, of course, subject to disillusionment and deidealization just as the parents were. At other times, the adolescent may revere and glorify the ruthless and seductive men and women who represent aspects of the parents that are devalued and embody the very erotic temptations the adolescent is struggling to control. Or, as happened with Chatterton, when he turned away from Rowley to vulgar Ossians and satire, the devalued aspects of manhood become the source of new literary inspirations.

While recovering from the heartbreak of a love affair or from the loss of some adored person or passionately held belief, the youth is hesitant to risk another romantic submersion, another idealistic dream. He retreats from the world to catch his breath and nurse his wounds. For a time his passions are bound up in grieving for lost glories. In this state of semiwithdrawal the youth is quietly mobilizing new resources, finding new solutions to his dilemmas. And because his passions and longings are so insistent, they are soon set free for a new love, a new belief, a new way of thinking about the world.

The new beliefs will be embraced with as much fervor and passion as the ones that have just been mourned and recognized as lost forever. Because he is incomplete, torn between the child he once was and the adult he is in the process of becoming, the adolescent yearns for experiences that convey wholeness and unity.... Religion, Politics, Nature.... Such cultural obsessions can be enlisted in the service of self-enhancement.

During the summer of 1769, Chatterton was not completely inactive. There was the outraged Walpole poem, an Ossian imitation, three elegies, a musical burletta, and a confused satirical poem about the conflict between the satirical impulse and self-interested prudence. Each of these verses hinted at a poetic style that Chatterton would adopt during the coming year.

Several of the central characters of the satirical poem Chatterton wrote at this time were the political figures surrounding King George III. This last poem of that relatively barren summer presaged the major thrust of Chatterton's next literary adventures. The social and political realities of eighteenth-century England were about to harness the unbound passions of the Rowley romance. The idealizations of manhood that had been attached to Rowley and Canynge would be attached to the leading freethinker of eighteenth-century England, John Wilkes. The men who exemplified his devalued images of manhood would become the subjects of Chatterton's satirical freethinking writings. The poetic rhythms of Chaucer, Dryden, and Pope that had governed the world of Canynge would be overshadowed by the loose verse forms of Charles Churchill, a friend of Wilkes's and one of the most popular and wealthy poets of the day. For his prose, Chatterton would impersonate the style of the anonymous journalist and letter writer, Junius. Sadly though, after the loss of Rowley, Chatterton's beliefs would never again rise to the purity and nobility of that romance. The impostor-poet gradually became an acknowledged writer and man of the world, but in doing so he lost the central motive for his poetic impulses. Had he lived, he might have continued the mourning process and perhaps regained a capacity for belief.

The first indication of the end of Chatterton's mourning of Rowley and the beginning of his metamorphosis comes in a verse letter to John Baker entitled *Journal 6th*. The letter, begun on September 6 and completed on the last day of the month (evidently written at odd hours when his master, the poetry-scorning Lambert, was not around), consists of three experimental satirical poems arbitrarily strung together, each one declaring a different facet of Chatterton's new, as yet tentatively formulated freethinking creed: libertine sexuality, contempt for religious orthodoxy, and a scornful superiority to those ordinary mortals who are deceived by corrupt gurus peddling religious belief for a fee. For the moment, Chatterton's freethinking consisted of disparaging and demeaning any tendencies toward belief and trust.

He presents the sexual aspect of his new creed in the form of poetic recommendations to Baker on the most advantageous approaches to the young ladies. There is nothing here of the tentative gentility of his pseudonymous addresses to Miss Hoyland, or the buoyantly waggish spirit that designed the Rumsey genealogy. This is the sophisticated satire of disillusionment, the bravado of a sexual rake.

> *Oft have I seen the wounded Swain*
> *Upon the rack of pleasing Pain*
> *Full of his flame, upon his tongue*
> *The quivering Declaration hung*
> *When lost to Courage Sense and reason*

THE IMPOSTOR-POET THOMAS CHATTERTON

> *He talkd of Weather and the Season.*
> *Such Tremors never coward me*
> *I'm flattring impudent and free*
> *Unmov'd by frowns and lowring eyes*
> *'Tis Smiles I only ask and Prize*
> *And when the Smile is freely given*
> *You're in the highway Road to Heaven*
> *Those coward Lovers seldom find*
> *That whining makes the Ladys kind*
> *They laugh at silly Silent Swains*
> *Who're fit for nothing but their Chains*

Chatterton follows this advice with some lines comparing the sexual attitudes of the rake and the buck, presumably recommending the sexual and moral advantages of rakedom:

> *A Rake, I take it, is a Creature*
> *Who winds thro' all the folds of Nature*
> *Who sees the Passions and can tell*
> *How the soft beating heart shall swell*
> . . . .
> *Who looks above a Prostitute, he*
> *Thinks Love the only Prize of Beauty*
> *And she that can be basely sold*
> *Is Much beneath or Love or Gold*
> *Who thinks the almost dearest part*
> *In all the Body is the Heart*
> . . . .
> *A Buck's a Beast of th'other Side*
> *And real but in Hoofs and Hide*
> *To nature and the Passions dead*
> *A Brothel is his House and Bed*
> *To fan the flame of warm desire*
> *And after wanton in the Fire*
> *He thinks a Labor; and his parts*
> *Were not design'd to conquer hearts*
> *Serene with Bottle Pox and Whore*
> *He's happy and requires no more*

The mischievous misogyny of Chatterton's expressed attitudes toward love never change. Nevertheless until the very last weeks of his life, flickering in the background of many of his poems and satirical letters on matrimony is the figure of the faithless Miss Polly Rumsey. He starts the new year off with a short poem, *The Advice,* addressed to Miss R*****, of Bristol, condemning her for her insincere admiration for the numerous swains who adore and flatter her. He relinquishes her with a gesture of mock gallantry to his narrow-minded rival Fowler—"Fly to your worthiest lovers arm / To him resign your swelling charms, / And meet his gen'rous breast." Yet Chatterton still yearns for his Polly.

The parallels between Chatterton's new sexual creed and his new sociopolitical creed are already apparent in *Journal 6th.* He had adopted both facets of his freethinking from the two eighteenth-century writers he turned to after losing Rowley and Canynge.

Chatterton never did meet John Wilkes, whose attitudes toward sexual and political freedom so influenced him. And Charles Churchill, the most prominent verse satirist of his day when Chatterton was still at Colston's, had died of a mysterious fever at the age of 32 in 1764. Nevertheless, Chatterton was strongly influenced by Churchill's satirical methodology, his libertine sexual attitudes, and his knowledge of how to make political satire pay off; the young poet had "pretty well dipped into" all of these before he left for London.

In London no chaste Thomas Rowleys or noble William Canynges would serve as models for Chatterton's poetic, religious, political, sexual, and personal sentiments. His new inspirations, already adopted during his last year in Bristol, would be two worshipers of the mysterious powers of the phallus, two champions of liberty who often mistook license for liberty.

PART II

A NOBLE INSANITY OF THE SOUL:

CHATTERTON'S

SEARCH FOR AN

EIGHTEENTH-CENTURY

FATHER

SIX

The Rage of Satire

*Chatterton adopts the Churchillian poetic morality—
"Written in gold let REVOLUTION stand."
The Articles of Belief of Me Thomas Chatterton.
The debate between Chatterton and Vicar Alexander
Catcott. Chatterton's "fake" suicide note,
his Will, composed on the day before Wilkes is
released from prison, becomes
his ticket to freedom.*

AS Rowley wrote for the benevolent causes of Canynge, so Churchill wrote for Wilkes and the radical causes of the Patriot party. The journalists who defended the policies of King George III referred to this champion of freedom and independence as "the Hireling slave of Faction and Spite." In the four short years of his literary career, Churchill published thousands of lines of verse, much of it pro-Wilkesian political satire, for which he was paid handsomely. Churchill was famous for the fact that he never let his prodigious literary output interfere with his hedonistic pursuits. Because of his popularity and prolific output, he acquired the funds to fulfill his avowed aim in life, "To live as merry as I can."

Very likely Churchill, whose writings opposed tyranny in any form—public opinion, superstition, privilege, government, the literary establishment—lusted for independence as passionately as he did because he had been enslaved to respectability and a traditional way of life. At the age of eighteen he embarked on a season of rebellion by eloping with his childhood sweetheart, though neither had any money. But he soon returned to follow his father, who was a vicar, into the church. Churchill dedicated the next four years of his life to preparations for the priesthood and in 1756 was ordained and appointed curate to his father. To supple-

ment the meager income on which he could barely support his wife and three children, he turned to teaching, another calling for which he had little genuine inclination. But despite his hard work, by 1760 he was on the threshold of debtor's prison.

At the last minute, poetry came to his rescue. Destitute as Churchill was, he took the chance of publishing, at his own expense, his satirical commentary on the world of theater, *The Rosciad.* Like the clergyman Laurence Sterne, whose *Tristram Shandy* had catapulted him to fame and fortune, the curate Churchill became an immediate critical and financial success. It was suggested in *The Monthly Review* that "the present age may, perhaps, be as much distinguished for its merry Parsons, as the reign of Charles II was for a set of waggish and witty Courtiers."

Churchill's next maneuver was to clip the chains of marital bondage. He separated from his wife. Though he remained a clergyman for three more years, Churchill's life was from then on consecrated to poetry, pleasure, and politics. A focal point of his merry new life was his position as coeditor with John Wilkes of the *North Briton,* a radical newspaper whose principal target was the government of George III. He and Wilkes dined frequently at the Sublime Society of Beefsteaks, where members and their guests, among them Garrick, Boswell, Hogarth, and Lord Sandwich, convened to eat good, honest, English beef, "have wine and punch in plenty and freedom," engage in schoolboyish heckling of one another, and exercise their wits by composing spontaneous verse, much of it obscene.

And after his separation, Churchill acquired mistresses aplenty. In a letter to Wilkes, who became his most intimate friend and colleague, Churchill advertised his sexual pleasures as items in a regime of physical discipline. "Breakfast at nine, two dishes of tea and one thin slice of bread and butter—Dine at three—eat moderately—drink a sober pint—Tumble the bed till four—Tea at six—walk till nine—Eat some cooling fruit and to bed. There is regularity for you—" In honor of his lifelong devotion to pleasure, Churchill's tombstone was inscribed, "Life to the last enjoy'd, here Churchill lies."

For all his hatred of tyranny of any sort, Churchill was a religious and sexual tyrant in his own right. He was one of the prominent anti-Semites of his day. When it came to homosexuality he could be savage. His moral outrage against that sexual deviance was vented in his satire entitled *The Times*: "Sins worse / Than plagues, which truly to unfold / Would make the best blood in my veins run cold, / And strike all Manhood dead. . . . For those who thus offend amongst Mankind, / A fire more fierce, and tortures more refin'd." But then Churchill interrupts his tirade against homosexuality to lament that women are becoming out-of-date. His anti-Semitism was personal. But in his satirically lofty attitudes toward women as in his homophobic attitudes, Churchill expressed the obligatory prejudices of his age.

Churchill's brand of libertinism was quite at home with the condescending sentimentality that he accorded the weaker sex. Lest any of his friends interpret his sentimentality as sexual flabbiness, he portrayed his "healthy" lustings for the opposite sex in a satirical mode. Women, with their unconditional love and grace and softest arts, humanized men. With their tears, they would "melt the rugged temper of our Isle." The raptures of physical love with a woman were what made a man a man:

> *No more the Heart, that seat where Love resides*
> *Each Breath drawn quick and short, in fuller tides*
> *Life posting thro' the veins, each pulse on fire,*
> *And the whole body tingling with desire.*

Journal 6th, the verse-letter Chatterton sent Baker at the end of September 1769 that had tentatively proclaimed his freethinking creed, was not yet modeled on the Churchillian stance. Fashioned on Pope, with some Gay, some Swift, and some Butler here and there, *Journal 6th* was as crude and amorphous in its stylistic format as it was in its formulation of the meaning of liberated thought. In October, Chatterton kept struggling to achieve a greater coherence of thought and expression. Finally, during the last five days of the month, the unifying principles of modern satiric verse as practiced by Charles Churchill came to him.

Chatterton's excitement over this revelation was evident by the feverish rate at which he began to write. Of the 614 lines he completed between October 27 and October 30, 408 were "Churchill Chattertonized." The last of the verses, a 144-line fragment of what had been intended as a much longer poem, was written in two hours. From then on, for better or worse, Chatterton was wedded to the satirical style of Charles Churchill.

Every verse satirist of the eighteenth century, including those like Churchill who were eventually recognized for a poetic style of their own making, was influenced by Alexander Pope. Even Rowley, the fifteenth-century priest, almost gave himself away, so closely were some of his phrases modeled on Pope. When Rowley's audacious creator abandoned Canynge's world for the eighteenth-century social order, he liberated himself from Pope by becoming a near clone of Charles Churchill. Pope, who was no freethinker, had served as the immediate source of Churchill's satirical mode. Churchill then adapted Pope to suit his own temperament and literary purposes. And Churchill's adaptation seemed to have been made in heaven for the evolving freethinking philosophy of Thomas Chatterton.

Pope's satirical mode had created a way to explore nature, religion, politics, the human condition. Pope's method of looking at the world depended on his poetic stance. With Churchill, the poet's stance itself became the central subject of the poem. This was just what Chatterton had been searching for. Pope had been a suitable model for Rowley's high-minded commentaries on life and art. But Rowley had been rejected. Chatterton found a new ideal: a poetic form in which the poet's plight commands the interest and sympathies of the audience, a poetic form in which the poet's wit and intelligence emerge as superior to all that he surveys.

Whereas Pope strove to contain the satiric emotion within a strict, ten-syllable couplet, thereby demonstrating the power of the poetic structure, Churchill wanted to exemplify the overpowering nature of the satirical emotion. With Churchill's Poetics, the satiric impulse is *supposed* to break through and overcome the structure. The reader is meant to be swept away by the spontaneity and expressiveness of the poet's feelings and temperament. The poet's contempt and rage are the essence of the Churchillian satiric mode.

What Chatterton first seized from Churchill was his overall oratorical style and his abhorrence of obedience in any shape or form. For Churchill, as for Chatterton, any unquestioning obedience to rules was equated with slavery. The traditional theater critics in *The Rosciad* were depicted as a "servile race," "Who blind obedience pay to ancient schools / Bigots to Greece, and slaves to musty rules."

Churchill had declared his opposition to Pope—"E'en excellence, unvary'd tedious grows"—and sworn his allegiance to Dryden's "halting rhime," his "gen'rous roughness of a nervous line." Churchill's own poetic genius emanated from a careless ingenuity that drew its life from "those bold and daring strokes of fancy, those numbers so hazardously ventured upon and so happily finished." Proud of his rough, careless creativity, Churchill referred to his poems as "rude, unfinish'd brats."

It was only as the friendship between himself and John Wilkes deepened that Churchill became committed to political satire and his topical, public, declamatory style flourished. It was then, too, that Churchill severed his bonds with Dryden. Whereas the poetic revolutionary Dryden was ideologically a firm adherent of law and order in civil life—"What Prudent men a settled Throne would shake?"—Churchill proclaimed that what was far more important was freedom to act as one wished: "thro' ev'ry age, in ev'ry land / Written in gold let REVOLUTION stand."

While Chatterton was mourning in near silence during that summer of 1769 there were hints that he was awakening politically. But what he needed first was a style and mode of expression congenial to his iconoclastic temperament. From Churchill, an established and well-paid poet, Chatterton got his license for poetic freedom. He began entrusting himself to the force of powerful sentiments, especially rage.

On October 27, Chatterton wrote the fifty-six-line *Intrest thou universal God of Men,* in which he voices for the first time the conflict that will be implicit in much of his future satirical verse. The conflict itself, between prudence and personal courage, derives directly from Churchill. Should the poet heed the commands of prudence, thinking first of his own self-interest? Or should he obey his conscience and say what he truly believes? "Can honest Conscience of doing Right / Provide a Dinner or a Girl at night?" To this initial posing of the question, Chatterton tentatively concludes, "Flattery's a cloak and I will put it on." But the passion of Chatterton's beliefs, his rage at the merchant mentality of the Bristol elders, overtakes the prudence he seems to be advising. "The rage of satire" seizes his brain. Rage is the overpowering emotion of the poem.

Rage is decisive in shaping the outcome of the poetic conflict. Chatterton will continue to flatter Burgum and Catcott with his genealogies and panegyrics. The poem recommends prudence and flattery. But Poets will perceive his elegant rage and contrast it with the dull mentalities of those he praises. In the end *Intrest* arrives at an ingenious compromise. Prudence will keep watch over the poet's self-interest, but his satirical stance will legitimize the personal outrage that has seized his heart and brain.

What better model for the lowly, imprisoned apprentice scrivener than a famous poet who had found a way to earn a sizable income—providing himself with a merry life full of grand dinners and magnificent girls—while simultaneously giving free expression to his haughty scorn? With Churchillian satire Chatterton could have his rage along with the benefits of a merry life. It was said that "every writer of abusive verse during the decade following 1764 looked to [Churchill] as a model or was in some way affected by his spirit." Would Chatterton follow Churchill's quest for political justice? Or would he merely imitate him without sharing his underlying beliefs? Would Chatterton become just another hack scribbler who had entered Churchill's quarrels "without his provocations and inherited his spirit of abuse without his capacity, his virulence without his poetry"?

One day in late November or early December, Chatterton brought to George Catcott a copy of the latest version of his freethinking creed. It was mounted on parchment, which had a portion cut out at the top so that the title would always be clearly visible, even when the parchment was folded.

THE ARTICLES OF THE BELIEF OF ME THOMAS CHATTERTON

That God being incomprehensible: it is not required of us, to know the mysterys of the Trinity &c. &c. &c. &c.

That it matters not whether a Man is a Pagan Turk Jew or Christian if he acts according to the Religion he professes

That if a man leads a good moral Life he is a Christian

That the Stage is the best School of Morality and

The Church of Rome (some Tricks of Priestcraft excepted) is certainly the true Church.

And indeed this did become Chatterton's creed. He was attracted to Catholicism, the simple piety of the Franciscan monks, and also to Muhammad, and the rituals of African savages. And when the machinations of London politics finally left Chatterton on the verge of financial disaster, he turned to the stage for his next literary adventure.

Chatterton wrote *The Articles of the Belief* in the middle of a philosophical debate with Alexander Catcott, the vicar of Temple Church and the elder brother of the fame-seeking George. Chatterton's final article about the Church of Rome was not a true belief. It was a kiss good-bye to Anglican orthodoxy, a calculated affront to the vicar. No living person had presented more of a challenge to Chatterton's freethinking than Alexander Catcott.

From the opening gambit of their chary, mutually ambivalent relationship, the vicar made no bones about his estimation of Chatterton's moral deficiencies. Several months before Chatterton first wrote to Walpole, the vicar had warned his brother that there was no possibility whatsoever of there being any papers of poetical or historical value in the William Canynge coffers. Therefore, the young man who so often visited their house must be a forger and a liar. To check out his impression, the vicar questioned Chatterton closely on Rowley's account of the rebuilding of Temple Church and found him, just as he had expected, cleverly evasive and lacking in credibility. An observant man who had trained himself to pay attention to the minutest details of fossils, rocks, and other geological phenomena, Alexander also noted Chatterton's keen eye for any book in the parsonage library which might help him with his forgery.

But there was also a degree of gingerly respect between the poet and the vicar. Alexander Catcott spoke of Thomas Chatterton as a lad equal to anything, a most extraordinary genius. Chatterton, though he attacked the vicar personally along with every one of his beliefs, was willing nevertheless to recognize him as one of the few men of substantial or trustworthy intellect in all of Bristol. He boasted to his friends and relatives that the vicar admitted him to his study and not infrequently consulted him in matters of antiquity. The truth was that Alexander had very little to do with Chatterton. Furthermore, no one, not even his brother or sister, had free access to his study. And, after the poet's death, if Alexander had had his way, the Rowley manuscripts would have been burned—certainly not collected and published.

When he first met Alexander Catcott, Chatterton was too immersed in creating the world of William Canynge to wage battle with the vicar's theories on the creation of man. But the next year, as his skepticism evolved toward a freethinking position, Chatterton, who had always been exquisitely attuned to the natural world, set about to learn how that world worked. As he read and pondered, the vicar's theories were always in the back of his mind. Shortly before Christmas of 1769, Chatterton composed his *Epistle to Catcott*, attacking the vicar's learned, ponderous, and dreary attempt to harmonize his geological interests with his religious calling by reconciling the biblical account of the creation with eighteenth-century geological studies. Chatterton, who had been grappling for several months with the philosophical dilemmas inherent in the relationship between God's handiwork and the laws of nature, now felt himself mentally and morally equipped to challenge each of Catcott's geological fantasies as presented in his *Treatise on the Deluge*.

The opening lines of Chatterton's satirical attack strive toward an elegance of expression that brings to mind Dryden:

> *What strange Infatuations rule Mankind,*
> *How narrow are our Prospects how confin'd*
> *With universal Vanity possest*

But soon the fledgling satirist succumbs to the rougher rhythms of Charles Churchill:

> *Your Zeal for Scripture hath devour'd your Sense.*
> *Apply the Glass of Reason to your Sight*
> *See Nature marshal evry Atom right*
> *Think for yourself for all Mankind are free*
> *We need not Inspiration how to see*
> *If Scripture contradictory you find*
> *Be orthodox and own your Senses blind.*

At his most brazen, Chatterton did not seem to realize the extent of his grandiosity. But at other, more prudent, moments he conceded that he was a relatively small person taking on a mighty one. In a mildly apologetic postscript, he confesses, "this Poem is an innocent Effort of Poetical Vengeance, as Mr. Catcott has done me the honor to criticise my Trifles." And he takes some of the sting out of his poetic attack by conceding some admiration for a few of the vicar's thoughts. But scorn finally wins out over prudence as Chatterton concludes with his more customary bravado, "The many Admirers of Mr. Catcott may on Perusal of this rank me as an Enemy; but I am indifferent in all things. I value neither the Praise or Censure of the multitude."

Another Churchill posture that appealed to Chatterton's grandiosity was the use of the familiar tone as a weapon. Chatterton had already displayed a glimmering of this mode of address in his angry attack on Walpole. But in *Epistle to Catcott* Chatterton's insolence is a calculated stance, designed to lure the reader into sympathy with a young, modern-thinking critic who boldly places himself in opposition to an old, orthodox, closed-minded, rigid pedant who "racks each Metaphor upon a wheel," to prove his stodgy hermeneutics. The virtue that blazons its mark across the "scientific" arguments is the haughty impudence of a courageous young poet embattled with the old guard. The sustained satirical tone of the 270-line *Epistle* shows that in barely two months Chatterton mastered the essence of Churchill's poetic morality.

Chatterton ends the year 1769 with the seventy-line *The Defense,* written on Christmas Day, in which he declares that "The Church and all her Arguments are dust / Religion's but Opinions bastard Son":

> *I own a God immortal boundless wise*
> *Who bid our Glorys of Creation rise*
> *Who form'd his varied Likeness in Mankind*
> *Centering his many Wonders in the Mind*
> *Who saw Religion a fantastic Night*
> *But gave us Reason to obtain the Light*

Chatterton ushers in the New Year of 1770 with two literary gestures related to Polly Rumsey, both of which pay off by being published in the January issue of *Town and Country*. He composes his *Advice Addressed to Miss M***** R******, *of Bristol*[1] and the *Astrea Brokage* letter in which a young lady of genteel tastes and literary sensibilities with a special admiration for modern theater laments that she has been forced to relinquish her true love. The genteel lady explains that the man she really loves is "a young author, who has read more than Magliabechi, and wrote more love-letters than Ovid; but he never pays a compliment to my person without a concomitant one to my understanding." The lady is about to be married off by her rich merchant father to a Mr. Barter, an uncivilized Bristolean, an insignificant wretch, "who has never read further than the Gazette, or Tables of Interest," "a devil of a Buck." Chatterton's small revenge would be the day when Polly Rumsey and Jack Fowler might read these lines in *Town and Country* and blush.

Later that week Chatterton converted his bloody Welsh heroic *Hirlas,* written the past summer in more or less plain English, into the even more bloody Ossian-style *Hirlas II*, which was also published in *Town and Country*. His next literary venture was the first of his African eclogues.

---

[1] Maria R***** was a disguise for Polly Rumsey.

As Chatterton voices the vengeful passions of the heroic black man, Gaira, who has been separated from his beloved Cawna by the Lilly, a pallid race of slave traders, we see Rumsey in the shadows being abducted by the villainous Fowler. Chatterton conveys through Gaira the intensity of his own sympathetic rage.

> There Cawna mingled with a worthless train
> In common slav'ry drags the hated Chain
> Now judge my Heccar have I cause for Rage?
> Should aught the thunder of my Arm asswage?
> In ever reeking blood this Javlin dy'd
> With Vengeance shall be never satisfied
> I'll strew the Beaches with the mighty dead
> And tinge the Lilly of their Features red

No child growing up in Bristol, where the slave trade was the mainstay of the import-export industries, could remain unaffected by the implied and blatant violences of the enchained black slaves being transported to other parts of Europe or the unchained ones in domestic captivity as butlers, footboys, valets, cooks for the wealthy shipowners and merchants. That first week in January, rage commanded most of Chatterton's writings, including the African poem. It was as though the bloody warriors from his Ossian had leapt into the African landscape, "Where the sharp Rocks in distant Horror seen / Drive the white Currents thro' the spreading green / Where the loud Tiger pawing in his rage / Bids the black Archers of the wilds engage." Only after he has escaped from his slavery in Bristol, will the "red sword of war" be temporarily banished from the African landscapes. Only then is the raging Tiger tamed and can the romantic Africa of Chatterton's imagination burst into life:

> On Tiber's [sic] banks, where scarlet jasmines bloom,
> And purple aloes shed a rich perfume:
> Where, when the sun is melting in his heat,
> The reeking tygers find a cool retreat;
> Bask in the sedges, lose the sultry beam,
> And wanton with their shadows in the stream.

This gentler landscape, "where the blue blossom of the forky thorn, / Bends with the nectar of the op'ning morn," and "the purple, plum'd maccaws . . . skim along the silver shore" would become as vivid to Chatterton as the gates, archways, towers, and spires of fifteenth-century

Bristol. Meanwhile Gaira's bloody sword and the legitimacy of his rough rage were among the several themes that were moving Chatterton inexorably toward the Wilkesian political stance that would bring him to London.

As the first week in January drew to a close, Chatterton turned one of his less-successful October Churchills, *The Constabiliad,* a mock-heroic on the gluttonous behavior of some of Bristol's parish constables, into a satire, *The Consuliad: An Heroic Poem,* on the leading lights of King George's ministry. The king's men are depicted as squabbling over political spoils with lusts akin to the oral greed of the Bristol aldermen. The revision was uncomplicated. Chatterton accomplished it within a day or two, simply switching his ordinary scorn for Bristol politics into the more fashionable and well-paying contempt for the king's ministers. This first of Chatterton's purely political satires derives its satirical power from the graphic descriptions of the gluttony and repulsive table manners of King George's ministers. As the eloquent and compassionate Sir William Canynge had embodied all the virtues that Chatterton had conjured for an ideal father, just as surely did these gentlemen represent the vulgar and meaner qualities that were sometimes attributed to Thomas Chatterton, Sr.

Nine months earlier, in May of 1769, the virtuous Sir William Canynge had written an urbane, twelve-line poem describing the gluttony of the Bristol aldermen he was sometimes forced to associate with:

> *The Ealdermenne doe lye arounde*
> *Ande snoffelle oppe the cheorte steeme*
> *Lyke asses wylde ynne desarte waste*

Now Chatterton, teetotaler and ascetic, wallows in the disgust evoked by the obscene table manners of the gentlemen who serve the politics of King George. For this poem, Gregory's critique of the bloody *Battle of Hastings* is fitting: not one episode enlivens this rude brat of a poem. Few poetic beauties "relieve the mind of the disgusting subject." Just as the Chatterton known to be gentle and considerate in his personal relations had reveled in the gore and mangled bodies of *Hastings,* so now the Chatterton who boasted that he could just as well dine on bread and water here allows himself to binge on the intensity of his antigluttonous sentiments:

> *The mangled pigeon thunders on his face:*
> *His op'ning mouth the melted butter fills,*

> *And dropping from his nose and chin distills.*
> *Furious he started, rage his bosom warms;*
> *Loud as his lordship's morning duns he storms.*
> *Thou vulgar imitator of the great,*
> *Grown wanton with the excrements of state*

Easily recognizable in this antiministerial and therefore pro-Patriot satire are all the major figures satirized by Churchill for the Patriot hero John Wilkes—Wilkes's betrayer Jemmy Twitcher (the nickname of Lord Sandwich), the princess dowager, her lover the earl of Bute, and the king's current first lord of the Treasury, Grafton. Chatterton achieved his first link to pro-Patriot literature by borrowing Churchill's rough satirical style and wholeheartedly adopting his political causes.

In *The Consuliad,* Chatterton was forced to leave all but the most obvious London political figures cloaked in their Bristol disguises with Swiftian names like Mab-Uther, Curraras, Doglostock, Quarlendorgongos. He was not yet familiar with the subtler ins and outs of court politics, but he banked on the probability that his readers—and London magazine editors—would take the peculiar names as a code to be deciphered, even associating characters in the poem with real-life London ministers. His sleight of hand worked. When the satire was published in the January issue of Isaac Fell's *Freeholder's Magazine,* Chatterton was paid the decent sum of ten shillings sixpence.

Though Chatterton never forgot Polly or his other literary possibilities, the publication of *Consuliad* launched his career as a political journalist. Beginning in mid-February of 1770, Chatterton became a confirmed Patriot and a published one. In no time at all he mastered the tone and language of Patriot vs. ministerial politics, and he familiarized himself with all its minor figures and issues. He caught on to these details with the same facility and dexterity with which he had taken on the satirical style of Churchill. In one of his verse satires of this period, *The Whore of Babylon,* thirty of his targets are identical to those chosen by Churchill to advance Wilkes's cause. The Bristol apprentice was realizing that his antityranny, proliberty verses were relatively easy to publish. Early in March he received a letter from Fell, agreeing to publish in two issues the 820-line political satire, *The Resignation,* requesting "the rest of your productions," and promising "a Compliment equal to merit."

It was this letter from Fell which finally gave Chatterton the courage to escape from the oppressive security of his apprenticeship. Chatterton was not so naive or so grandiose as to expect political writing to be his only financial mainstay, but it did seem like his best bet. By then he had adopted radical Patriot politics as a congenial addition to his *BELIEFS* and John Wilkes and others associated with the Patriot causes had become his intellectual mentors. The young poet, who just the year before had been the respectful, worshiping son of Canynge, had found a new father. In 1770 he became a prodigal son, hoping to hammer out his own identity through rebellions, defiances, and declarations of independence while simultaneously winning the affection and admiration of his Patriot father, John Wilkes.

Ten days before he left for London, Chatterton composed his *Will*. The document is a peculiar amalgam of the jocularity and ironic bitterness that is characteristic of much of Chatterton's non-Rowleyan writing and it is that mixture which makes a definitive interpretation virtually impossible. Was this a tongue-in-cheek fake suicide note or a genuine declaration of the poet's intent to commit suicide? Doubtless Chatterton himself drew an uncertain line between elated denial and black despair. At the time he conceived of this exuberant suicide note he was truly desperate about his ignominious situation and oppressed by the narrowness of Bristol. He no longer had the Rowley romance to bolster his spirits and sustain his pride. It was essential to his sanity that one way or another he break the chains of his apprenticeship and declare his independence. Suicide was one way out. A cleverly worded suicide note that would frighten the upright, law-abiding John Lambert might do the trick just as well.

The occasion of his *Will* was not the first time that suicide had seemed like a real possibility to Chatterton. In August a friend had been reprimanded by his father for keeping bad company and, in reaction to his father's harsh words, that very night had retired to his room and taken his own life. At first Chatterton believed this friend to have been William Smith, one of his closest companions. With one eye toward publication and the other toward expressing his genuine distress, he composed an elegy in which tender grief—"I lov'd him with a brothers ardent love, / Beyond the Love which tendrest brothers bear,"—is swiftly overshadowed by rage at the injustices that had driven his friend to take his life:

> *Despis'd: an alien to thy Fathers breast,*
> *Thy ready Services repaid with Hate . . .*
> *Ye Callous breasted Brutes in human form*
> *Have you not often boldly wishd him dead?*
> *He's gone Eer yet his Fire of man was warm,*
> *O may his Crying blood be on your head.*

When the next day Chatterton discovered that the suicide had been William Smith's brother, he appended a footnote to his elegy: "Happily mistaken having since heard from good Authority it is Peter." This offhand dismissal is suspiciously carefree since Peter was also an acquaintance and, in fact, had many times incurred his father's wrath for his association with profligates such as Thomas Chatterton. The way in which Chatterton and his friends reacted to the Peter Smith suicide suggests that suicide was a topic frequently discussed and debated—particularly among freethinking youths. One of the Patriot tenets was that it was far better to rush bravely into death than to die slowly as a slave.

Chatterton had repeatedly intimidated the household servants at Lambert's by telling them that he meant to take his own life. It was rumored that he carried about a loaded pistol, which he would take out when the topic of suicide came up and put the barrel in his mouth, regretting that he lacked the courage to pull the trigger. With these antics he blurred the border between manic theatricality and true despair. As with all young men devoted to practical joking, whenever Chatterton could trick some other person into believing something which was not true, he was reassuring himself about his own bodily and mental integrity. Nevertheless, there is no doubt that after he became a committed freethinker, Chatterton genuinely believed in one's right to end one's own life when that life became insupportable.

Vengeance always played a significant role in Chatterton's visions of suicide. A prose tale entitled *The Unfortunate Fathers,* composed shortly after the 1770 New Year, concludes with the pistol suicide of the hero and the ensuing deaths from heartbreak and remorse of the father who had wronged him, the young lady he had loved and lost through the machinations of his father, and finally that young lady's father. The youth leaves a suicide note addressed to his father in which he reconciles his act with religious belief and high-minded motivations. "Suicide is sometimes a noble insanity of the soul: and often the result of a mature and deliberate approbation of the soul."

Chatterton used the natural death of his beloved Thomas Phillips, the only Colston's teacher to have shown an appreciation of his literary gifts, as a way to meet Michael Clayfield, the man whose freethinking convictions were sometimes later held responsible for Chatterton's belief in the legitimacy of suicide. In a verse-letter to Clayfield depicting his grief over their mutual friend's death, Chatterton addressed him as "long renowned the Muses friend," and a "friend to Genius, Sciences and Arts." Clayfield's opinions on religion, politics, and nature probably had far more influence on the young apprentice than he knew or intended. Mary mentions briefly in her letter to Croft, "At about 17 he became acquainted with

Mr. Clayfield, distiller in Castle-street, who lent him many books on astronomy." From one of Clayfield's volumes, Chatterton got the design for his poem, *The Copernican System,* which was printed in the December issue of *Town and Country.* After reading this poem, the astrologer Ebenezer Sibley was convinced that Chatterton knew enough about the stars to foresee "the evils he had to combat, and the fatal termination of a life, which his own folly had rendered insupportable." When Clayfield learned of Chatterton's suicide, he asserted that their friendship had nowhere near the intensity implied by Chatterton's expressions toward him. He recollected having loaned Chatterton only two books on astronomy. He maintained that Chatterton had been much too volatile to read seriously or deeply into any subject. Certainly he did not have the abilities to compose the Rowleys. "They were no more his composition than mine."

The distiller from Castle-street may not have considered himself to be much of a friend to Chatterton, but it is clear that Chatterton looked up to him as a man of honest values. About six weeks before he wrote the *Will,* Chatterton had composed another suicide note. This one, which he also left open on his desk for Lambert to discover, had been addressed to Michael Clayfield. After listing his distresses and complaints, Chatterton concluded by declaring that by the time Clayfield received the note, he, Chatterton, would be no more. Clayfield never saw the letter because Lambert had it delivered at once to William Barrett, the man he assumed might be in a good position to talk some sense into his troubled apprentice. Barrett summoned up a lecture about what a horrible crime self-murder was, an insensitive gesture that demonstrated how little appreciation he had of Chatterton's mentality. After their disagreeable meeting, Chatterton wrote to Barrett, attempting to portray his state of mind:

> You must know that the 19/20th of my Composition is Pride—I must either live a Slave, a Servant; to have no Will of my own, no Sentiments of my own which I may freely declare as such;—or Die—Perplexing Alternative!

For two years, nine months and six days Chatterton had been resentfully serving out the seven-year term of his apprenticeship. He held no grudge against Lambert and never used his satirical pen to wreak vengeance on him. As he wrote later to his mother, "Tho', as an apprentice none had greater liberties, yet the thoughts of servitude killed me: now I have that for my labour, I always reckoned the first of my pleasures, and have still, my liberty." To affirm that liberty he had to declare his independence—by whatever means he could.

Chatterton's *Will* starts out convincingly enough:

> *All this wrote between 11 and 2 o'Clock*
> *Saturday in the utmost Distress of Mind*

but is followed by a warning that a Genius[2] can pretend anything and will generally be believed. This ambiguity is followed by fifty-four lines of straightforward satirical verse addressed to his Bristol patrons Catcott and Barrett, and to Catcott's partner in the pewter trade, Henry Burgum, beginning,

> *Burgum I thank thee thou hast let me see*
> *Tht Bristol has impress'd her Stamp on thee*
> *Thy genrous Spirit emulates the May'rs.*

Burgum's unreliable generosity is sometimes thought to be the occasion for Chatterton's desperation to escape Bristol by any means, even by suicide. Chatterton was in debt, "in the whole not Five Pounds" and he had counted on Burgum's continuing gullibility to rescue him. If he would simply pay five pounds for a few more items for his pedigree, Chatterton could pay off his debt. But apparently Burgum drove a hard bargain for "futurity."

> *Gods! what would Burgum give to get a name*
> *And snatch his blund'ring Dialect from Shame*
> *What would he give to hand his Mem'ry down,*
> *To times remotest Boundary—a Crown.*
> *Would you ask more? his swelling Face looks blue*
> *Futurity he rates at Two Pounds Two.*

Catcott fares somewhat better than Burgum, but Chatterton nevertheless mocks his mercantile mentality: "Thy Friendship never could be dear to me / Since all I am is opposite to thee." For Barrett, the educated surgeon-historian, there are some words of admiration:

---

[2] In his 1930 biography of Chatterton, Meyerstein cites an eighteenth-century authority on an alternative meaning of the word *genius:* "The modern acceptation of the word [genius] by which it signifies a very silly young fellow, who from his extravagance and debauchery has obtained the name of genius, like *lucus a non lucendo,* because he had no genius at all. *The Connoisseur* No. 90, 5th Ed., 1767."

> *To Barrett next. He has my Thanks sincere*
> *For all the little Knowledge I had here*
> *But what was Knowledge: could it here succeed*
> *When hardly twenty in the Town can read*

Immediately following the fifty-four-line farewell to the elders of Bristol, the *Will* proper begins:

> This is the last Will and Testament of me Thomas Chatterton of the City of Bristol being sound in Body or it is the Fault of my last Surgeon. The Soundness of my Mind the Coroner and Jury are to be judges of—desiring them to take notice that the most perfect Masters of Human Nature in Bristol, distinguish me by the Title of the Mad Genius therefore if I do a mad action it is conformable to every Action of my Life which all savored of Insanity.

The next item of the will contains instructions for burial. "Cause my Body to be interred in the Tomb of my Fathers" with a monument raised "over my Body to the Height of 4 feet 5 Inches." Engravings, some in Latin, were to be carved into the six tablets that would be placed at its base. The third engraving, in Roman characters, was an epitaph for Thomas Chatterton, Sr.:

> Sacred to The Memory of Thomas Chatterton Sub Chanter of the Cathedral of this City whose Ancestors were residents of St. Mary Redclift since the Year 1140
> He dyed the 7th. of August 1752.

The fourth tablet, also in Roman characters, was the epitaph that the nineteenth-century vicars of St. Mary's finally allowed to be inscribed on the monument dedicated to Chatterton:

> To the Memory of Thomas Chatterton. Reader—Judge not: if thou art a Christian, believe that he shall be Judged by a Superior Power; to that Power only is he now answerable—

Following the instructions for his burial and monument, Chatterton parceled out his fortune to various friends and foes: To George Catcott, he bequeathed all his vigor and fire of youth, "being sensible he is in most want of it—." To the Reverend Alexander Catcott he left "some little of My freethinking that he may put on the Spectacles of reason and see how vilely he is duped in believing the Scripture literally." To this bequest Chatterton adds, "I wish he and his Brother would know how far I am their real Enemy but I have an unlucky way of railing and when the strong fit of Satyre is on me Spare neither Friend nor Foe." To Michael Clayfield he gives his sincerest thanks and gratitude, and directs, "that whatsoever any Person may think the Pleasure of reading my Works worth they immediately pay their own valuation to him since it is then become a lawful Debt to me and to him as my Executor in this case." To the young ladies he left one moiety of his own modesty, at least "to any young Lady who can prove without blushing that she wants that valuable Commodity." To these ladies he also left all the letters they had from him and assures them all "that they need be under no Apprehensions from the Appearance of my Ghost for I dye for none of them." He concludes, "I Leave my Mother & Sister to the protection of my Friends if I have any."

The playful tone of the *Will,* written in the mock will style, a common literary genre of Chatterton's day, would seem to belie its serious intent. But, as Freud once remarked:

> Might we not say that every child at play behaves like a creative writer, in that he creates a world of his own, or, rather, re-arranges the things of his world in a new way which pleases him? It would be wrong to think he does not take that world seriously; on the contrary, he takes his play very seriously and he expends large amounts of emotion on it. The opposite of play is not what is serious but what is real.

The creative alteration of unpleasant or threatening realities was habitual for Chatterton. And whether it was a real threat or a tongue-in-cheek creative act, his suicide testament was taken seriously. Lambert, fair-minded as he tried to be, had absolutely no sympathy for his peculiar apprentice who idled away his free hours reading books and writing poetry. Supposing the boy to be slightly lunatic, Lambert also feared him, and Lambert's panicky overreaction to the Clayfield threat made Chatterton persist in the plot to frighten his master into releasing him from his indentures. It worked.

Alarmed at his own possible implication in the suicide that Chatterton threatened would take place the next evening, "before 8 oClock being the feast of the resurrection," Lambert, with the encouragement of his mother who was terrified of the peculiar presence in their household, hastily canceled Chatterton's indentures, releasing the boy from his hateful condition as a lowly lawyer's scrivener.

Less than a week after his release Chatterton packed his clothing, books, and papers, and made his farewells to friends and family, some of whom donated a guinea each toward his traveling expenses. For several weeks prior to the writing of his will, Chatterton, who must have had some degree of confidence in his plans to escape from Bristol, had been writing to London editors and booksellers, some of whom had already published his social and political satires under the pseudonyms of Decimus and D.B., inquiring about his prospects as a journalist. Apparently the publishers were encouraging, for on Tuesday, April 24, he set out for London.

At 9:00 PM Thomas Chatterton boarded the One-Day post chaise for London. For the first two hours he rode as an outside passenger in the "basket," a contraption slung onto the back of the coach where only the most hardy and economical passengers rode. At Brislington, he "mounted the top of the coach, and rid easy: and agreeably entertained with the conversation of a quaker *in dress,* but little so in personals and behaviour." When they reached Bath two hours later, it was raining, so Chatterton decided to pay the extra fare and so have the comfort of riding inside for the remainder of the night. In fact, according to Chatterton's account, he had made a sensible decision, as the rain soon after turned to snow and it snowed all the night as the Coach crossed to the Marlborough Downs. By morning the snow was nearly a foot high.

At 7:00 AM Chatterton breakfasted at the halfway mark to London. When he remounted the coach box for the conclusion of his journey, he was in good spirits, as the day was remarkably fine. And when the coach stopped at noon, Chatterton allowed himself a luxurious dinner with illustrious company, "a young gentleman who had slept all the preceding night in the machine; and an old mercantile genius." He arrived in London at 5:00 PM and immediately called upon four of the booksellers he had written from Bristol, Edmunds of the *Middlesex Journal,* Fell of the *Freeholder's Magazine,* Hamilton of *Town and Country,* Dodsley of the *Annual Register.* All welcomed him warmly and renewed their promises of support. Fell made the day by promising to introduce him to Wilkes.

If, after twenty hours of travel, Chatterton had gone directly from the stagecoach terminal at Piccadilly to Shoe Lane, then to Paternoster Row, then to St. John's Gate, then to Dodsley's office at Pall Mall—all considerable distances from one another and also from Chatterton's boarding house in Shoreditch—then we have a good measure of his impatient ambition. On the other hand, the cheery letter in which he gave this account probably contained a few exaggerations. Chatterton's letters to his family from London smacked of bravado and elated denial. If ever he allowed himself to think of his worries, he certainly kept them from his mother and sister.

Before the evening was over he was settled in with his cousin, Mrs. Ballance, in Shoreditch. In a letter to his mother dated April 26, 1770 he proclaims his good spirits. Ten days later he writes home:

> What a glorious prospect! Mr. Wilkes knew me by my writings since I first corresponded with the booksellers here. I shall visit him next week, and by his interest will ensure Mrs. Ballance the Trinity House. He affirmed that what Mr. Fell had of mine could not be the writings of a youth: and expressed a desire to know the author. . . . I am quite familiar at the Chapter Coffee-house, and know all the geniuses there. A character is now unnecessary; an author carries his character in his pen.

SEVEN

Freedom of the Press, Revolution, and Obscenity

The Wilkesian Platform. Issue #45 of the North Briton *and* The Essay on Woman. *Lord Sandwich betrays Wilkes, and the firebrand of liberty becomes an extinct volcano. Chatterton's scandalous infidelities are revealed:* The Exhibition, *Chatterton's bitter farewell to Bristol. Exhibitionism: the humiliation and rage of an impostor. The genital largess of* The Letter Paraphras'd.

CHATTERTON had not leapt aboard the One-Day Express to London without a plan. It is clear from his letters home and from what he wrote during his first month in London that he craved to distinguish himself as a brilliant journalist who spoke out for the antigovernment position. He envisioned that his political letters and essays would bring him to the attention of the heads of the Patriot party, especially John Wilkes. With Wilkes as his patron and sponsor, Chatterton hoped to become the official writer for the Patriot party.

On May 6 his spirits were still high. He writes again to his mother:

> The poverty of authors is a common observation, but not always a true one. No author can be poor who understands the arts of booksellers—Without this necessary knowledge, the greatest genius may starve; and, with it, the greatest dunce live in splendor. This knowledge I have pretty well dipped into.

But by May 14, two of his editors-to-be had been imprisoned. Mr. Fell, the editor who had first published Chatterton's political verses and promised him an introduction to Wilkes, had finally managed to offend certain

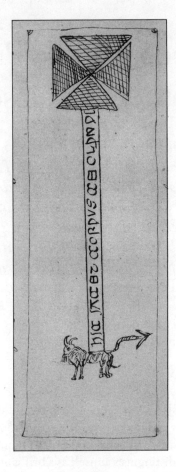

government officials and was put away in King's Bench as a debtor. Mr. Edmunds was tried before the House of Lords, sentenced with a fine, and thrown into Newgate Prison. These ominous events Chatterton reports to his mother with a characteristic optimism: "Matters go on swimmingly." Such misfortunes, it seemed, would not hinder Chatterton's success. As far as he was concerned, Mr. Wilkes had already heard of him, and whether or not the introducer was in jail, Chatterton was sure he would soon meet Wilkes.

For all the years of Chatterton's boyhood and adolescence, at first as a Blue-Coat boy merely imagining a family romance and then later as an apprentice creating the narratives of the world of Canynge, the heroic figure of John Wilkes was in the background. During Chatterton's third year at Colston's he surely heard the song celebrating Wilkes's release from the Tower of London. In 1763 Wilkes had been imprisoned for several weeks on charges of "an infamous and seditious libel, tending to inflame the minds, and alienate the affections, of the people from his Majesty, and to excite them to traitorous insurrections against his government." The song entitled "Wilkes and Liberty" was sung to the tune of "Gee ho Dobbin." Some of the concluding lines were "And *Wilkes* was discharged without Guilt or Disgrace. / O *brave* Liberty! Wilkes and Liberty!" "We have *Wilkes*—aye and *Wilkes* has his freedom again. / O *brave* Liberty! WILKES *and* Liberty! / Old English Liberty, O!"

In the summer of 1768, while Wilkes was serving another prison term, the drama of the London trials over the publication of Issue #45 of the *North Briton,* which had led to Wilkes's earlier imprisonment, was very much alive in Bristol. At the Cock Inn of St. James's Courtyard, 45 Wilkites sat down to a #45 dinner of 45 hams, 45 fowl, 45 cucumbers, 45 cabbages, 45 gallons of ale, 45 glasses of brandy, 45 papers of tobacco, and so on.

Chatterton had kept tabs on all events Wilkesian. And in all likelihood the subtle allusions to Wilkes in his *Will* were intentional. The fake suicide note, dated April 14, was calculated to release him from his indentures the same week that Wilkes, having paid at last for all his traitorous and libelous acts, was released from prison. Chatterton's instructions for the size of his monument—4 feet 5 inches—were a prankish personal tribute to the #45 brouhaha. Chatterton knew only the most public events of the life of this very flamboyant political figure, but these offered just the right mixture of heroism, scandal, and rebellion to appeal to a young man of Chatterton's proud and volatile temperament.

John Wilkes, born in 1725, was the second and favorite son of a prosperous distiller. His mother, an extremely inconsistent woman, was a rigid Presbyterian who promoted clean linen and moral rectitude while collecting pagan art, among which were six statuettes of the naked or half-clad Bacchus. Some accounts portray Mrs. Wilkes as the dominant spirit of the household, a powerful woman who overshadowed her husband's influence. But even these rather biased reports concede that when it came to John's upbringing, she and her husband saw eye to eye. John was to become the gentleman in the family—a very special sort of gentleman. Wilkes was thoroughly pampered and raised to be anything but a conformist. His tutor was chosen by his father allegedly because of his devotion to paradox and heresy. At nineteen Wilkes was sent off to Leyden University, chaperoned by his eccentric tutor. Wilkes's college days have the ring of a Churchillian regime: "I never read steadily. My father gave me as much money as I wanted. . . . Three or four whores—drunk every night—sore head the next morning. I'm capable to sit thirty hours over a table to study."

Wilkes was a strikingly ugly man, with squint eyes, a flattened nose, a long and projecting upper lip, and a crooked, square, protruding jaw. The artist William Hogarth, after being gravely insulted by Wilkes at the Sublime Society of Beefsteaks, made much of these features in his numerous anti-Wilkes cartoons.

As soon as he returned from Leyden at the age of twenty-two, Wilkes married a plain but extremely rich older woman. From that union Wilkes's much adored and only legitimate child, Polly, was born in 1750. Polly was a father's daughter and when her parents separated seven years later, custody was awarded to him. Later Wilkes would say of his loveless marriage, "To please an indulgent father, I married a woman half as old again as myself of a large fortune,—my own being that of a gentleman. It was a sacrifice to Plutus, not Venus." But Wilkes gave a lifetime of emotional commitment to Polly. He lavished her with gifts, made sure she attended the best schools, and sent her to Paris to finish her education.

By upbringing Wilkes may have been a rebellious eccentric. But he was also something of a conformist, ambitious for a place in high society. He wanted to be regarded as a scholar and a gentleman. In fashionable society he was addicted to classical allusions and known to quote pedantically and at great length from the Greek and Latin classics. However, it was his gift for clever obscenities that brought him linguistic notoriety. Even before the trials for salacious libel that sent Wilkes to prison and into exile, Gibbon spoke of him as "a thorough-going profligate in principle as in practice, his life stained with every vice and his conversation full of blasphemy and indecency."

Wilkes was a member of the most infamous of what were popularly known as Hell Fire clubs. His was the "Company of the Monks [or Knights] of St. Francis," a secret male fraternity which met at the newly redecorated Medmenham Abbey. Churchill was an occasional guest at the club, but even the loose-living merry parson was offended by some of the goings-on at Medmenham, which he satirized in his poetry. Members of the Hell Fire club, which included the rakish Lord Sandwich, apparently came to meetings garbed as Franciscan monks. Wilkes came as Brother

John of Aylesbury, but as he pointed out, penitence was not the favorite doctrine at the abbey. In the center of the orchard was a monument to Priapus, the Roman god of male generative powers, inscribed with the motto, "PENI TENTO NON PENITENTI." Among the invited guests were a variety of eminent London ladies, many of whom were probably prostitutes. In keeping with the general motif, some of the ladies dressed as nuns. The "monks" incanted hymns to various pagan gods and goddesses, most notably Venus. The gardens, which had been laid out according to the plans of Rabelais's Thélème Abbey, had over the entrance the libertine motto of Rabelais's Abbey, "Fay ce que Vouldras."

In his public life Wilkes served faithfully as a captain of the militia, a turnpike trustee, a justice of the peace, and a governor of a foundling hospital. In 1757, the same year he concluded his loveless marriage, Wilkes became a member of Parliament. His efforts to make his mark as a distinguished orator before the House of Commons were dismally unsuccessful. Four years later he started to write political journalism and soon after that he and Churchill founded the *North Briton* (the title mocked the stodgy progovernment *Briton*). The newspaper, which soon became required reading in every coffee shop, was blatantly antigovernment and opposed as well to all those who appeared to be government sympathizers. Wilkes and Churchill were the primary contributors. In one of the earliest issues, Samuel Johnson was chided for accepting a government pension, "pay given to a state hireling for treason to his country." Hogarth was denounced for becoming Serjeant Painter to the king for "gain and vanity," and his title was said to refer to "what is vulgarly called house painter." When Wilkes's old Medmenham crony Lord Sandwich was appointed ambassador to Spain, the *North Briton* advised the notorious profligate not to fight duels but "to make all your thrusts at the women, . . . first carry the breastwork, then take the demi-lune and at last plant your victorious standard in the citadel of every fair Donna." When Sandwich once attacked Wilkes by saying he would either die of the pox or at the gallows, Wilkes replied, "That depends, my lord, on whether I embrace your mistress or your principles."

All of this was meant in the spirit of elite manly play. The success of the *North Briton* came from its artful amalgam of scandal and "liberty of the press," which it declared as "the birthright of every Briton." As time went on, Wilkes's attacks on the administration became less playful and more realistically political in nature. His principal target was the earl of Bute, who was George III's first lord of the Treasury and the presumed bedfellow of the king's widowed mother, the Princess Dowager Augusta.

In a March 1763 issue Wilkes made much of the fact that George III, like the young Edward III, was a puppet king who was, he said in one issue, "held in the most absolute slavery by his mother and his minister." Within a few days after the next issue, in which Wilkes predicted that the king would remove his unpopular minister, Bute resigned. Wilkes was triumphant. But he knew his work was not done. Bute was still a principal adviser to the king, and the new minister Grenville was even more intent on suppressing the opposition than was his predecessor.

On April 23, two weeks after Grenville's appointment, Wilkes published Issue #45, entirely devoted to attacking a speech given by George III that proposed placing severe limitations on the freedom of the opposition. Wilkes could be wildly reckless, but on this occasion he started off treading cautiously, trying to observe the proper boundaries. He attacked the speech but not the king directly, implying that the speech was not his. "Every friend of his country must lament that a prince of so many great and admirable qualities ... give the sanction of his sacred name to the most odious measures." With all his efforts at respectful restraint though, Wilkes finally went too far. In writing about the honor of the Crown he could not resist a gratuitous provocation: "I lament to see it sunk even to prostitution." The king and his ministers realized that Bute's resignation had not and would not silence Wilkes's insulting smears on the government. A general warrant was sent out for the writers, printers, and publishers of the *North Briton*.

Wilkes handled his trial in much the same self-defeating way he had composed Issue #45. He started out winningly, but then took a few rash steps that once again put him in jeopardy. The trial was a great public event and Wilkes made the most of his immense popularity. He proclaimed that "the liberty of an English subject is not to be sported away with impunity in this cruel and despotic manner." A few days later Wilkes shrewdly waved his political colors: "The liberty of all peers and gentlemen and (what touched me more sensibly) that of all the middling and inferior people who stand most in need of protection, is in my case this day to be decided upon; a question of such importance as to determine at once whether English liberty shall be a reality or a shadow."

The judge, protecting his own neck and wisely estimating the riotous mood of the mass of middling and inferior people who revered Wilkes, declared that there was no evidence of treason or felony, and the only other reason to overrule the privilege of a member of Parliament—breach of the peace—was too uncertain to be considered. Wilkes was released after being in prison for only the few weeks of the trial.

Had it not been for his stubborn disregard of his publisher's warnings and his desperate need for money, all might have gone well. However, Wilkes insisted upon reprinting Issue #45 and all the back issues of the *North Briton*. He was certain that the sale of these issues would bring in a large sum. Since his usual publisher would not participate in such a reckless plan, and he could not find another willing to cooperate, Wilkes moved some presses to his home and ran off the copies himself. While waiting for the type to be set, Wilkes impulsively printed a dozen copies of some pages from a blasphemous treatment of Pope's *Essay on Man*, written over a decade earlier by himself and a friend and entitled *Essay on Woman*.

It was these ill-considered gestures of defiance that led to his eventual exile. Of the 2000 sets of the *North Briton* he had printed, only 120 were sold. He borrowed enough money to pay back some of his debts and his printing bills and then sealed his invitation to punishment by running off to France to visit his daughter, carelessly leaving behind the presses, copies of the *North Briton,* and evidence of the salacious poem. He was charged with reprinting the treasonous antigovernment newspaper and with printing the libelous poetic essay. This time the government would be shrewder in preparing its case against Wilkes.

While Wilkes was in Europe, the opposition gathered its forces. King George's ministers devised a scheme whereby Wilkes would be prejudged in Parliament before he was tried in court and be prevented from asserting his privilege as a member of Parliament. Seven weeks after Wilkes returned, on November 15, 1763, the government's two cases were ready. In the House of Commons, Wilkes was brought up on charges of seditious treason for the printing of Issue #45. In the House of Lords, Lord Sandwich read aloud from the *Essay on Woman* to support the charges of salacious libel. The second charge and the scandalous content of the *Essay* soon stole the scene from Issue #45. Within a week there were at least fourteen fraudulent copies of *Essay on Woman* on the London book market, some of them far more prurient than the original and others so mild that customers demanded their money back.

The unctuous piety of the noted lecher Lord Sandwich, who had taken it upon himself to lead the attack on his old Medmenham companion (Sandwich had been expelled from the rather lenient Society of Beefsteaks for blasphemy), was, a few days later, easily identified with some lines in the *Beggar's Opera*. Macheath's remark on finding that he has been betrayed by a member of his own gang, "That Jemmy Twitcher should peach on me, I own surprises me," brought down the house. Thereafter Lord Sandwich, who allegedly invented the idea of meat between two slices of bread so that his gambling and fornication would not be interrupted by mealtimes, was known less for his sandwiches than as Jemmy Twitcher, the betrayer of John Wilkes.

Wilkes's infamous *Essay on Woman* begins with a parody of Pope's first page. The essay was said to be written by Pego Borewell, Esq., pego being popular slang for penis. The footnote commentaries (about one dozen salacious explanatory lines for every line of salacious verse) were attributed to the Rev. Dr. Warburton, bishop of Gloucester, a House of Lords spiritual, and Pope's pedantic and long-winded editor. The dedication in Greek is to Miss Fanny Murray, who at the time of the writing of the *Essay* was the reigning harlot of Covent Garden, much pursued by Lord Sandwich. Years later, when Sandwich stood before the House of Lords reading the essay, Miss Murray was and had been for some time the respectable wife of a Scottish actor. The dedication to her in Greek, citing the Odyssey, Book XI, reads, "Such is the truth that there is nothing more dread nor more shameless than a woman." Prominently displayed just below, on the bottom third of the page, was a copper engraving of an erect phallus marked in Greek with the title, "Creator of the World" and with a Latin phrase just below, *In Recto Decus*. Beneath that, also in Latin, was the inscription, "From the original frequently in the crutch of the most Reverend George Stone, Primate of Ireland, more frequently in the anus of the intrepid hero George Sackville." Much of the poetry that follows is a line-by-line copy of Pope's words interlaced with recitals of the female or male genitals and their assorted activities—all of which produced merely lewd and singularly unoriginal poetry. Thus, the poem proper begins:

> *Awake, my Fanny, leave all meaner things;*
> *This morn shall prove what rapture swiving brings!*
> *Let us (since life can little more supply*
> *Than just a few good fucks, and then we die)*
> *Expatiate free o'er that loved scene of man,*
> *A mighty maze for mighty pricks to scan;*
> *A Wild, where Paphian thorns promiscuous shoot,*
> *Where flowers the monthly Rose, but yields no fruit:*
> *Together let us beat this ample field,*
> *Try what the open, what the covert yield,*

> *The latent tracts, the pleasing depths explore,*
> *And my prick clapped where thousand were before.*[1]

The drawn-out, pedantic prose commentaries, written by Wilkes in the name of the Reverend Warburton, have only slightly more grace. Of line 12, for example, the good reverend has this to say:

> The first edition has it, and my Prick *crown'd*, which I take to be the true reading. It means the *Corona Veneris*, the Glory of the Goddess *Venus* around the head of the beloved: and the Passage seems a Parody to Lucretius, *Insignemq;* meo *Capiti* petere inde Coronam unde prius nulli, &c.
> WARBURTON

As Lord Sandwich read, one or two of the lords covered their ears and begged him to stop. But those feeble cries were muffled by the impatient shouts of the rest, "Read on!" "Read on!" Sandwich obeyed, selecting those portions that would most offend, savoring and underscoring each salacious reference. The owner of Medmenham's, now Lord le Dispenser, said of Sandwich's performance that he had never before heard the devil preach against sin. Reverend Warburton's reaction was described by Walpole: "Foamed with the violence of a Saint Dominic; vaunted that he had combatted infidelity, and laid it under his feet, and said, the blackest fiends in hell would not keep company with Wilkes, and then begged Satan's pardon for comparing them together."

By December 1, 1763, both houses had voted that the #45 should be burned by the hands of the common hangman, who was assigned this task in the statutes on treasonous libel. Wilkes was ordered to appear before the Court of King's Bench to face sentence for his crimes. Knowing he

---

[1] The first lines of Pope's *Essay on Man* were:

> *Awake, my St. John! leave all meaner things*
> *To low ambition, and the pride of Kings.*
> *Let us (since Life can little more supply*
> *Than just to look about us and to die)*
> *Expatiate free o'er all this scene of Man;*
> *A mighty maze! but not without a plan;*
> *A Wild, where weeds and flow'rs promiscuous shoot;*
> *Or Garden, tempting with forbidden fruit.*
> *Together let us beat this ample field,*
> *Try what the open, what the covert yield;*
> *The latent tracts, the giddy heights, explore*
> *Of all who blindly creep, or sightless soar.*

could expect an unfavorable outcome, perhaps even life imprisonment, on Christmas Eve Wilkes slipped past the king's agents and fled to France. He was officially expelled from the Commons and declared an outlaw. And the next month, when the case was heard at the Court of King's Bench, he was found guilty for publishing and printing the *North Briton #45* and for printing the *Essay on Woman*.

After a glamorous, licentious, intellectually exciting, but unproductive four years in exile (marred by the death of Churchill, a devastating loss that would reverberate in Wilkes's thoughts for many years to come), Wilkes was heavily in debt. He decided to return home and to resume his political career.

His first move was to stand for the Middlesex seat in the Commons. After some misadventures with the government he achieved a resounding victory. A mob of his "middling and inferior supporters" forced all of London including the houses of the rich and the great to be lit with candles all night in honor of Wilkes. Even the king's relatives had to obey. Every carriage without a number 45 painted on it was stopped to have one scratched on. Benjamin Franklin, who happened to be in town, calculated that in two nights London had used over £50,000 worth of candles. He was amazed at the 45's printed on the windows and shutters of all houses within a fifteen-mile radius of the city and astonished at Wilkes's popularity. "Tis really an extraordinary event to see an outlaw and exile of bad character... set himself up as a candidate for the capital of the Kingdom."

Walpole, one of those who had no liking at all for Wilkes, summed up his political career: "Though he became a martyr of the best cause, there was nothing in his principles or morals that led him to care under what government he lived. To laugh and riot and scatter firebrands with him was liberty—Despotism will for ever reproach Freedom with the profligacy of such a saint!"

Though his reputation as a firebrand stuck, Wilkes had returned to London with a more sober attitude. His next move was a carefully calculated risk. On April 20, 1768 he presented himself before the King's Bench to demand justice. The judge, who wanted as little trouble as possible from Wilkes, reversed his previous judgment of outlawry. This time he committed Wilkes to King's Bench Prison for twenty-two months for the printing and publishing of the two blasphemous works.

King's Bench Prison was a London precinct, a sort of miniature village where the great and near-great who could afford it lived in style while serving out their sentences. Wilkes chose to pay for one of the best accommodations, an "apartment de luxe" with a view of St. George's Fields. There were shops and stalls, a tennis court, a bowling alley, a coffee shop where the prisoners could read their newspapers, and a tavern. Wilkes was allowed any visitors he wanted, including women galore. Gifts came pouring in: hams, cheeses, fish, hampers of wine, expensive silverware, and numerous assorted packages each weighing forty-five pounds. A hogshead of tobacco came from America. From his headquarters at King's Bench, Wilkes launched numerous political campaigns, beginning with his attempts to stand again for the Middlesex seat in the Commons. The causes he fought for from his prison headquarters involved his own personal freedoms but by extension the constitutional rights of all English citizens. To pay for his political expenses and his debts, which may have been as high as thirty thousand pounds, Wilkes, on the advice of a wealthy supporter, formed the Society of the Supporters of the Bill of Rights. He received large amounts of money from prosperous London businessmen and from the American colonies. The legislature of South Carolina sent fifteen hundred pounds sterling. Wilkes had faithful admirers from all rungs of society. Merchants, artisans, and shopkeepers were the backbone of his support. Workingmen, workers on strike, and those out of work also viewed Wilkes as their spokesman. Many intellectuals, like Dr. Thomas Fry, president of St. John's College at Oxford, and even some religious leaders, sympathized with him.

After standing three times for the Middlesex seat in the Commons and each time winning by a huge margin before being rejected by Parliament, Wilkes urged his constituency to fight for the right of the electorate to choose its own representatives. Wilkes claimed this liberty was a basic right of every citizen. When released from prison in April 1770, Wilkes continued to fight for parliamentary reforms and extension of the voting franchise. Among his other causes were more frequent parliamentary elections, humane prison treatment, better working conditions for apprentices, the elimination of favorites (placemen) in Parliament, the right of the press to report on parliamentary debates, the rights of the American colonies. Even when the war came and patriotism made this last form of opposition unpopular, Wilkes defended the American fight for independence.

After his return from exile, Wilkes became a more practical politician. His thinking was less audacious. He did not so recklessly display his personal life to the public. He began to express the more generalized and vague "humanitarian" visions of the Enlightenment. In fact, though he had been something of a radical, he was never a revolutionary. The bloody spirit of the French Revolution offended him. In a few years, younger political reformers found him irrelevant, and by 1780 he had become, as he put it, "an extinct volcano."

He spent the last years of his life in quiet dignity with a kindly mistress, attended by his devoted Polly and several illegitimate children. Some of his old enemies became his friends. At parties he and King George occasionally enjoyed amiable conversation. He started writing scholarly editions of Greek and Latin classics. Of his more or less conventional old age, Wilkes had this to say: "Adversity may be a good thing to breakfast on; nay a man may dine on it. But believe me, it makes a confoundedly bad supper." He died on Boxing Day, 1797, at age 72. His epitaph, which he had requested, was "John Wilkes, a Friend of Liberty."

Between May 1 and May 3, 1770, while becoming acquainted with London politics and waiting for his interview with Wilkes, Chatterton crowned his scornful farewell to Bristol by writing *The Exhibition*, a 444-line satire that emulated the spirit of Wilkes's blasphemous *Essay on Woman*. Now that he had given up the saintly Rowley and Canynge, Chatterton began a fling with the sinners. Freethinking was his ticket to Liberty. And Liberty à la Wilkes meant one thing above all—freedom of the press. Where Prudence would position herself among all this freedom was uncertain.

So far as we know, the Rowley works, although they were subject to all manner of antiquing and deantiquing, were not censored by his editors, largely because their few sexual innuendos are well cloaked in thick Rowleyese. But after his death, Chatterton's various editors and biographers did not hesitate to censor his freethinking writings. Contrary to the generous impression created by some of Chatterton's early biographers, Chatterton's literary infidelities were more along sexual lines than religious ones. At times, though, as in *Journal 6th*, he ingeniously combined the two.

Until quite recently, Chatterton phrases with explicit genital reference, almost all of which are from his London letters and his satirical poetry, could be read only at the British Museum or the Bristol Public Library and Art Gallery. Elsewhere these scatalogical odds and ends, words here and there, double entendres, puns, were simply excised, allowing the satires and letters to be published without doing injury to the poet's reputation or to the morals of his readers. Those who might have been tempted to peek at the awful words could do so only at the museums, and working their way through the holographs and original transcripts, they were free to read the parts that had been removed from the published texts.

Two works were thoroughly scandalous. Mere excision could not do the job. Therefore, *The Exhibition: A Personal Satire,* and *The Letter Paraphras'd* were kept out of all biographies and all editions of Chatterton's poetry. For over a century, those two most depraved Chatterton works could be read freely only at the museums. Biographers and other Chatterton commentators alluded to obscenity and blasphemy, and some hinted at the nasty Chatterton secrets contained therein. But none would reveal what the manuscripts actually contained. Their tones ranged from patronizing regret about the poet's adolescent excesses to voyeuristic elitism. Readers of these critiques, naturally, were aroused to wild interpretations.

In 1892, the fifty-fifth year of the sixty-four-year reign of Queen Victoria, *The Letter Paraphras'd* was deemed so explicitly pornographic that it was removed from its folio at the British Museum, hidden away from public view altogether, put under lock and key in the curator's office, and shown only to applicants with the right scholarly credentials.

In 1910, an expurgated version of *The Exhibition* was published for the first time. John Ingram was granted permission by the British Art Gallery Committee, who had possession of the manuscript, to publish the poem in his biography of Chatterton, *The True Chatterton.* Whether such permission was granted "only with conditions" is uncertain. Ingram's introduction to his version of *The Exhibition,* in which he assumes full responsibility for the expurgated text, is discreetly tucked away in the appendix. The appendix opens with an explanation of George Catcott's reasons for originally suppressing this poem. The eighteenth-century lover of antiques became alarmed that it might be included in collections of the young poet's writings and therefore "protested most energetically and effectively against the publication of a work which reflected so seriously and libelously upon many of his [Catcott's] relatives and friends." Ingram then goes on to explain his own reasons for publishing the poem and *his* rationale for continuing the censorship:

> Owing to the suppression of the poem and its supposed unsuitability for publication, editors of Chatterton's works have been deterred from including it in their collection of his writings.
>
> Notwithstanding the circumstances connected with the suppression of the poem, and allowing for the inequality of merit of the various portions, there does not seem to be any real reason, nowadays, why "The Exhibition" should not be published, *provided the few offensive lines be omitted,* [ital. added] although Professor Wilson may be justified in remarking of what he probably never read, "It would have been well had it perished with its

evidence that youthful purity had been sullied, and the precocious boy was only too conversant with forbidden things."

After Ingram had thoroughly perused the poem, he decided to adopt for himself the role of its protector. Thus, when the poem was included in Ingram's biography, published in London and in Leipzig in 1910, it was missing a total of 164 lines. A few scattered lines were omitted for mysterious reasons having to do with offense to the Anglican Church, but mainly large chunks of consecutive verse were excised because they described the size and movement of the exposed penis of the clergyman exhibitionist, the central character of this poem, and the reactions of Bristol ladies who were privy to this wondrous sight.

Chatterton launches his attack on the citizens of Bristol with a description of the penis of the Reverend Alexander Catcott. George Catcott's energetic efforts on behalf of his relatives and friends are understandable.

> *. . . Catcott's Heavenly Heart*
> *Is never mov'd but in the better part,*
> *Devotion only warms his freezing Blood*
> *Lust never melted up the sizy Flood.*
> *And should his last Degenracy of Mind*
> *Be to the Pleasures of the World inclin'd*
> *Sickly desire is all his little Crime*
> *For Catcott's stretch'd beyond his trying time*
> *Like his dull Brother, frigid, cold, and dead*
> *He'd sleep unsullied in a Harlot's Bed.*
> *And in defyance of the stroaking Hand*
> *His matters like his Reason, would not stand*

The furtive exhibitionist turns out to be the hero of the piece. He is held up as a victim of the prurient Bristol mentality. The respectable citizens of Bristol are preoccupied with ferreting out the sinfulness of every private sexual act. Yet they blindly entrust their civic justice and morality to the clerical and medical professions whose corruption and folly Chatterton savagely exposes. While his primary targets are the clerics and surgeons, the Royal Academy, the prurient citizens, the small-minded artists and musicians who catered to the ostentatious tastes of the average Bristolean also get their due. The poem struggles throughout to adhere to the mock contention satirical style, a convention in which each side of a dispute is given opportunity to do itself in by its own characteristic arguments and rebuttals. The subtlety of this convention is hindered by

Chatterton's crude rage and blunt contempt. The poem loses its poetic structure to his scornful rage.

Chatterton ends up with an uneven, unsuccessful poem. At the same time, the poetry itself does succeed in rendering precisely the spirit of exhibitionism. Like any perverse sexual activity, "indecent exposure" always represents an artful compromise between sexual necessity and a triumphant revenge on a world experienced as rejecting and gratuitously hostile. In every perverse act there is contempt for the straight world, the world of deceptive adults who are too stupid to really appreciate what sex is all about. With the perversion, the once-rejecting insiders become outsiders. Three weeks before he wrote this poem, Chatterton had put one over on the lumbering, dim-witted giants of Bristol with his fake suicide note. Now, with *The Exhibition,* he takes one last scathing look back at the Bristol that he had once tried to glorify but now could only mock and despise. *The Exhibition* is his revenge on the grown-ups.

Unlike the tired matters of Alexander Catcott, the exhibitionist's penis is far from cold and dead. It is a jewel, a living work of art:

> *In the dark Covert of a Shed arrayd,*
> *Delia the young, saw mighty ——— stand*
> *His Sacerdotal Truncheon in his Hand;*
> *Which as he whiskd about from Side to Side*
> *In the exulting of a decent Pride,*
> *By just Degrees to greater Glorys spread*
> *And the bright Jewel glow'd a stronger red.*
> *Why modest ——— didst Thou creep away*
> *To hide thy beauties from the glare of Day*
> *Merit like Thine, so thick, so very long*
> *If lost or hid, it does the Public wrong.*
> *Uncommon Parts, and Blessings of the Mind*
> *Were sent, my Friend, to benefit Mankind.*

Chatterton's choice of the metaphor of exhibitionism to express his own ambivalent relationship to his childhood home was entirely unconscious. It was not, however, accidental or coincidental. Exhibitionism figures prominently in the sexual and moral plight of the impostor. The imposture is designed to cloak a deformed, fragmented sense of self with one that is experienced as intact, magnificent, enviable. Exhibitionism and other perverse sexual acts have as their aim an attempt to prove that one's genitals are superior to the ordinary kind and therefore impervious to damage or insult.

The impostor is not a mere criminal. Nor is he a simple show-off or poseur whose obvious flamboyance deceives no one for very long. The impostor assumes false identities because he must hide from himself and from everyone else the inadequacies of his actual self, including a basic sense of genital inadequacy.

There are different forms and varying degrees of imposture. The arch-impostor has a vast repertoire of accessory behaviors in which he resembles other men who, in their talents, character structure, and/or sexual orientation also exhibit a certain degree of imposturousness. The blatant impostor may forge, plagiarize, counterfeit, and swindle, and in these behaviors he resembles the men who make careers of such pursuits. Like magicians, gurus, mediums, occult healers, who also have a considerable talent for dissembling, the impostor appreciates that his acts of conjuring depend upon the suspension of disbelief in his audiences. The victims are his abetting audience, the unconscious conspirators who are as hungry as the perpetrator to consummate the illusion. The impostor is frankly exhibitionistic: he changes costumes frequently and also has a voyeuristic relationship to his audience.

Some of these accessory behaviors, such as forgery and counterfeiting, are props for the impostor's artful deceptions. Others, such as exhibitionism and voyeurism, while they serve the deception, are also direct expressions of the impostor's shaky masculine identity. The impostor is predisposed to acquiring actual perversions such as transvestism, fetishism, exhibitionism, voyeurism. Impostors also suffer from potency problems, so that when they do engage in heterosexual pursuits they are pseudogenital. That is, while they employ their genitals heterosexually, they emphasize scoring, performance, the imitation of fantasized ideal males, orgasm in the partner not as the giving of pleasure but as a vanquishment and defeat, and they view erection as risk, enmity, deception, survival.

With respect to his pseudomanhood, the impostor resembles the Casanova, the bigamist, the supermacho male. In his enormous grandiosity and with the fanatical ploys with which the impostor fends off disclosure, he resembles certain paranoid characters, such as the founders of religious cults and members of secret male societies. Men who suffer from these other disorders—the perversions, the pseudogenital pursuits, the grandiose paranoias—have some features in common with full-fledged impostors. They too are pretenders to adult sexuality. They feel entitled to be treated as moral exceptions and thus achieve power over others through acts of dissembling.

In some persons, men *and* women, the imposture may consist of relatively minor, restricted episodes of dissembling identity or falsifying achievements. In these less desperate, less repetitive versions we inevitably discover that the dissemblers are very much like the arch-impostor in that their sexual and moral immaturities are hidden beneath a cloak of narcissistic entitlement. And in their childhood histories we usually find the two basic elements in the etiology of the full-fledged impostor: the person was expected to mirror an exalted sexual ideal of one parent, and the other parent was an emotional or actual absentee.

No little boy, not even one whose mother has roused him to greater and greater heights of exhibitionism, can really vanquish his father. The knowledge that his own penis is puny, insignificant, and vulnerable compared to the awesome genital wherewithal of the stupid, ignominious giant that the mother has banished from the bedroom fills him with mortification and a nameless dread of retaliation. Whether or not he has an actual bodily deformity (which some famous impostors have actually had), the potential impostor grows up with the entrenched conviction that his body, especially his genitals, is inferior and defective.

The full-fledged impostor suffers from a profound impairment of his sense of identity, the core of which is a defective sense of gender identity. He knows that he is not the person he pretends to be, but he feels that he *must* be some person greater or more magnificent than the ordinary mortals he sets out to deceive. His behavior is driven and repetitious. His very existence depends on the success of his trickery. The central motive, the one that drives the imposturous behavior, is an inordinate anxiety over genital intactness.

Technically speaking, Chatterton is only half-deserving of the title "Impostor." He never tried to misrepresent his identity by presenting *himself* to the world with a fictitious name or history. However, he did fabricate a Thomas Rowley according to an imaginative conception of a ideal masculine self, a virtuous self that had been connected with St. Mary's Church since "time out of mind." He did try to impose that fabrication on the world. As for the gender confusions that may have driven his impostorous behaviors, we shall never know if Chatterton, like Rousseau, Boswell, Johnson, Wilkes, and other prominent men of his day, ever engaged in a compulsive sexual activity whose purpose was reassurance about his genital integrity. There is no evidence that he was a blatant exhibitionist, fetishist, flagellant, Casanova. But the mental preoccupation with genital integrity which he not-so-elegantly disguised in the act of the disgraced clergyman was even more evident in the second of his banished obscene texts, *The Letter Paraphras'd*.

More shocking to some eyes than the clergyman's exposed sacerdotal jewel was the very brief exchange of genital innuendos between Chatterton and, as she has come to be remembered, "an unknown girl." This girl apparently wrote only once to Chatterton. He never delivered his reply, a paraphrase interpretation of her letter, but he enfolded it in his notebook for safekeeping along with the girl's original. Evidently the young poet found some special delight both in the young lady's letter, which has touches of literary grace, and in his spirited doggerel response. Chatterton received the letter sometime during his last year in Bristol.

> Sir
>   I Send my Love to you and Tell you Thiss if you prove Constant I not miss but if you froun and Torn a way I Can make cart of batter Hay pray Excep of me Love Hartley and Send me word Cartingley Tell me How maney ouncs of Grean Ginger Bread Can Sho the Eaker of Honiste
>   My House is not belt with Stavis I not be Coarted by Boys nor Navis I Haive a man an man Shall Haive me if I whaint a fool I send for the
>   if you are going to the D. I wish you good Gonery

In effect the unknown girl is saying in a direct and playfully abusive manner, "I'll not be courted by boys or knaves. I'll give my self only to a man. If I want a fool, I'll send for thee." As a final good-bye touch she wishes Chatterton a good case of gonorrhea. Chatterton responds in kind. Since she wounded his pride by her assault on the size and erectile capacities of his penis, he insults her by focusing on the inordinate size of her genitals and the depravity of her huge, appetitive lust.

The Letter Paraphras'd

My Loving Dear I send thee this
To tell thee that I want to piss
Pray let me speak the matter blunt
I want to stretch my narrow Cunt
But if you frown and turn away
Go, with the devil dance the Hay
Pray send me back a swelling Prick
To touch my Matters to the quick
But if your Roger cannot fill
The water brook that turns my Mill
Go fuck Green Sickness Girls and Wenches
On Bulks, in Lanes on Tombs on Benches
By God I want a strapping Man
My cunt is more than twice a Span
And Faith I speak it without Joking
Last Night I put a Cartwheel Spoke in

> Then if your matters can not do
> By God I never will have you
> Unless I dangle with thy Prick
> Piss in thy face and let thee lick

Were Chatterton's genital preoccupations, as expressed in *The Exhibition* and *The Letter Paraphras'd*, so different in kind or degree from those of any boy just on the verge of manhood? Pubescent boys are obsessed with the reality of their erections, which are visible and difficult to control. This fact alone leads to uniquely male experiences of pride and humiliation. The penis is regarded as a thing that has a life of its own. As he approaches full genital maturity the boy is preoccupied with watching his penis and testicles grow in volume and length, his scrotum becoming looser and more pigmented. His erections become more frequent and last longer. There is an increasing capacity for larger amounts of ejaculate in more frequent succession, events that are greeted with pride but also with an awesome fear of genital damage. The association between genital adequacy and self-adequacy haunts the mental life of adolescents, boys and girls alike. Typically a boy is more desperate about sexual prowess. He is convinced that he must prove himself by the performance of his penis.

Whereas most boys somehow gain reassurance, at least partially, by the signs of their approaching manhood, the potential imposter becomes more desperate. With the advent of puberty, the prospect of having to prove himself a real man looms ominously. The average boy begins to give up the family romance that has softened his disillusionment with his real parents and helped him to bear the humiliation of oedipal defeat. The potential impostor, on the other hand, grows more reluctant to relinquish the fantasies and daydreams that have so far held together his shaky sense of identity. As he approaches manhood, the imposturous boy not only clings more desperately to the family romance scenario, he now elaborates and refines it. He begins to enact the scenario in his everyday life.

At the time that Chatterton composed these two obscene poems, he had given up Sir William Canynge and the family romance that had once endowed him with an inner sense of wholeness and unity. Now his rage at the deceptive adults was out in the open, and the more subtly hostile role of the impostor-poet was no longer an urgently felt need. Ironically, though, as he gave up the beautiful poetry that expressed his romance of a pure and noble father, benefactor of St. Mary's Church, patron of the arts, owner of the most affluent merchant fleet of Bristol, five-time mayor of a Bristol deserving of admiration and belief, he was also giving up his blatantly imposturous behavior. For Chatterton, the end of crime went hand in hand with the end of romance. Chatterton's energies would now be focused on the real world. He was ready to take on the challenge of proving himself a real man.

The Exhibition expresses the mood of vengeful disillusionment with which Chatterton left his native city, saying bitter farewell to his childhood illusions and turning his face toward the social realities of his day. It is, as he put it, a *personal* satire. The *Letter Paraphras'd,* on the other hand, was a fairly ordinary piece of eighteenth-century doggerel, typical of the double-standard sexual sentiments of the average eighteenth-century Englishman who, if we are to judge by the variety of sexual specialties in the London brothels, was as plagued by the association between genital adequacy and personal power as the average apprentice youth. One doesn't have to go too far to conclude that the genital preoccupations expressed in Chatterton's paraphrase have been the concern of all men, in all places, in all eras. What is original about the poem is not its sentiments but its form—the certainty and agility of Chatterton's rhyming scheme.

As Chatterton boarded the One-Day Express for London, he thought he was leaving his impostor days behind. He believed he was on his way to becoming a genuine man of the world. And indeed, he would soon be more of an everyday imposturous type than the out-and-out impostor-poet of his early adolescent years. The great impostor was becoming a garden-variety narcissist.

Of vaunting and obscenity, those everyday socialized varieties of exhibitionism, Chatterton would certainly perform his share. Within weeks of arriving in London, the blustering charmer of the ladies of Redcliffe Hill was busily transforming himself into an enchanting and captivating London personality. During his Rowley year, he had demonstrated many of the behaviors and attitudes of a character perversion. He was a pathological liar, a practical joker and hoaxer consumed by his efforts to prove that something which was not true was true. During his four months in London, while not an out-and-out liar, he became addicted to exaggerating the extent of his power and influence in the world of men. He was also learning how to transform genuine art into the pleasing product the public wanted. And when his idol Wilkes eluded him he simply transferred his affections to where the money was. In no time at all he became a master of what he all-too-knowingly referred to as "The Art of Puffing."

> *Versed by Experience in the subtle Art,*
> *The mysteries of a Title I impart*
> *Teach the young Author how to please the Town,*
> *And make the heavy drug of Rhime go down.*

EIGHT

The Great Impostor Becomes a Garden-Variety Narcissist

Chatterton adopts the new coffeehouse hero, London's Lord Mayor William Beckford, as his new father. What the Shoreditch household thought of the poet in their midst. The downward plunge begins. The death of Beckford and the move to Brooke Street. Chatterton's suicide: What happened to the freethinking journalist who cared more for truth than for prudence? The relationship between crime and art. The poets of imitation. Madness and infidelity.

WHEN in the middle of May his two major resources, Fell of the *Freeholder's* and Edmunds of the *Middlesex Journal*, were thrown into prison, the adaptable Chatterton rapidly switched allegiances to Hamilton, the editor of *Town and Country Magazine* and newly appointed editor of the *Middlesex Journal*. Chatterton assured his mother that these apparent misfortunes were good fortune, that the sorry luck of the Patriot publishers "will be to me of no little service." Already a dyed-in-the-wool literary warrior, he steps up his coffeehouse campaigns:

> Last week being in the pit of Drury-Lane Theatre, I contracted an immediate acquaintance (which you know is no hard task to me) with a young gentleman in Cheapside; partner in a music shop, the greatest in the city. Hearing I could write, he desired me to write a few songs for him: this I did the same night, and conveyed them to him the next morning. These he showed to a doctor in music, and I am invited to treat with this doctor,

on the footing of a composer, for Ranelagh and the gardens. *Bravo, hey boys, up we go!*—Besides the advantage of visiting these expensive and polite places, gratis; my vanity will be fed with the sight of my name in copper-plate, and my sister will receive a bundle of printed songs, the words by her brother. These are not all my acquisitions: a gentleman who knows me at the Chapter, as an author, would have introduced me as a companion to the young Duke of Northumberland, in his intended general tour. But alas! I speak no tongue but my own!

With Fell in prison, Chatterton's meeting with Wilkes had to be indefinitely delayed. But Chatterton's increasing familiarity with London politics inspired him to try another route to fame and wealth. Although the case of Wilkes and Liberty still monopolized the domestic political scene, a new incident had temporarily claimed the foreground.

The chief conversation at the coffeehouses was of Lord Mayor Beckford's challenge to King George III. Beckford was Wilkes's most powerful political ally. Some of Wilkes's foremost defenders, as well as fellow advocates of freedom of the press and the right of free election, were members of the Corporation of the City of London, which was then under Beckford's leadership.

In March the king had imperiously rejected a strong remonstrance from the City deploring the Ministry's handling of the Middlesex elections and calling for new elections and the dissolution of Parliament. Faced with this setback Beckford became even more openly aggressive. As soon as Wilkes was released from King's Bench in April, Beckford had him sworn in as an alderman of the City of London. At his instigation the Patriots were continuing with their plan to bring the case of Wilkes before both houses nearly every day of the January 9 through May 19 session with the goal of readmitting Wilkes to the House of Commons. If they succeeded, they would win a major battle in the struggle for free elections.

Beckford would not let Parliament's summer recess silence the causes he championed. The week after Parliament adjourned, on May 19, leaving the issue of free elections and Wilkes's right to a seat in the Commons up in the air, Beckford requested an interview with King George.

There was another Londoner in whose interests it was to keep the Patriot fires burning. On May 18, the day before Parliament was to recess, the pseudonymous political writer Probus submitted a letter addressed to the Lord Mayor to the *Middlesex Journal*. Whether he wrote as Probus or as Decimus, Chatterton now knew exactly where the political action was. He had quickly realized that Lord Mayor Beckford could be his entry to the Patriot camp.

Probus' letter starts off with a burst of rage toward the "tyrannous junto of slaves, who would mutilate every shadow of right, law and justice." This flamboyant attack is cleverly balanced with a flow of panegyrics to the mayor's personal and political integrity. The letter urges Beckford to again seek redress from King George III. Chatterton closes with a few suggestions on how the lord mayor might proceed with his noble assignment:

> Should you address again, my Lord, it would not be amiss to tell his Majesty, that you expect *his* answer, and not the answer of his mother or

ministers.—You complain not to them, but of them; and, would they redress our grievances, they can only do it by doing justice on themselves, and being their own executioners. Your perseverance in the glorious cause will check the rapid progress of oppression, and extort a conclusive answer from the ministry, through the mouth of his Majesty. . . .

Let us, with one united voice, demand redress, if again refused: let us take the sword of justice in our hands, and punish the wretches whose evil councils have estranged his Majesty from the good of the subject, and robbed him of his surest safeguard, the love of the people.

Chatterton's timing and tactics were just right. It was almost as though the seventeen-year-old newcomer to London politics had read the lord mayor's mind. The *Middlesex Journal* did not publish the Probus letter until May 25, but a copy was sent to Beckford so that he would have ample time to study it before his second meeting with King George. There is something marvelously presumptuous about a seventeen-year-old instructing a lord mayor on how to deal with a king. That the unknown Bristol youth's inflammatory sentiments might have had some influence on Beckford's subsequent actions is not entirely out of the question.

Certainly what the mayor decided to do stoked Chatterton's grandiosity. On May 23, a day or so after reading the letter from his anonymous adviser, Beckford presented his second remonstrance to King George, following it up with an extemporaneous appeal to the king to heed the concerns of his fellow citizens, and reject the advice of any court minister who tried to alienate His Majesty from his loyal subjects. Beckford's appeal fell on deaf ears and the king refused to back down. But Beckford's audacity endeared him further to his fellow Londoners and to all Englishmen of Patriot persuasion. To have walked away from the king's second rejection would have weakened Beckford's standing with his constituency, but now he was the hero of the day. For a brief time his name and his speech were in every newspaper and on everyone's lips. For a moment Beckford eclipsed Wilkes.

A week later, on May 30, Chatterton wrote to Mary from Tom's Coffee-House:

You have, doubtless, heard of the Lord Mayor's remonstrating and addressing the King: but it will be a piece of news, to inform you that I have been with the Lord Mayor on the occasion. Having addressed an essay to his Lordship, it was very well received; perhaps better than it deserved; and I waited on his Lordship, to have his approbation, to address a second letter to him, on the subject of the remonstrance, and its reception. His Lordship received me as politely as a citizen could: and warmly invited me to call on him again. The rest is a secret.—

We now know Chatterton's secret. He planned to publish Probus' second letter on the remonstrance, which he had composed on the eve of Beckford's triumphant challenge to the king, in the *North Briton*. That newspaper, which had ceased publication after its forty-sixth number, had been revived in 1768 by a Patriot printer named William Bingley. But Bingley had been committed to the King's Bench for refusing to testify against Wilkes in the Spring 1769 trials. From his prison headquarters he continued to publish a small folio version of the old *North Briton*. Each issue consisted of one highly significant, elegantly printed essay of about six columns. And Bingley was to be released from prison during the first week in June.

Almost as soon as Bingley arrived at his new premises, Chatterton called on him with the second Probus letter and Bingley accepted it at once. In the meantime the first Probus letter, which had been printed on May 25 in the *Middlesex Journal,* was accepted for reprinting in the widely read *Political Register*. Both letters were promised for publication toward the end of June. By the end of June, then, Chatterton hoped to realize his fantasy of becoming the second-most popular Patriot journalist (the first, of course, would be Wilkes). Politicians from both sides would be asking after him. His name would be on everyone's lips.

Chatterton's self-congratulatory letter to his sister was written before his second Probus letter was accepted in the *North Briton*. Yet with all his exalted daydreams Chatterton was remarkably savvy about his burgeoning career. The voice of Prudence was always there. And now that most Patriot publishers were either imprisoned or intimidated by the government, writing in their cause had ceased to be lucrative for Chatterton. Chatterton let his sister in on his qualms and reservations. "There's no money to be got this side of the question." "But," he adds, "he is a poor author who cannot write on both sides of the question." He confesses to Mary the awkwardness of attempting to publish political essays:

> Essays on the patriotic side, fetch no more than what the copy is sold for. As the patriots themselves are searching for a place, they have no gratuities to spare. . . .
> —On the other hand, unpopular essays will not even be accepted: and you must pay to have them printed, but then you seldom lose by it— Courtiers are so sensible of their deficiency in merit, that they generally reward all who know how to daub them with an appearance of it.

While he waited to see the effects of the simultaneous publication of his two letters to Lord Mayor Beckford, Chatterton wrote no more essays on the Patriot side, attempting instead a few on the ministerial side. After his death, remnants of these proministerial writings were found among his papers. One, composed on the same day as his second Beckford letter (even before the letter to Mary, he had commenced writing "on both sides of the question"), speaks of Wilkes as a "Pretended Patriot," "the Epitome of the Faction, Selfinterested, Treasonable, and Inconsiderable."

Any ambitions Chatterton might have had for making an impact on the Patriots were soon totally dashed. The lord mayor died suddenly on June 21 from a cold which had developed into rheumatic fever. Beckford's glorious remonstrance was yesterday's news. Now, elegies to him were the hot items, paying twice and three times more than the usual half-guinea per political piece. Chatterton's second essay was pulled from publication.

His Shoreditch cousin, Mrs. Ballance, reported that "when Beckford died the young poet was perfectly frantic and out of his mind and said that he was ruined." Yet it appears that he was one of a whole legion of aspiring writers who tried to make literary hay out of the lord mayor's death.

Some weeks later Chatterton sent the manuscript of his second Beckford essay to his Bristol friend, Thomas Carey. All that survives are a few jottings for the opening passage. "When the endeavors of a Spirited people to free themselves from an insupportable slavery &c." "This is as violent an abuse of Government for rejecting the remonstrance." On the back is Chatterton's computation of how much was lost by the defeat of his *North Briton* scheme:

Accepted by Bingley—Set for, and thrown out of, the *North Briton*, 21st June, on account of Lord Mayor's death:

	£. s. d.
Lost by his death on this Essay	1 11 6
Gained in Elegies. . . . . . . £ 2 2 0	
" in Essays. . . . . . . £ 3 3 0	
	5 5 0
Am glad he is dead by	3 13 6

According to Chatterton's emotional accounting, his interests were advanced by the death of Beckford. But his five pounds' worth of elegies and essays on Beckford may never have been published. Even if they were, no scholar has been able to distinguish Chatterton's handiwork from the hundreds of anonymous Beckford elegies and essays that appeared after the lord mayor's death.

Mrs. Ballance, a sensible woman of very modest education and financial means, was unimpressed by the literary mannerisms of her young cousin from Bristol. She was somewhat bewildered by the way he carried on about the death of Beckford, but since everything Chatterton did struck her as wild, odd, peculiar, his latest rantings came as no surprise. First of all he was "proud as Lucifer." One day when she had attempted some family intimacy by calling him "Cousin Tommy," he had one of his tempers and scolded her as though she were the child, "Who ever heard of a poet called Tommy?" Mrs. Ballance did not let him get away with that one. She told him she didn't know much about poets but who did he think he was, setting himself up as a gentleman? When his two editor friends, Edmunds and Fell, were thrown into prison, Mrs. Ballance advised Tommy to get a proper job. In response to that Chatterton stormed about the room like a madman, threatening to gain fame and fortune by having himself imprisoned in the Tower. And when he wasn't storming about, he might be performing his other distinctive variety of fit, especially when there was company about, by staring into a person's face without speaking or even seeming to see him for nearly a quarter of an hour, his thoughts apparently elsewhere, but who knew where. When Mrs. Ballance reported these characteristics of her cousin several years after his death, she also lamented that she had not then appreciated his talents. Had she known he was such a great man, she certainly would have been more tolerant of his eccentricities.

The Shoreditch rooming house was run by a Mr. and Mrs. Walmsley, with whose nephew, a boy of fourteen or fifteen, Chatterton shared a bed. The younger boy regarded his bedmate with a certain perplexity. Most nights the new boarder never came to bed at all, staying up scribbling away until three or four in the morning. On the nights he did sleep he was up again at five or six. Every morning the floor would be covered with small bits of torn-up paper containing the poet's rejected words. He was very thin. He never ate meat but seemed to live on bread, water, an occasional tart. Once he ate a sheep's tongue. He was surely a very haughty person but taken all in all there was something nice about him. It was impossible not to like him.

This young man's sister, a girl of seventeen or eighteen, said she had assumed Chatterton to be nothing more nor less than a mad boy full of flights and vagaries. Yet if it had not been for his youthful face and her knowledge of his real age she never would have reckoned that he was only seventeen himself. He seemed unusually manly for his age. And though no woman ever came to visit, it was obvious to her and to everyone else that Tommy was terribly fond of women. He was "a sad rake," and sometimes quite saucy to her. In general he was good-tempered, agreeable, and likable. But there was no way not to notice his pride and haughty ways: he was always putting on airs and acting as though nothing in the world were too good for him, and for his mother, his sister, and his grandmother. Like everyone else at Shoreditch, the Walmsleys' niece commented on Chatterton's strange eating habits. She added the fact that her brother had been a little frightened to lie with him: what with Chatterton not eating and not sleeping the boy sometimes imagined the poet was more a spirit than a real person.

As for the landlord's wife, Mrs. Walmsley, she spoke well of her peculiar tenant. He was very civil when they met, never molested her in any way and never stayed out past family hours except for once. Although he did not ever want his room to be swept, even this annoying oddity Mrs. Walmsley shrugged off. She attributed it to poetry; poets did not like brooms. What "poet-folks" are good for is to sit in a garret and starve. Of all the Shoreditch household, Mr. Walmsley had the most easygoing attitude toward Chatterton. He approved of the youth who in his eyes seemed a wholesome sort—manly, pleasing, and "did not dislike the wenches."

Even though they gradually adjusted to the exotic presence in their midst, Mrs. Ballance and the Walmsleys were probably somewhat relieved when, shortly after Beckford's death, Chatterton decided to move from Shoreditch to Brooke Street, where, as Mrs. Walmsley might have predicted, he would sit in a garret and starve.

As the lord mayor was dying of rheumatic fever, Chatterton acquired "an horrid cold," "a most horrible weezing in the throat," which lasted until the last days of June. Sometime during his recuperation, Chatterton made the move to Brooke Street, one of the poorest and most disreputable neighborhoods of London. Compared to his shabby attic room at Mrs. Angel's, the room he'd shared with the Walmsleys' nephew had been working-class elegance.

In whatever real way Chatterton may have been affected by the death of Beckford, that event served as the marker between hope and despair. After June 20, there would be one or two more dizzying peaks of elation, promise, even faith, but essentially the road would be straight downhill. After the initial triumphs, when his poems and letters were appearing everywhere—*Freeholder's, London Magazine, Court and City Magazine, Town and Country Magazine,* and nearly a dozen in the *Middlesex Journal*—every plan, every offer of employment, real or fantasized, failed to materialize.

By the end of his first month in London, though he clung to the daydream that the two Probus letters would bring his name to the attention of politicians on both sides of the question, the prudent side of Chatterton was coming to terms with the futility of trying to earn a living as a writer. At the end of May he was already considering going to sea for the East India Company, although he reassured his sister, "I shall not take a step to the sea, whilst I can continue on land." Chatterton knew as well as Boswell that company at sea could be worse than in prison and that the food served to ordinary seamen made starvation seem preferable. An enterprising youth like Chatterton would not have taken the East India offer seriously had he not thought of a way to survive at sea. While under Barrett's wing, Chatterton had read a great many medical books and also picked up the rudiments of surgical technique. He wrote to his Bristol collaborator requesting the necessary papers to apply for a position as surgeon's mate. In all likelihood the clever and resourceful young poet would have been better at the tasks of bleeding, shaving, evacuations, and tooth extraction than most of the men who performed those services at sea, but on that occasion Barrett chose to comport himself with professional scrupulosity and refused to send the papers that would allow Chatterton to pose as a surgeon's mate.

In a letter to Carey, dated July 1, which for the most part flies high on the ecstasies of rakedom and the glory of seeing his writings in all the famous journals, Chatterton concludes with a sad commentary—probably a more accurate account of the state of his fortunes than the innuendos of sexual adventure and boasts of literary success that precede:

> The Printers of the Daily Publications are all frightened out of their Patriotism, and will take Nothing unless tis Moderate or Ministerial, I have Not had five Patriotic Essays this fortnight. All must be Ministerial or Entertaining.

After the loss of Wilkes and Beckford, Chatterton searched about for something or someone he could believe in—or at the very least some writing assignments. Early in July there were two bursts of renewed optimism. From his attic room at Mrs. Angel's, Chatterton made one last try as Thomas Rowley with *An Excelente Balade of Charitie: as wroten bie the gode Prieste Thomas Rowley, 1464* and sent it off to the editors of *Town and Country*. An accompanying letter, dated July 4, 1770, is signed with the anonymous D.B. Chatterton had felt it necessary to ensure his disguise by having someone, probably Barrett, post the poem, which is postmarked Bristol. The letter says, "If the Glossary annexed to the following piece will make the language intelligible; the Sentiment, Description, and Versification, are highly deserving the attention of the literati." D.B. explains in one of those ingenious Chatterton footnotes that the poet Rowley "was born at Norton Mal-reward in Somersetshire, educated at the Convent of St. Kenna at Keynesham, and died at Westbury in Gloucestershire." Thus, in his last appearance, Rowley finally acquires a birthplace.

The *Balade* is ranked with *Aella* as a Rowleyan masterpiece. Critics have admired the clever touches of Chaucer and the Miltonic measure with its royal rhyme and final alexandrine. The poem is exceptional in that it portrays Thomas Rowley on his own, with no reference to William Canynge, St. Mary's, or Bristol history. Chatterton was now standing alone. All his fathers had deserted him. He was at the mercy of strangers. The poem is put forth as Rowley's version of the parable of the good Samaritan, yet the surface narrative on the loneliness and rejection of the Samaritan has been considered less poetically significant by critics than Rowley's descriptions of nature. His depiction of the approaching storm has been said "not to be excelled either in ancient or modern poetry." That scene is recognized as having been influenced by the storm scenes of the long-forgotten poet James Thomson, Chatterton's "only 18th century competitor in capturing the movements of Nature."

> *The gatherd storme is rype; the bigge drops falle;*
> *The forswat[1] meadowes smethe,[2] and drenche the raine;*
> *The comyng ghastness do the cattle pall,[3]*
> *And the full flockes are drivynge ore the plaine;*
> *Dashde from the cloudes the waters flott[4] againe;*
> *The welkin opes; the yellow levynne[5] flies;*
> *And the hot fierie smothe[6] in the wide lowings dies.*
>
> *Liste! now the thunder's rattling clymmynge sound*
> *Cheves[7] slowlie on, and then embollen[8] clangs*
> *Shakes the hie spyre, and losst, dispended, drown'd,*
> *Still on the gallard[9] eare of terroure hanges;*
> *The windes are up; the lofty elmen swanges;*
> *Again the levynne and the thunder poures,*
> *And the full cloudes are braste[10] attenes in stonen showers.*

---

[1] forswat—sunburnt
[2] smethe—smoke
[3] pall—appall, frighten
[4] flott—fly
[5] levynne—lightning
[6] smothe—steam
[7] Cheves—moves
[8] embollen—swelled
[9] gallard—frightened
[10] braste—burst

Despite the storm scenes and the copious and learned footnotes supplied by D.B., the editors of *Town and Country* were not convinced of the worthiness of the *Balade of Charitie*. That magazine had been regularly publishing Chatterton's modern works under his various pseudonyms. But after not responding at all to the *Balade* for several weeks, the editors rejected Rowley's verse with the following notice, which appeared in their columns a few days after Chatterton's suicide. "The pastoral from Bristol, signed D.D. [sic] has some share of merit: but the author will, doubtless, discover upon another perusal of it, many exceptional passages."

Though he did not live long enough to read his rejection notice, it proved once again that Chatterton was correct in his decision to give up Rowley. The world was not ready for something so completely inventive and idealistic as the poet-priest Thomas Rowley. Chatterton's artistic wit and good common sense were right in urging him away from the fifteenth century and toward the artistic and commercial possibilities of realistic, up-to-date literary modes.

In July, Chatterton's *Bravo, hey boys, up we go!* fantasy about composing for the musical theater also became a near-reality. *The Revenge, A Burletta* was purchased to be performed at Marybone Gardens. Chatterton had patched together this musical romp of jealousy, matrimonial infidelity, lovers' quarrels, and lovers reunited, starring Jupiter, Juno, Bacchus, and Cupid from his earlier works *Amphitryon* and *Aella*, as well as bits of Dryden. Though only a few airs were in rehearsal, the entire burletta would soon be performed, according to Chatterton's July 1 letter to Carey, and was sure to be a rousing success:

> A song of mine is a great favourite with the Town, on Acct of the fulness of the Musick has much of Mr. Allens Manner in the Air, You will See that, and Twenty more in print, after the Seasons over, I Yesterday heard Several Airs &c, of My Burletta sung to the Harpsichord, Horns, Hautboits, Flutes, Bassoons, and Violins &c and will Venture to pronounce, from the Excellence of the Music, that it will take with the Town.

The song Chatterton refers to was to be sung by two of the stars of Marybone Gardens, Mrs. Barthelemon and Master Cheney, a young boy of thirteen:

THE FAMILY ROMANCE OF

MAY

Sung by Master Cheney at Marybone Gardens

THE FAMILY ROMANCE OF

THE IMPOSTOR-POET THOMAS CHATTERTON

The Revenge was almost certainly never performed at Marybone Gardens or any of the other London music gardens.[11] The greatest good fortune of *The Revenge* was that Chatterton was paid the most money he had ever earned from one piece of writing:

> Receiv'd July 6th., 1770 of Mr: Luffman Atterbury, Five Pounds, Five Shillings, being in full for all the Manuscripts contain'd in this Book, of which I am the Author: for which consideration of Five pounds, Five Shillings I hereby give up my sole right and property in, and the liberty of printing and disposing of the same to the said Luffn. Atterbury only, and in such a manner as he thinks proper—As witness my Hand this 6th: Day of July 6th: 1770.

With that sum, he fulfills one promise of his childhood days. The second week in July he is out to the shops, purchasing finery and gifts for the women he left behind in Bristol. For his mother there is a cargo of patterns, a French snuff box, some British herb snuff, two fans— "the silver one is more grave than the other, which would suit my sister best. But that I leave to you both." His grandmother gets her favorite British herb-tobacco to fill her pipe. For Mary there are six cups and saucers and two basins with the promise of a china teapot and a cream pot if they are desired. Later that week he writes to Mary, advising her on matters of fashion, "I have sent you some china and a fan. You have your choice of two. I am surprized that you chose purple and gold; I went into the shop to buy it; but it is the most disagreeable colour I ever saw; dead, lifeless and inelegant. Purple and pink, or lemon and pink, are more genteel and lively." On July 20 he writes another letter to his sister. The cheery words are belied by the scanty details, brisk pace, and unaffectionate tone:

> I am now about an Oratorio, which when finished will purchase you a gown. You may be certain of seeing me, before the 1st of January, 1771.— The clearance is immaterial.—My mother may expect more patterns.— Almost all the next Town and Country Magazine is mine. I have an universal acquaintance: my company is courted every where; and, could I humble myself, to go into a compter, could have had twenty places before now; but I must be among the great: State matters suit me better than commercial. The ladies are not out of my acquaintance. I have a good deal

---

[11] There is some dispute as to whether or not *The Revenge* was performed. There is no record of it from the announcements of Marybone Gardens. See Notes for chapter 8.

of business now, and must therefore bid you adieu. You will have a longer letter from me soon—and more to the purpose.

Yours,
T.C.

Mary never received the promised gown or even another letter from her beloved brother. The oratorio was never performed or published. It may have ended up among the scraps beside his deathbed.

For the five remaining weeks of his life Chatterton cast about for inspiration and money. All that survives from these weeks are a few satirical letters on love bought with gold, on matrimonial "bliss" and matrimonial betrayal, his cynical verse, *Art of Puffing,* on how to make "the drug of rhime" go down, a bloody Ossian, a short pastoral in oratorio form celebrating the African landscape and the sexual consummation of black lovers, in which the natural beauties and noble love from this far-off land have been neatly Anglicized à la Collins. A short story, *Maria Friendless,* published in July's *Town and Country,* was later discovered to have been plagiarized nearly word-for-word from a short story in Samuel Johnson's *Rambler.* Except for some lines that betrayed his unquenchable longings for Polly Rumsey and the Anglo-African arias, there is very little in all these lines of poetry and prose that reveals any faith in human nature. Instead the works betray restlessness combined with deep melancholy. Had Chatterton survived the summer of 1770 and gone on to some new mode of literary enterprise, the tormented emptiness of his last weeks might have been interpreted as another period of normal mourning similar to the previous summer when he had lost all hope for Rowley and Canynge. The difference was that in the summer of 1770, Chatterton's moral and emotional plight was desperate.

In his early days in London he had bravely stated to his mother, "A character is now unnecessary; an author carries his character in his pen." There is truth in this. The moral ambiguities expressed in Chatterton's writings are central to his character—and they also created the climate in which suicide could be seen as a "noble insanity of the soul."

As an impostor, Chatterton created the glorious imaginary world of William Canynge, a world constructed with such narrative sophistication that even the most anti of anti-Rowleyans, like Walpole and Johnson, were amazed that an untutored Bristol youth had been the actual author. As Thomas Rowley, Chatterton spoke with an honest and noble poetic voice, but when he turned from the false, imagined world to the true, modern world, he produced, for the most part, rather commonplace and imitative art. In essence, his counterfeits were an honest expression of his inner dilemmas, while his acknowledged freethinking pieces were instruments of expedience. The life and death of Thomas Chatterton evoke the same perplexing relationships between art and crime that are reflected in Thomas Mann's evaluation of the fictional impostor Felix Krull: "It is in essence the story of an artist; in it the element of the unreal and illusional passes frankly over into the criminal."

A less daring mind than Mann's could not regard this easy association between art and crime with such playful equanimity. The deadly solemn Rowleyan Jacob Bryant was appalled. To him the very notion of an impostor-poet was a monstrous aberration: "If a young lad of little or no principle should find a treasure of old poetry, and put it off for his own; I should not much wonder. But that such a person should compose to this amount, and then give the credit of it to another, is past my comprehension. It is repugnant to nature, and contrary to all experience."

But Mann had the right idea. Krull, liar, thief, and seducer of married women, rises to creative heights only after he begins to impersonate Marquis Venosta. The life history of an impostor-artist poses questions central to the creative impulse itself. Are we not often bewildered by what we take to be the vast discrepancy between an artist's sublime work and his mundane or violent personal life? Moreover, is it not true that the unreal and illusional world created by the artist is always a sleight of hand, a confidence game in which we, the illusion-hungry audience, are abettors to a falsehood? Yet at the same time both artist and audience agree to enter into a shared illusion which ennobles them through the beauty of a fabricated world.

Where do the Rowley narratives fit in? Are they a species of criminality? Or are they expressions of the truth-telling aspect of art? And what of the moral character of Thomas Chatterton? Was he inspired by criminal passions or artistic ones? He surely was a lying boy who hid beneath the habit of a virtuous priest, a self-seeking flatterer who one month paraded as a freethinking Patriot and the next preened himself to wear the purple robes of a proministerial journalist, an author who could write as well on one side as the other provided he was paid well enough. What are we to make of his professed love for Wilkes, whom he so easily labels a treasonous Pretender Patriot, or his adoration of Beckford, who is flattered for "the goodness of your heart," "the soundness of your principles," "the merit of [your] cause," and "the rectitude of your conduct," and yet whose death makes the writer gladder by three pounds, thirteen shillings?

What had happened to the audacious freethinker, the aloof, indifferent

Chatterton who valued neither the praise nor censure of the multitude, the young poet whose consciousness of doing right, whose rage of satire took precedence over a dinner or a girl at night? Had Chatterton simply abandoned the struggle to balance ideals and self-interest, a conflict which was once a "curst Tormentor" of his inner peace? Had he decided it was no longer worth raging against the social and political injustices of his time? Had he, after all his protest, adopted the motto of the prudent, "Flattery's a cloak and I will put it on"?

From his first published writings, this conflict between belief and self-interest had blazed. The same ten-year-old who composed the lines celebrating the birth of Christ—"The God from whom Creation sprung / Shall animate my grateful Tongue; / From him I'll catch the Lay,"—was already turning out the satiric poems and letters addressed to Apostate Will, "a preacher and what not / as long as money could be got," to Sly Dick, whose angelic voices justify and inspire him to heavenly theft, to the church master who gets "a *profitable Job* out of the Church," by carting off graveyard clay to his brick-making shop.

His Rowley year was a celebration of men who cared less for fame, wealth, or family interests than for painting, sculpture, architecture, poetry, theater, and the honor of Bristol. Like *Last Epiphany* and *Hymn for a Christmas Day,* the Rowley works are clear statements of belief: belief in the goodness and nobility of the founders of Bristol, belief in art and nature. But the freethinking months recall Sly Dick and Apostate Will, when the Colston Blue-Coat boy had taken up his pen to mock the Bristol elders, mock their mercenary mentality, expose all those guilty of cowardly orthodoxy, and all who placed personal and financial gain above true belief. Later, as a scrivener's apprentice, just before he left for London, Chatterton damned all of Bristol: "The Muses have no Credit here; and fame, / Confines itself to the mercantile name."

Even in Chatterton's scornful attacks his struggle to remain true to his beliefs is always just below the surface. As we bear witness to his confrontations with the perversions and villainies to which all humans are prey, it becomes clear that a youth who rages so violently against the corruptions of the world around him is warring with the corruptions in his own soul.

What cruel internal scenarios were afflicting the seemingly intrepid youth who set out so bravely for London, the freethinker who had forged his personal declaration of independence out of his loathing for slavery of any kind?

Bristol may keep her prudent Maxims still;
I scorn her Prudence, and I ever will.

> *Since all my Vices magnify'd are here,*
> *She cannot paint me worse than I appear,*
> *When raving in the Lunacy of ink,*
> *I catch the Pen and publish what I think—*

In the short time, somewhat less than a year, between ceasing to fabricate the world of Sir William Canynge and beginning to produce for the eighteenth-century literary marketplace, Chatterton mastered the writing styles of his day. His precocity with language and prosody combined with his distinctive gifts of attunement and imitation enabled him both to "know" the ear of his audience and to be able to please it. But then every modern poet, from the most individual to the most conventional, is at some time, to some extent, a fabricator or impersonator. For example, were it not for Ezra Pound's "caesarian operations" on *The Wasteland*, the young T.S. Eliot might have published a poem ringing with imitation and stylistic allusions. The first four sections were introduced by parodies of "the music hall monologue of a rake, the stiffened replica of Elizabethan narrative, . . . a piece of misogynistic satire in the manner of Pope." As Peter Ackroyd, Eliot's biographer, comments on these excised sections, "If these passages veer close to parody or pastiche, they are not simply imitations but rather creative borrowings of another style and syntax which releases a plethora of voices and perceptions."

James Joyce, too, invented a world founded on the reproduction of literary voices. The Joycean world which begins with Homer and ends with Joyce's Dublin achieves its historical continuity with journalese, Anglo-Saxon, scientific prose, romantic narrative. Eliot closes *The Wasteland* with allusions to Dante, Kyd, de Nerval, Sanskrit. Pound did not excise these, but he did rescue Eliot from his more self-conscious imitations, releasing in the process the underlying poetic cadences. The cadences, not the pirated words and phrases, are what bring the reader into contact with the lush poetic world beneath the broken images, stony rubbish, dry stones, dead trees, brown fog. The images of *The Wasteland* are both Eliot's and not Eliot's. As Ackroyd says, there is "a continual oscillation between what is remembered and what is introduced, the movement of other poets' words just below the surface of his own."

Eliot proclaimed the artistic principle underlying his inspired pirating from the past.

> . . . the historical sense involves a perception, not only of the pastness of the past, but of its presence; the historical sense compels a man to write not merely with his own generation in his bones, but with a feeling that the

whole of the literature of Europe from Homer and within it the whole of the literature of his own country has a simultaneous existence and composes a simultaneous order.

Eliot questioned the tendency to praise a poet most for "those aspects of his work in which he least resembles anyone else":

> We dwell with satisfaction upon the poet's difference from his predecessors, especially his immediate predecessors. . . . Whereas if we approach a poet without this prejudice we shall often find that not only the best, but the most individual parts of his work may be those in which the dead poets, his ancestors, assert their immortality most vigorously. And I do not mean the impressionable period of adolescence, but the period of full maturity.

Robert Browning, in *Essay on Chatterton,* judged Chatterton's peculiar poetic fate to have been induced by the liabilities of imitation.

> Genius almost invariably begins to develop itself by imitation. It has, in the short-sightedness of infancy, faith in the world: and its object is to compete with, or prove superior to, the world's already recognised idols, at their own performances and by their own methods. This done, there grows up a faith in itself: and no longer taking the performance or method of another for granted, it supersedes these by processes of its own. It creates, and imitates no longer. . . . This first instinct of Imitation, which with the mediocre takes the corresponding mediocre form of an implied rather than expressed appropriation of some other man's products, assumed perforce with Chatterton, whose capabilities were of the highest class, a proportionably bolder and broader shape in the direction his genius was to take. And this consideration should have checked the too severe judgment of what followed. For, in simple truth, the startling character of Chatterton's presentment, with all its strange and elaborately got up accompaniments, was in no more than strict keeping with that of the thing he presented.

Browning was not the first to recommend the literary merits of Chatterton's gift for imitation. George Gregory, Chatterton's official and very proper eighteenth-century biographer, grasped that Chatterton's premature genius, lamentable as it was in so many other respects, at least enabled him to resist the "puerile affectation" that generally guided young aspiring poets. Those pretentious chaps, impressed as they were by the naive premise that worthwhile literature should borrow *nothing,* strove for complete originality. But the poetic virtuoso Chatterton knew better. "He knew that original genius consists of forming new and happy combinations rather than in searching after thoughts and ideas which never had occurred before; and that the man who never imitated has seldom acquired a habit of good writing."

Of course, when he posed as Rowley, Chatterton was neither a plagiarist nor an imitator. He invented an entire imaginary world and the writings that explained, supported, and celebrated that world. It was only afterward, when he tried to become a legitimate eighteenth-century writer, that Chatterton resorted to imitation and plagiarism. Even Chatterton defenders, like Browning and Gregory, became confused on these distinctions.

Another of Chatterton's champions was Anna Seward, herself a well-known eighteenth-century writer and author of nearly a dozen volumes of letters. As she takes it upon herself to defend the legitimacy and beauty of Chatterton's non-Rowleyan poetry she uses the opportunity to explain her own plagiarism of some lines from Chatterton. "Certainly the resemblance between Chatterton's personification of winter and mine are too strong to have been the result of coincidence, and must be unconscious plagiarism and that on my part . . . I conclude some features of Chatterton's impersonation of that season came forward, from the large deposit of English poetry in my brain, and rendered me an unconscious plagiarist."

From April 26, when he had arrived, buoyant and confident, in London, until the beginning of July, Chatterton tried valiantly to tailor his talents to the London literary marketplace. The first week in May brought success and promised more. From one magazine, the young author was receiving four guineas a month. The *History of England* he was planning would bring at least double his earnings. He was hoping to write occasional pieces for several daily newspapers. He was hoping to meet Wilkes. He knew all the intellectuals at the coffeehouses, and he was promising his Bristol writer friends he would use his vast influence to get their journal articles published.

When the aspiring Patriot journalist heard of Beckford's death, he went to pieces. His own fever, acquired just a day or so before Beckford's death, hung on for nearly two weeks. Around this time he moved to the disreputable Brooke Street—one more portent of his ineluctable, irreversible downward plunge.

For a brief moment things reversed. The first three weeks in July swooped Chatterton to a precarious pinnacle of success. He had adjusted to Beckford's death. With the three pounds, three shillings earned from the Beckford elegies and the five guineas, five shillings from his burletta,

Chatterton was at last able to visit the London shops and fulfill his childhood promise by purchasing china, fans, patterns, and other finery for his mother and sister. He was composing an oratorio, promising his sister a new gown and planning a visit home.

Between that last letter home on July 20 and the mixing of the arsenic potion on August 24, there is a peculiar exchange with George Catcott,[12] and a heady letter to William Smith, the Bristol friend who had introduced him to Catcott. The Smith letter dispenses entirely with any news of actual life in London. After some excited salutations, Chatterton simply runs on with a string of the hardest words in the Kersey dictionary:

> ... The Poem ran thus. The first Line, an Acatalectos, the second an Aetiologia of the first. The third an Acyrologia; the fourth an Epanalepsis of the third, Fifth a Diatyposis of beauty. Sixth a Diaporesis of success. Seventh a Brachycatalecton; Eighth an Ecphonesis of Ecplexis. In short an Enypnino, could not contain a greater Synchysis, of such accidents without Syzygia. I am resolved to forsake the Parnassian Mount and would advise you to do so too, and attain the Mystery of composing Smegma. Think not I make a Mycterismus in mentioning Smegma. No; My Mnemonsyne will let me see (unless I have an amblyopia) hour great Services which shall be always remembered by:
>
> Hasmot Tnchaorett

The hypermanic tone and medical allusions that characterize the Smith letter hint of mental agitation and venereal disease. It was written on the anniversary of William's brother's suicide the previous August 12. For news of Chatterton after mid-August, we have only the few sketchy details revealed by Chatterton's neighbors, some unauthenticated last poems, and the unverified rumors that continued to accumulate around Chatterton's name for several decades after his death.

Unlike Browning, Gregory, and the graciously unconscious Seward, the average commentators on Chatterton's fate were not favorably impressed with the poetics of imitation. For them Chatterton's poetry could only be judged while simultaneously apportioning the good and evil in the young poet's soul. Chatterton's detractors seemed to delight in ferreting out his moral indiscretions. His protectors went to great lengths to dignify every word or act that might connote immorality.

Said one of these protectors, "I fear thou hast uttered impious and blasphemous thoughts, which none can defend and which neither thy

---

[12] See chapter 9.

youth, nor thy fiery spirit, nor thy situation can excuse." Nevertheless, with some righteous indignation toward those who were defaming the dead youth, this same champion of Chatterton protested, "Let many of thy bitterest enemies reflect what were their own religious principles, and whether they had any, at the age of fourteen, fifteen, and sixteen."

His suicide alone would have been sufficient to condemn Chatterton to everlasting infamy. Even his most loyal defenders were at a loss to invent justifiable motives for that heinous act. After all, to take one's own life was a sin and a crime, an act committed by a criminal, one whose soul was already depraved. Throughout Europe, degradation of the bodies of suicides was commonplace. A suicide could be punished by having his dead body bound to the back of a cart and dragged to a public square, where it might be hung upside down for a day or so. A suicide's corpse could be burned and thrown onto the garbage heap. The body might be put in a barrel and floated down the river out to sea. In some cities suicides who died in bed or in the kitchen or the attic could only be taken from the house through a window so as not to contaminate the doorways through which the survivors must pass. In burial, stones were placed on the head and stakes driven through the chest as though a suicide were as fiendish as a vampire. Bodies of unclaimed suicides were carted off to anatomy classes. Most suicides, especially those of low social station, were denied the rights of burial. Unsuccessful suicides were sent to jail. A suicide's property was confiscated and turned over to the state, depriving his family of their rightful inheritance.

As the eighteenth century progressed, the laws on suicide were humanized. The family of the suicide was granted the right of appeal. The bereaved could have their beloved dead one declared *non compos mentis*. So many families used the *non compos* loophole to seek emotional and financial redress that in 1755 the English jurist William Blackstone felt it urgent to warn the juries:

> But this excuse ought not be strained to the length to which our coroner's juries are apt to carry it, vis., that every act of suicide is an evidence of insanity; as if every man who acts contrary to reason had no reason at all; for the same argument would prove every other criminal *non compos*, as well as a self-murderer.

Blackstone's cautionary morality notwithstanding, coroner juries were turning in the verdict of *non compos* more and more. The verdict of the inquest into Chatterton's death was suicide by reason of insanity. Was it a real *non compos mentis* or merely a legal one? In 1810, Robert Southey disclosed that Mary had once been confined to a mental asylum. Thereafter, the judgment of a taint of madness in Chatterton's character was said to have been confirmed.

If one believed that only madmen committed suicide, then there was proof of madness in Chatterton's expressed beliefs on the topic of suicide. And there was Chatterton's little morality tale on love and suicide, *The Unfortunate Fathers,* which he wrote in late December 1770. Though Chatterton pretended that the beliefs of his love-thwarted hero were not necessarily his own, the suicide note that the hero dashed off to his father before ending his life did make a good New Year's sermon for the readers of *Town and Country.*

> There is a principle in man, (a shadow of the divinity) which constitutes him the image of God; you may call it conscience, grace, inspiration, the spirit, or whatever name your education gives it. If a man acts according to this regulator, he is right: if contrary to it, he is wrong. It is an approved truth, that this principle varies in every rational being. As I can reconcile suicide to this principle, with me it is consequently no crime. Suicide is sometimes a noble insanity of the soul: and often the result of a mature and deliberate approbation of the soul. If ever a crime, it is only so to society: there indeed it always appears an irrational emotion: but when our being becomes dissocial, when we neither assist or are assisted by society, we do not injure it by laying down our load of life. It may seem a paradoxical assertion, that we cannot do wrong to ourselves, but it is certain that we have power over our own existence.

Suicide was still on Chatterton's mind in the last weeks of January 1770. He composed a short poem, *Sentiment:*

> Since we can die but once what matters it
> If Rope or Garter Poison Pistol Sword
> Slow wasting Sickness or the sudden burst
> Of Valve Arterial in the noble Parts
> Curtail the Miserys of human Life
> Tho' varied is the Cause the Effect's the same
> All to one common Dissolution tends.

As Chatterton's bold deliberations on death and suicide were being published, the liberated Enlightenment philosophers he emulated were still exercising great caution on those subjects. Hume's *Essay on Suicide,* written during the 1750s and certainly more eloquent and carefully reasoned than the brazen sentiments of the young Bristol poet, was not made available to the general public until after his death in 1777. Though many of Hume's philosophical meditations were at least somewhat familiar to educated readers, his words on suicide were considered dangerous to public morality and injurious to his own reputation. Almost as soon as the essay was finally published, it was suppressed again.

Hume differed from Chatterton in his idea that only the person, not the society, is harmed by an act of suicide. But like Chatterton, he felt compelled to reconcile a belief in God with the act of suicide.

> Were the disposal of human life so much reserved as the peculiar province of the Almighty that it were an encroachment on his right, for men to dispose of their own lives; it would be equally criminal to act for the preservation of life as for its destruction. . . . It would be no crime in me to divert the *Nile* or *Danube* from its course, were I able to effect such purposes. Where then is the crime in turning a few ounces of blood from their natural channel?

Not long after Chatterton's suicide, despite the risks of speaking freely about the subject, enlightened men began to openly criticize the view that consigned suicides to everlasting shame and degradation. Even a vindictive man like Walpole would not abide the severe morality that denigrated and abused the reputations of those who chose self-destruction. Far from condemning Chatterton for his suicide, Walpole sympathized with the young man's pride, which he assumed had been its cause. Walpole, of course, had to transmute what might have been taken as weakhearted mercy into his customary vitriol. His generous moral convictions were allowed only in the context of his contempt for the commonplace moralities of his day. At first he found the topic of suicide excellent meat for his gossipy letters, in which he treated suicides of noblemen as signs of noble character. A bit later into the century, as the act of suicide began to attract some sympathy if not general acceptance, Walpole denounced the entire topic as a matter of utter boredom. "It is very provoking that people must be hanging or drowning themselves or going mad . . ."

On the Continent, though the number of suicides was probably about equal to that of the Britons, it was generally assumed that suicide was an English specialty, a reflection of the bittersweet melancholia of that gray island. For the romantics, the real suicide of Chatterton in 1770 and Werther's fictional one four years later were feats of triumph, supreme gestures of contempt toward the corrupt values of bourgeois society. By the end of the nineteenth century, as the science of sociology gained respectability, suicide was seen no longer as a heinous private exploit but as a grievous social problem. Finally, in fact as late as thirty years ago, the legal sanctions punishing the suicide and his family melted away. Nowadays neither gallows nor prison await the unsuccessful suicide but, as Alvarez writes in his classic study of suicide, *The Savage God*, "at worst, a period of observation in a psychiatric ward; more often he faced nothing more piercing than his own continuing depression." Like most suicides, Chatterton's reflected what Alvarez refers to as "this constant impurity of motive." The motives for Chatterton's suicide are as elusive as his motives for posing as Rowley. And both actions have been seen as manifestations of the same depravity.

In the decades immediately following Chatterton's death, commentators on his case paused briefly to speculate on the psychological motives for his two unlawful deeds—his counterfeiting of antique poetry and his suicide by arsenic poisoning. Madness could explain both these infamous acts. Yes, Chatterton must have been mad, truly *non compos*. Had he not marched about the streets of Bristol with a loaded pistol in his vest declaiming his readiness for suicide? Had he not publicly defended suicide, even reconciled it with a belief in God? Had he not terrorized the other servants at Lambert's by loudly announcing his intentions to commit suicide? And then, of course, there was that impulsive letter of suicidal intent to his freethinking friend Clayfield, written weeks before Lambert discovered the outrageously irreverent *Will*. And what about the testimony from his old school chum, Thistlewaite? That friend, himself a well-known liar and plagiarist whose testimony was always suspect, claimed that Chatterton had told him his goals when he left for London. "My first attempt shall be in the literary way: The promises I have received are sufficient to dispel doubt; but should I, contrary to my expectation find myself deceived, I will in that case turn Methodist preacher: Credulity is as potent a deity as ever, and a new sect may easily be devised. But if that too should fail me, my last and final resource is a pistol."

If insanity explained the boy's death, if it drove him to forgery, it was also used to explain his purported sexual profligacy. And although not every madman is an irreverent infidel, the consensus from admirers and attackers alike was that Chatterton was, at heart, a confirmed infidel, a godless person for whom suicide was a fit and just ending. Everything boiled down to the issue of godlessness. With that—the insanity and the religious infidelity together—the question of motives for suicide was laid to rest. No deeper explanation was required or sought.

Even as he calls attention to Chatterton's generosity and attachment to his mother and sister, "the unremitting attention, kindness and respect, which appear in the whole of his conduct towards them," Gregory, a charitable and sympathetic biographer, feels compelled to footnote his favorable commentary: "It can never be sufficiently lamented, that this aimiable propensity was not more uniform in Chatterton. A real love for his relations ought to have arrested the hand of suicide; but when religion is lost, all uniformity of principle is lost."

Gregory did deplore the Bristol youth's infidelity and his devotion to the speculative excesses of Hume and Voltaire, but his account was considered far too generous by many Britons. A goodly number of the upright citizens of the gray isle where eccentrics were usually tolerated were not to be swayed from their focus on the malevolence in the boy's character. Chatterton was to them the ultimate affront.

As he pondered the intensity of the indignation and hatred expressed toward the dead youth, a contemporary of Gregory's resolved, "There seems to be a general and inveterate dislike to the boy, exclusively of the poet; a dislike which many will be ready to impute, and, indeed not without the appearance of reason, to that insolence and envy of the little great, which cannot bear to acknowledge so transcendent and commanding a superiority in the humble child of want and obscurity."

After all, this impudent stripling had duped some of the most honored scholars of his day. The fact of his age, which might have protected him from the wrath of his mighty elders, seemed rather to rub salt in their wounds. His enthusiasms, his noisy proclamations of freethinking, his fiery temperament, his sexual vitality, his opposition to greed and tyranny, his proud spirit, all characteristics that in an older person might have been admired, winked at, or at least tolerated, were, because they came from an adolescent, feared and envied.

Even in these psychologically enlightened times, the bold narcissism, crude aggression, and fulminating sexuality of the adolescent can strike terror into the hearts of usually well-intentioned, liberal-minded adults. The attitude toward some of the more violent casualties that befall the younger generation—for example, death from drugs, alcohol, and speeding cars—is often expressed with a careless shrug: "What do you expect? It was a group of teenagers." When a child is becoming an adult, society is always at risk. The elders are fearful. The adolescent strains against personal limits and the personal risks he takes threaten tradition. With his towering physical and psychological presence, he is also a reminder of fecundity and new life. He is the germinator of new life. Will he leave us behind in the dust? We had better tie him down, flagellate him, consign him to seven years of apprenticeship, send him off to war, carve his body into our kind of manhood, indoctrinate him to the tribal laws and make sure he kneels before the power of the elders. Thomas Chatterton, the epitome of everything the average citizen feared and envied about the younger generation, did not submit.

For the romantics, Chatterton became an emblem and a source of inspiration. Though the romantics overdid the adulation, Chatterton was a fit image for their poetic morality. The poets could penetrate beneath the violence at the surface of Chatterton's actual life to the inner moral passions that had propelled him. They grasped that Chatterton, the fatherless boy, had no choice but to forge his own conscience. From early boyhood, the contamination of religious sentiments by lust for financial gain had deeply distressed him. He might have toyed with becoming a Methodist preacher as a way of salvaging his own freedom, but he never took that option. He may have been a freethinker in religion and politics but he never fooled himself about the corruptions of the Methodist mentality that was sweeping the land: "These Representatives of God / In Color, way of Life and Evil / Should be so very like the Devil" or the hymns they sang, "composed so oddly / Youd swear twas bawdy Songs made godly."

Almost to his last days in London, Chatterton continued to search for someone or something to which he could be true. But his curious way of intermingling sexual escapades with spiritual chastity and infidelity with political and religious purity was never discreetly hidden. His brazen opposition to what ordinary mortals regarded as sacred was always out in the open, plainly exhibited for all the world to behold, yet most people could not discern the virtue in his honest stance. All they could grasp was that something must be seriously wrong with that young man from Bristol.

In *Love and Madness,* a best-selling novel of 1780 based two-thirds on the murder of Lord Sandwich's mistress by the love-thwarted Reverend Hackman and one-third on the suicide of Chatterton, the author adapted Dryden's notion of the relationship between understanding and madness to support his own idiosyncratic interpretation of Chatterton's poetic genius. "I am sure," he proclaimed "that love and madness are near relations." If it wasn't the madness and the infidelity that explained one another, the suicide, the forgeries, and everything else, then it must have been the sex. And in those days the most direct and common route from sexual profligacy to moral and psychical insanity was venereal disease.

NINE

The Makings of a Romantic Hero

Fornication, Prostitution, Perversion, Gonorrhea, Syphilis, Opium, Suicide. Was Chatterton a profligate or a dreamy-eyed saint? The rationalizations and denials of Chatterton's biographers.
The sexual proclivities of the average eighteenth-century male. The follies and foibles of youth. Brothel specializations and the cult of virginity. Was it opium or arsenic that killed Chatterton? Was it gonorrhea or syphilis? From external behavior to internal reality.

"AS Saturn is posited in a sign out of all his dignities and is the lord also of the eighth house, his influence is implicative of certain ruin by means of wicked and debauched women, described by Venus conjoined by the worst rays of Saturn." Sibley the astrologer was one of those who ascribed to and promulgated the venereal disease theory of Chatterton's suicide. Mercury and Jupiter, the Sun and the Moon might play their little parts, but for a suicide, Saturn played the commanding role—with Venus as his handmaiden.

During the early rumblings of the Rowley controversy, the image of a dreadful libertine, a syphilis-ridden profligate and forger had become synonymous with the name Chatterton. The stains on Chatterton's character, his volatile temperament, his reputation as a villainous forger, his satirical attacks on organized religion, even the fact that he had been raised in indigence by an ignorant woman provided all the context necessary to

make of flimsy evidence an entirely plausible case that the precipitating cause of Chatterton's suicide was his salacious sexual appetite. Sibley's morality tale written in the heavens was a reflection of the widely held theory that Chatterton had severe untreated syphilis, which his champions alluded to as gonorrhea; not wishing the dreadful secret to become known, he was driven to suicide. One of his early biographers had asked, "Can anyone be sure he was not determined to seal his secret with his death?" Merely because he posed such a question, this scholar later became part of the argument in support of the venereal disease hypothesis. His question, however, probably referred to the secret of the Rowley forgeries.

More to the point, but in view of the source hardly conclusive, is the memorandum of the eighteenth-century antiquarian Michael Lort, who was determined to uncover the true facts of the life and death of Chatterton. He reports his interview with Thomas Cross, the apothecary from whom Chatterton purportedly obtained the fatal dose of arsenic: "Mr. Cross says he had the Foul Disease which he would cure himself and had calomel and vitriol of Cross for that purpose. Who cautioned him against the too free use of these, particularly the latter."

Lort was a shrewd scholar. He was measured and circumspect in his methods of interviewing and cross-questioning. However, since Lort was a personal friend of Horace Walpole, the writer often held responsible for Chatterton's suicide, he may not have been entirely objective when it came to evaluating Chatterton's character. If Chatterton were found to be a truly innocent youth, then Lort's friend and colleague Walpole would look worse. Among Lort's observations on Chatterton are the following:

> Both Mrs. Newtons and Mr. Thistlewaytes (sic) testimony in favour of C's moral character is to be received with grains of allowance for the [prejudices?] of a sister and a friend.
> Chatterton's Bristol acquaintance of the most abandoned sort.
> Regularity of his attendance not true [a comment on Lambert's favorable testimony] he was sometimes about at nights, and not in the best of company.
> It is certain that much of his time was spent in the company of disreputable young men.
> Profligacy equal to his abilities. Considering the magnitude of the latter I am inclined to think this is rather too hard a censure but surely not without good foundation.

Thistlewaite, a humdrum journalist, as usual defended his now famous childhood friend with words cleverly chosen to highlight every vice or failing that Chatterton had ever been accused of:

> It has been said that he was an unprincipled libertine, depraved in his mind, and profligate in his morals; whose abilities were prostituted to serve the cause of vice and whose leisure hours were wasted in continuous scenes of debauching and insanity.

Not so! protested Thistlewaite.
The following six lines from one of Chatterton's unauthenticated sui-

cide poems have been interpreted as a description of the mental and physical anguishes of the venereal disease that precipitated his suicide:

> *Life's thorny path incautiously I've trod,*
> *And bitterly I feel the chastening rod:*
> *O! who can paint the horrors of my mind,*
> *The stings which guilty conscience leave behind:*
> *They rage, they rend, they tear my aching heart,*
> *Increase the torment, agonize the smart.*

Those who wish to validate the poem's venereal implications and thereby prove Chatterton's profligacy will speculate that the poem never achieved its deserved status as genuine Chatterton because his idealizers refused to acknowledge anything that did not demonstrate his sexual innocence. If, however, Chatterton's suicide poem was written by a forger, then the foul disease deduction falls apart. A genuine poem implies an unchaste Chatterton. A forged poem implies an innocent Chatterton.

A nearly convincing confirmation of the venereal hypothesis was penned by the poet himself in the conclusion of his August 12 letter to George Catcott:

> Heaven send you the Comforts of Christianity: I request them not, for I am no Christian. Angels, according to the Orthodox Doctrine, are Creatures of the Epicene Gender, like the Temple Beaux: the Angel here, is of no such materials; for staggering home one Night from the Jelly house, I made bold to advance my hand under her covered way, and found her a very very Woman. She is not only an Angel, but an arch Angel; for finding I had Connections with one of her Assistants, she has advanced her demands from 6s. to 8s.6. per Week, assured that I should rather comply than leave my Dulcinea, and her soft Embraces.

Most of Chatterton's idealizers simply declare that the lines are a plumped-up exaggeration, a false claim to manliness by an inexperienced boy who wished to impress his sexually vigorless Bristol patron. Some biographers, however, would not resort to such an easy way around the problem. In 1930, the restrained, excruciatingly objective E. H. Meyerstein leaned heavily on his interpretation of the Angel pun as he plodded his way through and around the sexual-moral dilemmas of Chatterton's character.

Meyerstein first questions Chatterton's change in accommodations. After living nearly two months in Shoreditch, a poor but respectable working-class neighborhood, why would Chatterton have made such an abrupt move to the lodgings of Mrs. Angel? Mrs. Angel's house, Meyerstein reports, was located in the Upper Liberty of St. Andrews Holborn, in that "lowest of regions" where in 1720 "so many pretty gentlewomen are retain'd for the use and behalf of too many gentlemen in this great Protestant city and suburbs," and where by the turn of the century "children were brought up in such a way that the boys mostly become thieves and the girls prostitutes"; it was an address that would have conveyed "a poetic license disquieting enough."

That Mrs. Angel was a sack-maker and conducted her trade in the building of which she was also landlady is put forth as further evidence that Chatterton had, knowingly or innocently, "stepped into the forefront of 18th century London's temptation." Some dressmaking or mantua-making establishments were covers for Jellyhouses or houses of resort. As for Mrs. Angel's sack-making, says Meyerstein, "between a sacque and a mantua, in this connection, there is about as much difference as between a Johnsonian louse and flea—always allowing that Mrs. Angel, who was not to be found when Croft sought her, may have been a wholly respectable matron."

Meyerstein's trail of sexual innuendos goes on for several pages until readers are prepared to hear that when Chatterton says "she has advanced her demands from 6s. to 8s. 6 per week," he means that the Angel had raised the fees for sexual favors. However, Meyerstein arrives at an unexpected destination. Chatterton, he asserts, is alluding to rental fees. His six shillings "savours of braggadocio," and was obviously intended to deceive his Bristol acquaintances about the quality of his new dwelling place. "Six shillings for a garrett, even with two windows, as this seems to have had, was too much." Meyerstein follows this surprise interpretation with a scholarly discourse on comparative rentals, a precise description of the furnishings of a comparable attic room, concluding at last with a verification of his hypothesis, "six shillings a week would, in 1770, have been excessive." The question of the poet's sexual habits is dropped until some fifty pages later, when Meyerstein gets back to it via the issue of Chatterton's motives for suicide.

Meyerstein's interpretation of the apothecary's brief testimony to Lort is discreetly hidden away in the footnotes. Here Meyerstein explains the common uses of calomel, "used to cure the pox without spitting," and vitriol, "an emetic and detergent," and arsenic magnet, "a caustic for breaking venereal buboes."

From these fragments, Meyerstein momentarily revives the possibility that Chatterton had a severe, untreated case of what he called gonorrhea (the medicines described in the footnote were well-known treatments of syphilis). Then, presumably in the interests of absolute objectivity, Meyerstein neither validates nor rejects the gonorrhea theory. Instead he leads us once again to a murky region. "There is abundant motive for the poet's fate *without* this." Other problems were pressing on the boy's mind: his lack of literary success, the possibility that he would have to return to Bristol as a failure, his hunger and poverty, his loneliness. Meyerstein hedges, "Even if it [gonorrhea] could be proved the solution," that fact would not degrade the poet's character. And finally, in a burst of uncharacteristic geniality, Meyerstein wonders, "Is it likely that a mind so ardent, hasty, and inquisitive would be content to meet death wilfully with no previous experience, at first hand, of the sexual adventure?" Even Meyerstein, who forswears the sentimental, poor, helpless, starving boy motif, who proclaims his lack of interest in "the romantic child whose day dreams were peopled by 15th century familiars," succumbs finally to the emotional temptations that had become the hallmark of most modern biographical studies of Chatterton. The affectionate protectiveness he came to feel for the poet ultimately undermines his staunch scholarly resolutions.

Within the larger puzzle of the relationship of Chatterton's sexual life to his moral values and his eventual suicide is a smaller but no less pertinent one: why did his biographers adhere to such fastidious sexual attitudes? Using a range of rationalizations and denials, Chatterton's idealizing biographers replaced the unlikely portrait of syphilis-ridden profligacy with an equally fanciful picture of total and marvelous innocence.

As Chatterton began to substitute freethinking for the romantic mythology of Rowley and Canynge, he also began to substitute lines on rakedom and buckdom for the relatively conventional sentiments he had earlier composed on the relations between men and women. This change posed a considerable challenge to his biographers, who wondered whether or not the advanced sexual knowledge contained in those lines of poetry had come to Chatterton via direct experience. The fact that his sexual recommendations appeared in *Journal 6th,* which also demonstrated his exquisite familiarity with all sorts of religious and political heresies, did not advance the case for Chatterton's sexual innocence.

The nineteenth-century Chatterton authority Daniel Wilson is more realistic than some of his sentimental colleagues. He presents a logical and sympathetic argument that "Chatterton's masking began as an innocent dream of the child poet," that it was cherished as "an ideal reality," but that it soon became a deception supported by falsehood, spurious manuscripts, and fictitious details. He finds no evidence of the systematic profligacy described by others, but regrets "there are passages in Chatterton's modern prose and verse, and allusions in his letters, which repel by their irreverence and at times by their impurity." Wilson, who is referring here to *The Exhibition*, and *The Letter Paraphras'd*, goes no further in his descriptions of these passages.

John Nevill, a contemporary of Meyerstein's and one of Chatterton's more open-eyed biographers, surveys the evidence and concludes that Chatterton's readiness to portray himself as a monster of iniquity was actually his best defense. Had the youth really been so thoroughly libertine he would have kept his mouth shut.

> The dreamer, the child idealist who had peopled the silent spaces of St. Mary's with heroic visions of the Middle Ages, was overlaid by that obverse side of his dual personality—the sharp-witted, cynically minded young man of the world, who might have been twin-brother to Tom Jones. To show how little he cared what was said or thought about him, he flouted public opinion, boasted of his promiscuities, and greatly fancied himself in the role of a local Don Juan. Precocious in all ways, in sex experience as in everything else, this was precisely the sort of exhibitionistic attitude one would have expected him to adopt.

By hook or by crook, the most sentimental of Chatterton's biographers managed to sustain their belief in the marvelous boy's essential if not actual chastity. Although most of them presumably had not seen *The Exhibition* or *The Letter Paraphras'd*, Chatterton's infamous reply to the infamous letter from Miss Esther Saunders, an exchange that took place shortly before Chatterton departed for London, was challenge enough to their wishful images of an innocent Chatterton. Miss Saunders wrote:

> Sir:
> to a Blage you I wright a few Lines to you But have not the weakness to be Believe all you Say of me for you may Say as much to other young Ladys for all I now But I Cant go out of a Sunday with you for I ham a fraid we Shall be Seen to Go   Sir if it agreeable to you I had Take a walk with you in the morning for 5 I be Belive we Shant be Seen a bout 6 a Clock But we must wait with patient for ther is a Time for all Things.
>
> April 3, 1770
Esther Saunders

Appended is Chatterton's reply—which was never sent to Esther Saunders or to whomever else it might have been intended—epitomizing the way Chatterton could scornfully reject all who might ignore or reject him. Both items of correspondence were found among his papers after his death, sealed with red wax and unaddressed:

> There is a time for all things—Except Marriage my dear.
> And so your humble Servant
> T. Chatterton
> April 9th—

This Affair began Mar. 19th.70 and broke off April 9th.70—The young Lady wants to be married and can't keep her own Secrets—NB. Having no great Stomach for the Amour for divers good Causes and Considerations she therefrom otherwise moving, and having been forc'd into Correspondence by the Officiousness of B. was very indifferent about it and far from being chagrin at dismission Had also the Pleasure of seeming to break first—

☞ The Lady is not handsome but a great Fortune
✱ Miss W. a very pretty Girl now in Chace

Charles Edward Russell, author of the 1910 *Thomas Chatterton: The Marvelous Boy,* which is by far the most sentimental version of Chatterton's life, had no trouble enlisting Miss Saunders's letter and his marvelous boy's commentary for his hero's defense:

> Every line of his writing, every chance expression in his letters, every unfavorable recollection of those that had not liked or had envied him, has been exhumed and twisted into a derogatory significance. Following the licentious manner of the times, he gave pen to much idle and some objectionable matter, and all this has been cited as proof that he was a libertine and depraved person. . . . His innocent addresses to various young women of Bristol have been tortured into meaning that he was a sad rake, his admiration for Wilkes and his bold attacks on monarchy have been used to show his revolutionary and dangerous character, and over all have been spread the lurid colors of that word, "forgery."

Even a consummate sentimental like Russell might be at least partly right. Certainly the Saunders-Chatterton "affair" sounds like the sort of innocent activity Mary describes when she protests that her brother was wrongly accused of sexual profligacy. "He would frequently walk the colledge green with the young girls that statedly paraded there to show their finery. But I really believe he was no debauchee (tho some have reported it)."

Whether or not Chatterton himself was an actual innocent as Mary and Russell maintained, the playful tone of the "innocent adresses to various young women of Bristol" suggests that they were more innocent than not. In the middle of Chatterton's May 14 letter to his mother, he sends personalized regards, one by one, to what must have been nearly all the dear young ladies of Redcliffe. Tucked in (as though carelessly) among the other messages was an invitation to Polly Rumsey. The mixture of sexual longing and plain loneliness in Chatterton's plea to Polly is reminiscent of Baker's letters to Chatterton from Charleston, but most of these messages are light and witty.

> My sister will remember me to Miss Sandford. I have not quite forgotten her; though there are so many pretty milliners, &c. that I have almost forgot myself.
>
> Miss Rumsey, if she comes to London, would do well, as an old acquaintance, to send me her address.—London is not Bristol—We may patrole the town for a day, without raising one whisper, or nod of scandal: if she refuses, the curse of all antiquated virgins light on her—
>
> Miss Rumsey will tell Miss Baker, and Miss Baker will tell Miss Porter; that Miss Porter's favoured humble servant, though but a *young* man, is a very old lover; and in the eight and fiftieth year of his age: but that, as Lappet says, is the flower of a man's days: and when a lady can't get a young husband, she must put up with an old bedfellow.
>
> I left Miss Singer, I am sorry to say it, in a very bad way; that is, in a way to be married.
>
> Miss Thatcher may depend upon it, that, if I am not in love with her, I am in love with nobody.
>
> If Miss Love has no objection to having a crambo song on her name published, it shall be done.
>
> Begging pardon of Miss Cotton for whatever has happened to offend her, I can assure her it has happened without my consent.
>
> Let my sister send me a journal of all the transactions of the females within the circle of your acquaintance.
>
> Let Miss Watkins know, that the letter she made herself ridiculous by, was never intended for her; but another young lady in the neighbourhood of the same name.

John Ingram, less a sentimental denier than a champion rationalizer, explains the suggestive undertone to many of Chatterton's remarks to the young ladies of Redcliffe: "Chatterton's words home about the many girls he seemed to have been acquainted with prove that they were only acquaintances; that they must have been respectable girls, or he would not have named them to his mother as he did."

When pushed against the wall, however, as when he must juggle with the Jellyhouse-Dulcinea references in the August 12 letter to Catcott, Ingram resorts to blatant denial: although he quotes the letter in his biography, the Dulcinea section is excised. Ingram's notations concerning that letter must have been bewildering to his readers since the offensive lines he takes such pains to exonerate are absent, leaving only a scant, tantalizing whisper of their content.

> It will be plainly seen that the letter is filled mainly with nonsensical aimless gossip, including a few lines of unpublished, unreliant boyish braggadocio respecting certain amorous exploits of the writer, which those people familiar with his strong imagination will give not more credence to than they do to any other of his mythical confessions.

Though he too had his blind spots, George Gregory was at least aware of how his own character influenced his interpretations of his subject's. Gregory conceded his tendency to present Chatterton "in the pleasing light of an ingenious and virtuous youth." After recognizing that this was a personal reaction, Gregory was able to give the poet's character a rounded reading. Gregory strained against his tender impulses toward the youth and admitted, albeit regretfully, that he had acquired the "tincture of infidelity." "Infidelity or skepticism at least, may be termed the disease of young, lively and half-formed minds." As Gregory posed it, the crucial question was whether Chatterton had descended from speculative to practical irreligion. Was he among the "wretched," one of those impetuous youths who, once "released from all the salutary restraints of duty and religion," must thenceforth "seek for happiness in the vicious gratifications of this life"? Did Chatterton advance to actual sexual profligacy? Here Gregory drew the line. He refused to side with those who had "sullied the youth of Chatterton with the imputation of extraordinary vices or irregularities." Gregory's eighteenth-century good common sense, combined with a great deal more literary keenness than many of his contemporaries possessed, let him point with clear conscience to the grave fallacy of carelessly condemning Chatterton's character on the basis of the profane and immoral trends in his writings.

Nevertheless, when it came to everyday life, Gregory allowed his sentimental inclinations full rein. He insisted that with the exception of Polly Rumsey, to whom Chatterton wrote some poems and for whose family he composed an imaginary genealogy, the youth had little close acquaintance with any young lady. As for the celebrated Miss Rumsey, in every likelihood her relationship to Chatterton was purely literary. "A kind of Laura to his Petrarch," Gregory supposes, Polly served only to "polish his manners and exercise his fancy."

Gregory treats Chatterton's obviously libertine writings as unmentionables. Try as he may, he cannot vindicate them. With a sincere, almost fatherly compassion, he wishes aloud that Chatterton had never written such offensive lines. Yet even here Gregory distinguishes between his subject's character and the repugnance he feels toward these passages. This distinction protects the youth both from defamations resulting from literal readings of his satirical works and overidealizations resulting from conferring on Chatterton the virtues he had attributed to Rowley. Gregory's interpretive flexibility alone places him among the great intellectual adventurers: he refuses to make that easy reading from art to actual life which so often mars discussions of Chatterton—and became the curse of later literary interpretation.

Also to Gregory's credit is the fact that his portrait of the artist takes into account the fact that Chatterton did not grow into maturity and therefore never had the opportunity to rectify, explain, or censor his own impetuous youthful outpourings. If critics had treated, for instance, T.S. Eliot the way they treated Chatterton, our idea of Eliot would be drawn from the images in *The Love Song of St. Sebastian* (1914), a poem in which the speaker imagines flagellating himself while he strangles the woman performing fellatio on him; or seen from his *King Bolo and His Great Black Queen*, a pornographic epic abounding in allusions to buggery, penises, sphincters, and sexual parts and adventures of every imaginable sort. On the other hand, though no one nowadays sees Eliot as a combination of St. Sebastian and King Bolo, it is acceptable critical practice to presume Eliot's own genital hesitancies informed those of his sexually anxious Prufrock.

In his forties, Eliot could tell the world that he had written these perverse extravaganzas because he had been, and often still was, obsessed by the meaninglessness of human affairs. Torments of religious martyrdom and gross sexual indulgences had caught his youthful literary imagination, he said, because they helped alleviate his great anxieties. Eliot claimed that these anxieties derived from his precocious grasp of the central emptiness of feeling that characterized human existence.

As early as 1914, his last year at Harvard, Eliot started controlling which of his juvenile efforts he would allow to be published. Privately he continued to compose comic doggerel about King Bolo and send extracts to friends. On occasion he pretended to be Bolo's transcriber or editor. But in accordance with his wishes, the Bolo poems have never been published.

Chatterton, of course, took no such self-protective measures. Despite his thirst for preeminence, he did not suppose that his letters to Baker, his mother and sister, Catcott and Barrett, or his reply to Miss Saunders's letter would ever be published. At seventeen he did not have the foresight or inhibitions that Eliot had acquired by age twenty-six. And aside from Mary's occasional restraints and the calculated editing of his coconspirators Catcott and Barrett, no one advised or cautioned the young poet. Chatterton, however, could be a scrupulous editor of his own work. He usually tore up what he judged to be unworthy of his talents—although he saved scraps of letters and bits of poetry or prose, worthy or otherwise, that had some personal meaning to him. We will never know whether with advanced maturity he would or would not have chosen to censor any of his writings.

For two centuries, Chatterton biographers of vastly differing social values, writing styles, degrees of honesty, and intellectual range all tried to uphold the honor and chastity of the impostor-poet Thomas Chatterton. Each dutifully recorded the remark of one of Chatterton's London acquaintances that Chatterton was "guilty of no other follies and foibles than most young men are, at his age." None of these gentlemen had difficulty reporting on the customs and traditions of eighteenth-century England, mentioning the situations of housing, education, trade, religion, politics. But, with the exception of Meyerstein, who went farther but never far enough, they barely touch on the sexual atmosphere of eighteenth-century England, even though Chatterton's own sexuality is a specter that haunts each volume. When they do refer to his sexuality they do so only to discount it. Are they all exhibiting the adoptive instincts of the male sex toward a fatherless boy? Is their hesitancy based on a moral delicacy about the ambiguities of Chatterton's character? Or is it the direct influence of our straitlaced Anglo-American morality?[1] While there have been many rea-

---

[1] The French have not done much better by Chatterton's sexual passions. In 1832, in his novel *Stello* and in his *drame bourgeoise* entitled *Chatterton*, Alfred de Vigny portrays the young poet as a symbol of the imaginative and emotional sides of man's nature, of misunderstood genius ignored and victimized by materialistic society. In the *drame*, Chatterton's passions are pledged to the perfectibility of man. As a result of this moral purity he is totally unaware until moments before his suicide of his sexual love for Kitty Bell, the wife of the inhuman factory owner John Bell. On her side, Kitty's sexual impulses are held in check by shyness, reverence, purity, and sensitive maternal compassion. There is no sudden irresistible romantic passion here. So subtle are the desires of

sons why the sexual dimensions of Chatterton's character have been masked, the commanding motive concerns the apparent irreconcilability of the nobility of Rowley's moral sentiments with the obvious sexual vigor of young Chatterton.

In mid-eighteenth-century England, sexual straitness was associated with poetic and moral uprightness. To validate the grandeur of the poetry, the soul that produced it had to be proved untainted. It was incomprehensible that a sexually active being could be a morally active one. In the 1850s Delacroix wrote, "Real superiority admits no eccentricity—. The great genius is simply a being of a more highly reasonable order." Yet only three decades later Rimbaud spoke of the poet as the great Sick Man, the great Criminal, the great Accursed. By the twentieth century the sexual-moral eccentricities of poets was becoming an acceptable—indeed essential—ingredient of their life histories. The predicament of reconciling the highest order of imaginative beauty with the "baser" human emotions would become a preoccupation of modern consciousness. Nowadays, sexual normality and moral straitness are equated with a dullness of mentality. The poetic gifts of the pediatrician and the insurance executive are greeted with wonderment. Poets are supposed to be deranged, mad, perverse. As Eric Bentley says of Rimbaud's conception, "for a while startling, [it] is by now a received idea. By the standards of the modern man on the street, a Dylan Thomas is obviously a poet while William Carlos Williams is not. To justify his men or women, the biographer has to go back to the detail of their lives and discover the sinister, or at least the scandalous element. Ruskin, who had seemed one's primmest uncle is brought back—vindicated—as a child molester."

In a similar vein Gore Vidal has this to say about the cult of the mad poet: "Although poetry is no longer much read by anyone in freedom's land, biographies of those American poets who took terrible risks not only with their talents but with their lives are often quite popular; and testimonies, chockablock with pity, terror and awe provide the unread poet, if not his poetry, with a degree of posthumous fame." And, Vidal concludes, "If nothing else, suicide really validates, to use lit-crit's ultimate verb, the life if not the poetry."

Poor Chatterton just missed the boat to modernity. First he was dismissed as an unprincipled impostor and incorrigible profligate, but then he was sentimentalized into a pale powder by those who were trying to

---

Chatterton and Kitty that they must be informed by a Quaker friend that they are in love. Later that century, Rimbaud and Baudelaire, who extolled madness and sexuality for themselves, carried on the tradition of revering Chatterton as a martyred saint.

protect him. Less than a half century after his death, the English romantics were permitted risky lives, drugs, luxurious sexuality, and suicide. Posthumously as their emblem, Chatterton too was allowed his madness but only as that saintly impossibility, "the marvelous boy." Even as Chatterton was inventing his Rowley, composing his last will and testament, churning out his journal pieces and burlettas, Jean-Jacques Rousseau, the herald of modernity, was living in England under the protective wing of the speculative philosopher David Hume. Rousseau, the exiled *philosophe,* now in his late fifties, was writing up his adolescent indulgences, his masturbatory torments, his lust for flagellation, his exhibitionistic exploits in the alleys and byways of the Parisian countryside, his sexual initiation by the woman he called "mamma," Mme. Louise de Warens, his passion for his mistress Thérèse Levasseur, his abandonment of the five children she bore him. Like Chatterton, Rousseau had escaped from his apprenticeship. At sixteen he ran away from his master, an engraver who "managed in very short time to quench all the fire of my childhood, and to coarsen my affectionate and lively nature; he reduced me in spirit as in fact to my true condition as apprentice."

Rousseau's confessed passions were not merely the distinctive property of his eccentric nature. Nor were they, as is so often supposed, especially characteristic of the French. They resemble in deed and spirit the follies and foibles of English youth of the eighteenth century and those of the majority of their elders. In 1766, Rousseau permitted his precious Thérèse to accompany the twenty-five-year-old Boswell on a journey from Paris to London. (The facts of this journey we learn from Boswell's "confessions," not from Rousseau's.) The passages in which Boswell describes his eleven days of continual fornication with Thérèse have been destroyed, but the knowledge of what he wrote has been passed on through literary gossip. Apparently his first attempt with Thérèse was a total fiasco. The second time he did much better, so much so, he thought, that he was prompted to congratulate Thérèse, a woman twenty years his senior, on her marvelous fortune in having attracted a Scotch lover. Thérèse was diplomatic. "I allow," she said, "that you are a hardy and vigorous lover, but you have no art." She proceeded to instruct the young Boswell in the art of love, how to be gentle but ardent, how not to hurry. She reminded him of the great things that could be achieved by men's hands. Her inspired teaching had some effect. Boswell learned the rudiments of the art, and Thérèse had, at least, the satisfaction of having been an exceptional teacher. Boswell, who went on to derive all his sexual satisfaction outside his marriage, confessed to nineteen episodes of "urethetitis," at least a dozen of which were fresh gonorrheal infections, the others probable recurrences. Boswell made no secret of his own appetites, his gambling, drinking, running amok in the street, seducing married women; Samuel Johnson tolerated them with good-natured amusement. Boswell in turn kept details of Johnson's rumored indulgence in flagellation off-the-record. Samuel Johnson represented the letter of eighteenth-century sexual mores, but Boswell was the spirit. Somewhere in between was probably the actuality.

Any English youth inclined toward sexual or other extravagances had elders enough to emulate, as well the unspoken apprentice code of behavior to guide him. The rules of indenture—"Fornication he shall not commit. Matrimony he shall not contract"—were honored more in legal documentation than in observance. Many of the working- and middle-class boys who signed such documents were notorious for finding ways around the sexual starvation imposed upon them by their indentures.

As formal higher education does now, so apprenticeship then acted as the crucible for adolescent identity. During the seventeenth and eighteenth centuries there was a sizable urban apprentice subculture renowned for its riotous living, lust, cockfighting, defiance of authority. By the eighteenth century these young men between the ages of fourteen and twenty-one were viewed as "a constant threat to the social order." Some social commentators observed, and with reason, that the intensity of a young man's sexual and aggressive passions might be directly correlated with the harshness of his apprenticeship existence.

In the eighteenth century, the interval between pubescence and marriage steadily increased in all segments of society—at least for males. Unless they resorted to prostitutes, more and more young men spent longer and longer portions of their sexually mature years with no other sexual outlet than masturbation. The first popular pamphlet on the moral and physical dangers of masturbation was published in 1710. By 1760, this pamphlet, written by a clergyman who chose to remain anonymous, had gone through nineteen English editions and sold thirty-eight thousand copies. It was entitled *Onania, or the heinous sin of self-pollution and its frightful consequences for both Sexes considered.* For all his terrifying clerical admonishments, the author of *Onania* recognized that genital arousal was not a torment exclusive to the male sex.

The insistence on virginity before marriage for respectable girls, the unprecedented growth of lifelong bachelorhood for the younger sons of the upper class, the increasing delay in age of marriage, and the overall increase in urban population was accompanied by a steady rise in the number of prostitutes in urban centers like Bristol and London.

Prostitution was an indelible feature of daily life. Visits to brothels were standard items in the budgets of middle- and upper-class bachelors. For those without sufficient income, there were nighthouses, coaches, dark alleys where a man might give a girl an evening meal or a bottle of wine in return for her favors. What was unique about eighteenth-century English prostitution was its diversification. Brothels and nighthouses, though nominally illegal, abounded and catered to every class, pocketbook, and sexual taste. Some of the diversification arose out of the need to accommodate the twenty to thirty thousand bachelor apprentices who came to England's commercial cities.

There were the grand courtesans and the elegant villas from which they operated. And strolling street whores could be seen clustering around the Strand or St. James's Park, available for mere shillings. The gentleman with a large pocketbook could satisfy or acquire more exotic sexual tastes. For the wealthiest there were the lavish balls at which men did nothing but meet, examine, and bargain with courtesans. Judging by the entrance fee of Mrs. Prendergast's erotic balls at Pall Mall—five guineas, or the sum that Catcott paid to Mrs. Chatterton for her son's writings—these were very expensive and available to few. Then there were the highly celebrated specialty brothels and flagellation houses—which were also quite costly and considered by other Europeans to be an English specialty. While the whole spectrum of London sex habits was an affront to the respectable, it was homosexuals who attracted the most virulent criticism. The brothels that were most harassed by the authorities were the "molly houses," establishments reserved for homosexual practices.

As prostitution and its erotic specializations flourished, so did the double standard that gave rise to the cult of female chastity. The latent association between prostitution and virtue could assume diverse and manifestly contradictory forms. For example, the second most popular perversion after flagellation, more widespread in eighteenth- and nineteenth-century England than anywhere else in the world, was defloration—a brothel specialization that became a mania, creating an unprecedented demand for virgin prostitutes. The view of the prostitute as the most efficient guardian of virtue derived from the Bible and ancient Greece. Augustine expressed it succinctly: "Remove prostitution from human affairs and you would pollute the world with lust." In 1714, Bernard de Mandeville proposed the establishment of state-licensed brothels to protect the innocent from venereal disease and other evils. In "A Modest Defense of Publick Stews," Mandeville argued that his plan would not only reduce venereal disease, it would eradicate masturbation, cut down on too frequent or immoderate enjoyment of intercourse, and halt the debauching of modest women. Mandeville's proposals did not get very far. Nor did a counterproposal of another social reformer who suggested polygamy as the antidote to venereal disease and the prostitution problem.

From the fifteenth to eighteenth centuries, the variety of treatments for venereal disease, especially gonorrhea, increased. The three most common subjects in the advertisement columns of English eighteenth-century periodicals were cures for venereal disease, cosmetics, and books—in that order. By the early 1700s there were enough men and women afflicted with venereal disease to create an embarrassing dilemma for the medical profession. An inquiry into hospital practices conducted in 1736 revealed that venereal disease was thought of as a form of punishment for sins of the flesh, a transgression of Christian morality. Therefore, at most large hospitals, venereal disease patients were either not admitted at all or accepted at a very large contribution. Any venereal inpatient who had inadvertently gained admission for the treatment of some other illness "was to be discharged immediately without awaiting cure." Presumably this regulation was meant for the protection of other patients.

The treatment of venereal disease was left to private practitioners, who fell into two categories: physicians who were philosophers, medical scholars, or theorists; and surgeons. The surgeons then fell into three classes: those who could perform surgery; barber-surgeons (like William Barrett); and apothecaries (like Thomas Cross). The physician and the surgeon, who usually had hospital appointments, were looked up to by the public, who rarely had the opportunity to see either of them. The barber-surgeon and the apothecary did most of the general practice. Gradually the surgeon-apothecary became the specialist in the treatment of urinary disorders and skin complaints. Indeed, it was "the cure of Venereal Disease, upon which alone the Subsistence of three Parts in four of all Surgeons in town" depended. And though they did not consistently distinguish syphilis and gonorrhea by name, most barber-surgeons and apothecaries were well versed in the differential symptomatology and treatment approaches.

While Boswell was on the high side of the frequency calculations, one scholar has estimated, perhaps fancifully, that the average sexually active bachelor or dissatisfied husband could count on a half dozen or so attacks of gonorrhea; gonorrhea was as everyday an occurrence as the practice of prostitution. By 1700 the Latin terms "ardor" or "incendium" to describe gonorrhea and their anglicized equivalents, "brenning" or "burning" had fallen into disuse. But the word "piss" and the expression "pissing pins and needles" were in common use. The gonorrhea terminology of Continental Europe had its equivalents. In a letter to Voltaire, Frederick the Great reports: *"J'eus l'honneur / De recevoir, par mon malheur-* / *D'une certaine imperatrice* / *Une bouillante chaud pisse.* [2]

In short, gonorrhea was a rather unremarkable fact of a sexually active young man's life in the London of 1770. So commonplace an infection would not be regarded as a dread secret. Some might even boast of it. It was not likely to provoke thoughts of suicide.

There are speculations that Chatterton may have had gonorrhea and then died of an accidental overdose of some combination of drugs. Mr. Cross, the apothecary, enjoyed exchanging ideas with the eccentric young poet and might have regularly supplied him with a number of medications in addition to those he confessed to when cross-examined. Very likely, the apothecary would have given Chatterton opium, which was popular then as a stimulant and painkiller. Chatterton wrote to his sister shortly after his move to Mrs. Angel's house, "But, I don't repent that I have this cold; for there are so many nostrums here, that tis worth a man's while to get a distemper he can be cured so cheap." In his *History of Bristol*, Barrett reports of Chatterton's death: "He took a large dose of opium, some of which was picked out from between his teeth after death, and he was found the next morning a most horrid spectacle with limbs and features distorted as after convulsions, a frightful and ghastly corpse."

The surgeon Barrett would have known that opium alone, in any dosage, could not have caused such bodily contortions. Nevertheless, two possibilities at least are raised by Barrett's authoritative qualification of the coroner's arsenic diagnosis. One is that Chatterton used some opium to anesthetize the pain caused by the arsenic potion. Another is that Chatterton did not consciously set out to destroy himself. He might have taken arsenic and opium in combination in order to simultaneously cure his venereal disease and alleviate the painful and discomforting symptoms. If this were the case, his death could have been accidental.

The possibility that Chatterton was a habitual user of opium was given some validation in 1947 when a puzzling deep stain running through nineteen pages of his London notebook was subjected to chemical analysis. The forensic expert who conducted the analysis reported that a sample of the stained section contained the opium alkaloid. Whether Chatterton's death was due to an accidental or intentional overdose of drugs, what type of venereal disease he did or did not have, whether that disease was related to his possible drug habits all remain something of a mystery, and presumably will always remain so. However, some conjectures are more plausible than others.

---

[2] I had the honor / to receive, worse luck / From a certain empress / a boiling hot piss.

The two remedies that the apothecary purportedly recommended to Thomas Chatterton, calomel—a white tasteless powder used as a fungicide and purgative, technically known as mercurous chloride—and oil of vitriol—sulfuric acid—were not typically suggested for an uncomplicated gonorrhea. Rather, they were among the more drastic remedies for the "foul disease" syphilis—an infection which was far more likely to provoke thoughts of suicide, especially in a proud young man like Chatterton.

In contrast to gonorrhea, syphilis was a comparatively rare and dreaded disease. The most severe form of syphilis, "the great pokkes," which spread in epidemic proportions across Europe during the fifteenth and early sixteenth centuries, was by the eighteenth century no longer characteristic, but syphilis was still referred to as "the evil pox," and nobody bragged of having acquired it. At all three stages, from the initial venereal cankers—"buboes"—to the secondary phase pustules that could erode pharynx, nose, or sexual organs and cause excruciating muscle pains and enlarged lymph nodes—"gummata as large as an egg"—to the third internal phase in which the disease could destroy heart, blood vessels, spinal cord, and brain and culminate in general paresis or death, the symptoms were debilitating, very difficult to alleviate, nearly impossible to eradicate totally, and as apt as not to leave telltale stigmata such as ulcerated skin scars, the eroded saddlenose, baldness, patchy loss of body hair including eyebrows and eyelashes. Gonorrhea would have marked Thomas Chatterton as just another careless London youth. Syphilis was something else again.

In his most impressive Rowley counterfeit, *The Rolle of Seyncte Bartlemeweis,* on the art treasures, architecture, theater, and statuary of Bristol, Chatterton inserts several footnotes designed to show the learned surgeon-historian that he is an expert on the fine distinctions between gonorrhea and syphilis:

> 6. The Burning. Rowley is not the only writer who comprehends the Leprosie of his time under the general name of the Brenning.
> 7. A Mormall is defined "a Sore whereynne the fleshe cleaveth to the Bone and the bone brastethe, spewinge oilie reinynge." I leave Mr. Barrett to determine whether this is not a Definition of Nodes and Tophs . . .
> 8. The watry, is also called the reining Leprosie. I have seen no particular Definition, but suppose it means the Gonnorrhea.
> 9. The blacke Maingere (says Rowley) taketh offe the h_____ and the bodie is hylte wythe bouches; and sharpe Peynis.

Because of the terror aroused by its ravages, syphilis acquired around it a mythology of xenophobia. Beginning in the fifteenth century, the

English referred to the French pox, as did the Germans, who called it *Frantzozischen Pocken* and the Italians, who called it *Mal Francese*. The French had their *Mal de Naples*. Syphilis was known as *Dutch Spaanse Pocken* by the Portuguese, the Disease of the Germans by the Polish and by the Russians as the Disease of the Polanders.

From the fifteenth century (and very likely much before) until Dr. Paul Ehrlich's discovery in the early twentieth century of the 606 arsenic compound, the standard treatment of syphilis was an ointment of mercury or some compound of mercury such as calomel. All along critics of the mercury cures pointed out that they could be as murderous as the foul disease itself. One eighteenth-century proponent of metallic mercury was nicknamed Dr. Quicksilver—a name that slipped first to quacksalver, then to quack.

Throughout the ages the mercury formulas differed, each practitioner favoring his personal ointment base. But the effective ingredient and proportion was from one-eighth to one-tenth mercury. Given the carelessness of the inquest and burial procedures that attended Chatterton's death, it is as reasonable to infer that he died from an overdose of mercurous chloride as from arsenic poisoning. Either way, the poet's death may not have been a suicide.

The argument for a causal relationship between Chatterton's venereal disease and his premature death, intentional or accidental, is fairly convincing only if we are satisfied with a normative view of Chatterton's life; that is, that he was vulnerable to the same follies and foibles as other young men his age and therefore was genitally active, at times with prostitutes who very likely contaminated him with gonorrhea. Even staying within these conjectures, the normative view quickly reveals its limitations. The questions remain: Did Chatterton contract the commonplace gonorrhea or the dread disease syphilis? Was the infection a direct motive for his suicide? Did the effects of the venereal disease—fever, loss of appetite, pain—affect his judgment and thus indirectly lead to his suicide? Was his death, in fact, a suicide, or was it due to an accidental overdose of drugs?

Chatterton was most likely an average youth, in many respects very much like other boys of his age, class, and station in life. The normative approach can yield valuable data on the typical and the probable and thus reveal a great deal about the quality of Chatterton's social environment. However, probabilities cannot tell us much about the personal dilemmas and predilections of that particular and exceptional young poet. Surely statistics cannot tell us how Chatterton actually behaved.

This impediment to grasping Chatterton's character is not as formidable as it might appear, since his attitudes and fantasies about sexual and moral issues are available to us through his writings. These reflections of his inner life reveal much of what we need to know about him.

Chatterton's inner emotional states are accessible to us even though we cannot be sure whether or not he had sex with a prostitute and/or contracted venereal disease. This shift from examining Chatterton's external behaviors to understanding his psychic reality entails a few alterations in our customary ways of pursuing "the truth." We must be willing to accept that there are always discrepancies between attitudes and fantasies described in writing and actions that take place in the real world. Moreover, we must accept the unfashionable idea that what we discover about the poet's psychological life can reveal more about him than knowing what he might or might not have done in certain situations.

For example, even in these days of liberated, free-for-all sexuality, a young man might not engage directly in sexual adventure until he has experienced a prolonged, committed attachment or even until marriage. Great will be that poor youth's torments over his lamentable, humiliating, and frightening virginity. Nevertheless, his mind and body will be flooded by erotic passions. And, sooner or later, like any other adolescent, he will have to find some way to direct those passions toward the outer world. More than birth, marriage, or death, adolescence entails a highly elaborated drama of passage from one realm of existence into another. The sexual and moral passions arise and attain maturity. The once-powerless and morally submissive child becomes caregiver and lawgiver to the next generation. The central dilemma of the adolescent passage is how to negotiate the challenges of adult genitality and yet manage to stay somewhere within the moral authority of the social order. How a person behaves may give us some clues to his personal solutions to that dilemma, but just as often behavior can be a deception which removes us from the truth. To many eighteenth-century adults, Chatterton appeared to be an unprincipled rebel out to destroy the structures of the society in which he lived. They would have been surprised to hear that he was an avid seeker of moral authenticity, an exceedingly courageous young man who wished above all to achieve some realistic power over the real world while remaining true to his values and ideals.

To appreciate the psychological dimensions of Thomas Chatterton's moral character, we must be comfortable with Geoffrey Scott's summation in his biography, *Portrait of Zelide,* of Madame de Charrière (whose path was also crossed by the wandering James Boswell). Scott comes to the question he supposed all his readers would eventually ask: Were Zelide and Benjamin Constant lovers? Scott replies, "The subject has its pedantries like any other—I will not explore them." He adds, "Psychologically, the character of their relation is abundantly clear, technically the inquiry would be inconclusive."

Certainly Chatterton was not yet, at the age of seventeen, the libertine or sexual profligate his attackers claimed. Nor was he the chaste innocent his more sentimental biographers wished him to be. What infuriated his detractors and so worried his idealizers was that the poet who had created a world of artistic and human nobility was the same young man who demonstrated such facility in describing the innuendos and hypocrisies of eighteenth-century sexual mores. His more deeply troubled detractors and sentimentalizers had no resort but to insist that they were two different people. But Thomas Rowley and Thomas Chatterton were the same person, proving that purified artistic sentiments and genital animation are not mutually exclusive. Ample evidence of Chatterton's advanced sexual knowledge can be derived from his poetry, his journal articles, and his correspondence with family and friends. The tone and spirit of these documents demonstrate clearly that he was a young man of enormous sexual vitality *and* moral vigor. Whether or not Chatterton's actual sexual experiences were commensurate with his spirited literary genitality will remain inconclusive.

TEN

Narcissism and Melancholia

*A replacement child: Deaths and other anniversaries.
The benevolent and punishing superego.
When Chatterton loses Sir William Canynge, he loses
the protecting aspects of his conscience. The savage
torments of melancholia. Deserted by all his fathers,
Chatterton lets himself die.*

MANY of the embarrassed antiquarians and literary dilettantes who had been deceived by the Rowley fabrications did not accept the sentimental view that religious infidelity was the cause of madness, sexual depravity, suicide, and every other perversity of human nature. Since men of their stature had been duped, the duper was a person of the meanest motivations. Greed had brought Chatterton low. Chatterton had become an impostor simply to make money. He killed himself when his driven financial ambitions were thwarted.

Walpole's response to this theory was surprisingly generous. The haughty literary giant who had been accused of causing Chatterton's suicide became his posthumous defender against those who condemned him for mercenary motives. Walpole believed firmly that pride and self-esteem counted far more to a youth like Chatterton than mere financial gain.

> It is just to Chatterton's memory to say, that his poverty never made him claim kindred with the richest, or most enriching branches, yet his ingenuity in counterfeiting styles, and, I believe, hands, might easily have led him to those more facile imitations of prose, promissory notes. Yet it does not

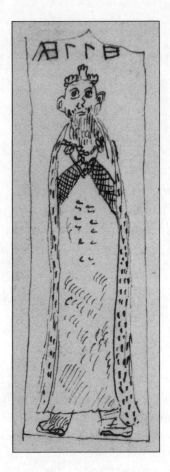

appear to my knowledge that his honesty in that respect was ever perverted. He made no scruple of extending the circulation of literary credit, and of bamboozling the misers of Saxon riches; but he never attempted to defraud, cheat, rob unpoetically. He preserved dignity in despair. . . .

A few other thoughtful scholars of the eighteenth century also refused to attribute such petty motives to Chatterton. They arrived at more complicated reckonings on the nature of the human psyche.

After giving Chatterton's life weighty consideration, Thomas Warton, the poet laureate, came upon the idea that there was in Chatterton a conflict between one type of self-aggrandizing motive and another. His ruminations led him finally to an insight that anticipates contemporary psychological appraisals of our own culture of narcissism. One of those taken in by Rowley's narratives, Warton was at first vexed and irritated by realizing the truth. He said that he regretted having "to pronounce the Rowley poems to be spurious," and he deliberated about why Chatterton had written them. Had the imposture promised a fast and easy way to earn a fortune? Or was it that Chatterton had been willing to sacrifice the vanity of being applauded for the greater vanity of enjoying the dexterity of his sleight of hand? Warton concluded that the motive underlying the fabrication of the imposturous Rowleys was "the pleasure of deceiving the world, a motive which in many minds, operates more powerfully than the hopes of gain."

Having identified the narcissistic advantages of imposture, Warton received his own narcissistic satisfaction: he was compensated for the embarrassment of having been duped and the pain of having to part with what he had believed was valuable antique English poetry by, as he deftly phrased it, "the more solid satisfaction, resulting from the detection of artifice and imposture."

During the last half of the twentieth century it has become fashionable to view all psychological disturbances afflicting modern men and women in terms of narcissistic defenses and strategies. Such diagnostic simplicity is alluring because it alleviates the need to grapple with certain intricacies and complications of the human mind. It is comforting, but of course only partly accurate, to suppose that everybody these days suffers to some degree from narcissistic disorders. Since narcissistic dilemmas are an essential part of human development, this is an obvious truth.

The twentieth-century catchall *narcissism* has taken the place of the eighteenth-century catch-all *infidelity*. And though the two terms have distinctly different meanings, they both carry similar automatic associations to madness, sexual perversity, criminal tendencies, and suicide. The term narcissism, as used by some psychoanalysts and the general public alike, refers to issues of pride and self-esteem, fantasies about the integrity or fragmentation of the sense of self, feelings of true-self and false-self. Seen in this light, the disturbances of narcissism include the actual perversions—sadomasochism, exhibitionism, fetishism, transvestism; perverse characters such as impostors, practical jokers, and petty liars; the so-called as-if personalities; the eating disorders and addictions; and certain forms of criminality such as swindling and counterfeiting. Clearly, narcissistic issues of one kind or another could play a significant role in the tale of the impostor-poet Thomas Chatterton, who wrote that he was fully aware that pride composed "19/20th" of his personality.

Evidence of the narcissistic features of Chatterton's character must be derived from very limited data on his infancy and early childhood. We have no direct access to his fantasy life or the fantasies of the two women who raised him. We do have the reminiscences of his bereaved mother and sister, whose retrospective accounts of his childhood have the ring of truth precisely because they are so innocently adoring. According to these accounts, Chatterton had all the makings of a narcissistic character. He was born posthumously, and thus it is likely that psychologically he replaced his dead father in his mother's affections. Moreover, as the replacement child for his dead brother, Giles Malpas, he would have been further predisposed to narcissistic conflicts.

Again we can only conjecture that Chatterton was treated by his mother as a replacement for her baby who had died at the age of four months. Infant mortality rates in eighteenth-century England were extremely high, and it has been argued that many mothers did not allow themselves to become too firmly attached to their newborns until they had proven their survival capacities. Giles Malpas, Sarah Chatterton's firstborn son, might have died too soon for his mother to form an attachment to him. But from what we know of Sarah's character, she was an unusually devoted and caring mother. The intensity of her emotional involvement with her surviving children would suggest that she had formed an early maternal bond with Giles as well. And at least one gesture could be interpreted as a wish that her second son would replace Giles. Sarah waited to have Thomas christened until New Year's Day of 1753, the two-year anniversary of Giles Malpas's christening. As we shall soon see, the date of Chatterton's suicide may also have been influenced by his feelings about his dead brother.

Whether or not he was an actual replacement child, Chatterton's role as the only surviving male in a family of doting women marked him as an exceptional child. Exceptional children tend to be grandiose and are thus predisposed to more than the usual share of narcissistic dilemmas. Thomas Chatterton grew up with all the burdens as well as the advantages of his special status in his family.

Perhaps the biggest burden for Chatterton was the deliciously grandiose fantasy that he was more powerful than his father. A little boy's fantasy that he, not his father, has been chosen to fulfill the mother's desires is a narcissistic triumph but a terrifying assignment. It is made all the more terrifying by the knowledge that his own penis is really small and inadequate, an idea that fills the little boy with a sense of mortification. With this realization, narcissistic triumph is transformed into narcissistic defeat. Added to this is the boy's nameless dread of retaliation from the lumbering giant who has been banished from his mother's bed. Every little boy experiences some castration anxiety for entertaining such wishes. But so extraordinary is the dread of the potential impostor, who believes that he has actually defeated his absent father, that his anxiety over bodily integrity fulminates into a pervasive mutilation anxiety rather than limiting itself to the more focused and ordinary castration anxiety.

Thus imposturous deeds must be able to achieve some extraordinary psychological compromises. For narcissistic motives the man must remain the champion. At the same time he must find a way to avoid the dread retaliation that has haunted him since childhood. Imposturous acts succeed in rectifying the narcissistic defeats of childhood. They also allay the inordinate dread of mutilation. Thus, imposturousness brings us to a central dynamic of narcissism and to an issue that is hidden behind commonly accepted terms like pride and self-esteem—that is, the issue of bodily integrity.

By proving that something which is *not* real is real, the impostor allays his mutilation anxiety. That peculiar logic derives from an image of something he has seen and found so frightening that he must prove it isn't real. The terrifying image that must be denied and reversed is that of the woman's penisless genitals, a sight that arouses anxiety in most little boys, but absolute terror in fatherless boys who have no masculine ally around to defend them from the all-powerful, swallowing-up mother.

The dynamic psychological relationship between falsehood and castration anxiety was first elaborated in 1929 by the psychoanalyst Otto Fenichel in "The Economics of Pseudologia Fantastica." Fenichel begins by presenting an adult patient's report of a childhood memory. The patient relates how he had once been frightened by seeing his father's penis, which had seemed to him awesomely large. The patient recalls wondering if his mother also had such a large penis. One day he managed to peek up his mother's skirt. To the little boy's relief and satisfaction, the reassuring penis was there. Fenichel comments:

> It became probable that the true state of affairs had been just the reverse. During an accidental exposure the boy must have caught sight of his mother's genital, been frightened by it, wondered if his father looked like that too, peeked under his father's nightshirt and seen with relief his large penis. . . . Indeed it is a special case which is reminiscent of an already

familiar one, namely, the perverse behavior of fetishists by which they seek to deny the woman's lack of a penis. . . . The fetishist and my patient's screen memory have a great deal in common.

In contrast to screen memories and fetishistic fantasies which follow circuitous routes in the effort to deny an unpleasant reality, pathological lying accomplishes denial directly. "The formula is: If it is possible to make someone believe that untrue things are true, then it is also possible that true things, the memory of which threatens me, are untrue."

The literary impostor says to potential mutilators—devouring mothers and castrating fathers alike, "You needn't envy me. This is someone else's poetry. I am merely the translator." As he obscures his real self behind the powers and virtues of his assumed self, the impostor can derive an enormous sense of power and mastery, not to mention the highly charged hostility his anonymity allows him to express toward his assumed audiences. And all without fear of retaliation.

Chatterton was not an outright impostor, but his character was structured around issues of falsehood. Falsehood as a method of fending off castration anxiety is not reserved for blatant perversions or arch-impostors. The psychoanalyst Jacob Arlow has described the emotional plight of certain men who never acquire actual perversions or rise to the rank of full-fledged impostors: these men suffer from character perversions. When they are young boys and adolescents, they struggle with perverse impulses and have brief adventures with fetishism, voyeurism, transvestism, exhibitionism. They are able, by the time they reach adulthood, to suppress the overt manifestations of their impulses and to quell their perverse desires. What remains of the struggle is a character structure that expresses the perverse impulses indirectly. Denial, lying, and trickery of one sort or another manage to both express the perversion and simultaneously defend against it. In other words, a compromise between desire and authority is often successfully effected, but there remains some deformation of the person's character.

Arlow refers to some of these men as unrealistic characters, men who always look at reality through a veil of uncertainty—compelled to peer through the veil in the hopes of seeing some unnameable reality but never allowing themselves to really see. Others become petty liars who use lying to disavow the fact of the woman's genitals; still others become practical jokers and hoaxers, who shock and deceive their unsuspecting audiences as they themselves have been shocked by the awesome knowledge of the difference between the sexes.

As Arlow portrays these idiosyncratic outcomes of castration anxiety he comments:

> The petty lie is the equivalent of the fetish—it is something which is interposed between the individual and reality in order to ward off the perception of the true reality and to substitute instead perceptions which facilitate ambiguity and illusion, both of which can temper for the patient the harsh reality of female anatomy. . . .
>
> It is a short step from grasping the fetish and having phantasies about women possessing penises to dressing up in a fetish-like outfit or in women's clothes and then acting out the phantasy of being a woman with a penis. These fundamental features of the transvestite may be transformed and may become the basis of the pathological character trait of the practical joker.

What Arlow is suggesting is that the practical joke is a sublimated and more socially acceptable version of transvestism. For example, a favorite practical joke of pubescent boys is to blacken one or two of their front teeth and then terrorize their unsuspecting mothers and sisters with the unexpected sight. How relieved mother is when she discovers that her precious boy is intact after all. Most practical jokes and hoaxes work on the same principle. First, the unsuspecting audience must be shocked. Usually but not always surprise is followed by relief that the terrible event is easily remedied. In a far less subtly disguised rendition of this scenario, the transvestite, whose get up is a caricature of femininity, is saying, "you think I am a woman without a penis, but at any moment I could reveal to you that I do have a penis. Under *my* skirt, as we all know, there *is* a penis."

As must be apparent even from these comparatively innocuous perverse scenarios, the term narcissism, as popularly used, no longer serves to adequately describe what is going on in the mental life of the various character types labeled narcissistic. The so-called narcissist is not without conscience. Nor is he withdrawn from other human beings. As it turns out, his conscience is unusually exacting and harsh, and he is perpetually involved, albeit not in deep or satisfying personal relationships, at least in interpersonal interacting. Therefore, in order to grasp the full range of motives and dynamics underlying the imposturous romance and tragic suicide of the adolescent impostor-poet Thomas Chatterton, our customary views of narcissism must be supplemented with a few of the more traditional psychoanalytic perspectives on character formation.

Sigmund Freud's revolutionary conceptualizations of the evolution of the superego, or human conscience, provide a necessary link between narcissistic issues and the manifold ways in which we negotiate the demands of relating to other human beings.

A narrow use of the term narcissism to signify a sexual perversion was introduced at the turn of the century by sexologists Paul Nacke and Havelock Ellis. Freud's 1914 paper *On Narcissism* begins with a reference to Nacke's description of a man masturbating while looking into a mirror. But that perverse behavior is merely the starting point of Freud's approach to the issues of narcissism. Narcissism, he stresses, should be understood as the *attitude* of a person "who treats his own body in the same way in which the body of a sexual object is ordinarily treated—who looks at it, that is to say, strokes it and fondles it till he obtains complete satisfaction through these activities." Freud goes on to point out that this narcissistic attitude is not limited to the perverse act and its sexual satisfactions, but is to be found as a regular feature in the course of *every* developmental history.

The narcissistic attitude has to do with the ubiquitous problem of adapting to the similarities and differences between self and other. *Every* child must adapt to the genital differences between the sexes and to differences between the generations. The father's presence in the mother's life and her presence in his make it evident to the child that there is a great deal more to the regulation of sexuality than the nursery morality of separation, weaning, controlling one's bodily functions. The triangle of mother-child-father announces the intimate connection between male-female anatomical differences and the fact that there are profound and unalterable differences between child and parent. There are those secret pleasures that Mother and Father share for which the child has no anatomical capacity. This oedipal defeat carries the child out of the nursery and into the larger social order, which at that point in the child's life is represented by the incest taboo. The child misapprehends the parents' motives. The mother and father simply wish to protect the child from precocious involvement in adult sexual behavior. The child, however, regards their protective gestures as a commentary on his own genital inferiority. He attributes his exile from the parental bedroom and his inability to participate in adult pleasures to his various emotional, physical, and moral inadequacies. To compensate for these unbearable humiliations, the child identifies with the power, the beauty, and the moral authority of the idealized others—his parents. In exchange for all that he has lost, the child acquires his own inner authority to rule over his own desires. This new acquisition is the most significant outcome of the infantile debate between desire and authority. It is the part of the human mental life that derives its force from absence, weaning, separation, withdrawal of love; it is the agency of authority that represents the lawfulness of the social order. It establishes itself as that aspect of a child's inner life that we call superego or conscience.

Freud's consistent response to any "agitated apprehensions as to the whereabouts of the higher nature of man" was to remind his anxious critics of the intimate relations between man's higher nature and the lower forms of mental life from which it derives. He spoke of the ego-ideal or superego as the primary representative of man's highest nature. "It is easy to show that the ego ideal answers to everything that is expected of the higher nature of man. As a substitute for a longing for the father, it contains the germ from which all religions have evolved." The superego is the outcome of the child's complicated relations to both parents. "When we were little children we knew these higher natures, we admired them and feared them; and later took them into ourselves." The ideals of the superego, among them our highest aspirations, are made up of the identifications, those aspects of our parents that become aspects of our own self. But as heir to the desires, anxieties, humiliations, and struggles of the Oedipus complex, the superego is also "the expression of the most powerful impulses and most important libidinal vicissitudes of the id." Thus our noblest wishes and hopes, and all that is highest in our natures, are inexorably bound up with the infantile desires that formed them. As an offshoot of our infantile erotic hungers the superego devours, scrutinizes, tempts, torments. It appears in our dream thoughts as threats of defilement, castration, starvation, exile. It is the dread shadow of the God of Job, who demands submission above all else. It is the voice of Tezcatlipoca, the savage god who was "able to enter everywhere, in the heavens, on earth and into the place of the dead."

The implacable god whose wrath and displeasure causes us to tremble is the same god we worship and adore. Freud underscored the contrasts between the punishing and protective aspects of the superego. "The superior being which became the ego ideal, once threatened castration, and this dread of castration is probably the nucleus around which the subsequent fear of conscience has gathered." On the other hand, the superego also "fulfills the same function of protecting and saving that was fulfilled in earlier days by the father . . ." Thus when the ego is deprived of the protecting superego, it will let itself die. The fear of death, which is part of melancholia, is really an intense fear of conscience—a castration fear that has gathered around it earlier fears of annihilation, and "the infantile anxiety of longing—the anxiety due to separation from the protecting mother."

These protective and punishing aspects of the superego can encompass the essential motives for Chatterton's imposturous acts and his final tragic suicide. When Chatterton lost Sir William Canynge, he lost the internal god that had protected and nourished him. Without Canynge, he fell prey to the torments of mutilation anxiety, that intensified form of castration anxiety that combines dread of annihilation, separation anxiety, and the awesome images of abandonment, defilement, exile from the human race; in short melancholia. When his family romance came to an end, Chatterton searched but found no other method to escape from the persecuting aspects of his own untamed and ruthless conscience.

Though it represents our personally created internal tormentors and protectors, conscience does not function independently of the external world. Misfortune tends to increase the severe and sadistic elements of the superego. Usually, good fortune will elicit the benevolent and nourishing aspects. True, when things are going "too smoothly" we can sometimes seek to punish ourselves for such undeserved good luck. But generally when all goes well we feel as though destiny loves us and so we love ourselves. The internal forces of conscience and the external happenings in the actual world work hand in hand to dole out the rewards and punishments of ordinary life. So with Chatterton, we must always wonder about the interplay between conscience and circumstance. To some extent the misfortunes of his last days were sought after and created by his implacable conscience. At the same time, it is certainly possible that some piece of good fortune, some act of generosity or benevolence, might have rescued him from his inner torments.

We assemble the bits and pieces of Chatterton's life during those four months in London. We scrutinize his activities for clues to his state of mind. Was there some actual event or series of events that could have precipitated the desperate act of suicide? Was there something or someone that could have saved him?

The most popular legend had it that Chatterton was driven to suicide for lack of actual nourishment. That version of the last days of Chatterton's life is derived from certain details in the inquest report, which were based on the scanty and probably not entirely reliable report given to the coroner by Frederick Angel, husband of Mrs. Angel. According to Angel, on the afternoon of August 22, Chatterton returned to his lodgings in a passion about the baker's wife, who had refused him a loaf of bread until he paid the three shillings he already owed to her. When on August 23, Chatterton still seemed extremely agitated, Mrs. Angel had inquired, "What ails you?" The young poet had replied, "Nothing. Nothing. Why do you ask?" Around 10 on the morning of August 24, he left with a bundle of papers under his arms saying that he was putting them in a place of safety lest they meet with an accident. Mr. Cross, the apothecary, saw him at 11:30 when he stopped in to ask for some arsenic, supposedly for an experiment he was conducting. Chatterton did not return to the Angels' until 7 P.M., and nobody seemed to know how Chatterton spent this last afternoon of his life or what happened to that bundle of papers. That evening he was pale and dejected. He sat with Mr. and Mrs. Angel moping about and muttering rhymes in some unintelligible language until retiring to his room a few hours later.

The assumption was that when the baker's wife had denied Chatterton a loaf of bread, the dignity of suicide was the proud boy's only option. Horace Walpole would announce to the world that Chatterton had "poisoned himself on being refused a loaf of bread." Thomas Warton would conclude that the young impostor-poet had "died for want of bread."

Mrs. Angel, his landlady, disappeared shortly after Chatterton's suicide. However, her friend the barber's wife maintained that her vanishing had nothing to do with feelings of guilt. Rather the friend recalled when Mrs. Angel noticed that her young boarder had not eaten for nearly three days, she of course offered him a free dinner. But the proud poet who lived in her attic would not accept charity. Mr. Cross, who was rumored to have given Chatterton his opium and his fatal dose of arsenic, also claimed to have offered his starving young friend some food. After numerous refusals, Chatterton had finally succumbed. Voraciously hungry, he devoured an entire barrel of oysters. But as some would later speculate, this eating binge may have led to a fatal case of food poisoning or perhaps a severe fever and debilitating illness. August had been a bad month for oysters.

The editor of one of Chatterton's first volumes of poetry recalled:

Every effort appears to have been insufficient to ward off the approach of poverty; and very soon after he settled in London his distress became so great, that he meditated a design of going to Senegal. This intention he never executed. He continued drudging for the booksellers a few months, when at last, oppressed with poverty and disease, in a fit of despair, he put an end to his existence.

William Blake took a playfully modern view of the entire Chatterton affair, linking his fellow poet's scholarly excitements with starvation, disease, and death by poisoning.

In the first place I think, I think in the first place that Chatterton was clever at Fissie Follogy, Pistinology, Aridology, Arography, Transmography, Phizography, Hogamy, Hatomy, & hall that, but, in the first place, he eat very little, wickly—that is, he slept very little, which brought into a consumption; & what was that that he took? Fissic or somethink,—& so died!

In a more direct and sober manner, many others interested in Chatterton's fate also associated his suicide with the poet's eccentric mental habits and peculiar temperamental displays. A London acquaintance described the changes in Chatterton's mental state during those last weeks: "He sometimes seemed wild, abstracted, incoherent; at others he had a settled gloominess in his countenance, the sure presage of his fatal resolution. In short, this was the very temperament and constitution from which we should, in similar circumstances, expect the same event."

These days that same eighteenth-century hypothesis would be dressed up in "scientific" language. On those rare occasions when Chatterton's name does come up at scientific meetings, one psychiatrist or another will suggest the possibility that Chatterton suffered from a bipolar manic-depressive disorder. When he could no longer swing back out of the depressive phase of his illness, his manic agitation finally drove him to the violent act of suicide. Inevitably this summation is coupled with the theory that the vast majority of creative persons have as the baseline of their personalities a manic-depressive mental disorder.

There is no doubt that this theory is a pervasive one. As Aristotle spoke of the artist's "divine madness," and Renaissance scholars referred to the "Saturnine temperament," so the self-consciously mad artist Strindberg boasted that few ordinary people were lucky enough to be capable of insanity. John Berryman also championed the poetic inspirations deriving from madness: "The artist is extremely lucky who is presented with the worst possible ordeal which will not nearly kill him."

Meyerstein, Chatterton's scrupulous twentieth-century biographer, shunned the language of contemporary psychiatry. The term *manic-depressive disorder* would have offended him. But he nevertheless ascribes to the ancient formula behind it that associates madness—and especially madness characterized by sudden mood swings—with poetic sensibility. Says Meyerstein, "The poetic consciousness has its abyss, as well as its height, and existence can, at any moment, be envisioned as the former."

From all descriptions of his overt behavior during childhood and adolescence, Chatterton the narcissist would certainly also qualify for the diagnostic label manic-depressive. But once again, the label explains neither the special qualities of his artistic genius nor the unique mental anguish that might have led to his early death.

According to another set of rumors, Chatterton's suicidal intentions are said to have been made apparent at least a few days before his death. According to one story, on August 21 he and a friend were reading the legends on some tombstones in St. Pancras Churchyard when Chatterton stumbled and fell into a freshly dug grave. Said Chatterton to the friend who helped him out, "My dear friend, I feel the sting of a speedy dissolution. I have been at war with the grave for some time, and find it is not so easy to vanquish it as I imagined; we can find an asylum to hide from every creditor but that."

Mrs. Edkins, who also supplied the fabricated story of Chatterton's reburial, purportedly told Cumberland of a letter sent to poor Mrs. Chatterton two weeks before her son's suicide. The alleged letter stated, "I am about to quit for ever my ungrateful country. I shall exchange it for the deserts of Africa, where tigers are a thousand times more merciful than man." In that same alleged letter is another version of Chatterton's flirtation with freshly dug graves:

> A week before the news of Chatterton's death reached his mother, she had received a letter from him, and sent for Mrs. Edkins to read it to her. She was in tears and very uneasy. . . . The letter stated, that walking in a church-yard a few days before writing, he had quitted the path, and wandering among the graves, he suddenly found himself on his face in one, by stumbling; but he added, in his humorous way, "it was not the quick and the dead together;" for he found the sexton under him, who was digging a grave.

This letter, which is taken to be a testimony to Chatterton's confused state of mind and suicidal wishes during the last days of his life, is probably another of Mrs. Edkins's or George Cumberland's fabrications. However, like the other accounts and interpretations of Chatterton's last days, it depicts Chatterton in a distraught state of mind.

Among the poems still attributed to Chatterton but never ascertained to be authentic are the two candidates for his last lines. Both are from copies at least twice removed from the supposed originals. One, given the posthumous title *The Last Verses Written by Chatterton,* dated August 24, 1770 and signed T.C., was said to have been found in Chatterton's pocket notebook after his suicide.

> *Farewell, Bristolia's dingy piles of brick,*
> *Lovers of Mammon, worshippers of Trick!*
> *Ye spurned the boy who gave you antique lays,*
> *And paid for learning with your empty praise.*
> *Farewell, ye guzzling, aldermanic fools,*
> *By nature fitted for Corruption's tools!*
> *I go to where celestial anthems swell;*
> *But you, when you depart, will sink to Hell.*

> *Farewell, my Mother!—cease, my anguished soul,*
> *Nor let Distraction's billows o'er me roll!—*
> *Have mercy, Heaven! when here I cease to live,*
> *And this last act of wretchedness forgive!*

Chatterton's other last lines, undated and unsigned, were supposedly written sometime near the eve of his death and then sent off to a friend in the East Indies, who twenty-five years later donated the poem to *The Bristol Mercury* as "a compliment to the City that gave him birth." Who this friend was and whether or not he was aware of the irony of his compliment are unknown.

> *Naked and friendless to the world expos'd*
> *Now every scene of happiness is clos'd;*
> *My mind distress'd, and rack'd with anguish drear,*
> *Adown my cheek oft rolls the falling tear:*
> *My native place I ne'er again shall see;*
> *Condemn'd to bitter want and penury.*
> *Life's thorny path incautiously I've trod,*
> *And bitterly I feel the chastening rod:*
> *O! who can paint the horrors of my mind,*
> *The stings which guilty conscience leave behind:*
> *They rage, they rend, they tear my aching heart,*
> *Increase the torment, agonize the smart.*
> *What shall I do, whither speed my way,*
> *How shun the light of the refulgent day?*
> *Each coming morn but ushers in fresh grief;*
> *No friend at hand to bring me sweet relief:*
> *The sigh I stifle, and the smile I wear,*
> *In secret, but increase my weight of care.*
> *One comfort's left, and that's in speedy death,*
> *What! rob myself of my own vital breath;*
> *Yes! for my frame's so torn, I can't abide,*
> *Of keen reflection the full flowing tide;*
> *Then welcome death: O God my soul receive:*
> *Pardon my sins, and this one act forgive:*
> *I come! I fly! O how my mind's distrest;*
> *Have mercy Heaven! when shall I find rest.*

These two "last poems" show a young poet suffering and alone in his last hours and thus appealed especially to the biographers of the sentimental school who wished to portray his virtue and nobility. On the other hand, since the "naked and friendless" lines also intimate a mysterious and possibly venereal infection, gradually his idealizers began to believe the second verse to be a forgery. Although the poem's sentiments have a few Chatterton-like touches, the blatant and manifest guilt, the repentance, the self-pitying tone are uncharacteristic. As for the awful *Last Verses,* the consensus is that "Any competent hoaxster would not have to have read far in Chatterton to pick up the tone and vocabulary of the first part." The second half is the sort of sentimental nonsense that only the Chatterton of the marvelous-boy myths might have written. But, even in the depths of despair, suffering from disease and poverty and contemplating suicide, it is unlikely that the intrepid, proud Chatterton would have descended to "Farewell, my Mother!—cease, my anguished soul, / Nor let Distraction's billows o'er me roll!"

We come finally to a collection of facts, possible events, conjectures, and outright fabrications that might add up to a reasonable explanation for the voluntary termination of one's own life—Chatterton's increasing isolation from friends, family, and familiar faces; the drying up of his publishing sources; poverty; starvation; the devouring of contaminated oysters; drug addiction; venereal disease; an unconscious wish to fall into the grave; a manic-depressive disorder that had gotten out of hand; a hypermanic-delusional state of mind that was exacerbated by hunger. Yet the impurity of motive that Alvarez describes makes it abundantly clear that tangible adversity rarely, if ever, is the direct cause of a suicide. A savage god had done the deed, a savage god who "gave riches, prosperity and fame, courage and command, dignities and honour, and took them away again as he willed. For this he was feared and reverenced, for it was within his power to raise up or to cast down."

The impurities of Chatterton's motives for suicide stem from the intangibilities of *melancholia,* the most savage of Tezcatlipoca's afflictions. The question of whether Chatterton's melancholia was the predictable accompaniment to a constitutionally based manic-depressive disorder or the more internalized but equally tormenting melancholia that Freud discovered is academic. Freud's version, however, provides a more profound appreciation of Chatterton's internal experience.

Freud came to his understanding of the psychological dynamics of melancholia a year or so after he had described the narcissistic attitude and its relationship to the formation of the superego. It was Freud's special contribution to our understanding of depression to distinguish the pathology of melancholia from normal mourning. Mourning is a process of coming to terms with loss, and as such is normal, expectable, and desirable.

Little by little and at a great expense of emotional spirit and energy, as each memory of the lost person is brought up for reinterpretation and reexamination, the finality of the loss is gradually accepted. In this slow, piecemeal way a terrible loss becomes a bearable reality. The lost loved one becomes part of the mourner's internal world, where the former can live on peacefully as a loving and benevolent internal presence. Mourning then is a way of defusing the hated and hating aspects of the dead person. When the mourning process is aborted, the slow and painful ordeal of recognizing the finality of loss is forgone. In its place comes the purgatory of melancholia. Here the dead one also becomes an internal presence, but in this instance a condemning, retaliatory tormentor.

Of all the torments the human soul may suffer, melancholia is the harshest and most perverse. Freud depicted its virulence: "We find that the excessively strong superego which has obtained a hold on consciousness rages against the ego with merciless violence, as if it had taken possession of the whole of the sadism available in the person concerned."

The melancholic takes ordinary misfortune and transforms it into tormenting self-hatred. If there is no misfortune for his anguishing soul to feed upon, he imagines it. If imagination is not up to the cruel task, the melancholic will court actual disasters. He begets the mire of misfortune into which he sinks. According to the perverse logic of melancholia, Chatterton's poverty, starvation, addiction, disease were as much the outcomes of his tortured state of mind as the causes of it.

Most suicides, whatever else their precipitating cause or causes, have as their predisposing cause an underlying melancholia. From the letters and other writings of suicides and from the "confessions" of foiled suicides we construe that the self-murder is directed at some inner tormentor, and *not* at the rest of the self, which actually longs to be set free to go on living.

When a person feels that he is exposed to dangers and humiliations that he can no longer overcome, he can only conclude that he has been deserted by his protecting inner presences, which he may call Fate, Destiny, Providence, God. In *The Unfortunate Fathers,* written the January preceding his suicide, Chatterton associates suicide with an internal presence that permits such acts of noble insanity. The hero writes to his father:

> I shall not accuse your conduct, for you are my father; I shall only endeavor to vindicate the action I am about to perpetrate. This will be easily done. There is a principle in man, (a shadow of the divinity) which constitutes him the image of God; you may call it conscience, grace, inspiration, the spirit, or whatever name your education gives it.

Freud's words on suicide were simple: "The ego gives itself up because it feels itself hated and persecuted by the superego instead of loved." The suicide tries to murder his internal persecutor. And with that very gesture he hopes to find his way back to the internal presences that once loved and protected him. Consciously or unconsciously, the suicide believes that in death he will be reunited with his loved ones.

Chatterton's life history begins with the deaths of his brother and Thomas Chatterton, Sr. It will end with a gesture unconsciously designed to reunite him with his father. Nearly all of Chatterton's suicidal writings associate that act with his father's death and to a lesser extent with the death of his brother. His *Will,* for example, written on April 14, the date of Giles's death, instructs that his own body "be interred in the Tomb of my Fathers." Next to the tablet commemorating his own death was to be placed another inscribed, "Sacred to The Memory of Thomas Chatterton Sub Chanter of the Cathedral of this City whose Ancestors were residents of St. Mary Redclift since the Year 1140. He dyed the 7th of August 1752."

Chatterton's life as a fatherless boy very likely predisposed him to the melancholia that underlies the suicidal gesture. Occasionally psychologists revive the theory that an individual suicide is part of a pattern that they refer to as a "death trend." Taken in its loose, general meaning, the term death trend means simply that one suicide or violent death encourages another. This straightforward contagion principle is meant to account for mysterious and otherwise unexplainable epidemic and mass suicides. The other meaning of death trend has a deeper psychological significance and shows it to be a more personal phenomenon. This interpretation is usually illustrated by the example of a child whose parent has committed suicide, died, or deserted the family and who is therefore predisposed to melancholic ruminations and suicide.

There is merit in the notion that without the sensitive guidance of the surviving parent or other intimate adult, a young child would not have the mental or emotional capacity to absorb the reality of the death of a parent. He would be incapable of the delicate and painful process of mourning and would be prone instead to melancholic mental and emotional reactions. Left to his own devices, the child would cope as best he could with the complex and unanswerable questions that inevitably arise when a parent dies. One set of questions concerns that child's fantasy that he or she is responsible for the parent's death. Even when the father dies before the child's birth, as in Chatterton's case, this does not prevent the child from imagining that he has gotten rid of his rival. A child could convince himself that his own fetal presence inside the mother was responsible for the killing of the father. According to such magical thinking the unanswerable, unconscious questions might go like this: Did my evil feelings and thoughts, my tempers, my furies destroy my father? Did my urge to possess my mother get so out of hand that I actually murdered my rival? Since I wished to destroy the cruel father who abandoned me, will he one day seek retribution? Will he return to seek revenge for my murder of him?

Hard enough is the task of mourning for any child who loses a parent, even one who for a time knew his living, breathing father or mother. That child would have come in contact with both the loving and angry sides of his parent, the protecting and punishing aspects. Such a child would have some way of measuring his internal representations of his parent against some external reality. But for a boy like Chatterton, who never knew his father at all, it would be nearly impossible to arrive at a realistic assessment of the father's powers—his protecting ones or his punishing ones. At the one extreme the father could be idealized as the most magnificent and benevolent father of all. At the other extreme he could assume the unmanageable proportions of an inescapable tormentor.

As does every adolescence, Chatterton's expressed a struggle between the forces of the past and those of the future. Each adolescent makes decisions, largely unconsciously but also consciously, about how much of the past and which of its aspects will be allowed to prevail in the future. In that regard the adolescent is a mourner, but a mourner who at first only dimly realizes what it is he is losing. What the adolescent is losing, and what is so difficult to relinquish, are his passionate attachments to the family and to the infantile scenarios that were once the center of his existence. Thus, the adolescent mourning process provides an opportunity to remodel the archaic conscience, which is made up of residues of the infantile scenarios—watchful eyes, prohibiting voices, demands for perfection. At the conclusion of the adolescent passage the watchful eyes might seem a bit friendlier, the no-saying voices less harsh. But the most significant change wrought by adolescence is the taming of the ideals by which a person measures himself.

Was Chatterton entitled to go on to the future? Could he have tamed and humanized his childhood conscience? Or did the claims of the past take priority over his passionate desire to move on to that future? We know for a fact that Chatterton conceived of suicide as an act that would liberate him from the torments and humiliations of his apprenticeship. He consciously and literally designed his *Will* as a declaration of independence, a passport to the merry life of a freethinking journalist. Yet some of the contents of the *Will* allude to Chatterton's ties to the past. The date of the *Will* alone is a clue to the inner struggles that beset him as he contemplated the approach of manhood.

The suicide was to take place the next evening, April 15, at 8:00 PM, "being the feast of the resurrection." Chatterton's suicide would be both a death and a resurrection. On the fourteenth, his idol John Wilkes was to be released from King's Bench Prison. Thus, the *Will* could be construed as a harbinger of the future. If the *Will* did indeed free Chatterton from his apprenticeship, his ambitions to become the favorite Patriot journalist would be realized.

But April fourteenth also represented the past. Since Chatterton's mother had had him christened on the same date as his brother Giles, no date could be more fitting for Chatterton's suicide than the date of his brother's death.

Replacement children grow up with a conviction that they do not have a right to their own lives. Surely they too are fated to die in childhood. Often the dead sibling lives on in the family in a concrete way. His birthdays are celebrated, overtly or silently. Around the anniversaries of the child's death, a sadness often permeates the household, inducing in the surviving or replacement children highly sensitized reactions to illness and death. These children are ever-watchful over their own physical health; some of them, like Chatterton, become noticeably ascetic in their personal habits. Nor is it unusual for the replacement child to feel the impact of the dead sibling's birthdates and death dates throughout his life.

For Chatterton April was a dangerous month, but the month of August held a few other Chatterton anniversaries. Sir Herbert Croft, the author of *Love and Madness,* confesses his puzzlement on the date of that violent act. Why did Chatterton choose August 24 for his suicide? There was no full moon on that date. And August was a bad month for oysters but not as depressing as the winter months. Croft is unable to come up with an answer to his tantalizing questions.

Ebenezer Sibley was certain that Chatterton knew enough about astrology to predict his suicide and the sign under which the deed would be done. Whether or not Chatterton indulged in astrological speculation, it is certain that Chatterton's thoughts on suicide were connected with thoughts about fathers and sons and in that sense August was indeed an ominous month. When the previous August 12 Peter Smith had shot himself with a pistol, Chatterton had no hesitation about where to pin the blame. "Despis'd an alien to thy Fathers breast . . . O may his Crying blood be on your head." Nearly half a year later, when suicide begins to seem a noble insanity of the soul, a benevolent option to a deprived existence, again the Unfortunate Fathers are to blame and are therefore condemned to pay the heaviest toll known to mankind—the self-murders of their own children.

Thomas Chatterton, Sr. was born on August 8, 1713 and died on August 7, 1752 of a cold and fever; he was buried two days later. The month of August could not have been an easy time for Chatterton—especially after he had lost the nurturing inner presence of Sir William Canynge.

The past eventually won out. Chatterton never completed the slow adolescent process of mourning for the attachments of his childhood. Though he struggled heroically and against enormous odds, the melancholia which had been crouching in the wings since his birth leapt into center stage and kept him captive to the past.

By the time he committed suicide, Chatterton had lost or surrendered the material items of everyday life that most of us take for granted. Illness, poverty, hunger, and lost love convinced him that he had been totally deserted by the powers that once protected and nourished him.

William Canynge had been an expression of the softer, more merciful conscience that might have saved the young poet from the torments of melancholia. Within two months of Chatterton's "disgusting" celebration of Saxon warriors who prove themselves by decapitating and disemboweling their enemies, looting the treasures and vandalizing the monuments of the enemy villages, Sir William Canynge had become a mason and builder of cities. Merely through his reasoning on issues of justice Sir William Canynge would be the epitome of a merciful and benevolent conscience. But Chatterton's heroic father has something deeper than reason to guide his morality. Underlying Canynge's rare interpretation of masculine virtue is his willingness to tame his aggressive impulses, his wish to transform narcissistic self-interest into a concern for the common good. He uses his wealth to support playwrights, poets, painters, and their artistic enterprises. His life is committed to the rebuilding of St. Mary Redcliffe and to the preservation of the artifacts and architecture of Bristol. Canynge was indeed "the Great, the Charytable and Good / Noble as Kynges if not of Kynglie Bloude."

Though most of the protagonists and antagonists in Rowley's dramas and poetry exhibit stereotypical rough-and-ready masculine characteristics, whenever Canynge appears he is portrayed as gentle and nourishing. Even his physical appearance is touched by a kind of feminine grace: "hys Aspecte sweete and Skynne blanche han he not soe moche nobinesse yn hys Fygure he woulde be Wommanysh."

With his begetting of Canynge, Chatterton had filled in the gap in his own identity. In fabricating a father who could represent what Chasseguet-Smirgel calls "the missing phallus," he simultaneously created an internal voice that would support his artistic talents and shield him from the mercantile vulgarity of the actual eighteenth-century Bristol in which he lived. When Walpole discovered the mischief and declared the Rowleys counterfeit, Chatterton was bereft. After all, Walpole was meant to have become the young poet's next patron. He was meant to be a living version of Canynge. Walpole could not have suspected the deeply personal motives that had stimulated Chatterton to produce *Historie of Peyncters yn Englande,* and therefore he could not know how deeply his rejection would penetrate. With one blow Walpole had managed to puncture the young poet's self-esteem and his hopes of salvation and protection by a benevolent father.

"Walpole, I thought not I should ever see / So mean a Heart as thine has proved to be." Chatterton vows to repay scorn with scorn, and pride with pride: "I shall live and Stand / by Rowley's side—when Thou art dead and damned." These words are the first outward signs of the deterioration of the benevolent aspects of Chatterton's conscience. Without Canynge as an internal source of fatherly nurturance, Chatterton's conscience gradually reverts to a primitive and archaic violence. The aggression and self-serving narcissism that had been tamed by his loving relationship with his imaginary father now erupt with the rage of satire. We can gauge the increasing severity of Chatterton's own conscience through the intensity of his contemptuous attacks on the citizens and institutions of Bristol. Men are represented as drunken sots, gluttonous barbarians, given to demeaned sentiments and violent temperamental outbursts. And women are depicted as harlots and whores and biddies, or young virgins whose sexual favors can be had by the highest bidder. As the voice of Canynge faded, the savage morality that would drive Chatterton to suicide grew more and more virulent.

Other than his gentle fifteenth-century merchant prince, Chatterton had turned sporadically to two additional ideal masculine images: the noble blacks of his African poetry—Gaira, Heccar, and Narva—and the assorted primitive warriors of his imitation Ossians—Ethelgar, Cerdick, Kenrick, Griffydh, Godred Crovan and Gorthmund. These heroes and the imaginary primeval worlds they inhabited were all that remained as genuine inspirations during Chatterton's last two weeks. While his first African eclogue of January is consumed by the despair and violent rage of the black prince whose wife has been sold into slavery, the London Africans, even the warlike ones, are suffused with the ecstasies of flowering life and the raptures of sexual desire. With *An African Song,* probably written near the eve of his suicide, the sexual union of Narva and Mored is consummated:

> Black is that skin as winter's skies;
> Sparkling and bright those rolling eyes,
>   As is the venom'd snake.
> O let me haste! O let me fly!
> Upon that lovely bosom die,
>   And all myself forsake.

Like chameleons of a thornier breed, the vengeful Ossian heroes blend in with their howling tempests and harsh, rugged cliffs, and with Old Testament overtones of the Lord's wrath and Job's sufferings. His first Ossian, *Ethelgar,* opens with, "Tis not for thee, O man! to murmur at the will of the Almighty. . . . The evils of life, with some, are blessings; and the plant of death healeth the wound of the sword." The August 1770 Ossian, *Gorthmund. Translated from the Saxon,* while not the bloodiest (to *Godred Crovan* of the previous August 12 goes that honor) is as savage as any of Chatterton's raging satires. Before the Danish Gorthmund is slain by the Saxon Segowald, his death is foretold in three progressively more horrible nightmares. As he "slept on his couch of purple; the blood of the slain was still on his cruel hand," Gorthmund hears the shrieks of those he has murdered and raped. In Gorthmund's nightmare voices, an amalgam of biblical and pagan malevolence, we hear the torments of the savage god:

> Thine are the bitter herbs of affliction; for thee shall the wormwood shed its seed on the blossoms of the blooming flower, and imbitter with its falling leaves the waters of the brook. Rise, Gorthmund, rise, the Saxons are burning thy tents: rise, for the Mercians are assembled together, and thy armies will be slain with the sword, or burnt in the image of Tewisk.

Here Chatterton appends a footnote:

> The Pagan Saxons had a most inhuman custom of burning their captives alive in a wicker image of their god Tewisk. Whilst this horrid sacrifice was performing, they shouted and danced round the flames.

He continues, "The god of victory shall be red with thy blood, and they shall shout at the sacrifice. Rise, Gorthmund, thy eyes shall be closed in peace no more."

Chatterton had assumed the voice of Rowley to fabricate a father who would love, honor, and cherish him. When he gave Canynge up, he could not recover his nourishing presence in any of the other imaginary or actual masculine idols that he tried to believe in. One by one all his living fathers had deserted him—George Catcott turned out to be a fool, his brother the Reverend Alexander belittled the Rowleys and ignored Chatterton's free-thinking arguments, Burgum would not pay for his new pedigree, his adored Clayfield hardly noticed the existence of the young poet-apprentice who appointed him as executor of his poetical works, Walpole demolished whatever remained of the Chatterton-Canynge romance, the poetic morality of Churchill just barely sustained him for a few months, Fell and Edmunds were imprisoned, Wilkes never summoned him, Beckford died. Finally his mentor and collaborator Barrett refused to give him the papers that might have allowed him to journey to Africa as a surgeon's mate. During his last two weeks his most nourishing and supportive acquaintance was the neighborhood apothecary. By the end of August, Chatterton had lost all hope of rescue by a protecting father. No good Samaritan would show the hapless pilgrim charity or cloak him from the storm. No one would answer the plea in Rowley's *Excelente Balade of Charitie*, "Where from the hail-stone could the almer flie? / He had no housen theere, ne anie covent nie." Chatterton had been abandoned, and he let himself die.

ELEVEN

The Rowley Controversy

*On the eve of Chatterton's suicide, Dr. Thomas Fry
travels to Bristol to adopt the young man
who discovered the Rowley documents.
Walpole's* Vindication. *Catcott and Barrett arrive
at their sorry ends. The ambiguities of Chatterton's
character inspire fraudulence: Chatterton's biographers
are caught in the web of deceit. Trustworthy witnesses.
The author of* Love and Madness *betrays Mary and
Sarah. Robert Southey rescues Chatterton's survivors.
The Bristol poet who committed suicide
in his attic room is rescued by
his romantic brothers.*

TOWARD the end of the last week in August, 1770, Dr. Thomas Fry, the president of St. John's College, Oxford, set out for his native city of Bristol. He was drawn there by stories of a Bristol youth named Chatterton who had discovered some ancient parchments containing hitherto unknown medieval writings.

Like so many of the characters who played a part in Chatterton's life, Fry is remembered because his name became associated with the name of Chatterton, the glorious poet, the villainous impostor. Since Fry arrived in Bristol so soon after Chatterton's suicide, it has become part of the Chatterton legend to speculate about what might have happened between the fatherless poet and the great Oxford don had that gentleman only thought to come to Bristol a week or two earlier. Would Fry have gone on to London to meet the young poet and save him from his fate?

Dr. Fry, a former Bristol schoolboy, had escaped the mercantile frenzy of that bustling port city at the age of fourteen and devoted himself

thereafter to the study of classical literature. The link between his boyhood and his present scholarly activities kindled the don's curiosity. If he moved quickly he might be one of the first to view the parchments and examine their writings. His excitement was such that he barely heeded his uneasiness concerning the authenticity of the fifteenth-century parchments. The supposition that Rowley's creations might be counterfeit was not farfetched, but Dr. Fry wanted to believe. The idea that his scholarly efforts might be instrumental in bringing before the world documents that transformed his native city into a place of virtue, heroism, and poetic nobility was motive enough to believe in Rowley.

Whether genuine or false, the poems might be remarkable. Whether transcriber or author, Chatterton must be an unusual young man. Either way, Fry was intrigued. He departed for his native city in hopes of verifying the Rowley parchments, but, failing that, of discovering a youth of notable literary gifts who could benefit from his tutelage. After learning of Chatterton's suicide, Fry called on George Catcott and William Barrett, who were rumored to possess the mass of Rowley narratives. Thomas Fry would have been a far better father to Thomas Chatterton than either of those men. He did turn out to be the first angel to trumpet the name of Chatterton over the world.

From his diaries we learn that Dr. Fry had a keen interest in the table and menus but disapproved of those who were "slaves to eating and drinking." He took his teaching and scholarly duties very much to heart. He kept himself up-to-date in classical readings and was shocked at those of his colleagues who allowed themselves to fall behind in their studies. At St. John's there were those who thought that Fry's standards were too high. It was true that he could be strict in some matters, but in others Fry was open-minded and tolerant. He believed that Methodists and other freethinkers, like his friend John Wilkes, should not be persecuted. Fry was a defender of those who held dissident views and a friend to free inquiry and liberty of the press. All in all, in theory at least, Thomas Fry, Doctor of Divinity, possessed the intellectual and moral values and steadiness of character eminently suitable to a rescuer of the proud, impetuous Thomas Chatterton.

Passionate young poets are not likely to form lasting friendships with Oxford dons. And Fry's patronage might not have survived Chatterton's volatile temperament. Eventually, the scrupulous scholar might have cared much more for the poems than the poet. On the other hand, as a defender of dissidents and a believer in freedom of the press, Fry might have encouraged the journalistic inclinations that had begun to emerge in Chatterton after he gave up the world of Sir William Canynge. Fry might have introduced the young man to his idol, John Wilkes, and thereby helped him to fulfill his ambition to become an offical spokesman for the Patriots. Although Chatterton might have had reservations about Fry's excessive interest in table matters, the Oxford scholar would have nodded to the youth's ascetic attitudes toward food and drink.

Whatever the potential fate of this potential father-son relationship,

Chatterton's suicide effectively prevented any actual relationship between poet and don. However, Thomas Fry, in the two years before he died on November 22, 1772, did become the first legitimate sponsor of Thomas Chatterton, or at least of his alleged transcriptions of Rowley. Fry died believing in the authenticity of Thomas Rowley's writings. Before he died he spread the word of Chatterton's discovery to his colleagues at Oxford.

Catcott had surrounded the Rowley relics with an aura of secrecy and mystery. With some hesitancy, he and Barrett agreed to loan Dr. Fry a few of the "transcripts," but only after extracting two promises from the esteemed college don. He must return the transcripts forthwith. He must agree not to show anyone the copies he made for his own use.

Fry returned the originals within three weeks. As for the second pledge, his enthusiasm could not be restrained. He spoke to a number of his fellow scholars about the remarkable ancient poems in his possession. To a few trusted friends he revealed the notebook pages into which he had copied the transcripts. And he proudly displayed the beginning stages of what he hoped would be the definitive glossary of Rowley's exotic fifteenth-century language. Word of Fry's remarkable find made the rounds at Oxford. In no time at all the Bristol proprietors of the Rowley manuscripts learned that Fry was not keeping to his vow of secrecy.

Perhaps the first intimation of Fry's scholarly exhibitionism was early that winter, when Dr. Francis Woodward, a member of St. John's College and also a former Bristol grammar school boy—and ironically enough, the surgeon in attendance at the death of Chatterton's father—wrote to his acquaintance, George Catcott, to request a copy of Rowley's *Bristowe Tragedy*. Woodward offered to pay. And as Fry had done, Woodward promised not to show the poetry to anyone.

Catcott reacted to Woodward's request with some ambivalence. The request was evidence enough that Oxford scholars had as hard a time keeping secrets as any ordinary person. He began to worry that he and Barrett might lose what he presumed to be their exclusive rights to the manuscripts. On the other hand, Catcott saw in his friend's request the prophecy of a lucrative trade in Rowleyana. Now that the scholarly world was showing an interest, Catcott's reservations about publishing the poetry could be put to rest. But he wished to have absolute control over the terms of sale. When, several months later, Dr. Woodward intervened on behalf of Oliver Goldsmith, who wished to purchase some of the Rowleys, Catcott responded: "Alas, Sir! I fear a poet's note of hand is not very current upon our Exchange of Bristol."

In all likelihood it was Fry who first drew Oliver Goldsmith's attention to Chatterton's discovery. Woodward, casually breaking his own vows of secrecy, then fanned the flames by reading some of the poems to Goldsmith. Finally, when Goldsmith announced the discovery at the first annual banquet of The Royal Academy in April 1771, the Rowley controversy officially began.

As Goldsmith related the amazing story of the father's discovery of the parchments in St. Mary's and the son's clever transcriptions, he impressed his listeners with his own belief in the authenticity and beauty of the poems he had been reading. Among the distinguished literary figures present at that dinner were Samuel Johnson and Horace Walpole, both of whom would soon earn the title of anti-Rowleyan (meaning they thought Chatterton a forger and the true author of the poems). Johnson scoffed at Goldsmith's naiveté and instantly identified the Rowley manuscripts as forgeries. He was, however, of two minds about their true creator, Thomas Chatterton. Later, as the Rowley controversy gathered steam, Johnson would refer to Chatterton as a "vulgar, uneducated stripling," but also as "the most extraordinary young man that has encountered my knowledge." How was that most realistic man of letters to reconcile glorious poetic narratives with deception, forgery, and criminal mentality of the worst sort?

Johnson decided on the side of art. He framed the conflict succinctly: "It is a sword that cuts both ways. It is as wonderful to suppose that a boy of 16 had stored his mind with such a train of images and ideas he had acquired, as to suppose the poems, with their ease of versification and elegance of language to have been written by Rowley in the time of Edward the Fourth."

Walpole had the most emotional reaction, though he dared not show it. Upon hearing Goldsmith utter the name Chatterton, Walpole at once realized that these so-called transcriptions were no novelty to him. Two years earlier, the boy had sent him a few Rowleys with the request that the famous writer help him to find a publisher. Had Walpole the inclination then, he might have "had the honour of ushering the great discovery to the world." When Goldsmith then told him that the boy had committed suicide, Walpole reacted with genuine shock. Though he would later deny all responsibility for the youth's unfortunate fate, it must have crossed his mind that his rejection of Chatterton had contributed to the young man's despair. The Walpole-Chatterton relationship, brief and tenuous as it had been, was to become one of the major sideshows of the spectacular controversy.

During the first two decades of the debate, when Walpole was, as he described it, blamed for "imaginary abortions which my freezing breath nipped in their pre-existent state" and "accused of blasting the promising genius and depriving the world of Lord knows what *Iliads* and *Lost Paradises,* which this youth might have procreated in his own or any other name—for in truth he was fonder of inventing great bards than being one," he would not deign to participate in what he regarded as a "silly dispute," a "fantastic" and "ridiculous" subject.

To the very end, even as he condescended to compose his lengthy *Vindication,* Walpole would claim, "as I was originally an actor in this interlude without my consent, so am I a spectator most indifferent how it shall terminate."

Occasionally, despite their scornful tone, Walpole's arguments arouse some sympathy for his side of the relationship with Chatterton. As usually happens in the unraveling of an imposturous deed, the one who blows the whistle becomes the villain and somehow begins to look like a paranoid maniac, an envious libeler, a cruel and insensitive betrayer. And that is how most scholars ended up evaluating Walpole. On the other hand, those who had believed in the Rowleys, like Catcott, Barrett, and the pro-Rowleyan scholars, were regarded as upright and honest men whose worst crime was to have been foolish enough to believe in the lies of a clever boy.

But in fact Walpole, though he was far from an innocent bystander in the outcome of Chatterton's life, was absolutely right about the role in which he had been cast. "Is it not hard that a man on whom a forgery has been tried unsuccessfully, should for that single reason be held out to the world as an assassin of genius?" He protested, again with good reason, that he would have deserved the reproaches hurled at him if he had cherished an impostor, that he would have been blamable to his mother and to society if he had encouraged the youth's propensity to forgery, "which is not the talent most wanting culture in the present age."

Walpole was, however, willing to concede the extraordinary literary gifts that had for a moment fooled even him. After condescending to get involved in the controversy and thus having to read all of Chatterton's writings, Walpole began to have some admiration for the boy who in life had nearly put one over on him and who now after death had come back to plague him for having caught him in the act. "Still the boy remains a prodigy, by whatever means he procured or produced the edifice he erected." He commended the marvelous vigor, the quick intuition, the humor, the vein of satire, the perfection of the boy's poetry, "the amazing number of books he must have looked into, though chained down to a laborious and almost incessant service, and"—for Walpole this last point was the ultimate in demeaning slavery—"confined to Bristol." Finally, Walpole succumbed to marveling over Chatterton's talent for imposturousness. This sort of glorification of artistic sleight of hand is another of the commonplaces in the tale of an impostor: we condemn the impostor, yet we stand in awe before his ability to trick us. "In short," concluded Walpole, "I do not believe that there ever existed so masterly a genius, except that of

Psalmanazar, who before twenty-two could create a language, that all the learned of Europe, though they suspected could not detect."

Walpole's appreciation of Chatterton's talents and character demonstrate a latent generosity of spirit surprising in a man who was notorious for acrimony and arrogance. But his admiration for the boy's skillful counterfeiting was also true to form. As his critics were fond of pointing out, Walpole's literary brilliance and occasional shows of virtue did not prevent him from being hypocritical and outright dishonest when it suited his purposes. Many of the eminent scholars who participated in the Rowley debate were not nearly as clever as Walpole, and some of them were entirely misguided in their evaluation of the authenticity of Rowley's works. However, they knew better than to trust the veracity of this illustrious writer who had become the wealthy and powerful fourth earl of Orford. Walpole, whose literary fame is based largely on his elegant, witty, and frequently malicious letters, used his pen as a weapon. For a clever turn of phrase he would betray his closest friends. He would not hesitate to denigrate their characters and destroy their reputations. After his death, Walpole was characterized as a "bundle of inconsistent whims and affectations. His features were covered by mask within mask." His telling phrase, "all the house of forgery are relations," would be used to highlight the deceits of his own literary career. A review of Walpole's *Memoirs* concluded by warning readers to "receive with extreme caution and doubt the evidence of a witness who in so many weighty points has been, we may almost say *convicted* of all the arts of calumny, misrepresentation and falsehood."

It is important to remember that Walpole had had brief flings with literary imposture himself. In 1765, he had palmed off his novel, *The Castle of Otranto*, as a translation from the Italian printed at Naples in 1529. Another of his playful hoaxes was to write a counterfeit letter to Rousseau, whom he hated, offering the destitute and exiled author asylum in Austria. This cruelly deceptive letter Walpole boldly autographed with the signature of Frederick the Great. Even among those who deplored Chatterton's villainous character, Walpole's testimony had little currency. It was said, "If literary forgery were the capital offense, the same gallows would have sufficed for Walpole and Chatterton."

When he was accused of having rejected a poor, starving poet, Walpole's first impulse was to cover up. He asserted that Chatterton had lied about their correspondence, confident that the public would surely trust the word of a nobleman over that of an ignominious youth. He denied any exchange of letters with the boy. Then, after learning that Barrett was in possession of his correspondence with Chatterton, Walpole allowed that he must have returned Chatterton's letters and then either lost or mislaid the very last one, in which Chatterton demanded the return of his manuscripts. Some years later, after Walpole's death, the entire Chatterton-Walpole correspondence, including all the missing letters, showed up intact in *The Works of Horace Walpole.*

It also came out that he *had* received Chatterton's letter to him requesting the return of his manuscript. Walpole tried to justify his failure to reply in several ways. First, he claimed he had been out of the country when the letter arrived. Sometime later, he said that he had written a reply and then burned it, "reflecting that so wrong-headed a young man, of whom I knew nothing, and whom I had never seen, might be absurd enough to print my letter." The "burned" letter, however, appears in Walpole's collected papers with the following explanation:

> N.B. The above letter I had begun to write to Chatterton on his demanding his MSS. but not chusing to enter into a controversy with him, I did not finish it, and only folding up his papers, returned them.

Upon learning of the embarrassing preservation of the supposed nonexistent exchange of letters between himself and Chatterton, Walpole not only acknowledged that correspondence but haughtily demanded that the full extent of it be ascertained and published. He expressed his confidence that neither Rowley, should he rise from the dead, nor Chatterton, should he do the same, could prove that he had used the boy ill.

Walpole, of course, had never been privy to the "Walpole, I thought I should not ever see," verse which was not published until 1837, 40 years after his own death. Nevertheless, not long after Chatterton's suicide, Walpole, like everyone else, became aware that the pseudoanonymous Decimus-D.B.-Harry Wildfire satires in the 1769 and 1770 issues of *Town and Country Magazine* and *The Middlesex Journal* had been written by the young poet-turned-journalist. In these pieces, Walpole appears as Baron Otranto, Horatio Otranto, the great Dr. Trefoil who discovered "that the word *kine* came from the Saxon *cowine,*" or simply as Horace. In a Decimus article, "An Exhibition of Sign Painting," Walpole appears in one sign along with his aging mistress, the actress Kitty Clive. "A Piece of Modern Antiquity, by Horace Walpole. This is no other than a striking portrait of the facetious Mrs. Clive. Horace, finding it too large to be introduced into his next edition of Virtu,[1] has returned it on the town."

Walpole's sole acknowledgment of Chatterton's satires on him was to

---

[1] There is a triple pun here. *The Virtu* was an arts magazine. Walpole's *Anecdotes of Painting* was derived from the notes of the antiquarian artist, George Vertue.

belittle those who imagined his feelings could be touched by anything the boy had written about him. "He [Jacob Bryant, an affirmed Rowleyan] says Chatterton treated me very cruelly, in one of his writings; I am sure I did not feel it so. I suppose Bryant means under the title of Baron of Otranto, which is written with humour: I must have been the sensitive plant, if anything in that character had hurt me!"

The two Bristoleans who had adopted Chatterton, abetted his counterfeiting, and profited by his suicide eventually fared worse than Walpole. George Catcott, who had expected that his reputation and finances would swell through growing interest in the writings of Thomas Rowley, was disappointed. Whatever small fame he acquired concerned his propensities and his foolish acts of heroism.

His ridiculous behavior is recorded in *Life of Johnson*. When Boswell and Johnson visited Bristol in 1776, Catcott seized the occasion to convert the disbelieving Johnson to the Rowleyan faith. He asked him to read aloud some of the verses, as though just hearing the ancient words would constitute proof of their authenticity. To assure the great man's belief, he then invited Johnson to see with his own eyes the Muniment Room in the tower of St. Mary Redcliffe and the chest where the parchments had been found. Boswell reports:

> Dr. Johnson good-naturedly agreed; and though troubled with a shortness of breathing, laboured up a long flight of steps, till he came to the place where the wonderous chest stood. "There, (said Catcot, with a bouncing confident credulity) *there* is the very chest itself!" After this *ocular demonstration,* there was no more to be said.

Shortly after his brother's death in 1779, Catcott found himself heavily in debt. Though he made some profit from the Rowleys (a good deal less than he had wished for), the money was far from sufficient to pay off the huge losses from his pewtering business. His partner, Burgum, a "musicomaniac," had neglected the mundane affairs of the pewtering trade to listen to Handel and collect music manuscripts. When the business failed he would not assume any responsibility for the money he and Catcott owed. Catcott wrote of his ex-partner, "He has completely ruined himself, his wife and family, and by his haughty and artful behavior made all his best friends his greatest enemies. As it is I shall lose upward of 2,500 pounds by his dishonesty and subtle evasions." Though he managed eventually to pay his debts, Catcott lost his business and was forced to seek employment as an assistant shopkeeper to another pewterer, where he served customers and wrapped packages. Until a few years before his death in 1802, he labored from the break of day until eight or nine in the evening. His employer treated him as though he were an apprentice, without any rights or privileges. Catcott would lament that it was very trying indeed for a man of his age to be reduced to a condition of such humiliating servitude.

William Barrett, the man who had the most to gain by believing in Rowley, came to the most embarrassing end. As was fitting, part of his humiliation came about through his connection with Rowley. Barrett remained faithful to Rowley throughout the Rowley controversy. Even when the majority of learned men had finally accepted Chatterton as the true author, Barrett, whose *History* was documented by Rowley, was a steadfast Rowleyan.

In 1772, as the controversy gathered momentum, a red-faced Barrett stumbled through Michael Lort's penetrating queries: "As I told you before, I will not vouch for the authenticity of all; the originals I will abide by: and the minstrels songs; tho' the originals are destroy'd, I really believe to be authentic: tho' Chatterton might have thrown the Tragedy of Ella into its form, much of it I believe to be the genuine production of Rowley. . . ."

Five years later, Barrett wrote again to Lort with virtually no revision in his opinion: "There is a great deal to be said on both sides of the question—the medium perhaps is the truest—that they are not wholly genuine nor all forg-d—tho' some bear certainly the marks of modernity—yet it is improbable & almost impossible that all that I have seen & have in my possession under that name should be forg'd."

All during this time Catcott was growing more and more impatient that Barrett get on with his history and finally get it published. They could be the first then to publish works discovered by Chatterton. In 1778 the pewterer wrote to a renowned Rowleyan complaining about Barrett, "as he has for some years amused the world with the idea of an approaching Publication I will by no means be responsible for his veracity in fulfilling his engagements to the public." When the novel *Love and Madness* was published with a full account of Chatterton's life and some of his poetry, Catcott was visibly annoyed. Because of Barrett's hesitation to publish, Catcott had been scooped on the Chatterton story. And this only a year after his other crony, Burgum, had betrayed him and cast him into perpetual servitude.

At last, in 1789, the surgeon yielded up his manuscript to a publisher. The volume was dedicated to Levi Ames, the mayor, and the aldermen and common council of Bristol. The price was two guineas. Upon learning that nearly all of Chatterton's original parchments were printed in Barrett's history, Lort expressed his amused astonishment: "He appears to have adopted them all indiscriminately, and as the old saying is 'without either fear or wit,' . . ." Catcott, who had procured 178 subscribers and delivered the books personally, griped that "the name of Catcott does not once appear throughout the whole."

Barrett's thirty-year labor was greeted with derision. Every review was negative, some mocking, a few overlaid with strained courtesy. His Bristol friends and acquaintances regarded him with embarrassed silence. He received anonymous letters complaining about the quality of the engraving plates and the language. Barrett died in October of 1789, too late to avoid some notices, too soon, luckily, to read them all. The items that gave the critics and anti-Rowleyans the most pleasure were Rowley's drawings. Horace Walpole was triumphant: "I am sorry, very sorry, for what you tell me of poor Barrett's fate. Though he did write worse than Shakespeare, it is a great pity he was told so, as it killed him."

Even had he not relied so heavily on Chatterton's counterfeits, Barrett still would not have received glowing notices. The surgeon had been too lazy and too immersed in the pleasures of everyday life to have produced the monumental history he had envisioned. But had he not been so caught up in the Rowley mythology, his work, which had some value, might at least have been regarded as another dull but respectable scholarly treatise. As it is, Barrett's *History of Bristol,* when it is remembered at all, is remembered as one of the major fiascos of the Rowley controversy. If Barrett had truly believed in Rowley, he was a fool. And if he had known the truth, then he was Chatterton's abettor, as guilty of counterfeiting as the young man he had taken under his wing.

Barrett was not the only eighteenth-century scholar who was belittled for the tenacity of his belief in the Rowleys. The eminent antiquarian Jeremiah Milles, Dean of Exeter and one of the major contestants in the Rowley controversy, devoted several years of his life to collecting data that would prove beyond a doubt that an uneducated stripling like Chatterton could not possibly have composed beauteous poetry such as *Aella,* a tragic drama that, "required not only an elevation of poetic genius far superior to that possessed by Chatterton, but also such moral and mental qualifications as never entered into any part of his character or conduct and which could not possibly be acquired by a youth of his age and inexperience."

The learned Dean would muster in support of his pro-Rowleyan thesis some of the dreariest arguments in eighteenth-century English letters. Coleridge would refer to Milles's ruminations on Rowley's poetry as "An owl mangling a poor dead nightingale." And though he had his serious reservations about the nightingale, Walpole had this to say about Milles and the other leading Rowleyan, Jacob Bryant: "I had rather believe in Rowley than go through their proofs."

Edmund Malone, who had for a brief time believed in Rowley but became one of the more vocal anti-Rowleyan scholars, recommended that Milles and Bryant be brought to their senses by being incarcerated in the Muniment Room of St. Mary Redcliffe and set to measuring the empty chests or computing the precise number of parchments of a size they could hold in their hands.

Ambiguities of veracity and authenticity are challenges expected by all biographers, even those investigating relatively straightforward personages who are still alive to verify the facts of their lives—at least as they think them to be. With the history of an impostor—dead or alive—such ambiguities constitute the very substance of the narrative. First, there are the uncertainties created by the duplicities of the impostor. These are then compounded by the dubious motives of those who have directly abetted or otherwise hoped to profit from the imposture. The tale begins to include a small army of imposturouslike characters, many of whom are far more deceitful and much less sympathetic than the impostor himself. Whoever attempts the biography of an impostor must expect to compose a history of the ethical and moral duplicities of the age in which the impostor lived.

Not surprisingly, in one way and another, a number of Chatterton's biographers became entangled in the web of misrepresentation and fraudulence. The first widely published account of Chatterton's life appears in the 1780 *Love and Madness: A Story Too True / In a Series of Letters between Parties, whose / Names would perhaps be mentioned, were / they less known or less lamented*. About the only merit to this "scandalous" 296-page novel, supposedly an exchange of letters between a love-crazed reverend and the famous but unresponsive actress he murdered—a work in fact composed entirely by the supposed editor, Sir Herbert Croft—is that it contained a 120-page narrative, totally irrelevant to the reverend's homicide, about the life of Thomas Chatterton. Every succeeding biography would use as one of its primary sources the research and findings of the author Sir Herbert Croft.

Appearing nine years after Croft's reliable but self-serving account of Chatterton's life was *The Life of Thomas Chatterton with Criticisms on His Genius and Writings* by George Gregory, Doctor of Divinity, Author of Essays Historical and Moral. Gregory, a fair-minded and honorable scholar, relied heavily on Croft's version of Chatterton's life. But his starting point was the research of Michael Lort, longtime friend and colleague of Horace Walpole. As he proceeded, Gregory found himself in need of more direct sources of information. At that point Lort loaned him his personally notated copy of *Love and Madness* and his collection of Chatterton's non-Rowleyan poetic and journalistic efforts from *Town and Country Magazine*. He also gave Gregory a copy of his interview with the attorney with whom Chatterton had served the two years of his apprenticeship. When Gregory completed his labors in the fall of 1788, he sent a manuscript to Lort for correction. Lort added his notes, signed them with a mysterious *O*, but would not allow his name or authorization to appear in support of Gregory's text.

Several of Lort's *O*'s vindicated Horace Walpole. In a letter to Walpole dated November 10, 1788, Lort writes:

> A MS of Chatterton . . . has been lately put into my hands, in which I made some alterations and corrections of facts better known to me than to the writer. In the account given of the transaction between you and Chatterton, it seemed to me that the writer had leaned too much on the side of the question unfavourable to you, as given by ignorant or prejudiced persons, and I think I convinced him that he had done so.

Evidently Gregory was entirely convinced by Lort's commentary. He deleted all unfavorable references to the transactions between Chatterton and Walpole. He combined into one long note all of Lort's correctives and concluded, "to ascribe to Mr. Walpole's neglect, (if it can merit so harsh an appellation) the dreadful catastrophe, which happened at the distance of nearly two years after, would be the highest degree of injustice and absurdity."

While it is to Gregory's credit that he respected most of Lort's corrections, he was too quick to absolve Walpole of all wrongdoing. Gregory was never guilty of outright misrepresentation, but he had a suggestible streak and could be taken in by the lies, biases, and prejudices of others. Thus, the deceptions and self-deceptions of writers like Croft and Milles are rendered in his book as gospel. He often permitted testimony to stand without comment even when that testimony was from a source whose own character was questionable. A notable example are his lengthy quotations from James Thistlewaite, the clever liar and plagiarist, whose envy of Chatterton muddied all his testimonials in favor of his friend. In defending Chatterton against the charges of forgery and counterfeiting, Thistlewaite claimed that it would have been impossible for someone with such an "eccentric" intellect, a dilettante who one day "was busily employed in the study of Heraldry and English antiquities" and the next "deeply engaged, confounded and perplexed, amidst the subtleties of metaphysical disquisition or lost and bewildered in the abstruse labyrinth of mathematics" could have composed the Rowleys. To clinch this pro-Rowleyan position Thistlewaite argued that "vanity and an inordinate thirst after praise" distinguished Chatterton from his peers, therefore, "I conceive myself at liberty to draw the following inference, that had Chatterton been the author of the poems imputed to Rowley . . . he would have made it his first, his greatest pride."

An adapted version of Gregory's biography served as the introduction to the 1803 collection of Chatterton's writing, the three-volume *Works*. Quite remarkably, Gregory's introduction to this charitable venture, given that it was derived from the commentaries of the pedantically incorrect Rowleyans, the scandalous novel of the self-serving Croft, the testimonies of the envious and disreputable Thistlewaite, and the Lort whitewash of Walpole, survives as a creditable treatment of the life of Chatterton. Though he tended toward the sentimental view of Chatterton that was to dominate nineteenth-century versions of the poet's life, Gregory was aware of some of his own personal biases and prejudices. He conscientiously tried to present both sides of Chatterton's character, his speculative infidelities as well as his noble poetic spirit.

About a decade into the nineteenth century, John Dix began to write the first full-scale biography of Chatterton, promising to bring out new, previously unpublished data on the life of the poet. That calamitous volume was published in 1837 with a second edition in 1851. In its general outlines it is a portrait of Chatterton as an innocent child betrayed by the world. Deliberately or as a result of his own innocent credulity, Dix produced an essentially fraudulent piece of work. Whatever is accurate in Dix's sentimental rendering of the poet's life was lifted from the old familiars—*Love and Madness,* Dean Milles's *Dissertation,* Gregory's *Life.* Of the seemingly new material, nearly half is a straightforward appropriation of Horace Walpole's lengthy vindication letter in which some of Chatterton's satirical poetry and anonymous journal articles had been printed for the first time. The rest of the so-called new and previously unpublished data is contained in Dix's appendices and in the narrative sections derived from them. The appendices and everything in them are entirely untrue, either fabricated by Dix personally or by one of his research collaborators, all of whom were either outright dishonest or being deceived by their own informants who were themselves lying, senile, or just plain fanciful. The frontispiece of Dix's *Life of Thomas Chatterton* is a counterfeit life portrait of Chatterton as a child.

Then in 1871 came the Walter Skeat edition of Chatterton's writing, an honest effort to lay the ghost of Rowley to rest and vindicate Chatterton while simultaneously proving that he was a forger. Through his scholarly efforts, Skeat was able to deduce which dictionaries and other linguistic references Chatterton had used for his invention of the fifteenth-century language of Rowley. Skeat, however, managed single-handedly to create a new realm of Chatterton misrepresentation by deantiquing the Rowley language into something presumably resembling the Anglo-Saxon rhythms and words that originally had sprung forth from the young poet's mind.

So it went, each biographer interweaving the fundamental *Love and Madness* narrative with his own prejudices, romantic fancies, wishful thinking, and then incorporating into his own emerging tale the errors and misrepresentations of his predecessors.

Well into the twentieth century, biographers were reluctant to recognize the proud, melancholic, cynical, impulsive, ambitious young man beneath the garb of the virtuous priest, as though such cognizance would be tantamount to a betrayal of his wholesome traits—his affectionate concern for family and friends, his literary enthusiasms, his emotional vitality, his prodigious intellectual and poetic gifts. A classic of the idealizing genre is Charles Edward Russell's 1909 biography, the title of which conscientiously echoes the lines from William Wordsworth's *Resolution and Independence:*

> *I thought of Chatterton, the marvellous Boy,*
> *The sleepless Soul that perished in his pride.*

Russell's fanciful construction of Chatterton's life, *Thomas Chatterton, The Marvelous Boy, The Story of a Strange Life*, begins:

> I have tried in these pages to set forth the plain records of this extraordinary story with hope to do something, however little, however poor and inadequate to clear from calumny and undeserved reproach the memory of one of the greatest minds and sweetest souls that ever dwelt on this earth.

Having so frankly and so unabashedly revealed his adoration of his marvelous boy, Russell does not hesitate to pick and choose every detail that will prove the shining innocence of that sweet soul. Every shred of evidence, however slight or doubtful, is marshaled to damn those who brought the boy to his ignominious end. Foolish Catcott and scheming Barrett get their due. Walpole comes off as a selfish, deceitful, petty, vindictive scoundrel. Russell sifts the facts he requires from *Love and Madness*, from Gregory's biography, and then elaborates on the false testimonies from Dix's biography in order to construct his wishful version of Chatterton.

The moral ambiguities in Thomas Chatterton's character, with its exotic amalgam of artistic genius and imposturousness, infected those who set out to understand him. As his biographers and critics attempted to decipher Chatterton's "true" character, they necessarily evolved their own mythologies of good and evil, virtue and vice, veracity and falsehood. They approached the great issues of belief and faith with a kind of religious fervor. Where in these narratives of corrupted innocence will we find the trustworthy witnesses?

In any common court of justice two people would be summarily dismissed as untrustworthy informants on the life of Thomas Chatterton: his mother Sarah and his sister Mary. During his lifetime their love for him was a blend of intimidated wonderment and unqualified admiration. A lacing of skepticism scarcely balanced the potion. After his death the two women gave out narratives to the world that were innocent, yet crafty. The considerations that claimed their attention were the honor of their beloved boy and the facts that would substantiate that honor.

Nevertheless a biased account is not the same as a fraudulent account. Nor, if one grasps the unique rules of evidence of such an account, is it necessarily unreliable or untrustworthy. In the tale of an impostor the evidence necessarily unfolds along the bias.

As Sarah and Mary reminisced on their "dear boy," they composed what can be taken as a reliable portrait of the impostor-poet Thomas Chatterton. For all their desire to protect his image, the two women did not hesitate to speak of Tom's bewildering peculiarities. With regard to the Rowley creations, Sarah and Mary, like Chatterton himself, were steadfast. They had seen the boy laboring night and day on his translations. He had been exactly what he claimed to be, a translator of ancient poems.

The tenacity with which Sarah and Mary clung to their belief in Tom's innocence suggests that love and loyalty were not their sole motives. The charges against the dead youth must have had a profoundly disturbing effect on them. Infidelity and debauching were humiliating enough, but words like "forgery" and "counterfeiting" would have terrified these two respectable, law-abiding women. In their most anxious moments they even imagined they could be hanged for Thomas's crimes. Much as they adored their beloved Tom, Sarah and Mary also had their doubts, doubts which they could barely admit to, even in the privacy of their own thoughts.

In the end, Sarah's and Mary's blind devotion to their "lost darling" is a testimony that rings true. As they were, in the strict interpretation of the law, "false" witnesses after Chatterton's death, so in his lifetime their passionate veneration of him steamed up the emotional atmosphere in which imposturousness thrives. What they have left to history as the record of Chatterton's infancy, childhood, and young manhood may not be the whole truth, but it is a truth that counts.

Caught up as they were in defending his innocence, neither woman could comprehend that Thomas Chatterton would be far more valued as a forger than as a mere transcriber. If, between the ages of fourteen and sixteen, he had invented the Rowley poems, plays, and narratives, then he was a prodigy whose writings now that he was dead might also be worth a sum of money. Sarah and Mary did not immediately grasp the literary merit of Chatterton's writing. In fact they found the ancient Rowley poetry strange and incomprehensible. But there were many others no more intelligent who nevertheless calculated the market value of anything Chatterton.

The two women were besieged by callers. They were interviewed, questioned, cross-examined by all manner of self-seeking visitors. There were the journalists who saw exciting copy in the story of the suicide on Brooke Street, a dead poet, a forger, a poor misguided youth. There was, of course, Catcott. The pewterer, who had already amassed a sizable collection of Chatterton's ancient poetry, persuaded Mrs. Chatterton to part with all that remained, thereby cornering for himself and Barrett practically the entire market on Rowley manuscripts. For this bounty he grudgingly reimbursed Sarah five guineas. Barrett, though he willingly accepted copies of the Rowleys collected by Catcott, did not participate in the actual looting. Nor did he pay a condolence call on the mother of the boy who for two years had supplied him with documentation for his mighty *History of Bristol*. Finally, the church authorities swooped down on Mrs. Chatterton and demanded that she return all the parchments that her husband had "stolen" from the Muniment Room forty years earlier. In the bargain they also convinced the confused woman to surrender to the church most of the copybooks and papers belonging to her son.

Mrs. Chatterton capitulated to the powerful men who visited her home partly to protect the honor of her son, partly to quell her anxiety. Mary was less intimidated than her mother, but, in her desire to enhance the reputation of her brother, she also complied. As the full truth about her brother's genius dawned on her, Mary became more wily. Whereas in the early days after her brother's suicide she would insist on the phrase "the poems my brother copied from Rowley," later on at the merest suggestion that her brother had actually composed the whole of the Rowley narrative, she would reply archly, "Aye, to be sure; anybody might have seen that with half an eye."

Mary and her mother were predictably congenial to the Rowleyans who left generous donations and whose literary arguments depended on proofs of the boy's honesty and upstanding character. The Rowleyans, among them Dean Milles, who interviewed Mrs. Chatterton extensively, walked a delicate balance. They had to demonstrate Chatterton too untutored and unskilled to have written such beautiful poetry, but then again he had to have been at least clever enough to recognize the worth of the ancient documents and sufficiently literary to transcribe them. Mary and Sarah walked the balance along with their interrogators with one thought only: to prove that Tom was a diligent, honest, respectable translator. Their compliance was mixed with pride and considerable amazement at the extraordinary attention given to the name of Chatterton.

Unsettled as they were by their private doubts, the two women were easily intimidated by the pressure of male authority. They had the presence of mind to hold onto the Walpole verse and a few other personal items, but within a decade after Chatterton's suicide Mary and Sarah had loaned or given away most of the poetry, letters, and papers in their possession.

On July 23, 1778 Herbert Croft, then a young man of twenty-seven and not yet a reverend, not yet a baronet, appeared in Bristol to gather information on Chatterton. After managing to entice the tenaciously possessive George Catcott into loaning him some Chatterton poems (among them *Happiness*), Croft called on Mary in her new home on Somersetshire Square, where she now lived with her husband, Thomas Newton, a glass cutter. Croft, who presented himself as a defender of Chatterton's honor, prevailed on Mary Newton to allow him to borrow, "for one hour only," the letters her brother had written to her from London. Mary was thoroughly impressed by Croft's soft-spoken, clerical manner. She consented to his request, without pausing to ask for his name or credentials. Croft paid Mary one guinea as the fee for his one-hour loan. He then paid a visit to Sarah Chatterton, made a similar request of her, reimbursed her with a half-guinea, and soon afterwards departed Bristol with several of Chatterton's earliest poems and with the entire collection of Chatterton's letters to his sister and mother under his arm. Neither woman ever saw him again.

After two weeks of bewildered anxiety, they heard from Croft. He wrote, this time promising that their "little treasure" would soon be returned. In August, Croft wrote again asking that Mary Newton write up a memorandum of her recollections of Thomas's infancy and childhood. The sister assented to Croft's wishes. The man's unreliability, his inconsiderate delay in returning the letters he had borrowed, seemed less important to her than the dedication with which he appeared to be pursuing the life of her dear brother. Within the month, Mary had fulfilled her assignment. That autumn, having copied the letters, Croft did send back all but Chatterton's last letter to his mother which he later claimed Mrs. Chatterton had suffered him to keep as a memento.

Mary Newton's letter of September 22, 1778 to Croft survives as one of the crucial documents on the life and character of Thomas Chatterton. In her interview accounts to Dean Milles or Michael Lort she embroidered on the facts outlined in that letter and occasionally added or altered a detail or two here and there, but the basic narrative she had entrusted to the author of *Love and Madness* would never change.

That heartfelt letter, printed for the first time in Croft's best-selling novel, opens with Mary's touching commentary on the paucity of her own literary gifts and her high regard for a gentleman such as Herbert Croft—who surely would do honor to the "sacred name" of Thomas Chatterton.

> Conscious of my own inability's to write to a man of letters. And reluctant to engage in the painful recollections of the particulars of the life of my poor deceased brother. Together with the ill state of health I've enjoyed since it has been required of me, are Sir, the real causes of my not writing sooner. But I am invited to write as to a friend, inspired with the sacred name, I will forget the incorrectness of my epistle and proceed.

When it came to her brother's life history, Mary's truthfulness was both tactical and psychologically keen. She could be enchantingly circumstantial with events that would enhance her brother's reputation. She was adept at sidestepping those that might in any way belittle him. In her letter to Croft she handles her brother's early school failure with grace. She does not mention that he had been remanded to his mother by the new schoolmaster as a probable dullard, incapable of improvement, but instead underscores the splendid originality of her brother's reading tastes: he "always objected to read in a small book." In an unconscious assessment of the psychological meaning of her brother's fate, she rightly intuited precisely which events would proclaim him to Croft as a boy destined for artistic renown.

After receiving Mary's letter, Croft extended his researches to London, where he conducted detailed interviews with all those who might have had recollections of the last months of the poet's life (Croft was the landlord of the Walmsleys, who had rented a room to Chatterton during his first nine weeks in London). He then interviewed Chatterton's Brooke Street neighbors.

Many later biographers dutifully credited Croft for his exhaustive research and then went on to assail him for his unscrupulous behavior toward the Chatterton family. They charged that he deceitfully gathered data on Chatterton while planning to use the information in his unsavory, pseudobiographical novel, *Love and Madness*. However, on this score Croft's accusers go too far. The historical events that inspired that notorious volume did not occur until April 1779, some eight months after Croft began his Chatterton researches. Therefore it would have been impossible for him to have been deliberately scheming all along to deceive Mary and Sarah. He had probably begun his project with only some minor duplicities in mind, like keeping the letters for more than one hour and copying them without permission. The grander deception grew on him with the march of events.

Though it came as an afterthought, Croft's decision to include Chatterton's letters and life in *Love and Madness* was duplicitous enough. Not only did he neglect to inform Sarah and Mary of his new inspiration, he never bothered to apply for their permission to reprint Tom's letters, an application the two women surely would have refused had they been aware of the context in which those treasured letters would appear.

When the women discovered how they had been taken in by Herbert Croft, they were appalled. He had seemed to them to be one of the finest and most respectable of the many interviewers. In March 1780, Sarah and Mary had the shock of seeing the letters printed entire in a titillating novel based on the murder of the mistress of Lord Sandwich by James Hackman, the clergyman who was hanged for the crime. By adding suicide and forgery to the already tantalizing combination of lust and murder, the inclusion of the Chatterton material increased considerably the sales of Croft's novel.

Mrs. Chatterton wrote to Croft denouncing him for his breach of trust. In response she received from Croft ten pounds to be divided between herself and her daughter, along with his written assurances that the family of Thomas Chatterton "would never be forgotten by H.C." Croft, by then the author of a best-seller in its second edition, considered his payment and his generous sentiments to be ample compensation.

Perhaps his conscience did bother him just a bit. The next year he was moved to make yet another promise he would never keep. He wrote to Mary Newton inquiring about the circumstances of the Chatterton survivors and proposed that he might start a subscription for their financial aid. Mary, no longer an obliging innocent, wrote back a letter that could be interpreted as a polite thank-you note—or as a cagey rebuke. She acknowledged the ten pounds she and her mother had received the previous year and then stated that this sum was the only benefit her family had ever reaped from the labors of her dear brother.

There the correspondence between the Chattertons and the Reverend Sir Henry Croft rested until 1796, when Mary, then ten years a widow who had lost all but one of her four children, solicited Croft for the financial aid he had offered some fifteen years earlier. Croft was indignant. He declined to respond directly to Mrs. Newton. "The sort of threatening letter which Mrs. Newton's is will never succeed with me; but if the clergyman of the parish will do me the favour to write me word, through Mrs. Newton, what Chatterton's relations consist of and what characters they bear, I will try, by everything in my power to serve them; yet certainly not if any of them pretend to have the smallest claim on me."

In view of the sizable profits he had made on *Love and Madness,* Croft's suspicious attitude and surly tone were gratuitous. But Croft, like Chatterton's Bristol collaborators, Catcott and Barrett, was about to come to the end of his glory days. One year after this letter, the reverend was imprisoned for debt. Two years later, upon his release from Exeter Gaol, his mistreatment of Sarah Chatterton and Mary Newton would be made public through the efforts of the Bristol poet Robert Southey.

Between the time of Chatterton's suicide in 1770 and Southey's interventions on behalf of his survivors, the English romantic movement had begun to blossom. Chatterton's fate was no longer in the hands of antiquarians and journalists. He would belong to the poets.

NOTES

I am deeply indebted to E. H. W. Meyerstein, who died in 1952, some twenty years after completing the definitive biography of Chatterton, *A Life of Thomas Chatterton*. Meyerstein can be as guilty as any biographer of wishful thinking, introducing pleasing conjecture as though it were proven truth. Nevertheless, his determined efforts to untangle truth from falsehood have defined the directions that I did or did not explore on my own.

In putting together my portrait of Chatterton, I found every biography listed below useful, even those notorious for their falsehoods. Since Meyerstein occasionally relies on these secondary sources, I was wary of some of his interpretations. Finally, though, when pressed, I usually went along with Meyerstein, whose judgment, on the whole, is relatively free of the vulnerabilities of other Chatterton studies. Eventually, the naiveté, errors, bias, inconsistency, and conscious or unconscious falsehoods of Chatterton's various biographers became a minor theme of my own narrative.

Whenever feasible, with the able and devoted assistance of Helen Foster (see Acknowledgment), I have checked holographs and other primary sources in Bristols Avon County Reference Library, the British Museum, the New York Public Library, and the Phoenix collection at Columbia University.

Each biographical study of Chatterton will be cited hereafter by the author's initials, followed by page number(s).

Chatterton Biographies
Croft, Sir Herbert. *Love and Madness*. London: G. Kearsly, 1780. (HC)
Dix, John. *The Life of Thomas Chatterton*. London: Hamilton, Adams and Company, 1837. (JD)
Gregory, George. *The Life of Thomas Chatterton, with Criticisms on his Genius and Writings, and a Concise View of the Controversy Concerning Rowley's Poems*. London: G. Kearsley, 1789. (GG) A version of this book also served as the Introduction to *The Works of Thomas Chatterton*, 3 vols., ed. Joseph Cottle and Robert Southey. London: Longman and Rees, 1803.
Ingram, John H. *The True Chatterton*. London: T. Fisher Unwin, 1910. (JI)
Maitland, S. R. *Chatterton: An Essay*. London: Rivington, 1857. (SM)
Masson, David. *Chatterton, A Biography*. New York: Dodd, Mead and Company, 1856; rev. 1899. (DM)

NOTES

Meyerstein, E. H. W. *A Life of Thomas Chatterton.* New York: Scribners, 1930. (EM)

Nevill, John Cranstoun. *Thomas Chatterton.* London: Frederick Muller, Ltd., 1948. (JN)

Russell, Charles Edward. *Thomas Chatterton: The Marvelous Boy.* New York: Moffat, Yard and Co., 1908. (CR)

Wilson, Daniel. *Chatterton: A Biographical Study.* London: Macmillan and Co., 1869. (DW)

The Writings of Thomas Chatterton

The Complete Works of Thomas Chatterton, ed. Donald S. Taylor, in association with Benjamin B. Hoover. Vols. I and II. Oxford: The Clarendon Press, 1971. Citations will appear as DT vol.: p. I am grateful to Taylor and Hoover for bringing together this definitive edition of Chatterton's writings and for their excellent notes and critical evaluations.

The Psychology of Adolescence

Kaplan, Louise J. *Adolescence: The Farewell to Childhood.* New York: Simon and Schuster, 1984. Citations appear as *Adolescence.*

INTRODUCTION

"The Impostor," *Adolescence,* pp. 283–317.

Phyllis Greenacre, "The Impostor," in *Emotional Growth I;* "The Family Romance of the Artist," and "The Relation of the Impostor to the Artist," in *Emotional Growth II* (New York: International Universities Press, 1971).

Thomas Mann. "it is in essence," preface to *Stories of Three Decades,* trans. H. T. Lowe-Porter (New York: Modern Library, 1936), p. vii; hereafter referred to as Mann.

The formula for the relationship between perversion and pathological lying appears in Otto Fenichel, "The Economics of Pseudologia Phantastica," in *Collected Papers of Otto Fenichel,* 2nd ser. (New York: W.W. Norton, 1954), p. 133; hereafter referred to as Fenichel.

Jacob Arlow, "Character Perversion," in *Currents in Psychoanalysis,* ed. Irwin M. Marcus (New York: International Universities Press, Inc., 1971), pp. 317–336; hereafter referred to as Arlow. "The petty lie is," p. 326.

Literary Impostors in Eighteenth-Century England

Murray Warren, *A Descriptive and Annotated Bibliography of Thomas Chatterton* (New York and London: Garland Publishing, Inc., 1977), pp. 13–15. Warren presents a heavily abbreviated list of English literary impostors, among them Thomas Birch (1705–1766), who fabricated England's first

NOTES

newspaper, *Englishe Mercurie, imprinted at London by Her Highness's Printer, 1588;* Charles Betram (1723–1765), who produced an alleged ancient manuscript by Richard of Cirencester; John Jordon (1746–1809), the composer of some fraudulent tales on the life of Shakespeare; John Pinkerton (1758–1826), author of the spurious *Select Scottish Ballads;* and Allan Cunningham (1748–1842), who contributed many spurious entries to a collection of the *Remains of Nithedale and Galloway Song.*

Then, of course, there was Horace Walpole, the first person to detect the imposturous nature of Chatterton's poetry. He set an example for legitimate scholars by announcing on the title page that his own *The Castle of Otranto* was translated by a fictitious William Marshall, Gent. from the original Italian of Onuphrio Muralto, Canon of the Church of St. Nicholas, at Otranto, and claiming that the work, originally printed at Naples in 1529, was "found in the library of an ancient Catholic family in the north of England."

Horace Walpole's literary imposture: Wilmarth Sheldon Lewis, *Horace Walpole,* Bollingen Series xxxv, 9 (New York: Pantheon Books, 1960), 157.

Stanley Kunitz, "The Poet's Quest for the Father," *New York Times Book Review,* 22 February 1987, p. 37.

Judith Rossner, discussion on "Perversion, Falsehood, Creativity," by Louise J. Kaplan, at conference on *Character Perversions,* Council of Psychoanalytic Psychotherapists, October 19, 1986.

Chapter One

The Death of Chatterton was first exhibited at the Royal Academy in 1856. Ruskin said of the painting, "Faultless and wonderful: a most noble example of the great [pre-Raphaelite] school. Examine it well inch by inch: it is one of the pictures which intend and accomplish the entire placing before your eyes of an actual fact—and that a solemn one. Give it much time." As scandal surrounded the name Chatterton, so scandal "became inextricably intertwined with the history of the painting." Wallis selected his friend George Meredith, a struggling young writer, to pose. It is Meredith's head with the flowing chestnut hair but without his beard. Wallis subsequently eloped with Meredith's wife. *The Pre-Raphaelites* (The Tate Gallery: Penguin Books, 1984), pp.142–144. A smaller replica of this painting is at Yale University, and a small sketch hangs in the Birmingham Art Museum.

Coleridge had been working on the *Monody* since the age of thirteen, when he composed a few lines as a school exercise. He wrote the first draft of the longer version at sixteen and recopied it at eighteen. Coleridge continued to add, correct, and delete lines until his death in 1834.

Byron, "Chatterton is never vulgar," George Gordon Byron, *Works* VI:413, as cited by EM, p. 507 (no publisher given).

Newspaper stories: butcher boy: *Lloyds Evening Post,* 27 August 1770; stabbed

NOTES

widow: *Middlesex Journal,* 28 August 1770; bargaining salesman: *London Evening Post,* 28 August 1770.

On Bristol in the Eighteenth Century

General: John Latimer, *The Annals of Bristol in the Eighteenth Century;* hereafter referred to as Latimer.

Defoe quotation: Peter T. Marcy, *Eighteenth Century Views of Bristol and Bristolians* (Bristol: Bristol Branch of the Historical Association, 1966), p. 2; "glass bottles," p. 3; descriptions of the riverways, tides and the Severn, pp. 8–10; hereafter referred to as Marcy.

Defoe's *Tour* was known to be composed partially of his plagiarisms from other accounts. Later, his work would be freely plagiarized by other writers. This state of affairs was not thought unusual "in an age during which appropriation was as common as original writing," (Marcy, p. 1).

Trade and population: Marcy, pp. 3–7.

Nikolaus Pevsner, *The Buildings of England, North Somerset and Bristol* (Middlesex: Penguin Books, Ltd., 1958), p. 362.

Walpole, "dirtiest great shop," Marcy, p. 8, as cited in *The Yale Edition of Horace Walpole's Correspondence,* ed. W. S. Lewis (New Haven: Yale University Press, 1951) x. 253; hereafter referred to as WSL 51.

Description of Bristol: "streets narrow and ill-paved," Marcy, p. 10; "timbers and plastic," p. 10; "pavement worn smooth," p. 11; "another narrow," p. 15.

Pope, "no civilized company," Marcy, p. 15, as cited from George Sherburn, ed., *Correspondence of Alexander Pope,* 5 vols. (Oxford:1956): IV:204.

Summary of Chatterton's Life

Specific citations will be given under notes for ensuing chapters, particularly the notes for chapter 2. The summary, the family romance, and the replacement-child interpretations are mine. Fuller explorations and references for these interpretations appear in later chapters, particularly 2, 8, and 10.

Mary's descriptions of her brother's early childhood: "thurst for preeminence," the commander over his playmates are from her letter to Sir Herbert Croft: HC, p. 144.

Carey's elegy: *Town and Country Magazine* (October 1770).

Story of the delft cup: JD, p. 6 and Michael Lort's testimony on anecdotes of Chatterton from his sister: Bristol's Avon County Reference Library, 11457, f. 130–133; hereafter referred to as B11457. That story first appeared in *Public Advertiser,* 8 June 1772, and then in *European Magazine* (April 1792).

Mary's description of her brother's reading habits: HC, pp. 143–144.

Mary's description of life at Colston's: HC, p. 144.

Mary's description of Chatterton's moods: HC, p. 144.

"God has sent his creatures," JI, p. 94; GG footnote, p. lxxii.

Thomas Chatterton, Sr.: EM, p. 7; CR, pp. 13–16; JI, pp. 20–25, 29–30; JN, pp. 10–11.

Family romance: The concept of the family romance originates with Sigmund Freud's paper, "Family Romances," in *Standard Edition* (London: The Hogarth Press), 9:236–241. The writings of Sigmund Freud are hereafter referred to as *SE* vol:p. Applications of that concept to the life of Thomas Chatterton appear in Greenacre, "The Family Romance of the Artist," pp. 510–513.

Jack-and-the-Beanstalk as an idiosyncratic romance, from "The Impostor," in *Adolescence*, pp. 297–298.

Will, DT I:501.

"Here I am," DT I:510.

Sibley, "accumulated malevolence," *A New and Complete Illustration of Occult Sciences* (London: 1797), p. 808.

Rossetti on Chatterton: J. Knight, *Life of Rossetti*, p. 28, cited by EM, p. 516 (no publisher given).

Reburial Stories

Mrs. Edkins: JI, Appendix, pp. 308–309.

Cottle story: *ibid*. Cottle's embarrassing volume of poetry and essays received universally bad notices and succeeded in alienating the former bookseller and editor from all those he had imagined would become his fellow poets. Southey was among those who deserted him. Cottle's motive for including the Chatterton story was probably to remind the public of his association with the great poets.

Mrs. Stockwell's version: JD, Appendix A, by George Cumberland, pp. 299–300.

The architectural writer is George Pryce, *Memorials of the Canynges Family* (Bristol: The Author, 1854) citing the letter from George Cumberland, excerpts of which appear in JI, pp. 309–311. Pryce amends his story: JD, p. 311.

Displacements of Chatterton's Bones

Fleet Street Market erected over the Shoe Lane Workhouse: EM, pp. 444–445.

Farringdon Avenue to Little Ilford: EM, p. 445, citing G. W. Wright, *Notes and Queries*, 15 December 1928.

"This does not exhaust all the possibilities," EM, citing *Low Life* in footnote to p. 445.

Chatterton's Monument

"Proclaim our darling Son, our pride, our glory . . ." CR, p. 260. These lines appear in an ode read in honor of Chatterton in a commemorative program at the Assembly Room, Prince's Street, Bristol, December 3, 1784.

> *Strike the Lyre, the trumpet sound*
> *Wake to Joy each silent string,*
> *Let the vaulted Roof rebound*

NOTES

> *While the immortal Bard we sing*
> *While we proclaim our darling Son*
> *Our pride, our glory—Chatterton!*

The celebration and the full ode: CR, pp. 259–260.

Story of Chatterton's monument: CR, pp. 261–263, and "Chatterton Memorials" in *Bristol Mercury*, 4 November 1887, as cited in Reece Winstone's photographic essay, *Bristol Past and Present: a pictorial record of the ancient City of Bristol* (Headington, England: Oxford Illustrated Press, Ltd., 1976), p. 8; hereafter referred to as Winstone.

Inscriptions: As cited on p. 9, Winstone.

"To the Memory of," *Will*, DT I:501.

The present-day museum staff believes that the vicar in the 1960s disliked the idea of a suicide's statue being in the churchyard. Other contemporary Bristoleans have suggested that the statue was aesthetically offensive—not worthy of St. Mary's. Or perhaps, since the monument had been crumbling and neither the church nor the Bristol Council could, or would, pay for the repair, there was no choice but to dismantle it. This information was reported in interviews with museum staff and other Bristol citizens by Helen Foster, January 1985, June 1985, and also in a personal communication to the author from J. Bryant, Department of Archaeology and History, City of Bristol Museum and Art Gallery, 20 June 1985.

CHAPTER TWO

Sibley, "was a native of Bristol," p. 808.

Thomas Chatterton, Sr., believer in magic, "deeply read in Cornelius Agrippa," as recalled by Edward Gardner in his October 8, 1802 letter, *The Works of Thomas Chatterton III, containing Miscellaneous Pieces in Prose* (London: Biggs and Cottle for T.N. Longman and O. Rees, Paternoster-Row, 1803), p. 523; hereafter referred to as *Works*.

Significance of Redcliffe neighborhood and St. Mary's: Keith Brace, *Portrait of Bristol* (London: Robert Hale, 1971), pp. 52–54.

Chatterton on St. Mary's: July 1, 1770 letter to Carey, DT I:640.

Mary's October 17, 1802 letter to the editor of *Works*, p. 525.

Michael Lort's scrutiny of the "time out of mind" legend, B11457, f. 173–188.

Redcliffe parish accounts on the Chatterton family: EM, pp. 1–6.

Writing on tomb of Sir William Canynge: CR, p. 11.

Thomas Chatterton, Sr.: EM, pp. 1–10; JI, pp. 24–25; JN, pp. 10–11; CR, pp. 14–16; GG, p. ii; "a complete master," *Works*, p. 523; record of marriage: EM, p. 10.

Relationship between Sarah and Thomas Chatterton, Sr.: "and little enough afterwards," EM, p. 10; "decent, plain woman," CR, p. 15; "a dim and negligible woman," JN, p. 10; "a colourless personality," EM, p. 10; "no shining abilities," JI, p. 29; "cannot . . . be classed among . . . remarkable mothers," EM, p. 10; "the first of those misfortunes," EM, p. 11.

Catch for Three Voices (words and music) *Works* III:495; description of Pineapple Tavern "excessive drinking," CR, pp. 14–15; "exuberant," "gregarious habits," "rough and boisterous conviviality," JN, p. 11; Thomas Chatterton, Sr.: "ordinary stock," "no scholarly habit," "not quite a sot," CR, p. 14.

Sarah: "large, motherly soul, simple, unimaginative, affectionate," CR, p. 16.

Thomas Chatterton, Sr.: "shiftless and improvident," CR, p. 16; "handful of books," CR, p. 16; "more than ordinary ability," CR, p. 16; "he possessed eccentricities . . . however abnormal they may appear," JI, pp. 24–25. The statement about talking to himself was taken from the novel containing the life of Chatterton, *Love and Madness* (1780) by Sir Herbert Croft. It is believed that Croft was probably referring to the young poet and not the father, but some Bristoleans, Chatterton biographers and critics speak of this behavior as characteristic of Thomas, Sr. Whether Thomas ever heard his father spoken of in this manner is uncertain.

Sarah: "fair share of educational," JI, p. 29. The comment on professors is intended as a sly poke at those foolish, misguided scholars who were taken in by Rowley's fake Middle English. "Children of poor of those times," JI, p. 30; "one of the best of women," JI, p. 30; "devoted more care and intelligence," JN, p. 11.

Thomas: "heavily handicapped for life's race," JI, p. 30.

Mary's description of the Rowleys as reported to Dean Milles: "The language was so old," "all a mere blank," Thomas's grandmother and mother fear he will get into some terrible scrape, "what I sickened my poor brother," JI, p. 79.

George Gregory on the topic of *Hastings:* GG, p. cxvi.

Altruistic surrender: My interpretation of Mary's relationship to her brother is based on the chapter, "A Form of Altruism," in Anna Freud, *The Ego and the Mechanisms of Defense* (1936), rev. ed., *The Writings of Anna Freud* II (New York: International Universities Press, 1966).

The Exception: My interpretation of Chatterton's character is based on Sigmund Freud's paper, "Some Character Types Met with in Psychoanalytic Work I, The Exceptions," *SE* 14:311–315.

Colston's
JI, pp. 33–50; GG, pp. v–vi; EM, pp. 25–36.

CR, JI, refer to the uniforms as yellow and blue. But EM is insistent that they were, in fact, orange and blue.

First report of Colston's being built on the site of a Carmelite priory is JI, p. 34.

Virtually all children and adolescents slept two or more to a bed in the eighteenth century, certainly all boarding school boys and apprentice boys—Prof. Margaret Hunt (see Acknowledgment).

"I wish I knew the classicals," B11457, f. 130–133.

NOTES

The founder of Colston's: Brace, p. 34.

Qualifications for headmaster: EM, p. 29; GG, p. 7; EM, p. 57 citing *Copies of Mr. Colston's Settlements* (no page or publisher given).

"He was a lover of truth," HC, p. 144.

Haynes's testimony: EM, p. 30.

Carey's testimony, April 14, 1776: *Works,* p. 482.

Character of boys at Colston's: "for running away," EM, p. 35.

"No man a sailor," *Johnson's England* I, ed. A. S. Turberville (London: Clarendon Press, Oxford University Press, 1933, repr. 1967), pp. 39–65; "The Navy," by Admiral Sir Herbert W. Richmond, citing Boswell's *Tour to the Hebrides,* p. 39.

"10th year . . . chapters in Isaiah," HC, p. 144; "gloomy . . . saterical peicis," HC, p. 144.

Apostate Will, DT I:1; *Sly Dick,* DT I:2; *A Hymn for Christmas Day,* DT I:4.

On the Last Epiphany, DT II:688; *The Churchwarden and the Apparition, A Fable,* DT II:688; *'I've let my Yard, and sold my Clay,'* DT II:689.

Letter from Fullford, the Grave-Digger, DT II:690.

"The very parsons of Bristol," Latimer, p. 6, citing "Journey Through England," 1724; "all in a hurry," Marcy, p. 13.

Description of Lambert's: GG, pp. xix–xxi; HC, p. 145; JI, pp. 37, 50, 51; the indenture papers: JI, p. 5. In his typical Victorian fashion, John Ingram, author of the 1910 biography, *The True Chatterton,* leaves the phrase about fornication out of his text but includes on the following page a photograph of the indenture papers from the Bristol Art Gallery where the phrase can be read with no difficulty at all.

Apprentice life: Legal protection: Anne Yarbrough, "Apprentices as adolescents in sixteenth century Bristol," *Journal of Social History* 13 (1979):67–82; hereafter referred to as Yarbrough. S. R. Smith, "London apprentices as Seventeenth Century Adolescents," *Past and Present* 61 (1973): 149–161; Lawrence Stone, *The Family, Sex and Marriage in England, 1500–1811* (New York: Harper & Row, 1977); hereafter referred to as Stone; "exposed to unlimited sadism," Stone, p. 167.

Lambert's complaint re. Chatterton's threats: GG, p. xix. Gregory leaves out the last eleven words of Lambert's statement: B11457, f. 173. Mary's report on his hours: HC, p. 145. "19/20th," *To William Barrett, February or March 1770,* DT I:494.

Warton Lecture: Macneile W. Dixon, *Chatterton,* Warton Lecture on English Poetry, British Academy 1930, from the proceedings of the British Academy XVI (London: Humphrey Milford, Amen House, E.C): "The New Golden Age . . . the repudiated past," 4; "One might well suppose," 8. Dixon adds after "our understanding age," "as Addison complacently called it."

The ideas on Utopia are from *Adolescence,* pp. 122–127; pp. 150–153.

NOTES

Looking back to an ideal past, from *Adolescence,* pp. 151–152.
"Indifferent to females," HC, p. 145; the triumph of eros, *Adolescence,* p. 169; "introduced to Mr. Barret, Mr. Catcot," HC, p. 145.

Chapter Three

Three major Rowleys were written in early September preceding the *Bridge Narrative.* The rest were composed between October 1768 and May 1769. *Balade of Charitie* was completed in London in August 1770. It is not certain whether the so-called Rowleys written before the *Bridge Narrative* were attributed to Rowley and Turgot in their original versions or only later in October when Catcott and Barrett so desperately wanted Rowleys. The pre-*Bridge* Rowleys include *Bristowe Tragedie, Battle of Hastings I, Craishes Herauldry* (which includes a reference to Canynge but is not attributed to Rowley), and *A Brief Account of William Cannings from the Life of Thomas Rowlie, Preeste* (which includes the short poem, *Onn oure Ladies Chirch*).

The Bridge Celebration: Brycgstow, place of the bridge: Brace, p. 28; "More noise made about building this single bridge..." Event reported in Latimer, p. 335. The quotation is from Emmanuel Collins in *Miscellanies,* 1762, p. 136, cited by EM, p. 106. Social class in eighteenth-century Bristol: Marcy, p. 15.

As we shall see from his poetry and letters written while at Lambert's and later in London, Chatterton could count several young men among his intimates: his childhood friends Thomas Carey and John Baker; John Rudhall and Edward Gardner, who were privy to Chatterton's methods of fabricating ancient parchments; John Fowler, a fellow theater buff who betrayed Chatterton by stealing Polly Rumsey's heart; William Smith, who introduced Catcott to Chatterton and whose brother Peter committed suicide; and James Thistlewaite, a plagiarizer whose envy of Chatterton's literary gifts led him to subtly denigrate his friend's character and talents after he died. In Chatterton's May 6, 1770 letter to his mother, he instructs the following acquaintances to read his accounts in the *Freeholder's Magazine:* Messrs. Thaire, Gaster, A. Broughton, J. Broughton, Williams, Rudhall, Thomas, Carty, Hanmer, Vaughan, Ward, Kator, Smith, "&c, &c, &c." The next week his letter to his mother sends personal messages to nearly a dozen of the pretty ladies of Redcliffe.

Bridge Narrative: DT I:56–59.
Song of Saincte Werburgh: DT I:58–59.
The meeting with Catcott: Chatterton is questioned by the Bristol elders: EM, p. 110; CR, pp. 67–68; GG, p. xxii. Catcott is introduced to Chatterton: B5258. *Pious Meditation* by John Whitson. The testimony on Catcott by his nephews Richard and Henry Smith, hereafter referred to as B5258. Biography and incidents from Catcott's life, *ibid.*

NOTES

Happiness DT I:403.

Catcott's favorite author is Charles I: B5258.

The meeting with Barrett: Biographical information: EM, 129–130, citing G. Munro Smith, *A History of the Bristol Royal Infirmary* and *Bristol Times*, 19 March 1859.

Manufacturing the Parchments

As described by John Rudhall, JD, p. 48. On one occasion Rudhall added to his general account the detail that the *Bridge Narrative* had been written up on blackened parchment. That version appears in Thomas Warton, *An Enquiry into the Authenticity of the Poems Attributed to Thomas Rowley in which the arguments of the Dean of Exeter, and Mr. Bryant are examined*, 2nd ed. (London: J. Dodsley in Pall Mall, MDCCLXXXII, printed in *Essays on Various Subjects of Taste and Criticism*, London: C. Dilly, in the Poultry), pp. 122–123; hereafter referred to as Warton, *Enquiry*. Warton cites as his source Croft's letter to George Stevens of February 5, 1782.

Manufacturing parchments described by Edward Gardner in his letter of October 8, 1802: *Works*, p. 522; JD, pp. 49–50.

Manufacturing the ink and Chatterton's handwriting: EM, 122–123. EM cites a letter from Bishop Percy to Lord Dacre which was first published in *The Welsh Outlook*, June 1929, pp. 182–184.

The Construction of the Fake Middle English

Walter Skeat, *The Poetical Works of Thomas Chatterton with an Essay on the Rowley Poems by the Reverend Walter W. Skeat* I (and a memoir by Edward Bell, MA, II.) (London: Bell and Daldy, York Street, Covent Garden, 1871). Chatterton's four modes of forming words appear on pp. xxv–vi: (1) direct from Kersey and Bailey; (2) Kersey plus inverted endings; (3) capricious, such as anere for another; (4) coins words at pleasure, such as hoplem for hopelessness. Skeat also commented on other obvious signs of fakery: "The metres are mostly wrong, the rimes are sometimes faulty, the words are wrongly coined or have the wrong number of syllables and the phrases often involve anachronisms or occasionally plagiarisms," pp. x–xi. I have added to Skeat's four basics the general interpretations of DT II:1178–1180.

The 44 modern rules: DT II:1180. Selection of words from Glossary: DT II:1182–1228, primarily 1182–1186 words under A.

The Yellowe Rolle, DT I:63. It would seem that the fifteenth-century Rowley had read John Donne.

Englandes Glorye revyved in Maystre Canynge, DT I:65; *Purple Rolle or Explayneals of the Yellowe Rolle*, DT I:67–68.

Rowley's Collection for Canynge: The documents containing these artifacts and architectural phenomena are further discussed in chapter 4 in the context of Rowley's relationship with Canynge. *Rowley's Collection for Canynge Bristol Castle* DT I:117–119; *Three Rowley Letters,* 135–142.

The Rolle of Seyncte Bartlemeweis Priorie, DT I:143–152; quotation on venereal disease, 144–145.

The Collaboration Between Chatterton and Barrett

General comments: DW, pp. 76–79; JD, pp. 65–66; JI, pp. 128–130.

Mary's letter: "My brother read to me," *Works* 3:524; "found the argument and versified it," *ibid.*

Better than Chaucer: Mr. Seyer's MSS relating to history of Bristol: B4533.

Battle of Hastings I and II, EM, p. 142; JI, pp. 128–130; GG, p. cxxvii.

How did Barrett overlook Chatterton's common schoolboy confusion about years and centuries? Rowley the learned priest would have known that the Hastings battle of 1066 was in the *eleventh* century.

Ricart's *Kalender:* GG, p. cxlv; EM, p. 157. Spelling of Bawdin, Brandon, Baldwin, "one assisting the other when at a loss," B4533.

The mythical St. Andrew's Church: EM, p. 145.

"Approaches every man on his blind side," Joseph Cottle, *Reminiscences of Samuel Taylor Coleridge and Robert Southey,* 2nd ed. (London: Houlston and Stoneman, 65 Paternoster Row, 1848), p. 501.

"Absolute honesty . . . scarcely *demanded* of an antiquary," EM, p. 143.

The Climate of Belief

"Men who think," Dixon, p. 6; "this an age most unpoetical," p. 8. The crusade for antique literary treasures: Murray Warren, *A Descriptive and Annotated Bibliography of Thomas Chatterton* (New York and London: Garland Publishing, Inc., 1977), p. 14.

On the Scottish Highlanders and James MacPherson: *The Invention of Tradition,* ed. Eric Hobsbawm and Terence Ranger (Cambridge: Cambridge University Press, 1983), pp. 15–19.

James Macpherson: John Semple Smart, *James Macpherson* (London: D. Nutt, 1905). Macpherson's plan: pp. 92–93; Gray's involvement: pp. 95–96; quotation from Gray: *ibid;* Macpherson's letter to his sponsors: p. 99; Johnson's view on Macpherson: "In vain shall we look," p. 19; "many children," *ibid;* Hazlitt: p. 12; the English reaction: pp. 12–15; on the Continent: pp. 15–20; quotation from Voss: p. 11; "calculated to please," p. 9; the German reaction: pp. 12–13; Goethe and Werther: pp. 14–15; the French reaction: p. 16; Walt Whitman: p. 17.

Boswell on Johnson's feelings about Psalmanazar: James Boswell, *Life of Johnson,* III 1776–1780, ed. George Birkbeck Hill, D.C.L. (Oxford at the Clarendon Press MDCCCLXXXVII), Appendix A, 443–449; hereafter referred to as Boswell, *Life.* Psalmanazar had died May 16, 1763.

NOTES

Chapter Four

Chatterton's belief in the olden days: In February of 1769, Chatterton would write to the London publisher James Dodsley, "The Motive that actuates me to do this, [translate Rowley's play *Aella* for public edification] is, to convince the World that the Monks (of whom some have so despicable Opinion) were not such Blockheads, as generally thought and that good Poetry might be wrote, in the dark days of Superstition as well as in these more inlightened Ages." On Mirracles and Maumerys and noble Representations of Fame, DT I:148; "Our Amusement are the gaudy," 146; the superiority of maumeries, *Antiquity of Christmas Games*, 411.

Judging from Chatterton's behavior with Catcott and Barrett, there is some reason to infer that Canynge may have been invented first, with Rowley as a necessary afterthought. Possibly the footnote about Rowlie [sic] was invented after Chatterton realized that all the elders of Bristol were so keen on believing in the ancient origins of *The Bridge Narrative*. Chatterton always insisted that he was the true author of the first *Hastings* poem allegedly written by Turgot and translated by Rowley. Turgot and Rowley, then, both may have been invented after Canynge.

Bristowe Tragedie footnote introducing Rowlie: DT I:6; "truly elegant and pathetick," 8; "My noble liege—ynne enemies," 8–9; "teares began to flowe," 10; "tresses tere," 15; description of procession, 15; final footnote, 20.

Battle of Hastings I, DT I:28.

Craishes Herauldry, DT I:44–51; Chatterton-Canynge entries: 47.

A Brief Account of William Cannings, DT I:51–55. "A short Account" is a footnote: DT I:51. Dialogue between Canynge and Rowley: DT I:51. *Onn our Ladies Chirch*, DT I:53. "The dangers were nighe," 54; "Master Chaucer," 54; the owner "brent" it, 55; "Nowe growynge Auntiante," 55.

Prologue to male adolescence: *Adolescence*, pp. 166–168.

A Discorse on Brystowe by Tho. Rowlie, DT I:93–103. "The fyrst noticynge . . . Buylders in dyase of Yore," 93–94. Information on Turgot: DT II:826–827. "Turgotte so putteth," DT I:141, in *Three Rowley Letters*. "The inhabiters of Rudcleve ybuilden a Churche," *Discorse*, DT I:94; "This worke now fynished," p. 99; "Thou seest this Maystrie," p. 99.

"Sprung a mine," GG, p. lxxv. *Sprytes* is another of Rowley's anachronisms that Barrett did not notice. Actually speculative Masonic lodges did not begin to appear until the late seventeenth century. The whole Nimrod narrative very likely came from one of the many eighteenth-century books on Masonic pseudomythology. I thank Prof. Margaret Hunt for her suggestion that I see Margaret C. Jacob, *The Radical Enlightenment; Pantheists, Freemasons, and Republicans* (London: Allen and Unwin, 1981). *Parlymente of Sprytes*, DT I:106–116. For just one moment Rowley gives himself a coauthor, Sir John Iscam. A month earlier Chatterton, in the name of Iscam, had produced another short poetic interlude. In now naming Iscam as Rowley's coauthor, Chatterton was probably trying to justify that previous literary effort. Only four stanzas of *Sprytes* are attributed to Iscam, who is meant to look like an obviously lesser poet than Rowley. At Iscam's rare better moments, Rowley accuses Iscam of plagiarizing Rowley. Perhaps Iscam was a pseudonym for one of Chatterton's rivals at the Bristol playwriter's group, The Spouting Club: EM, pp. 100–101. Elle in *Discourse*, DT I:102; "But thou the Buylder . . . Kynglie Bloude," DT I:114; "Lyfe the beste," 116.

Aella DT I:174–228. "Canynge and I," 178; "Straunge dome ytte ys . . . ryse in estate," 176–177; Clemonde's lament: 179. Operatic reduction of Othello: Donald S. Taylor, *Thomas Chatterton's Art* (Princeton: Princeton University Press, 1978), pp. 125–127: "Ye Chrystyans . . . lowynge bedde," 202; "Lyche a rodde gronfer . . . wynne or die," 203; "O! synge untoe mie roundelaie," 210; "Whanne Autumpne blake," 186.

The emerging character of Canynge: "talle and stately," *Abstracts from Letters,* DT I:134.

Four Letters on Warwyke, DT I:121–124: "Ye would have me declare," 122; "Under Henrie," 123.

Lyfe of William Canynge, DT I:228–234: "beeynge of cleare Wytte," 231; "All thynges ynne readyness," 231; "Penne anne Entyrlude," 231; "Rowleie alleyne culde have plaied Aelle," 232; "Inne all haste," 233; Letter of 1467: 232; "Heere doethe ende," 233; *The Worlde,* 233–235; "To gettynge Wealthe," 234; "How villeyn Mynstrelles," 235.

Rowley's Heraldic Account, DT I:236–247: "a Manne well learned," 237; "Maste Canynge hymself is ne foule Payncter," 240; *On Happienesse,* 240–241; *The Storie of Wyllyam Canynge,* 241–247; lines from infancy, childhood and youth: 245; "But Landes . . . Goode contente," 246.

Beginning of the Walpole incident: *The Ryse of Peyncteynge,* DT I:259–261.

Fathers and Sons

Aaron H. Esman, "Giftedness and Creativity in Children and Adolescence," *Adolescent Psychiatry,* Developmental and Clinical Studies 13, ed. by Sherman C. Feinstein (Chicago and London: The University of Chicago Press, 1986): 62–84.

Footnote p. 78: "the *early* [ital. mine] flowering," p. 78.

"It was, I found, a portion," Sigmund Freud, Preface to *The Interpretation of Dreams,* 2nd ed. (1908) *SE:*4:xxvi.

George Pollock, "Process and Affect: Mourning and Grief," *The International Journal of Psychoanalysis* 59 (1978):255–276: "the creative process may reflect the mourning," 267.

The author of *The Orphans Lead the World* (Geneva: Educational Medical Hygiene, 1975) is Dr. P. Rentchnick, who is cited by Pollock, p. 268.

Janine Chasseguet-Smirgel, *Creativity and Perversion* (New York: W.W. Norton, 1984), p. 66; hereafter referred to as Chasseguet-Smirgel.

NOTES

Goddwyn, DT I:294–305. Two Ossians translated from the Saxon, *Kenrick,* 274–275; *Cerdick,* 276–279. *Eclogue the First,* 305–308. Dialogue between father and son, 307–308.

CHAPTER FIVE

The Baker-Chatterton Correspondence
John Baker died in 1775 in South Carolina a few months before the American War of Independence. The Chatterton letters and poetry were taken back to Bristol and placed in the hands of George Catcott. However, Baker's own letters to Chatterton were considered lost until Armistice Day of 1946, when the Chatterton scholar E.H. Meyerstein discovered them at Sotheby's in a sale of the Phillips collection.
The missing half of the correspondence, the two letters from Baker to Chatterton, were first printed in E. W. H. Meyerstein, "John Baker's letters to Chatterton," *Times Literary Supplement,* 26 April 1947, p. 204. Meyerstein then wrote "A Bristol Friendship," *Transactions, Royal Society of Literature* 25 (London: Oxford University Press, MCML) (in *Essays by Divers Hands*): 28–50. Meyerstein suggests that Baker was referred to in the incident of the bridge narrative as the gentleman who had hired Chatterton to write love poetry.
Baker's heraldic sign: DT I:45.
Baker's January 5th letter: "Bristol Friendship," *Essays,* p. 33; Information on Baker in footnote, p. 28.
Acrostic on Miss Eleanor Hoyland, DT I:159; Continuation of Baker's letter: *Essays,* p. 33.
Baker's second letter, February 18th, "Bristol Friendship," *Essays,* pp. 39–40.
Chatterton's letter to Baker, March 6, 1769, DT I:256–257.

The Walpole Incident
Anecdotes and *Otranto* as described by Wilmarth Sheldon Lewis, *Horace Walpole,* Bollingen Series 35, 9 (New York: Pantheon Books, 1960): 157 and 153–154.
Letter to Walpole, March 25, 1769, DT I:258; from *Ryse of Peyncteynge,* "payncted the Walles," 61; "Forfraughte wythe," 260; poetry by Johne Abbate: 261; Introduction to Canynge: 259; "T. Rowleie was a Secular Priest," 259.
Letter to Walpole, March 28, 1769, DT I:262; *Historie of Peyncters yn Englande bie T. Rowley,* 263–267; "inferior to Rowley," 266; "Botte now," 264; "When azure Skie," 264.
From Walpole's *Vindication,* the narrative of which was printed in the form of a letter at Strawberry Hill, Walpole's pseudo-Gothic villa and afterwards reprinted in *Gentleman's Magazine.* Other portions of the vindication are from letters to Reverend Milton Cole and are printed in Walpole's *Corre-*

NOTES

spondence. My references are from JD, who had published all of this as though for the first time in his biography of Chatterton.

Gray and Mason pronounce as forgeries: JD, p. 136; "I undeceived him," p. 137.

Letter to Walpole, April 14th, DT I:271; *Letter to Walpole,* April 8th (third draft as sent to Walpole), DT I:273–274; *Letter to Walpole,* July 24th, DT I:340.

The Account of the family of De Berghams DT I:316–338.

Barrett's collaboration: JD pp. 65–66; sources and construction of the *Account:* DT II:976–984.

"Walpole! I thought not I should ever see," DT I:341.

Adolescent mourning: *Adolescence,* pp. 133–134. Idealizations of members of the adult world: p. 188. Recovering from heartbreak of disillusionment: pp. 224–225.

Journal 6th, DT I:365–371; the wounded Swain, 370; The Rake, 370; The Buck, 371.

The Advice, DT I:427–428; "Fly to thy worthiest," 428.

References for Churchill: see notes for chapter 6.

"Pretty well dipped into," from Chatterton's letter to his mother, May 6, 1770, DT I:561.

Chapter Six

The references for the life and work of Charles Churchill are Wallace Cable Brown, *Charles Churchill, Poet, Rake and Rebel* (Lawrence, Kansas: University of Kansas Press, 1953); hereafter referred to as WB; Raymond J. Smith, *Charles Churchill* (Boston: Twayne Publishers of G.K. Hall and Co., 1977); hereafter referred to as RS; and Donald S. Taylor, "Satiric Worlds and Modes: 1769–1770," in *Thomas Chatterton's Art* (Princeton: Princeton University Press, 1978); hereafter referred to as DT 78.

The Life and Work of Charles Churchill

"The hireling slave," WB, p. 198.

"To live as merry as I can," RS, p. 13, citing Churchill's *The Ghost.*

Summary: embarked on a session of rebellion . . . debtor's prison, RS, pp. 13–21.

"The present age . . . merry parsons . . . witty courtiers," RS, p. 17, citing *The Monthly Review.*

Description of the Sublime Society of Beefsteaks, "had wine and punch in plenty and freedom," RS, p. 18, citing Boswell's *London Journal.*

Churchill's letter to Wilkes: "Breakfast at nine," RS, p. 18. The occasion for the letter was Churchill's latest love affair.

"Life to the last enjoy'd," RS, p. 13.

Quotation from *The Times,* "Sins worse," RS, p. 109. Churchill's attitude toward homosexuals was standard eighteenth-century homophobia, even his very standard Sodom and Gomorrah references. However, his virulent anti-

Semitism, while typical enough of anti-Semites, was not universally held among the British. I thank Prof. Margaret Hunt for referring me to Alan Bray, *Homosexuality in Renaissance England* (London: Gay Men's Press, 1982). Chapter 4 of that volume runs into the eighteenth century. Whereas Jews in eighteenth-century England had their defenders, homosexuals did not. Bray (pp. 81–114) reports on the homosexual "pogroms" of the first two decades of the eighteenth century, in which homosexuals were hounded, beaten, jailed, and sometimes driven to suicide. Similar attitudes toward homosexuals could be found manifested in equal virulence in the sixteenth and seventeenth centuries. The difference in the eighteenth century was that what had once been an unobtrusive, socially diffuse phenomenon became a visible social phenomenon. As Bray explains it, homosexuality became a continuing culture identified with clothing, gestures, language, buildings, and public places. "Its successor in the world of the molly houses was something that could be easily seen, and it was this that brought upon it the persecution which for so long had been no more than an unrealised potential. Its visibility was its bane" (p. 92).

"Melt the rugged temper," RS, p. 109; lines on desire from *The Times,* as quoted by RS, p. 109.

The Churchillian Stance

Descriptions of Churchill's satirical style and Chatterton's gradual adoption of the Churchillian satirical stance: "Satiric modes," DT 78; RS, pp. 23–25, 108–109, 120–121.

"Who blind obedience pay," RS, p. 27, citing Churchill's *The Rosciad.*
"Gen'rous roughness," RS, p. 13, citing Churchill's *The Apology.*
"Those bold and daring strokes," AH, p. 213.
"Rude, unfinish'd brats," RS, p. 123, citing Churchill's *Gotham.*
Dryden's code: RS, p. 129, from *Absalom and Achitophal.*
"Thro' ev'ry age," RS, p. 129.

The Earliest Freethinking Creed of Thomas Chatterton

Intrest thou universal God of Men, "can honest conscience," "Flattery's a cloak," DT I:377; "every writer of abusive verse . . . without his provocations," RS 128.

The Articles of the Belief of Me Thomas Chatterton, DT I:426.

Chatterton's relationship with Vicar Alexander Catcott: B5258; DT II:1015–1020; EM, pp. 306–307.

Epistle to Catcott, DT I:412–419; "What strange Infatuations," 412; "Your Zeal for Scripture . . . Senses blind," 414; postscript to *Epistle,* 419; "racks each Metaphor upon a wheel," 414.

The Defense, DT I:421–422; "The Church and all her arguments," 421; "I own a God . . . the Light," 422.

The New Year, January 1770: *Advice,* DT I:427–428; *Astrea Brokage Letter,*

NOTES

431–432; "a young author," "who has never read," "a devil," 432. *Hirlas I,* Composed by Blythyn, Prince of North Wales, DT I:401, and *Hirlas II,* Translated from the ancient British of Owen Cyfeliog, 428.

The African Eclogues

Heccar and Gaira. An African Eclogue, DT I:432–433; "There Cawna mingled . . . Lilly of their features red," 435; "where sharp Rocks," 434.

Death of Nicou, DT I:590–593; "On Tiber's bank . . . shadows in the stream," 590; "red sword of war," 591.

Narva and Mored, DT I:543–545; "where the blue blossom" 543.

An African Song, DT I:662–663; "purple plum'd maccaws," 662.

The Consuliad. An Heroic Poem, DT I:436–442.

The Acconte of W. Canynges Feast, DT I:294; "The Ealdermenne . . . desarte waste," 294.

From *The Consuliad,* "The mangled pigeon . . . excrements of state," DT I:437.

The Whore of Babylon, DT I:452–468. In Protestant countries, the whore is traditionally identified with the Roman Catholic Church. Chatterton alludes in his poem, however, to the princess dowager of Wales, mother of King George III, mistress to Wilkes's enemy, the earl of Bute. Either some mentor put a restraining hand on Chatterton or this satire was rejected by all the publishers he approached, including Fell. Catcott kept the poem and it was published after Chatterton's death in the 1803 *Works.*

From Isaac Fell, 13 March 1770, DT I:493.

Will, DT I:501–505.

Elegy on Mr. Wm. Smith, DT I:352–353; "I lov'd him," 352; "Despis'd: an alien . . . on your head," 353.

Chatterton on suicide: threats of suicide at Lamberts: GG, p. xix; B11457; he carried a loaded pistol: B4533; *The Unfortunate Fathers,* DT I:443–445; "suicide is sometimes a noble insanity," DT I:445.

Chatterton composed a premature elegy on Phillips's death and then revised that elegy several times after the death actually occurred a few days later. The three extant versions of the elegies contain some conventionally exaggerated elegiac sentiments as well as some of the more lyrical and eloquent examples of Chatterton's non-Rowleyan writings.

Relationship with Clayfield: *Epistle to Clayfield,* DT I:393–394; "long renowned the Muses friend, . . . friend to Genius," DT I:393. Mary's comments on Clayfield, HC, p. 145. *The Copernican System,* DT I:419. Sibley's comment on Chatterton's knowledge of astronomy: Sibley, p. 811. Clayfield on Chatterton's abilities: "They were no more his," EM, p. 306, citing Jacob Bryant's interview with Clayfield.

Lambert cancels Chatterton's indentures: "You must know that the 19/20th," *To William Barrett February or March 1770,* DT I:494.

"Tho' as an apprentice . . . my liberty," DT I:570–571; *To Sarah Chatterton, 14 May 1770,* DT I:570–572.

Will, "all this wrote," DT I:501; "Burgum I thank thee," 501; "Gods! what would Burgum . . . Two pounds Two," 501; "Thy friendship," 501; "To Barrett next," 502; "This is the last Will . . . savored of Insanity," 502–503; "Sacred to the Memory," 503; "To the memory of Thomas Chatterton," 503; bequests to friends and family: 504–505; Sigmund Freud's comments on play and the creative writer, the child at play, "Writers and Daydreaming," *SE* 9:144.

Chatterton departs for London: The description of the trip from Bristol to London is from Chatterton's letter to his mother on April 26, 1770: *To Sarah Chatterton,* DT I:510–511. Details on the quality of the various coach arrangements are from EM, p. 351, citing *Felix Farley,* "The London, Bath and Bristol Machines in One Day," 21 April 1770. Chatterton's visits to the booksellers, *To Sarah Chatterton,* DT I:511.

Chatterton's first sentiments on life in London: "What a glorious prospect . . . character in his pen," *To Sarah Chatterton, Thomas Carey and others, 6 May 1770,* DT I:560–563.

Chapter Seven

First Weeks in London: "The poverty of authors . . . pretty well dipped into," *To Sarah Chatterton, 6 May,* DT I:561; "matters go on swimmingly," *To Sarah Chatterton, 14 May,* 570.

The Life and Works of John Wilkes

I thank Prof. Margaret Hunt for the Brewer and Rude references on the general background of Wilkes's politics. John Brewer, *Party Ideology and Popular Politics at the Accession of George III* (Cambridge: Cambridge University Press, 1976), hereafter referred to as JB; and George Rude, *Wilkes and Liberty: A Social Study of 1763 to 1774* (Oxford: Oxford University Press, 1962), hereafter referred to as GR.

Adrian Hamilton, *The Infamous Essay on Woman or John Wilkes Seated Between Vice and Virtue* (London: Andre Deutsch, 1972), hereafter referred to as AH; and Louis Kronenberger, *The Extraordinary Mr. Wilkes: His Life and Times* (New York: Doubleday and Company, Inc. Garden City, New York, 1974), hereafter referred to as LK.

Wilkes's imprisonment for "an infamous and seditious libel," LK, p. 37. Lyrics to Wilkes and Liberty: AH, p. 87. The #45 feast at the Cock Inn: Latimer, p. 391.

Wilkes's childhood, education, marriage, and young manhood: LK, pp. 1–6; "Three or four whores," LK, p. 5; "I never read steadily," AH, p. 11; "To please an indulgent father," AH, p. 12; "Sacrifice to Plutus not Venus," LK, p. 6, AH, p. 12; Gibbon on Wilkes: AH, p. 10.

On the activities and membership at Medmenham: AH, pp. 15–16; LK, pp.

NOTES

12–15. PENI TENTO NON PENITENTI [an untamed penis requires no penitence]. "Fay ce que Vouldras," p. 16. Churchill's reaction: WB, p. 68.

The *North Briton:* On Johnson "pay given to a state hireling," LK, p. 29; on Hogarth as a house painter: p. 30; on Lord Sandwich: "to make all your thrusts," p. 30; "your mistresses or your principles," LK, p. 30; AH, pp. 14–15; WB, p. 72. On George III: "held in absolute slavery," LK, p. 34.

Issue #45: "Every friend of this country," "I lament to see it," LK, p. 36. Wilkes's first #45 trial: "The liberty of an English subject," LK, p. 42; "The liberty of all peers," p. 43; the private printing of the *North Briton* and *Essay on Woman,* pp. 46–48.

The betrayal by Lord Sandwich: AH, pp. 104–108; LK, pp. 51–52. The incident at *Beggar's Opera:* AH, p. 120; LK, p. 53. Several years later when his mistress of fifteen years, the singer-actress Martha Ray, was killed by a love-starved clergyman, very few Englishmen had much sympathy for Sandwich. In the 1780 *Love and Madness,* a novelistic version of that crime, all the sympathy was with Miss Ray and her thwarted clergyman lover. Readers were also captivated by the strange little history embedded in one of the clergyman's letters to Miss Ray. He relates the sad fate of a young poet named Chatterton, who had ended his life in suicide. *Love and Madness* became the first unofficial biography of Thomas Chatterton. See chapter 11. Fanny Murray and Lord Sandwich: AH, p. 21; Martha Ray: AH, p. 105. False editions of *Essay on Woman:* AH, pp. 20, 120, 187. Sandwich reads from *Essay on Woman:* AH, pp. 107–108; LK, pp. 53–54. Excerpts from *Essay on Woman:* AH, pp. 195–230. Description of title page: AH, p. 195; "Awake, my Fanny . . . where thousands were before," AH, pp. 213–217; LK, p. 54. Footnote by Warburton: AH, pp. 213–217. Footnote citation of *Essay on Man:* AH, p. 217; LK, p. 54.

Reactions from the House of Lords: "Read on," AH, p. 108. Lord LeDispenser: AH, p. 108. Walpole reporting Warburton's reaction: "Foamed with the violence," AH, p. 108.

Wilkes's exile: LK, pp. 44–82, and return from exile: pp. 85–102. Benjamin Franklin on the #45: " 'Tis really an extraordinary event," p. 92. Walpole on Wilkes: "Though he became a martyr . . . such a saint," p. 10. Description of King's Bench: LK, p. 113. Wilkes at King's Bench: LK, pp. 113–115. Wilkes's political platform: JB, pp. 197–198; GR, *passim.* Wilkes becomes an "extinct volcano," LK, pp. 236–252; AH, p. 50. Wilkes's old age and death: AH, pp. 249–250; LK, pp. 242–244. "Adversity may be a good thing," AH, p. 50.

The Exhibition and *The Letter Paraphras'd*

John Ingram's publication of *Exhibition:* Catcott quote, JI, p. 295. Ingram's excuse: p. 296. Appendix to *The True Chatterton,* JI, pp. 295–304. Lines on the dull penis of Alexander Catcott: DT I:547. Mock contention style described in DT 78, pp. 226–227. Lines on the exhibitionist's penis: DT I:552.

Exhibitionism and imposturousness; accessory behaviors and other forms of perversion and character disturbance; the anxiety over genital intactness: *Adolescence,* pp. 290–291.

As late as 1930, E. H. W. Meyerstein appends a footnote to his biography of Chatterton, "The rest of the twenty lines [of *The Letter Paraphras'd*] are suppressed at the publisher's desire; I regret that the reader should be debarred from testing my judgment by the evidence, but I am told that the language is too outspoken to be printed." EM, p. 98.

Letter Paraphras'd: Lines from the unknown girl, DT I:686; Chatterton's paraphrase: DT I:686–687.

The adolescent preoccupation with the penis: *Adolescence,* pp. 167–168, 192–195.

The Art of Puffing by a bookseller's Journeyman, DT I:650–651; "Versed by experience," 650.

CHAPTER EIGHT

Beckford Becomes Chatterton's New Idol

"Will be to me of no little service," "Last week being in the pit . . . no tongue but my own," *To Sarah Chatterton, 14 May,* DT I:570.

Lord Mayor Beckford's first remonstrance with King George III: DM, pp. 187–191.

Probus. To the Lord Mayor, DT I:579–583; "tyrannous junto of slaves," 579; "Should you address again," 580; "Let us, with one united voice," 583.

Lord Mayor Beckford's second remonstrance before King George III: DM, pp. 141–143.

To Mary Chatterton, 30 May 1770, DT I:587–589; "You have, doubtless, heard," 587–588.

William Bingley, the printer, and his promises to Chatterton: DM, pp. 190–192.

"There's no money to be got . . . both sides of the question," *To Mary Chatterton, 30 May 1770,* "Essays on the patriotic side," "On the other hand," DT I:589; Pretended Patriot, etc., DT II:775, citing B11457, f. 316.

The death of Beckford: Chatterton's consolation, "Accepted by Bingley . . . am glad he is dead by," GG, p. lxii; DM, p. 194.

The Shoreditch testimony: HC, pp. 189–193; Mrs. Ballance: pp. 190–191; the Walmsley nephew: p. 193; the Walmsley niece: p. 192; Mrs. Walmsley: pp. 190–191; Mr. Walmsley: p. 191.

The Move to Brooke Street. The Downward Plunge Begins

To Mary Chatterton, 19, 29 June 1770, DT I:598–599; "an horrid cold," 598; "a most horrible weezing," 599.

NOTES

To Mary Chatterton, 30 May 1770, DT I:587–589; "I shall not take a step," p. 588.

To Thomas Carey, 1 July 1770, DT I:639–642; "The Printers of the Daily Publications," p. 642.

An Excelente Balade of Charitie, DT I:644–648; "If the Glossary," 644; the Rowley footnote: 645; critical evaluation of *Balade:* DT II:1113–1115; "not to be excelled," 1114; "movements of Nature," 1115; "The gathrd storme . . . stonen showers," DT I:646; Letter from *Town and Country,* "the pastoral from Bristol," 1113–1114.

The Revenge, A Burletta, DT I:601–631; "a song of mine . . . take with the Town," *Letter to Carey,* DT I:641; "Receiv'd July 6th," 631. Meyerstein leaves the dilemma about whether or not *Revenge* was staged in a state of ambiguity. Ingram is adamant, "It is frequently stated that 'The Revenge was performed at Marylebone [sic] Gardens,' but even this statement is incorrect. Dr. Arnold declared that owing to some unknown cause, the burletta never was performed. It was neither published nor performed, all statements to the contrary notwithstanding," JI, p. 254.

Music to *May* or *The Invitation to be sung by Mrs. Barthelemon and by Master Cheney:* "Away to the Woodlands" was set for soprano, two violins, cello, and reprinted in EM, p. 537. An untitled reprint for voice part only appeared in *Vocal Music* (London, 1772) as "A Favourite Glee for 3 Voices / Sung with Universal Applause at Vauxhall Gardens." Though Chatterton might have had a hand in the writing of some of the music, James Hook (1746–1827) is thought to be the composer of *May* and about two thousand other popular songs. Possibly Chatterton lived long enough to hear this song played and sung with his words, even though the entire *Revenge* was never performed. Mary Barthelemon (née Young) and Master Cheney were in the Marybone Company during the 1769–1770 season: DT II:1108–1109.

The Last Letters Home

To Sarah Chatterton, 8 July 1770, "the silver one is more grave," DT I:648; *To Mary Chatterton, 11 July 1770,* "I have sent you," "I am surprized," 649; *To Mary Chatterton, 20 July 1770,* "I am now about an Oratorio . . . and more to the purpose," 650.

To William Smith n.d., DT I:687. There is some dispute on the dating of this letter. The tone and content have convinced me of the authority of Jacob Bryant's dating, which he got directly from William Smith, "about a fortnight before he died, c. August 10, 1770," DT II:1136. Meyerstein also agrees and has estimated the date to be during the two weeks immediately preceding the suicide: EM, p. 430. T. O. Mabbott has also argued for this dating. In "Notes on Chatterton: Letter to William Smith," *Notes & Queries,* 2 April 1932, p. 242, as cited DT II:1137, statements regarding Chatterton's confusion and despair and his expressed wish to go abroad as a surgeon support Meyerstein's conviction. Meyerstein, in "Chatterton's

Last Days," *Times Literary Supplement,* 28 June 1941, p. 316, presents an argument based on the numerous references to the venereal disease which he believes may have preceded and precipitated Chatterton's suicide. Taylor, though he cites these arguments, finds the reasoning ingenious but based on slender evidence: DT II:1137.

The perplexing relationship between art and crime: Mann, "It is in essence," p. 3; "The Muses have no credit here," *Kew Gardens,* DT I:542. Chatterton's personal conflict between belief and self-interest may have been a reflection of the more-popular tensions between orthodoxy and anticlericalism. On the other hand, many eighteenth-century intellectuals found it quite possible to believe in God and still be critical of the clergy, many of whom were not truly pious or virtuous enough to inspire the well-intentioned but weak-willed to virtue, and some of whom were outright self-seeking men, like Apostate Will, who did not hesitate to proselytize the most lucrative side of any religious question. Chatterton still believed in God, albeit his own version, even after he became a satirist. "Bristol may keep her prudent Maxims . . . publish what I think," 542.

T. S. Eliot: Peter Ackroyd, *T. S. Eliot, A Life* (New York: Simon and Schuster, 1984). Pound's "caesarian operation," p. 117; "the music hall monologue," p. 117; "If these passages," "a continual oscillation," p. 120. Eliot's literary platform: "Tradition and Individual Talent," *The Sacred Wood* (London: Methuen and Company, Ltd., 1948), pp. 47–59.

Robert Browning, *Essay on Chatterton,* ed. Donald Smalley (Cambridge, Mass.: Harvard University Press, 1948). "Genius almost invariably . . . the thing he presented," p. 111.

George Gregory: "puerile affectation," "He knew that original genius," GG, p. lxxii.

Anna Seward, *Letters of Anna Seward written between the years 1784 and 1807* 5 (Edinburgh: George Ramsay and Company, 1811):272, hereafter referred to as Seward. In this letter to Thomas Park, January 30, 1800, she quotes Johnson's disparagement of Chatterton. See notes to chapter 11.

Immorality, Suicide, and Madness
"I fear thou hast uttered," GG p. lxxxiii.

Treatment of the bodies of suicides: Thomas Szasz, "The Case Against Suicide Prevention," *American Psychologist* (July 1986), p. 806. A. Alvarez, *The Savage God* (New York: Random House, 1971), pp. 46–47.

Though the word *suicide* begins to be used sporadically around the middle of the seventeenth century, the term was still sufficiently rare in Chatterton's day for it to be absent from Johnson's *Dictionary.* The common and legal language for suicide associated the act and the person with homicide—self-homicide, self-murder, self-destroyer, self-slaughter (Alvarez, p. 50).

Blackstone's statement on the *non compos mentis* plea: W. Blackstone, *Commentaries on the laws of England: Of public wrongs* (Boston: Beacon Press, 1962) (original 1755–1765), p. 212.

NOTES

Robert Southey on Mary Newton's insanity: EM footnote, p. 340, citing Southey's letter to John Britton, November 4, 1880. Southey claimed that a taint manifested itself in Mrs. Newton, who had to be confined to an asylum, and in her only surviving child, Marianne. "Insanity was hereditary in his family," JD, p. 291. Dix, though he gives no reference, is probably referring to Southey's letter.

The Unfortunate Fathers, "There is a principle . . . our own existence," DT I:445; *Sentiment*, DT I:446, "Since we can die . . . Dissolution tends."

David Hume, as cited in Alvarez, p. 172. Walpole's comment, as cited in Alvarez, p. 173.

Suicide as an English specialty: Alvarez, p. 84.

"At worst, a period of observation," Alvarez, p. 74.

"My first attempt . . . final resource is a pistol," GG, p. lii.

"The unremitting," GG, p. lxxix. "It can never be sufficiently," GG footnote, p. lxxix; "There seems to be a general . . . want and obscurity," GG, p. lxxxiv.

When a child is becoming an adult . . . power of the elders: a paraphrase of *Adolescence*, p. 116.

"These Representatives of God," DT I:447; *The Methodist*, DT I:446–447.

Sir Herbert Croft on love and madness: HC, p. 143.

Chapter Nine

The Venereal Disease Hypothesis

"As Saturn is posited . . . revolution of Saturn," Sibley, pp. 808–810.

"Mr. Cross says he had the Foul Disease," B11457, f. 137.

Lort's observations on Chatterton: *ibid*. The last item cited by Lort, "profligacy was, at least, as conspicuous as his abilities," is from the Preface to *Miscellanies*, ed. John Broughton (Fielding and Walker, Pater Noster Row, MDCCLXXVIII), p. 18.

Thistlewaite's defense of Chatterton: *Works* III:478.

Lines from Chatterton's suicide poem, *Naked and friendless to the world expos'd* DT II:734.

To George Catcott, 12 August 1770, DT I:670.

Meyerstein's report on the Brooke Street neighborhood: EM, pp. 388–393; "lowest of regions," p. 388; "so many pretty . . . gentlemen," p. 389; "children were brought up," p. 389; "a poetic licence," p. 390; "stepped into the forefront," p. 388; "between a sacque and a mantua," p. 390.

Meyerstein's reasoning on rentals: EM, pp. 391–392; "she has advanced," p. 391; "Six shillings for a garret," p. 391; "six shillings a week," p. 392.

Meyerstein on the venereal issue: EM, pp. 439–442; "used to cure," footnote, p. 441; "there is abundant motive," p. 442; "even if . . . sexual adventure," p. 442; "the romantic child," p. xv.

NOTES

The Moral Dilemmas of the Chatterton Biographers
Wilson, "Chatterton's masking," "There are passages," DW, pp. 127–128.
Nevill, "the dreamer . . . expected him to adopt," JN, p. 165.
From Esther Saunders, 3 April 1770, DT I:495–496.
Russell, "Every line of his writing . . . that word 'forgery,' " CR, pp. 240–241.
To Sarah Chatterton, 14 May 1770, "My sister will remember me to Miss Sandford . . . Let Miss Watkin know," DT I:570–572.
Ingram, "Chatterton's words home," JI, p. 275; "It will be plainly . . . mythical confessions," p. 277.
Gregory, "Infidelity or skepticism . . . vicious gratifications of this life," GG, p. xliv; "sullied the youth of Chatterton," p. xlvi; on Chatterton's relationship with Polly Rumsey: "Laura to his Petrarch," p. xlvii.

On the Censorship of Chatterton's Literary "Infidelities"
T. S. Eliot's youthful pornography: "The Love Song of St. Sebastian," "King Bolo and His Great Black Queen," Ackroyd, p. 52. Eliot's anxieties, the central emptiness of experience: Ackroyd, p. 53; he cites Eliot's letter to Paul Elmer More dated "Shrove Tuesday, 1928." Shrove Tuesday is the day of punishment for sexual offenses.
The Love Song of St. Sebastian can be read in manuscript form at the Berg Collection of the New York Public Library. However, the Bolo poems are not available to the public.
Eliot's distinctions between personality and art, artistic creation and emotion: "Tradition and Individual Talent," Sacred Wood, p. 58.
Follies and foibles of youth: EM, p. 441.

The Sexual Atmosphere of Eighteenth-Century England
Footnote on Alfred de Vigny's Chatterton, ed. with an intro. by A. H. Diverres (London: University of London Press, Ltd., 1967). Summary: pp. 11–45.
Delacroix, "Real Superiority," "Sweden's Nasty, Sexist, Racist Genius," book review by Eric Bentley, New York Times Book Review, 1 September 1985, p. 3. Rimbaud on "the Great Sick Man," "for a while startling . . . child molester," p. 3.
Gore Vidal, "Immortal Bird," a review of two biographies of Tennessee Williams, New York Review of Books, 13 June 1985, pp. 5–10. "Although poetry is no longer . . . if not the poetry," p. 5.
Rousseau "managed in a very short time," Confessions, trans. and with intro. by J. M. Cohen (New York: Penguin Books, 1953), p. 39.

Boswell and Johnson
Thérèse's sexual adventure with James Boswell is described in Mark Harris, Saul Bellow, Drumlin Woodchuck (Athens: The University of Georgia Press, 1980), pp. 26–28. The passages on Thérèse's sexual instructions are from

NOTES

Boswell on the Grand Tour 1765–1766, ed. Frank Brady and Frederick A. Pottle (New York: McGraw-Hill, 1955), pp. 293–295. Harris tells us that the passages from Boswell's private papers describing his eleven days of continual fornication with Thérèse were destroyed, but that the knowledge of what was in those "reprehensible passages" survives and is conveyed by his present editors: p. 26.

Boswell's nineteen episodes of gonorrhea: Theodor Rosebury, *Microbes and Morals: The Strange Story of Venereal Disease* (New York: The Viking Press, 1971), p. 156.

Boswell's sexual escapades and rumors of Johnson's perversity: Harris, p. 53.

Prostitution in Mid-Eighteenth-Century London

Like Basserman, Scott, and Riley (cited below), Harris may tend to overestimate the prevalence of perversity and prostitution in eighteenth-century urban society. Thus these writers have understated the repressive, moralizing side of eighteenth-century life. There was much popular and elite opposition to prostitution and brothels and many efforts at their suppression. Stone, cited earlier, presents a more sober and reliable account of these issues. Also, especially on the history of prostitution, see Leah Otis, *Prostitution in Medieval Society: The History of an Urban Institution in Languedoc*, (Chicago and London: University of Chicago Press, 1985).

The apprentice code: Yarbrough, pp. 68–70.

Masturbation: *Onania* as described by Stone, p. 514.

Brothels, nighthouses, coaches, dark alleys, and bagnios: Stone. Lujo Basserman, *The Oldest Profession: A History of Prostitution* (London: Arthur Barker Limited, 1967), p. 133; hereafter referred to as Basserman. George Riley Scott, *Ladies of Vice: A History of Prostitution from Antiquity to the Present Day* (London: Tallis Press, 1968), hereafter referred to as Scott. Hilary Evans, *The Oldest Profession: An Illustrated History of Prostitution* (Newton Abbot, England: David & Charles, 1979), hereafter referred to as Evans. G. L. Simons, *A Place for Pleasure: The History of the Brothel* (Sussex, England: Harwood-Smart Publishing Co. Ltd., 1975), hereafter referred to as Simons.

Public balls: Basserman, p. 137; five guineas at Mrs. Prendergast: p. 136.

From grand courtesans to street strollers: Stone, p. 601; Evans p. 89.

Specialty houses: flagellation: Basserman, p. 128 and Simon, p. 51; the molly houses: Evans, p. 92; defloration as a mania: p. 197 of Keith Thomas, "The Double Standard," *Journal of the History of Ideas* 20 (April 1959):195–216; hereafter referred to as Thomas.

The prostitute as the protector of virtue: Thomas, pp. 197–200; Augustine, "Remove prostitution," p. 197; Otis, p. 12.

Bernard de Mandeville: Thomas, p. 197; Bullough, pp. 161–162.

NOTES

Venereal Disease
Treatment: Rosebury, pp. 212–215.
Ranking of the medical profession: Sir D'Arcy Power, "Medicine," *Johnson's England II*, ed. A. S. Turberville (Oxford: The Clarendon Press, 1933), pp. 270–273; hereafter referred to as Power.
Terms for gonorrhea: Rosebury, p. 21, and E. J. Burford, *The Orrible Synne: A Look at London Lechery from Roman to Cromwellian Times* (London: Calder and Boyars, 1973), p. 163. Frederick's letter to Voltaire: Rosebury, p. 157.

Did Chatterton Have a Venereal Disease?
Letter to Mary Chatterton, 19,29, June 1770, DT I:598–599; "But, I don't repent . . . cured so cheap," 599.
Barrett's diagnosis: EM, p. 436.
The forensic report of 1947: p. 239 of Richard Holmes, "Thomas Chatterton: The Case Re-opened," *Cornhill Magazine* 178 (1970):238–249, quoting Dr. Walls of South-Western Forensic Laboratory. Holmes also develops the hypothesis that Cross had supplied Chatterton with opium as a painkiller and with other medications, perhaps hallucinogenics: p. 238.
Remedies for syphilis and gonorrhea: Rosebury, pp. 45–47.
Symptoms of the "great pokkes," Rosebury, pp. 42–45.
Chatterton on the differences between gonorrhea and syphilis: DT I:144.
The xenophobia of syphilis: Rosebury, pp. 30–31.
Cures for syphilis: Rosebury, pp. 45–47.
Dr. Quicksilver: Rosebury, pp. 48, 214.
The mercury formulas: Rosebury, pp. 46–47.
Geoffrey Scott's summation of Zelide's relationship with Benjamin Constant: *The Portrait of Zelide*. This passage is cited by Leon Edel, *Writing Lives: Principia Biographia* (New York/London: W.W. Norton and Company, 1984), p. 180.

CHAPTER TEN

Men of Reason reasoning on Chatterton: Walpole, "It is just to say," JD, pp. 128–129; Warton, "To pronounce spurious," "the pleasure of deceiving the world," Thomas Warton, *History of English Poetry* II (London: J. Dodsley, 1778): 158; "the more solid satisfaction," Warton, "An Enquiry," p. 164.
Chatterton as a replacement child: A. C. Cain, and B. S. Cain, "On Replacing a Child," *Journal of the American Academy of Child Psychiatry* 3 (1964):443–456. Hansi Kennedy, "Growing up with a Handicapped Sibling," *Psychoanalytic Study of the Child* 40 (1984):255–274.
Infant mortality rates: E. A. Wrigley and R. S. Schofield, *Population History*

284

of England, 1541–1871: A Reconstruction (Cambridge: Harvard University Press, 1981). Stone, p. 360; LK, p. 106; Power, pp. 279–281. The mortality rate among middle-class Bristoleans would have been somewhat lower than among lower-class Londoners, where Power suggests that the infant and young child mortality rate was nearly 100%: "It was said with some degree of truth that there was no third generation of true Londoners," p. 180. At one time Stone was considered the most reliable source for population statistics. The Cambridge History, which postdates Stone, does not absolutely confirm infant mortality rates in eighteenth-century England. Most sources report the rates to be very high among the lower classes. The 70% sometimes reported for the middle and upper classes is probably an overestimation. We do know that three of Mary Chatterton Newton's children died within the first three years of life. Her first child, named Thomas Chatterton, was born in 1779 and died in 1783. Issac Henry was born in 1782 and died in 1783. Hannah was born and died in 1785. Her surviving child, Marianne, was born in 1783 and died at 24, surviving Mary, who died at the age of 54, by only three years.

Psychology of the exception: Freud, "The Exceptions," *SE* 14:311–315.

Fenichel, "It became probable that . . ." pp. 129–130; "The formula is . . . are untrue," p. 133. On p. 131, Fenichel describes screen memories and screen ideas with another formula, "Not *that* is true, but *this*."

Arlow: the unrealistic character, the petty liar, and the practical joker: pp. 317–318; the unrealistic character: pp. 318–324; "the petty lie is," p. 326; "it is a short step," p. 326.

On Narcissism, *SE* 14:73–102; the attitude of a person "who treats his own body . . . through these activities," 73. In this initial formulation, Freud referred to conscience as ego-ideal. Several years later, as Freud advanced his structural theory of the human mind, the ego-ideal became only one aspect or function of the superego. The other two functions of the superego were criticism and prohibition. It remained for the ego-ideal to represent the standards for perfection by which we measure the value of our own self and others. *SE* 19: "any agitated apprehensions," 36; "It is easy to show," 37; "When we were little children," 36; "the expression of the most powerful," 36. Although in this work, *The Ego and the Id*, Freud distinguishes the ego-ideal from the rest of the superego, he still sometimes used the terms interchangeably.

The voice of Tezcatlipoca, "able to enter everywhere," Alvarez, epitaph citing Sahagun, *History of the Things of New Spain*.

SE 19: "The superior being . . . fear of conscience," 57; "fulfills the same function of protecting," 58; the ego lets itself die: 58; "the infantile anxiety . . . the protecting mother," 58. Although Freud here speaks only of the protecting mother, his comments are taken to imply the protecting functions of the father that are a reflection of the child's original relationship with the mother.

NOTES

Testimonies on Chatterton's Last Days
Frederick Angel's (spelled Angell) testimony to the coroner on Chatterton's last three days is reported in George Pryce, *Memorials of the Canynge's Family*, pp. 289–291.
Walpole: "refused a loaf of bread," JD, p. 129, from Walpole's vindication letter to Rev. Cole, February 22, 1782.
Mrs. Angel: offer of a dinner: HC, pp. 194–195; JD, p. 290.
Mr. Cross: barrel of oysters: Warton, *Enquiry,* pp. 107–108; GG, p. lxix; JD, p. 290. Barrel is a measure that varies with the product. Probably several dozen oysters.
Editor's recollection: "Every effort . . . end his existence," John Broughton, *Miscellanies,* Preface, p. xix.
William Blake, "An Island in the Moon," *Blake's Poetry and Designs,* ed. Mary Lynn Johnson and John E. Grant, Norton Critical Edition (New York: W.W. Norton and Company, 1979), p. 381.
London acquaintance: "He sometimes seemed wild, abstracted," EM, p. 440. Meyerstein is referring to statements of Archibald Hamilton, Sr. in a notice to *Love and Madness* in *Critical Review* (June 1782). Hamilton claimed that Chatterton had not died of want, since a respectable friend had loaned him a sum of money a few days before he died.

In order to cover those persons who only manifest "mild" versions of the manic-depressive mood oscillations, psychiatrists have now invented a new label, Bipolar II. In this way almost anyone who experiences periodic mood changes, no matter how subtle or infrequent, can fit this diagnostic category, which attempts to underplay mental phenomena in favor of a theory of constitutional endowment.

Creativity and the Manic-Depressive Hypothesis: Strindberg on those who are lucky to be capable of madness; John Berryman, "the artist is extremely lucky;" Stanley G. Freedman, "The Creative Spirit," *New York Times,* 17 November 1986, p. C1.
Meyerstein: "the poetic consciousness," EM, p. 438.
Falling in the grave: "my dear friend," at St. Pancras, JD, p. 290; Mrs. Edkins's rumor: DT II:778, citing a possible lost letter *To Sarah Chatterton* c. August 20, 1770, as reported in Forbes Winslow, *The Anatomy of a Suicide* (London, 1840). Cumberland's appendix to Dix is cited in support of Winslow's belief. Taylor does not accept the veracity of this tale, attributing it to the general Chatterton mythology: DT II:778.
The Last Verses written by Chatterton, DT II:735; "a compliment to the City," DT II:1159; *Bristol Mercury* of August 24, 1795: "The following lines were addressed by the late unfortune Tho. Chatterton, to a Friend of his, lately returned from the East-Indies. They have never appeared in print; and he now publishes them as a compliment to the city of his birth."

NOTES

Naked and friendless to the world expos'd, DT I:734–735; "any competent hoaxster," DT II:1160.

Mourning and melancholia: The savage god who "gave riches," Alvarez epigraph citing Sahagun; Freud, *Mourning and Melancholia, SE* 14:243–258; the normal mourning process: pp. 244–245; "we find that the excessively strong superego . . . the sadism available in the person concerned," *SE* 19:53.

The Unfortunate Fathers: "There is a principle," DT I:445.

"The ego gives itself up," *SE* 19:58.

Death trend: Alvarez, pp. 109–111.

Adolescence as a struggle between past and future: *Adolescence,* p. 19.

Replacement child: Kennedy, pp. 255–274; Cain and Cain, pp. 443–456; also G. H. Pollock, "Childhood Parent and Sibling Loss in Adult Patients," *Archives of General Psychiatry* 7 (1962):295–305; G. H. Pollock, "Childhood Sibling Loss and Creativity," *Annual of Psychoanalysis* 6 (1978):443–481.

The Loss of the Protective Father: On the death of Peter Smith: *Elegy on Mr. Wm. Smith,* DT I:352–353; Chatterton evoked the name of Canynge one more time, a few weeks before his suicide, in *Decimus To the Freeholders of the City of Bristol,* DT I:585–587. He recalled Bristoleans to their duty as citizens. He writes about "the infamous set of wretches" running the government and asks Bristoleans to consider the honor of their city as Canynge once did, "remember the speech of the glorious CANYNGE." *Ethelgar.* trans. from the Saxon, DT I:253–255; *An African Song,* DT I:663; "Tis not for thee," 253. *Gorthmund. translated from the Saxon,* DT I:677–681; "slept on his couch of purple," 677; "Thine are the bitter herbs . . . closed in peace no more," 678 and footnote.

CHAPTER ELEVEN

Dr. Fry's journey to Bristol: GG, p. lxxi; JD, p. 292; HC, p. 200; CR, p. 223.

Dr. Fry is, of course, remembered by his present-day colleagues at St. John's. Also, because Fry kept a diary during the last four years of his life, his fellow scholars have been able to construct a more thorough and colorful picture of a don of St. John's than is usually possible.

St. John's record of Dr. Fry: W. C. Costin, *The History of St. John's College, Oxford* (Oxford: Oxford University Press, 1958), pp. 217–222.

Fry's negotiations with Catcott and Barrett: EM, pp. 450–456.

Dr. Woodward matriculated St. John's March 23, 1737/38. As he lay on his deathbed, Thomas Chatterton, Sr. composed an anthem. Michael Lort states that this anthem was entrusted to Woodward, his attending physician, so that it could be played at his funeral, B11457. But the only surviving trace of music and song written by Thomas Chatterton's father is the *Catch for Three Voices.*

Woodward's request via Oliver Goldsmith, "alas Sir . . . exchange of Bristol," EM, p. 452.

NOTES

Goldsmith story: The reactions and the story as told by Walpole: JD, p. 139.

Johnson's Reactions

"Vulgar, uneducated stripling," *Seward*, p. 272. Johnson's full sentiments were "Pho, child! don't talk to me of the powers of a vulgar, uneducated stripling ... No man can coin guineas, but in proportion he has gold."

"The most extraordinary young man," Boswell, *Life* III: 51; "This is the most extraordinary young man that has encountered my knowledge. It is wonderful how the whelp has written such things."

"It is a sword that cuts both ways," *Johnsonian Miscellanies*, ed. George Birkbeck Hill D.C.L. (New York: Harper and Brothers, Franklin Square, 1897), II: 15.

Walpole

"the honor of ushering," vindication letter: JD, p. 139; "imaginary abortions," p. 116; "accused of blasting ... inventing great bards than being one," p. 119; "silly dispute," p. 148; "as I was originally an actor," p. 113; "Is it not hard ... assassin of genius?" p. 119; propensity to forgery "most wanting culture," p. 128; "Still the boy remains a prodigy," p. 108; "the amazing number of books ... confined to Bristol," p. 150; "except that of Psalmanazar," p. 41.

Characterizations of Walpole: "bundle of inconsistent whims," WSL, 60 p. 6, citing *Edinburgh Review* (October 1833); "all the house of forgery are relations," JD, p. 128; review of Walpole's *Memoirs:* "receive with extreme caution," JI, p. 307 citing *Quarterly Review* (July 1822); letter to Rousseau: JI, p. 306; "If literary forgery were the capital offense," CR, p. 243. Russell is quoting Prof. Daniel Wilson.

Walpole's description of his letters to and from Chatterton: JD, pp. 133–148.

Chatterton's descriptions of Walpole: *Memoirs of a Sad Dog* DT I:651–662; "discovered the word *kine* came from the Saxon *cowine*," 659; *Decimus. An Exhibition of Sign Paintings*, DT I:576–579; "A Piece of Modern Antiquity," 577.

Walpole's statement on Jacob Bryant, "I must have been the sensitive plant," JD, p. 106.

Catcott's defeat: "Dr. Johnson good naturedly agreed ... no more to be said," Boswell, *Life* II:34; "He has completely ruined himself," letter to Dr. Glynn, January 18, 1783: EM, p. 150; Catcott as a pewterer's apprentice in humiliating circumstances: letter to Dr. Glynn footnote: EM, p. 477.

Barrett's defeat: "as I told you before," letter to Lort, February 7, 1772: B11457, f. 72–73; "there is a great deal to be said," letter to Lort, May 14, 1777: B11457, f. 74–75; Catcott's distress with delay in publication "as he has for some years amused the world," comment to Dean Milles, January 1, 1778:

EM, p. 481; Lort's amusement at Barrett's reliance on Chatterton's documentation, letter to Horace Walpole, August 4, 1789: WSL 51, 16:222–224; "without either fear or wit," 223; Walpole's triumph at Barrett's bad reviews: "I am very, very sorry," letter to Hannah More, Wednesday, November 4, 1789: WSL 51, 31:331.

Jeremiah Milles: Jeremiah Milles "required not only an elevation of poetic genius" as quoted by Edmond Malone, *Cursory Observations on the Poems attributed to Thomas Rowley A Priest of the 15th Century* (London: J. Nichols, J. Walter, R. Faulder, J. Sewell, and E. Newberry, MDCCLXXXII), p. 34; Coleridge on Milles, "an owl mangling," EM, p. 283; Walpole on Jacob Bryant, "I had rather believe," JD, p. 103; Malone on the punishment for Milles and Bryant, as reported by Horace Walpole: WSL 51, 29:176.

The Chatterton Biographies
(see introduction of Notes for complete references)
Love and Madness.

Gregory's *The Life of Chatterton:* His correspondence with Michael Lort is described by EM, pp. 485–486; exchange of letters between Lort and Gregory: B11457, f. 90–93; Lort's letter to Walpole, November 10, 1778: WSL, 51, 16:219–222; "to ascribe to Mr. Walpole," GG, p. xliii; Thistlewaite's testimonials: *Works* III: 478.

Dix's *Life of Chatterton:* Dix's counterfeit portrait and other counterfeit portraits are described by Ingram, Appendix F, pp. 335–338 and Wilson, pp. 113–115. They are also described in Charles Kent's entry on Chatterton in *Dictionary of National Biography,* pp. 143–154. Kent's Chatterton account is filled with inaccuracies, many of them from Dix's biography. He speaks of eight counterfeit portraits, saying that only one of these is genuine: pp. 151–152. Ingram quotes Southey on the authentication of the portrait in Dix: "The portrait of Chatterton which Mr. Dix discovered identifies itself, if ever portrait did. It brought his sister, Mrs. Newton, strongly to my recollection. No family likeness could be more distinctly marked considering the disparity of years." The Dix portrait may be a engraving copy of a genuine painting by A. Morris, March 25, 1762: JI, p. 337. Ingram mentions several other supposedly genuine portraits discovered in April, 1883 by a Reverend Dr. H. P. Stokes.

Russell's *Thomas Chatterton: The Marvelous Boy:* "I have tried," p. xiii.

The Testimony of Sarah and Mary
Imagined they might be hanged for Thomas's crimes: HC, p. 139; Mary: "the poems my brother copied," EM, p. 470, citing an exchange between Mary and George Steevens in 1777; "aye to be sure," EM, p. 470, citing Joseph Cottle, *Malvern Hills* 4 (1829):412, and Cottle, *Early Recollections* I:257. Cottle's exchange with Mary would have been around 1800.

NOTES

The story of Herbert Croft's betrayal: EM, pp. 467–468, 491. Some of Mary's interviews with Lort, the scrupulous cross-examiner, are much more detailed than the letter to Croft. Ironically, Mary also gave some interviews to William Ireland, the Shakespeare forger. He was to report his conversations with Mary in his *Confessions* (1805). Though he himself was a well-known forger, Ireland was considered to be a reputable informant on the life of Chatterton. The opening lines of Mary's letter to Croft, "Conscious of my own inability," HC, p. 143; Croft's response to Sarah Chatterton's letter denouncing him: "never be forgotten by HC," EM, p. 468.

Southey's intervention: "the sort of threatening letter." Southey's printing of the two letters and his exposure of Herbert Croft's ill treatment of Sarah Chatterton and Mary Newton: *Monthly Magazine* (November 1799), pp. 770–772. B5258.

INDEX

abandonment anxiety of children, 3, 8
Account of the family of De Berghams from the Norman Conquest to this Time (Chatterton), 114
Ackroyd, Peter, 181, 282
adolescence, adolescents, 42, 51–52, 116–118, 189; adult views of, 189–190; anorexia nervosa vs. imposturousness, as pathological solution to problems of, 7–8; boys' assertion of masculinity, 85–86, 161; boys' retreat from the female, 53, 85; capacity for mourning in, 116–118, 230; as drama of passage from child to adult, 211, 230; fear of sexual inadequacy in, 161; perverse impulses of incipient impostors in, 220–221; struggle for gender identity in, 8–9, 21, 42–43, 100–102, 117
Adolescence (Kaplan), 1, 2, 6
Advice Addressed to Miss M****** R****** of Bristol (Chatterton), 120
Aella: A Tragycal Enterlude, or Discourseynge Tragedie (Chatterton/Rowley), 41, 90–93, 94, 108, 172, 173, 247, 270
African poems of Chatterton, 131–132, 178, 233–234, 275
African Song, An (Chatterton), 234
aggression: adolescent, 189; in men vs. women, 7
Agrippa, Cornelius, *De Occulta Philosophica,* 34–35
Alvarez, Luis Walter, *The Savage God,* 188, 227
Ames, Levi, 246
Amphitryon (Chatterton), 173
Anecdotes of Painting in England (Walpole), 110, 244n.
Angel, Frederick, 222–223, 286
Angel, Mrs. Frederick, 15, 170, 171, 194–195, 208, 222–223
Annual Register, 141
anorexia nervosa, 6–8
anticlericalism, 280; of Chatterton, 27, 47, 49, 118, 129–131, 190, 191, 280
anti-Semitism, 18th-century England, 125, 274

Apostate Will (Chatterton), 47, 72, 180, 280
apprenticeship: Chatterton's indenture, 26, 27, 44, 49–51, 97, 137, 140, 230–231; system of, 44, 49–50, 205
Aristotle, 224
Arlow, Jacob, 4, 218–219
Arnold, Matthew, 74, 279
art: and crime, 2, 179, 242; and madness, 224, 286
Articles of the Belief of Me Thomas Chatterton (Chatterton), 128–129
artistic creativity. *See* creativity
Art of Puffing (Chatterton), 162, 178
as-if personality, 215
Astrea Brokage (Chatterton), 131
astrology, 33–34, 191–192, 231
Augusta, Princess Dowager, 134, 147–148, 275
Augustine, 206
authority, desire's debate with, 220

Bailey's (dictionary), 63, 64, 268
Baker, John, 105–109, 118, 125, 199, 202, 267, 272
Balade of Charitie. See Excelente Balade of Charitie
Ballance, Mrs., 142, 168–169, 170
Baronettage of England (Collins), 114
Barrett, William, 61–63, 64–70, 72, 82, 91, 97, 137, 138, 202, 239, 240, 251, 253, 267, 270; barber-surgeon, 61, 171, 207; Chatterton introduced to, 53, 59; collaboration in Rowley narratives (unconscious and knowing), 63, 68, 69–70, 98–99, 269, 270, 247; his credulity used by Chatterton, 79, 86–88, 90; fails as paying patron, 110; *History of Bristol* of, 61, 66, 67, 69, 70, 77, 86, 113, 208, 246–247, 253; knowing use of Chatterton's Burgum pedigree hoax, 114; probable collaboration in Chatterton's Walpole scheme, 113, 114; in Rowley controversy, 242, 243, 245–247
Barthelemon, Mary, 173, 279
Battle of Hastings I (Chatterton/Rowley/Turgot),

291

INDEX

Battle of Hastings I (continued) 40, 61, 68, 81, 84, 87, 133, 267

Battle of Hastings II (by Turgot translated by Roulie for W. Canynge, Esq.) (Chatterton/Rowley/Turgot), 68–69, 81–82, 84, 87

Baudelaire, Charles Pierre, 203n.

Bawdin, Sir Charles (invented name), 68, 69, 79–81, 94

Beckford, William, 165–166, 167–168, 235; death of, and Chatterton's reaction, 169, 170, 171, 179, 183

belief: climate of, 70; vs. cynicism, conflict in Chatterton's poetry, 47–49, 118, 179–180; vs. self-interest, Chatterton's conflict, 118, 127, 167, 179–180, 280

Bentley, Eric, 203

Berryman, John, 224

Betram, Charles, 261

Bingley, William, 167

biographers of Chatterton, 28, 29, 39–40, 41, 154, 155–156, 182, 189, 194–201, 202, 248–251, 254–257, 259–260, 277

bipolar manic-depressive disorders, 224, 286

Birch, Thomas, 260

Blackstone, William, 185

Blake, William, 27, 223–224

Boswell, James, 46, 76, 125, 159, 171, 204–205, 207, 211, 245, 282–283

Brahms, Johannes, 75

Bridge Narrative (Chatterton), 55, 57–59, 64, 65, 79, 81, 87, 267, 268, 270

Bridge Stowe, Brycgstow, 20, 56; *see also* Bristol

Brief Account of William Cannings from the Life of Thomas Rowlie, Preeste (Chatterton/Rowley), 83–85, 267, 270

Bristol, England, 18–19, 20, 30, 42, 49, 133, 156, 180, 233, 287; bridges (old and new), 55–57, 60, 86–87; in *Camden's Britannia*, 81, 83, 88; history fantasies of Chatterton about, 20, 51, 55–59, 65–66, 70, 81–83, 86–88, 238; *History* of Barrett, 61, 66, 67, 69, 70, 77, 86, 113, 246–247; mythical St. Andrews Church, 70

Bristol Castle, 66, 89, 90, 91

Bristol Cathedral, 37

Bristoliensis, Dunhelmus. *See* Dunhelmus Bristoliensis

Bristol Mercury, The, 226, 286

Bristowe Tragedie, or the Dethe of Syr Charles Bawdin (Chatterton/Rowley), 61, 68, 69, 79–81, 84, 240, 267

British Academy, 1930 Warton Lecture at, 51, 266

Browning, Robert, 183, 184; *Essay on Chatterton*, 182

Bryant, Jacob, 179, 245, 247

Burgum, Henry, 60, 114, 128, 138, 235, 245, 246

Burns, Robert, 18, 74

Bute, 3rd earl of, 134, 148, 275

Butler, Samuel, 126

Byron, George Gordon, Lord, 18, 74

Camden's Britannia, 81, 83, 88

Canynge, Sir William, 10, 20, 25, 26, 28, 42, 51, 64, 65–66, 69, 77, 85–90, 111, 118, 126, 161; character of, 80–81, 86, 92, 93–95; as Chatterton's conscience, 221–222, 232–233; emergence in Rowley narratives, 79–85, 270; evolution of his person, 96–98, 100, 101, 102; as "father" (and "patron") to Chatterton, 5, 42, 93, 101–102, 133, 135, 232–233, 235; fictional vs. real, 84; linking of Chatterton name with, 82–83, 114; mayor of Bristol, 20, 82; relinquished by Chatterton, 102–103, 114, 115–116, 120, 161, 221, 235; tomb and inscription, 36, 49, 69, 84, 94

Carey, Thomas, 21, 35, 45, 168, 170, 173, 267

Castle of Otranto, The (Walpole), 110, 243, 261

castration anxiety, 9, 217, 221–222; and creativity, 101; relationship of falsehood to, 217–219

Catch for Three Voices, A (song), 38, 287

Catcott, Alexander, 60, 129–130, 139, 156, 157, 235, 245

Catcott, George, 59–62, 65, 67–68, 72, 82, 89, 97, 129, 138, 139, 155, 156, 202, 245, 251, 267, 270; and Burgum, 114, 128, 245; Chatterton introduced to, 53, 55, 59; Chatterton's late letter to, 184, 194, 200; Chatterton's manuscripts in possession of, 61–62, 66, 229–240, 253, 254, 272, 275; fails as paying patron, 110, 235; in Rowley controversy, 242, 245, 246

Catholicism, 128–129

character perversions, 2–4; in Chatterton, 162; kinds of, 4; in impostor, 2, 4, 8–9, 218–219; in men vs. women, 9–10; relationship to sexual perversions, 4, 218–219

Charles I, King, 61

Charles II, King, 124

Charrière, Mme. Isabelle de, 211

Chasseguet-Smirgel, Janine, 9, 101, 233

Chateaton, Chateau tonne, Chateautonne, Chaderton (heraldic fantasy names), 82–83

Chatterton (portrait), *frontispiece illus.*, xi

Chatterton (Vigny), 202n.

INDEX

Chatterton: A Biographical Study (Wilson), 260
Chatterton, A Biography (Masson), 259
Chatterton: An Essay (Maitland), 259
"Chatterton": Warton Lecture on English Poetry (Dixon), 51, 266
Chatterton, Giles Malpas (brother), 35, 216, 229, 231
Chatterton, John (great-uncle), 36
Chatterton, Mary (*later* Mrs. Thomas Newton, sister), 21, 22–23, 29, 35–36, 40–41, 42–43, 46–47, 177, 193, 202, 216, 252–256, 289–290; biographical notes on, 41, 254, 256, 285; Chatterton's letters from London to, 166–167, 170, 177–178, 184, 208, 254, 256; cited, on her brother, 21, 22, 44, 45, 46, 47, 50, 52–53, 57, 136, 198, 255, 265; mental illness of, 186, 281; views of her brother's writing, 40–41, 47, 67–68, 252–253; and Walpole incident, 114, 115
Chatterton, Sarah Young (mother), 20–21, 22–23, 28–29, 36, 37, 39–40, 42–44, 67–68, 141, 177, 216, 252–254, 255–256, 264–265; Chatterton's letters from London to, 27, 141–142, 143, 163–164, 177, 184, 199–200, 225, 254, 256; views of her son's writing, 40, 67–68, 252–253
Chatterton, Thomas: alleged "last poems" of, 193–194, 225–227, 286; ancestral heraldic fantasies of, 82–83; anticlerical sentiments of, 27, 47, 49, 118, 129–131, 190, 191, 280; artistic inclination of, 22, 23, 40–41, 90, 97, 99–102, 173, 179; birth of, 18, 28; character perversion evident in, 162; childhood of, 20–24, 35, 40, 42–47, 216, 229–230; his conflict between belief and self-interest/cynicism, 47–49, 118, 127, 167, 179–180, 280; death of, 15, 208 (*see also* suicide of Chatterton); defenders vs. detractors of, 184–190, 191–201, 202, 212, 213–215, 227, 240–247; his drawings for Barrett's *History*, 70, 247; his drawing for "Intrest thou universal God of Men," *illus.* 124; his drawings for the Rowley narratives, xi, *illus.* 16, 20, *illus.* 34, *illus.* 56, 66, 69, 77, *illus.* 78, 86, *illus.* 106, *illus.* 214, *illus.* 238; dual aspects of his personality, 26, 118, 178–181, 197, 210, 212, 241, 250–251; education of, 22, 23–24, 43–46, 49–50; family background of, 23, 35–40; a freethinker, 3, 35, 40, 47, 49, 99, 117–120, 126, 136, 154, 179–180, 190, 196; as impostor, 1–2, 9–10, 26, 42–43, 55–59, 86, 87, 98–101, 106, 159, 161–162, 178, 213–215, 216, 218, 221; indentured as lawyer's scrivener, 26, 27, 44, 49–51, 97, 137, 140, 230–231; a leader in childhood play, 21, 35; literary pseudonyms of, 87, 98, 141, 165, 244; his loneliness, 107, 172, 178, 196, 199; longing for a father, 5, 9, 21, 23, 42, 93, 100–103, 117, 133, 135, 229; his love for Polly Rumsey, 52–53, 82, 109, 120, 131, 134, 178, 199, 200–201; his love of reading, 22, 46, 255; misogyny of, 120, 233; monument to, 29–32, 44–45, 139, 145, 263–264; parchment fabrication by, 62–63, 69–70, 86, 267, 268; as prey of his conscience, 221–222, 230; his pride, 113, 137, 187, 213, 216, 223, 233; and religion, 47–48, 128–131, 190, 280; religious infidelity of, 188–189, 190, 191, 200, 213; as a replacement child, 216, 231; sexual creed and writings of, 118–120, 154–157, 159–161, 162, 196–197, 200, 211–212; sociopolitical creed and writings of, 120, 128–129, 132–134, 165–168, 179; supposed sexual profligacy of, 109–110, 159, 188, 189, 190, 193–200, 203, 211–212, 213; suspicions of venereal disease, 2, 184, 190, 191–196, 208–210; temperament of, 23, 52, 127, 145, 191, 224, 251; thirst for fame, 21–22, 24, 44, 82–83, 164–168, 202, 249; unknown burial site of, 27, 28–30; women's role in his life, 22–23, 42–43, 169, 177, 188–189, 198–201, 216 (*see also* mother-son relationship; sister-brother relationship); writings of. *See* literary voices; poetry, acknowledged; poetry, imposturous; prose writings; satirical writings; writings
Chatterton, Thomas, Sr. (father), 20, 23, 34, 35–36, 37–39, 44, 264–265; character of, 23, 133; death of, 18, 20, 37, 229–230, 232, 240, 287; and St. Mary's parchments, 20, 35, 60, 67, 241; son's epitaph to, 139, 229
Chatterton, William (uncle), 22
Chaucer, Geoffrey, 63, 64, 68, 71, 78, 84, 118, 172
Cheney, Master (actor), 173, 174, 279
Chesler, Phyllis, 7
childhood: absence of father in, 4, 5–9, 21, 42–43, 100–101, 159, 172, 216–217, 229–230; of Chatterton, 21–24, 35, 40, 42–46, 216, 229–230; death experience in, 229–230; family romance in, 24–25, 161; of impostor, 21–22, 157, 159, 216–217; mother-child-father triangle, 8, 217–218, 220–221; passing of, 116–117, 211; of replacement children, 216, 231
Churchill, Charles, 118, 120, 123–128, 130–131, 133, 134, 146, 147, 152, 273–274

293

INDEX

Churchwarden and the Apparition, The; A Fable (attributed to Chatterton), 49
Clayfield, Michael, 136–137, 139, 188, 235, 275
Clive, Kitty, 244
Coleridge, Samuel Taylor, 247; *Monody on the Death of Chatterton,* 17, 32, 261
Collins, Arthur, 114
Collins, William, 178
Colston, Edward, 44–45
Colston's Hospital School, 22, 24, 25, 32, 37, 41–42, 43–46, 49, 85, 136, 265
Complete Works of Thomas Chatterton, The (ed. Taylor, with Hoover), 260
Confessions of Felix Krull, Confidence Man, The (Mann), 1–2, 179
conscience, 220–222, 230, 231, 285; Chatterton's, Canynge as, 232–233; in narcissist, 219; *see also* superego
Constabiliad, The (Chatterton), 133
Constant, Benjamin, 211
Consuliad, The: An Heroic Poem (Chatterton), 133–134
Copernican System, The (Chatterton), 136
Cottle, Joseph, 29–30, 35, 67, 70, 259, 263, 289
counterfeiting, 62, 99, 158, 179, 188, 213, 215, 252
Court and City Magazine, 170
Craishes Herauldry (heraldic fantasy of Chatterton), 82, 105, 113, 267
creativity: absence vs. presence of father and, 100–101; manic-depressive disorder and, 224, 286; relationship to falsehood and perversion, 2, 3, 5, 9–10, 100, 179; role of imitation and plagiarism in, 99, 181–183; spurred by mourning, 100
crime and criminality, 215; art and, 2, 179, 242; gender difference and, 7
Croft, Sir Herbert, 136, 195, 231, 248, 249, 250, 254–257, 259, 265, 289–290
Cross, Thomas, 193, 207, 208, 222, 223, 284
Cumberland, George, 28–30, 225
Cunningham, Allan, 261
cynicism vs. belief, conflict in Chatterton's poetry, 47–49, 118, 179–180

D.B.. *See* Dunhelmus Bristolienses
death: fear of, and melancholia, 221; of parent, 229–230
Death of Chatterton, The (Wallis painting), xiii, 15, 261
"death trend," 229
Decimus (pseudonym of Chatterton), 141, 165, 244
Decimus To the Freeholders of the City of Bristol (Chatterton), 287
Defense, The (Chatterton), 131
Defoe, Daniel, 18, 262

Delacroix, Eugène, 203
De Occulta Philosophica (Agrippa), 34–35
depression, 7, 227–228; manic-depressive disorders, 224, 227; in mourning, 228
desire, authority's debate with, 220
Discorse on Brystowe by Thos. Rowleie wrotten and gotten at the Desire of W. Canynge Esqur. (Chatterton/Rowley/Turgot), 86–87, 89
Dix, John, 29, 250, 251, 259, 289
Dixon, Macneile W., lecture on Chatterton, 51, 266
Dodsley, James, 141, 270
Donne, John, 268
Dryden, John, 71, 118, 127, 130, 173, 190
Dunhelmus Bristoliensis (Durham Man of Bristol), 58–59, 87; D.B. as pseudonym of Chatterton, 87, 98, 141, 171, 173, 244

eating disorders, 215; *see also* anorexia nervosa
Edda, The Descent of Odin (Gray), 73
Edkins, Mrs., 28–29, 225
Edmunds (editor/publisher), 141, 144, 163, 169, 235
educational options, in 18th-century England, 43–44
Edward III, King, 148
Edward IV, King, 36, 80, 94, 102
ego, raging of superego against, 221–222, 228–229
ego ideal, 101, 221, 285; *see also* conscience; superego
Ehrlich, Paul, 210
Elegy to the Memory of Thomas Chatterton: Late of Bristol (Carey), 21
Elegy Written in a Country Churchyard (Gray), 72
Eliot, T. S., 181–182, 201–202, 282; *King Bolo,* 201–202, 282; *Love Song of St. Sebastian,* 201, 282; his Prufrock, 201; *The Wasteland,* 181
Ellis, Havelock, 220
Endymion (Keats), 17–18
Englandes Glorye revyved in Maystre Canynge (Chatterton/Rowley/Turgot), 65–66
English romantic movement, 17, 72, 190, 204; Chatterton as emblem of, 1, 15, 18, 27, 46, 204, 257
Enlightenment, Age of, 70–71, 153, 186–187
Epistle to Catcott (Chatterton), 130–131
erection: in pubescent boys, 160; impostor's view of, 2, 158
Esman, Aaron, 100
Essay on Chatterton (Browning), 182
Essay on Man (Pope), 149, 150, 151n.
Essay on Suicide (Hume), 186–187
Essay on Woman (Wilkes), 149–151, 152, 154

INDEX

Ethelgar. A Saxon Poem (Chatterton/D.B.), 108, 234
Excelente Balade of Charitie: as wroten bie the gode Prieste Thomas Rowley, 1464 (Chatterton/Rowley), 171–173, 235, 267
exceptional child, 216
Exhibition, The: A Personal Satire (Chatterton), 154, 155–157, 161, 162, 197
exhibitionism, 4, 155–159, 162, 215, 218; as adolescent proclamation of masculinity, 85; in Chatterton's writings, 155–157, 159–161, 197; impostor's predisposition for, 2, 157–158
Explayneals of the Yellowe Rolle (or *Purple Rolle*) (Chatterton/Rowley), 66

fabrication, 3–5, 26, 98–100, 159, 181, 218–219, 233; *see also* Middle English, fake; parchments, fabrication and counterfeiting of
falsehood, 218; of literary impostors and impostor-artists, 99, 179; relationship to creativity and perversion, 2, 3, 5, 9–10, 100, 179; relationship to castration anxiety, 217–219
family romance, 263; of Chatterton, 26, 41–43, 51–52, 65, 81–98, 101, 118, 144–145, 161, 222; impostor's vs. typical, 24–26, 161
father: absence of, 4, 5–6, 100–101, 172, 229–230; absence of, and imposturousness, 1, 5, 7–9, 10, 21, 23–26, 42–43, 85–86, 159, 216–217; absence of, as inspiration to poets, 6, 93; Chatterton's creation of images of, in his writings, 23, 42, 93, 101–102, 133, 232–235; Chatterton's living substitutes, 135, 235; longing for, in poetry, 5–6, 23, 93
father-son relationship, 5, 85, 100; ego-ideal projection, 101, 221, 285
Felix Farley's Bristol Journal, 47, 48, 55, 57, 59, 61
Fell, Isaac, 134, 141–142, 143, 163, 165, 169, 235, 275
femininity: infantile ideals of, 8; gender traits and pathology, 7; male adolescent retreat from, 53, 85
Fenichel, Otto, 3, 217
fetishism, 4, 215, 217–219; impostor's predisposition for, 2, 158
Fingal (Macpherson), 73, 75
flagellation, 205, 206
forgery, 99, 158, 250, 252
Fowler, Jack, 108, 109, 120, 131–132, 267
"Fragmentes of Anticquitie" (Chatterton/Rowley), xi, *illus.* 106, *illus.* 214

Fragments of Poetry translated from the Gaelic and Erse Languages (Macpherson), 72, 75
Franklin, Benjamin, 152
Frederick the Great, King of Prussia, 207–208, 243
freedom of the press, 147, 154, 239
Freeholder's Magazine, 134, 141, 163, 170
Freemasons, 86, 95, 270
Freud, Sigmund, 3, 100, 140, 219–221, 227–228, 263, 285
Fry, Dr. Thomas, 153, 237–240, 287

Gainsborough, Thomas, 28
Gardner, Edward, 62, 267, 268
Garrick, David, 125
Gay, John, 126
gender identification problems, 2, 8–9, 21, 26, 42–43, 100–101, 117, 159; Chatterton's solution to, 101–102
genital inadequacy, fear of, 157–158, 159, 161 216–217, 220
genius, 100, 182–183; 18th-century meaning of word, 138 and *n.*
George III, King, 110, 117, 123, 124, 133, 148, 149, 154, 164–166, 275
Goddwyn (Chatterton/Rowley), 102
Godred Crovan (Chatterton), 234
Goethe, Johann Wolfgang von, 75; *Sorrows of Young Werther,* 31, 75, 187
Goldsmith, Oliver, 240–241
gonorrhea, 204, 207–208, 209; speculated for Chatterton, 2, 192–193, 196, 208, 210
Gorthmund. Translated from the Saxon (Chatterton), 234–235
Gray, Thomas, 72–73, 74, 75, 112
Gregory, George, 41, 133, 182, 183, 184, 189, 200–201, 248–250, 251, 259
Grenville, George, 148
Grossman, William, 10

Hackman, Rev. James, 190, 256
Hamilton, Archibald, 141, 163, 286
Happiness (Chatterton), 60–61, 254
Haynes, Mr. (Colston teacher), 45
Hazlitt, William, 74
hebephrenia, 7
Henry II (Ireland imposturing Shakespeare), 4
Henry VI, King, 80, 94
Hirlas (Chatterton), 131
Hirlas II (Chatterton), 131
Historical and Geographical Description of Formosa (Psalmanazar), 4, 5
Historie of Peyncters yn Englande bie T. Rowley (Chatterton/Rowley), 111, 112, 233
History of Bristol (Barrett), 61, 66, 67, 69, 70, 77, 86, 113, 208, 246–247, 253

INDEX

History of the Holy Bible, 35
hoaxes and practical jokes, 3, 4, 215, 218–219; of Chatterton, 106–107, 162; Chatterton's bridge hoax, 57, 86; Chatterton's Burgum hoax, 114–115; Chatterton's suicide threats and fake notes, 27, 32, 136–140, 145
Hogarth, William, 28, 125, 146, 147
homosexuality, 18th-century England, 125, 206, 273–274
Hook, James, 279
Hoover, Benjamin B., 260
Hoyland, Eleanor, 106–107, 109, 118
Hume, David, 186–187, 189, 204
Hymn for a Christmas Day, A (Chatterton), 47, 180
hysteria, 7

id, 221
identity problems, 215; gender identity, 2, 8–9, 21, 26, 42–43, 100–101, 117, 159; of impostor, 2, 4, 5, 26, 42, 157–158, 159; true-self vs. false-self, 215
imitation, in creative activity, 181–183; by Chatterton, 183, 184
impostor-artist, 2, 179; *see also* literary impostors
impostors, 158–159, 215–218; bodily deformities in, 159; childhood circumstances of, 21, 157, 159, 216–217; character perversion in, 2, 4, 218–219; family romance of, 24–26, 161; identity problem of, 2, 4, 5, 26, 42, 157–158, 159; predisposition for exhibitionism in, 2, 157–158; predisposition for fetishism in, 2, 158; predisposition for transvestism in, 2, 158; predisposition for voyeurism in, 2, 158; pseudomanhood and pseudogenitalism of, 2, 158; *see also* literary impostors
imposturousness, 158–159, 215–218; absence of father and, 1, 5, 7–9, 10, 21, 23–26, 42–43, 85–86, 159, 216–217; and character perversion, 4, 8–9, 218; emergence in Chatterton, 42–43, 55–59; a male disorder, 1, 5, 7–8, 9–10, 20; narcissism and, 159, 215–217, 219; as pathological solution for adolescent, 8–9, 19, 42, 218; and sexual perversion, 2–3, 157–158, 218–219
indecent exposure, 157
indenture system, 18th-century England, 44, 49–50, 205
infancy, 8, 20, 114
infidelity (religious), 215; of Chatterton, 188–189, 190, 191, 200, 213
Ingram, John, 155–156, 199–200, 259, 266, 279
insanity, 188; in Chatterton family, 186, 281; *see also* madness

Interpretation of Dreams, The (Freud), 100
"Intrest thou universal God of Men" (Chatterton), 127–128; drawing for, xi, *illus.* 124
Ireland, William Henry, 4, 75–76, 289–290
Iscam, Sir John (fictional Chatterton co-author), 95, 270–271
I've let my Yard, and sold my Clay (attributed to Chatterton), 49

"Jack and the Beanstalk" (fairy tale), 25–26, 42, 98
John Seconde Abbot of Sayncte Augustyns (Abbot John), 97, 111
Johnson, Samuel, 74, 76, 147, 159, 178, 205; in Rowley controversy, 241, 245, 280, 288
Jordon, John, 261
Journal 6th (Chatterton), 118–120, 125–126, 154, 196
Joyce, James, 181
Junius (pseudonym), 118

Kalender (Ricart), 69
Keats, John: *Endymion,* 17; "O Chatterton!," 17
Kent, Charles, 289
Kersey (dictionary), 63, 64, 184, 268
King Bolo and His Great Black Queen (Eliot), 201, 282
Krull, Felix (fictional character), 1–2, 179
Kunitz, Stanley, 6

Lamartine, Alphonse de, 75
Lambert, John, 49–50, 97, 118, 135–136, 137, 140, 188, 193, 266
Last Verses Written by Chatterton, The (unauthenticated), 225–226, 227
Lessing, Gotthold Ephraim, 75
Letter from Fullford, the Gravedigger (attributed to Chatterton), 49
Letter Paraphras'd, The (Chatterton), 155, 159–161, 162, 197, 278
Levasseur, Thérèse, 204, 282–283
Life of Johnson (Boswell), 245
Life of Thomas Chatterton, A (Meyerstein), 259, 260
Life of Thomas Chatterton, The (Dix), 29, 250, 259
Life of Thomas Chatterton, The (Gregory), 248–250, 259
literary impostors, 4–5, 9, 71–76, 99, 110, 179, 242–243, 260–261
literary voices of Chatterton, 49; Rowleyan voice, 25, 47, 51, 64, 92, 99, 172, 178
literature of mid-eighteenth century, 71–72
London, 164–165; Chatterton in, 26–27, 35, 107, 120, 135, 140–142, 143, 162, 163–178, 183–184, 195, 222–225
London Magazine, 170

INDEX

Lort, Michael, 36, 193, 195, 246, 248–249, 250, 255, 287, 289
Love and Madness (Croft), 190, 231, 246, 248, 250, 251, 259, 255–257, 265, 277
Love Song of St. Sebastian, The (Eliot), 201, 282
Lyfe of William Canynge, The (Chatterton/Rowley), 95, 108
lying. *See* pathological lying; petty lying

Mabbott, T. O., 279
Macpherson, James, 5, 71–76, 77, 102, 112; *Fingal*, 73; *Fragments of Poetry translated from the Gaelic and Erse Languages*, 72; *Temora*, 73
madness, 215; alleged in Chatterton, 185–186, 188–190, 213, 224; and creativity, 224; love and, 190; of poets, 203–204, 224; and religious infidelity, 188–189; and suicide, 185–186, 224
Maitland, S. R., 259
Malone, Edmund, 248
Mandeville, Bernard de, 206
manic-depressive disorders, 224, 227, 286
Mann, Thomas, *Felix Krull of*, 1–2, 179
Maria Friendless (Chatterton), 178
masculinity: adolescent assertion of, 85–86; Chatterton's satisfaction of his image of, 101–102; mother-conveyed infantile ideal of, 4, 8, 21, 26, 42–43; gender traits and pathology, 7; *see also* gender identity problems
masochism, 7
Mason, Rev. William, 112
Masson, David, 259
masturbation, 205, 206, 220
May (song), 173–176, 279
Medmenham Abbey, 146, 147, 151
melancholia, 178, 187, 227–229, 232; fear of death a part of, 221
Memorials of the Canynges Family (Pryce), 29
Meredith, George, 261
Methodists, 190, 239
Meyerstein, E. H. W., 138n., 194–196, 197, 202, 224, 259, 260, 272, 278, 279
Middle English, fake, of Rowley narratives, 63–64, 240, 250, 265, 268
Middlesex Journal, The, 141, 163, 165–166, 167, 170, 244
Milles, Jeremiah, 247, 249, 250, 254, 255, 265, 289
Milton, John, 172
misogyny of Chatterton, 120, 233
Monody on the Death of Chatterton (Coleridge), 17, 32, 261
Monthly Review, The, 124
mother, as single parent, 4, 5
mother-daughter relationship, 5

mother-son relationship, 4, 5, 85, 216–218, 285; in Chatterton's case, 1, 21, 23, 24, 42–43, 177, 188–189, 216–217, 252
mourning, 228; adolescent capacity for, 116–118, 230; Chatterton's periods of, 116, 117, 178; and creativity, 100; for dead parent, 230
Murray, Fanny, 150
mutilation anxiety, 3, 8, 217–218, 222

Nacke, Paul, 220
Napoleon, Bonaparte, 75
narcissism, 4, 101, 189, 215–220, 232; an attitude, 220, 227; of Chatterton, 85, 162, 215, 216, 224, 233; as cloak of immaturity, 159; disturbances of, 215–217; and imposturousness, 159, 215–217, 219; terminology, 215, 219–220; triumph transformed into defeat, 217
Nevill, John C., 197, 260
New and Complete Illustration of Occult Sciences, A (Sibley), 33
Newton, Marianne (neice), 281, 285
Newton, Mary. *See* Chatterton, Mary
Newton, Thomas, 254
New York Times Book Review, 6
Night Thoughts (volume of verse), 31, 32
"Nine Deeds and Proclamations" (Chatterton/Rowley), drawing from, xi, *illus.* 34
North Briton, The (newspaper), 124, 147, 167, 168; Issue #45, 145, 148–149, 151–152
Novalis (Friedrich von Hardenberg), 75

obscenity, 162; *see also* pornography
oedipal defeat, 161, 220
oedipal triangle, 8, 217–218, 220
Oedipus complex, 221
Onania (anon.), 205
On Happienesse (Chatterton/Rowley), 98
Onn oure Ladies Chirch (Chyrche) (Chatterton/Rowley), 61, 67–68, 267
On the Last Epiphany, or Christ Coming to Judgment (attributed to Chatterton), 48, 180
opium-overdose theory of Chatterton's death, 208, 284
orgasm in partner, vs. vanquishment and defeat of partner, 2, 158
Orphans Lead the World, The (Rentchnick), 100–101
Ossian and Ossiana, 73, 74–75, 77; of Chatterton, 102, 108, 111, 114, 117, 118, 131–132, 178, 233–234
Othello (Shakespeare), 91
Oxford University, 43–44, 239–240; *see also* St. John's College

297

INDEX

paranoia, 7; grandiose, and imposturousness, 158
parchments, fabrication and counterfeiting of, 62–63, 69–70, 86, 267, 268
parents; and child, family triangle, 8, 217–218, 220; child and adolescent idealization of, 24, 116–117, 161, 220–221; death of, 229–230; *see also* father; father-son relationship; mother; mother-son relationship
Parlyamente of Sprytes, The: On the Dedication of St. Mary's Church (Chatterton/Iscam/Rowley), 89–90, 95, 96, 270–271
pathological lying, 3–4, 9, 218; of Chatterton, 99, 162
Patriot party, 123, 134–135, 136, 143, 163, 165–168
Percy, Thomas, 63, 64
perversion: relationship to falsehood and artistic creativity, 3, 5, 9–10, 100; and pathological lying, 3; *see also* character perversions; sexual perversions
Petrarch (and Laura), 201
petty lying, 4, 215, 218–219
Phillips, Thomas, 136
Pinkerton, John, 261
plagiarism, 3, 4, 183, 262; Chatterton and, 99, 107, 178, 183; in impostor, 158; vs. imposture, 1, 5, 99; unavoidability of some, 99
Poems and Essays (Cottle), 29
poetry, acknowledged or under pseudonyms: of Chatterton, 3, 26, 118, 126, 179, 183, 275; African, 131–132, 178, 233–234, 275; Colston beginnings (pocket-notebook), 46–49; Ossiana, 102, 108, 111, 114, 117, 118, 131–132, 178, 233–234; pornographic, 3, 76, 154–157, 159–162; post-Rowleyan, 115–116, 117–120; *see also* satirical writings; writings
poetry, imposturous, of Chatterton, 3, 5, 17, 20, 24–25, 26, 27–28, 98, 178–179; *Aella* praised, 91, 92–93; *Balade of Charitie* praised, 172; beginnings of, 23, 51, 55, 61–63; father images in, 23, 42, 93, 101–102, 133; love poems for Baker, 106–110; *see also* Rowley narratives; writings
poets: madness in, 203–204, 224; morality or immorality in, 203–204; their passion for the past, 51, 99
"Poet's Quest for the Father" (Kunitz), 6
Political Register, 167
Pollock, George, 100
Pope, Alexander, 71, 118, 126–127, 181; cited on Bristol, 19; *Essay on Man*, 149, 150, 151n.

pornography: of Chatterton, 3, 76, 154–157, 159–162; of Eliot, 201–202; of Wilkes, 149–151
Portrait of Zelide (Scott), 211
portraits of Chatterton, counterfeit, 28, 250, 289
Pound, Ezra, 181
power, impostor's pursuit of, 158, 162, 218
practical jokes. *See* hoaxes and practical jokes
Prendergast, Mrs., 206
pride, 215, 217; Chatterton's, 113, 137, 187, 213, 216, 223, 233
Probus (pseudonym of Chatterton), 165; letters, 165–167, 170
prose writings of Chatterton, 24, 116; genesis in early poetry, 45, 46–47; under Probus pseudonym, 165–167, 170; *see also* writings
prostitution, 205–207, 283
Prufrock (fictional character), 201
Pryce, George, 29–30
Psalmanazar, George, 4, 5, 75–76, 243
pseudogenitalism, 2, 158
psychosis, in men vs. women, 7
puberty, 6; of boys, 161
pubescence, of boys, 85, 161
Purple Rolle (or *Explayneals of the Yellowe Rolle*) (Chatterton/Rowley), 66

Rabelais, François, 147
rage, in Chatterton's satire, 127–128, 161
Rambler, (Johnson), 178
Ray, Martha, 277
reality, denial or fabrication of, 3–5, 26, 98–100, 181, 218–219
Redcliffe, Bristol, 37, 56, 66, 86–88; Parish Account, 36; *see also* St. Mary Redcliffe
Redcliffe and St. Thomas Charity School, 37
religion: Chatterton and, 47–48, 128–131, 188–189, 190, 191, 200, 213, 280; source of, 221
Reliques of Ancient English Poetry (Percy), 63, 64
replacement child, 216, 231
Resignation, The (Chatterton), 134
Resolution and Independence (Wordsworth), 251
Revenge, The; A Burletta (Chatterton), 173, 177 and n., 279
Rimbaud, Arthur, 203 and n.
Rolle of Seyncte Bartlemeweis Priorie (Chatterton/Rowley), 67; drawings from, xi, *illus.* 16, 67, *illus.* 192, *illus.* 238; footnotes of Chatterton to, 67, 77, 209; score from, xi, *illus.* 164
romantic movement, 187, 190; *see also* English romantic movement
Rosciad, The (Churchill), 124, 127
Rossetti, Dante Gabriel, 27

INDEX

Rossner, Judith, 9
Rousseau, Jean-Jacques, 159, 204, 243
Rowley, Thomas, 17, 20, 25, 42, 55, 77, 90, 95, 102, 159, 171–173, 188, 201, 203, 212; Chatterton's cover for, 87–88; evolution of his person, 66, 89, 95, 101–102, 110; introduction of, 51, 79, 270; relinquished by Chatterton, 113, 115–116, 117, 118, 120, 126, 173; source and spelling of name, 69
Rowleyan voice, 64, 92, 99, 172, 178; emergence of, 25, 47, 51
Rowley narratives, 20, 51, 55, 59, 61–70, 77–98, 126, 171–173, 213, 238–240, 267; controversy, 26, 27–28, 30, 36, 41, 45, 48, 63, 137, 154, 191, 240–257; drawings from, xi, *illus.* 16, 20, *illus.* 34, *illus.* 56, 66, 69, 77, *illus.* 78, 86, *illus.* 106, *illus.* 144, *illus.* 192, *illus.* 214, *illus.* 238; early suspicions about authenticity, 67–68, 129; footnotes of Chatterton, 67, 77, 89n. 171, 173, 209; genesis of, 24–25; introduction of Canynge in, 79–85; language of, 40, 63–64, 99, 240, 250, 265; psychological assessment of, 99–103, 215, 232–233; Turgot documents, 65–66, 68–69, 81–82, 86–88, 267; Walpole's rejection of, 26, 64, 98, 102, 112–113, 116, 233, 261; *see also* specific titles
Rowley's Heraldic Account of Bristol Artists and Writers (Chatterton/Rowley), 97–98, 101, 108
Royal Academy, 156, 241, 261
Rudhall, John, 62, 267, 268
Rumsey, Polly, 52–53, 82, 107, 109, 116, 120, 131–132, 134, 178, 199, 200–201
Ruskin, John, 203, 261
Russell, Charles Edward, 198–199, 251, 260
Ryse of Peyncteynge, yn Englande, wroten bie T. Rowleie. 1469 for Mastre Canynge (Chatterton/Rowley), 98, 111, 113

Sackville, George, 150
sadism, 7
sadomasochism, 2, 215
St. John's College, Oxford, 43, 237, 239, 240, 287
St. Mary Redcliffe, Bristol, 19, 20, 35, 48–49, 66; Canynge's tomb at, 36–37, 49, 69, 84, 94; Chatterton's fantasies on founding and rebuilding of, 20, 51, 82, 83, 86, 88–90, 94–96; fables of Chatterton's reinterment at, 28–29; monument to Chatterton at, 29–32, 44–45, 139, 263–264; parchments, 20, 35, 52, 59–60, 61–62, 67, 101, 240, 245, 253; in Rowley narratives, 66; "time out of mind" legend of "Chadderdon" family association with, 35–36, 67, 94
Sand, George, 75
Sandwich, John Montagu, 4th earl of, 125, 134, 147, 149–51, 190, 256, 277
satire, 18th-century, 126–127
satirical writings of Chatterton, 23, 40, 47, 49, 117, 118–120, 126–128, 130–134, 154–157, 160–162, 178; interpretations of, 191, 194–195, 196–197, 198, 200–201
Saunders, Esther, 197–198, 202
Savage God, The (Alvarez), 188, 227
Schiller, Friedrich von, 75
Schubert, Franz, 75
Scott, Geoffrey, 211
screen memory, 218, 285
self, sense of, 215; *see also* identity problems
self-esteem, 215, 217, 285
self-interest vs. belief, Chatterton's conflict, 118, 127, 167, 179–180, 280
Sentiment (Chatterton), 186
"Servant's Diary" (Shapiro), 9
Seward, Anna, 183, 184
sexual mores and practices, in 18th-century England, 203–208, 212
sexual perversions, 2–4, 157, 159, 206, 215; examples, 4; exhibitionism, 2, 4, 85, 155–159, 162, 215, 218; fetishism, 2, 4, 158, 215, 217–219; in impostor, 2–3, 157–158, 218–219; in men, 3; in men vs. women, 10; narcissism and, 219–220; relationship to character perversions, 4, 218–219; sadomasochism, 2, 215; transvestism, 2, 4, 158, 215, 218–219; voyeurism, 2, 3, 4, 158, 218
Shakespeare, William, 17, 71, 74, 75; Ireland's imposturous forgeries of, 4, 76; *Othello*, and Chatterton's *Aella*, 91–92
Shapiro, Nell, 9
Shelley, Percy Bysshe, 18
Shoe Lane Workhouse, London, 27, 29, 30
Short Account of Mr. William Canynge ..., A. See *Brief Account of William Cannings, A*
Sibley, Ebenezer, 33–34, 40, 136, 191–192, 231, 275
sister-brother relationship, 5; in Chatterton's case, 21, 22–23, 24, 42–43, 177, 188–189, 216, 252
Skeat, Walter, 63, 250, 268
slave trade, 132
Sly Dick (Chatterton), 47, 180
Smith, Peter, 135–136, 231, 267
Smith, William, 135, 184, 267
Society of the Supporters of the Bill of Rights, 153
Song to Aella (Chatterton/Rowley), 64
Sorrows of Young Werther (Goethe), 31, 75, 187

299

INDEX

Southey, Robert, 29, 35, 67, 185, 257, 259, 263, 281, 290
Speght edition of Chaucer, 63
Sprytes. See Parlyamente of Sprytes
Staël, Mme. de, 75
Stay curyous Traveller and pass not bye (Chatterton/Rowley), 88
Stello (Vigny), 202n.
Sterne, Laurence, 124
Stockwell, Mrs., 29
Stone, Rev. George, 150
Storie of William Canynge, The (Chatterton/Rowley), 98
Strindberg, August, 224
suicide, 215, 280–281; contagion principle, 229; Hume's *Essay* on, 186–187; "legitimacy" of, 136; "a noble insanity of the soul," 136, 178, 186, 232; of poets, 203–204; societal attitudes toward, 185–188; underlying melancholia, 227–228, 229
suicide of Chatterton, 15, 184, 185–189, 190, 208, 213; vs. accidental death, 208–210; arsenic diagnosis of, 15, 193, 208; date of, 216; his earlier "fake" note, 27, 32, 50, 135, 137–140, 145, 188; his earlier thoughts and writings on, 135–137, 186, 188, 228–229; inquest and report, 185, 210, 222–223; monetary motives discounted, 213–215; opium-overdose theory for, 208, 284; suicide poems (unauthenticated), 193–194, 225–227; theories on motives for, 2, 184, 187, 188, 191–196, 208–210, 221–231; venereal-disease theory for, 2, 184, 190, 191–196, 208–210, 280
superego, 219–222, 227–229, 285; *see also* conscience
Swift, Jonathan, 126, 134
swindling, pathological, 3, 158, 215; *see also* imposturousness
syphilis, 209–210; and Chatterton, 2, 192, 196, 209, 210

Tate Gallery, London, 15
Taylor, Donald S., 260, 280
Temora (Macpherson), 73
Tezcatlipoca (god), 221, 227
Thélème Abbey (Rabelais), 147
Thistlethwaite, James, 188, 193–194, 249–250, 267
Thomas, Dylan, 203
Thomas Chatterton (Nevill), 260
Thomas Chatterton: The Marvelous Boy (Russell), 198, 251, 260
Thomson, James, 172
"Three Tombs" (Chatterton/Rowley), drawings from, xi, *illus.* 78, *illus.* 144
Times, The (Churchill), 125

Tour Thro' the Whole Island of Great Britain, A (Defoe), 18, 262
Town and Country Magazine, 108, 131, 136, 141, 163, 170, 171, 173, 177, 178, 186, 244, 249
"Towre Gate" (Chatterton/Rowley), drawing from, xi, *illus.* 56
transvestism, 4, 215, 218–219; impostor's predisposition for, 2, 158
Treatise on the Deluge (Catcott), 130
Tristram Shandy (Sterne), 124
True Chatterton, The (Ingram), 155–156, 259, 266
Turgot (monk), 66, 87, 89, 270
Turgot documents, 65–66, 68–69, 82, 87–88, 267
Twitcher, Jemmy (Lord Sandwich), 125, 134, 150

Unfortunate Fathers, The (Chatterton), 136, 186, 228–229, 232; theme in Canynge eclogue, 102–103
"unknown girl" letter, 159–160
Utopia, 51

venereal disease, 206–209; theory for Chatterton's suicide, 2, 184, 190, 191–196, 208–210, 280
Vertue, George, 110, 244n.
Vidal, Gore, 203
Vigny, Alfred de, 202n.
Vindication (Walpole), 242, 250, 272
Virtu, The (magazine), 244 and n.
Voltaire, 71, 189, 207
Vortigern and Rowena (Ireland imposturing Shakespeare), 4
Voss, Johann Heinrich, 74
voyeurism, 3, 4, 218; impostor's predisposition for, 2, 158

Wallis, Henry, *The Death of Chatterton* (painting), xi, 15, 261
Walmsley family, 169–170, 255
Walpole! (Chatterton), 115, 117, 233, 244, 254
Walpole, Horace, 64, 71, 73–74, 129, 130, 178, 235, 243–244, 247, 248, 250, 251, 288; *Anecdotes of Painting in England*, 110, 244n.; *The Castle of Otranto*, 110, 243, 261; Chatterton's correspondence with, 110–114, 115, 243–244; and Chatterton's death, 187, 193, 213, 223, 241–243; cited, on Bristol, 19, 242; detection and exposure of Chatterton's forgeries by, 19, 26, 64, 98, 102, 112–113, 116, 233, 241–245, 247, 249, 261; literary imposture fling of, 110, 243, 261; *Memoirs* of, 243; *Vindication*, 242,

INDEX

250, 272; on Wilkes, 151, 152; *Works of*, 244
Warburton, Bishop of Gloucester, 150, 151
Warens, Mme. Louise de, 204
Warren, Murray, 260
Warton, Thomas, 75, 214–215, 223
Warton Lecture on English Poetry (British Academy), 51, 266
Wasteland, The (Eliot), 181
Werther. *See Sorrows of Young Werther*
Whitman, Walt, 75
Whore of Babylon, The (Chatterton), 134
Wildfire, Harry (pseudonym of Chatterton), 244
Wilkes, John, 118, 120, 123, 124–125, 127, 133, 134, 143–154, 159, 165, 166, 231, 239, 276–277; Chatterton's futile hope of meeting with, 141–142, 143, 144, 162, 164, 183; Chatterton's two-facedness about, 167, 179; *Essay on Woman*, 149–151, 152, 154; as father substitute for Chatterton, 135, 171, 235; Issue #45, 148–149, 151–152; political agenda of, 153
"Wilkes and Liberty" (song), 145
Will (Chatterton), 135, 137–140, 145, 188, 229; date of, 229, 231
Williams, William Carlos, 203
Wilson, Daniel, 155, 196–197, 260

women: attitude of adolescent boys toward, 53, 85; excluded from Rowley narrative, 84–85
Woodward, Francis, 240, 287
Wordsworth, William, 17, 39, 74, 251
Works of Horace Walpole, The, 244
Works of Thomas Chatterton (Cottle and Southey), 29, 35, 249–250, 259
Worlde, The (Chatterton/Rowley), 96–97
writings of Chatterton: acknowledged vs. imposturous, 3, 26, 178–179; conflict between belief and cynicism/self-interest in, 47–49, 118, 127, 179–180; father images and masculine idols in, 23, 42, 93, 101–102, 133, 232–235; language of, 63–64, 99, 181; posthumous misrepresentations and censorship by editors, 28, 154–155, 278; publication of, during his lifetime, 26, 47–49, 57–59, 131, 134, 136, 141, 165–166, 170–171, 173, 178; satirical, 23, 40, 47, 49, 117, 118–120, 126–128, 130–134, 154–157, 160–162, 178; style, 115, 118, 126–127, 181; *see also* literary voices of Chatterton; poetry, acknowledged; poetry, imposturous; prose writings

Yellowe Rolle (Chatterton/Rowley), 64–65, 66, 268

301

LOUISE J. KAPLAN is the critically acclaimed author of *Adolescence: The Farewell to Childhood, Oneness and Separateness: From Infant to Individual,* and the coauthor with Donald M. Kaplan and Armand Schwerner of *The Domesday Dictionary.* She has also published numerous essays and articles on child, adolescent, and adult development. Dr. Kaplan has been on the full-time faculty of the graduate clinical psychology programs at New York University, where she was Director of the Mother-Infant Research Nursery, and the City College of City University of New York, where she was Director of Child and Adolescent clinical services of The Psychological Center. The recipient of several awards for distinguished contributions to Psychology, she is a member of the Association for Child Psychoanalysis and the Professional Advisory Committee of The Margaret S. Mahler Research Foundation. Currently, in addition to her writing and private practice in New York City, Dr. Kaplan lectures at psychoanalytic institutes throughout the United States. She lives in Greenwich Village with her husband, Donald M. Kaplan, and is the mother of two grown children.